*And I looked, and behold a pale horse; and his name that sat on him was Death, and Hell followed with him.*
**Book of Revelation**

The Westerly Wind asserting his sway from the south-west quarter is often like a monarch gone mad, driving forth with wild imprecations the most faithful of his courtiers to shipwreck, disaster, and death.
Joseph Conrad

You know, when something like, even like a coal mine disaster, or something like this, you think that well everybody's going to make a run to be able to get out, but it happened too fast that they were just all dead.
Richard Grimes

Calamity is the perfect glass wherein we truly see and know ourselves.
Sir William D'Avenant

The earth is mankind's ultimate haven, our blessed terra firma. When it trembles and gives way beneath our feet, it's as though one of God's checks has bounced.
Gilbert Adair

The back motors of the ship are just holding it (uh) just enough to keep it from...It's burst into flames! It burst into flames, and it's falling, it's crashing! Watch it! Watch it! Get out of the way! Get out of the way! Get this, Charlie; get this, Charlie! It's fire... and it's crashing! It's crashing terrible! Oh, my! Get out of the way, please! It's burning and bursting into flames and the... and it's falling on the mooring mast. And all the folks agree that this is terrible; this is the one of the worst catastrophes in the world.   indecipherable   its flames... Crashing, oh! Four- or five-hundred feet into the sky and it... it's a terrific crash, ladies and gentlemen. It's smoke, and it's in flames now; and the frame is crashing to the ground, not quite to the mooring mast. Oh, the humanity !
Herbert Morrison

To suffering there is a limit; to fearing, none.
Francis Bacon

# AND HELL FOLLOWED WITH IT

## BY TROY TAYLOR AND RENE KRUSE

– A Dark Haven Entertainment Book from Whitechapel Press –

*For Adrian, who resides in the clouds and visits us in starlight.*
*For Aaron, Bethany, Elyse, Rachael, Kaitlynn & Gavin*
*And for the found friends, lost loves, eccentrics and second chances who*
*always manage to make life an adventure.*

## ORIGINAL COVER ARTWORK DESIGNED BY

©Copyright 2010 by Michael Schwab & Troy Taylor

Visit M & S Graphics at http://www.manyhorses.com/msgraphics.htm

## THIS BOOK IS PUBLISHED BY:

Whitechapel Press
A Division of Dark Haven Entertainment, Inc.
Chicago, Illinois / 1-888-GHOSTLY
Visit us on the internet at http://www. American Hauntings .org

First Printing -- May 2010
ISBN: 1-892523-70-1

Printed in the United States of America

# INTRODUCTION

There is not a single person reading this book who does not vividly recall the pictures of the jet airliners crashing into the World Trade Center in New York in 2001, or the great clouds of smoke as the Twin Towers fell. Images of this horrific disaster, which millions saw on television, will be etched in our memories for the rest of our lives. If the past is any indication, the terror attacks of 2001 will become a milestone in American history, just in the way that other catastrophes have become turning points in the timeline of our country. From the destruction of the New Madrid Earthquake to the Great Chicago Fire, the San Francisco Earthquake, the Great Spanish Influenza epidemic, the Dust Bowl era of the "Dirty Thirties," and "Hemingway's Hurricane" in 1935, disasters and catastrophes have become symbols of the era in which they occurred. And most of these great catastrophes have not only trigged changes in society – many of them have left hauntings in their wake.

Disasters and calamities have an important role in American history. They have occurred in all time periods and have taken numerous forms over the last few centuries. The goal of this book is to introduce the reader to the most destructive, horrific and blood-chilling of these events. We have collected stories of floods, hurricanes, epidemics, earthquakes, fires, explosions, shipwrecks, blizzards, train collisions, aircraft disasters, tornadoes and dust storms, as well as some unusual occurrences that are hard to classify but are still recognized as disastrous. We have collected these accounts, fittingly we thought, in categories divided among the four elements: earth, air, fire and water. However diverse and strange these stories might be, the array of disasters contained in this book has had an impact on American history and on the country's haunted history, as well.

Keep in mind, as you turn these pages that not every story in this book will be related to ghosts but you won't find them to be any the less horrifying. Some of them were simply so strange, and often so terrifying, that we had to include them. Disaster can strike anywhere and at any time – a bit of knowledge that can have you sleeping uneasily at night if you start to think about it.

The tales ahead of you may be both familiar and strange. Some of them you will have never heard before and some of them may be a little too close to home. But every single one of them has left a bloodstain on the history of America. Some of them may frighten you, others may disturb you and some of them may have you looking over your shoulder as you read. They are not tales for the faint of heart.

Happy Hauntings!
**Troy Taylor**
**Rene' Kruse**
**Winter 2009-2010**

# TABLE OF CONTENTS

# EARTH

## 1622: THE JAMESTOWN MASSACRE

On the cool, quiet morning of Friday, March 22, 1622, a band of Algonquin Indians slipped inside the defenses at Jamestown, Virginia and slaughtered more than 347 English settlers, many of whom were sleeping at the time. The settlement, which was the capital of the Virginia colony, had been established along the James River and was totally unprepared for the attack. The men who had risen in the morning chill greeted the Algonquin, who were not seen as a threat. But, as John Smith related in his *History of Virginia*, the Indians "came unarmed into our houses with deer, turkeys, fish, fruits, and other provisions to sell us." Suddenly the Indians grabbed any tools or weapons that were available to them and killed any settlers that were in sight, including men, women and children.

When the massacre was finished, nearly one-fourth of the English population of Jamestown had been brutally slain.

Before the establishment of the Jamestown colony in 1607, the English expressed both hopes of "civilizing" and fears of clashing with the Native Americans in the new colonies. Their belief in the right to trade with the natives was coupled with the arrogant assertion that whites were both morally and culturally superior to the "savages." The Indians were seen as a necessary nuisance and a hindrance to the progress and prosperity of the colony.

At first, the natives were willing to trade with the English but they resisted the settlers' attempts to convert them to Christianity. The Indians were happy to accept trade goods, especially metal tools, in exchange for food but by 1608, tensions were already beginning to rise. Not only were the English colonists impinging on the Indians' hunting and planting grounds, but they burned down the Indians' homes and destroyed their food supplies. These acts of violence resulted in a shortage of food for the colony, as the number of natives willing to trade with them quickly diminished.

The Virginia Company of London, which had financially backed the colony, had much to lose if war broke out between the settlers and the natives, so strict instructions were given ordering the colonists to remain on good terms with the Indians. It was soon realized that both groups could benefit by trading with one another and a semblance of peace was restored. In exchange for food, the Indians were again provided with metal hatchets and cooper cookware.

**An idyllic life at Jamestown in the early 1600s**

But the peace was an unsteady one. A number of the military men among the colony's leaders, including John Smith, Thomas Dale, Thomas Gates and others, began to see the Indians as essentially a military problem. They believed that any contact between the two groups was bound to end badly. Leaders among the Native Americans shared this opinion. Chief Powhatan knew that the Englishmen did not settle in Jamestown simply to trade with the Indians. The English wanted more; they wanted control over the land. As Powhatan stated, "Your coming is not for trade, but to invade my people and possess my country."

In 1610, the Virginia Company, ignoring its earlier concerns about preserving peace for the colony, ordered Sir Thomas Gates, the newly appointed governor, to Christianize the Indians and absorb them into the colony. He was ordered to force the Indians to ignore their leaders and to acknowledge no other lord but King James. Gates knew what a foolhardy idea this was and when he arrived in Jamestown in 1610. He decided to pack up everyone, set sail, and abandon the fort. But as they were leaving they were met by an incoming fleet commanded by Lord de la Warre. Taking command as governor, de la Warre ordered the fort reoccupied and began plotting the conquest of the surrounding tribes. In July, the sent Gates against the Kecoughtan Indians, which resulted in a brutal massacre. Gates lured the Indians into the open by means of a music and dance act that was created by his drummer, and when they approached he slaughtered them.

Sporadic warfare took place between the colonists and the Indians for the next four years, culminating in the capture of Pocahontas, the daughter of Chief Powhatan. She was held hostage until the Indians agreed to the colonists' demands, which included the release of all English prisoners, the return of English weapons taken by Powhatan's warriors and "a lasting peace." During Pocahontas' captivity, she met John Rolfe, learned the English language and converted to Christianity, being baptized and taking the name Rebecca. The only way to maintain peace between the Indians and the English, Rolfe stated, was for him to marry the attractive Pocahontas, not "with the unbridled desire of carnal affection but for the good of the colony and the glory of God. Such a marriage might bring peace between the warring English and Indians, just as it would satisfy Pocahontas' desire."

The marriage did bring about a time of peace between the colonists and the Indians of the Powhatan Confederacy. In 1618, after the death of Powhatan, his brother, Opechancanough, became leader of the Algonquin tribes. Unfortunately for the settlers, Opechancanough had little interest in peaceful relations. During the fighting of previous years, his entire command of warriors had been wiped out and he longed for revenge. To make matters worse, a rapid rise in the colonists' population had led to an increased encroachment on native lands. Between 1619 and 1621, 42 ships had arrived from England, bringing more than 1,1200 colonists. It was alarming increase since the arrival of the first one hundred and four settlers in 1607. In the spring of 1622, Opechancanough seized his moment, and launched a campaign of surprise attacks upon 31 separate English settlements and plantations, mostly along the James River.

During the attack, many smaller communities, which were essentially outposts of Jamestown, were decimated. At Martin's Hundred, over half the population was killed and at its principal development of

Wolstenholme Towne, only two houses and a part of a church were left standing. About four hundred colonists were killed and twenty women were captured and taken to live and work with the Powhatan Indians until their death or ransom. Henricus, one of the most distant outposts from Jamestown, was home to a recently started school for Indian boys and a college for the sons of colonists. The town and schools were destroyed.

**An illustration of the Jamestown Massacre**

The vicious slaughter of the colonists had harrowing consequences for both the English and the Native Americans. Many settlers died in the assault, and those who survived were reluctant to tend crops, fearing more attacks. Men who were needed for defense of the town were not able to work in the fields, thus diminishing the labor force even further. The colonists abandoned the farms that were furthest from town and consolidated their settlements in order to better defend themselves. Starvation followed on the heels of these developments and the scarcity of food, combined with epidemics, killed another five hundred to six hundred people in the year following the massacre.

But things could have been much worse. Instead of engaging in further fighting, and wiping out the entire colony, Opechancanough withdrew after the massacre. He believed that the colonists would react as an Indian tribe would by either abandoning Jamestown or by learning their lesson and respecting the power of the Algonquin. He told his allies that he expected "before the end of two moons there should not be an Englishman in all their Countries." However, this proved to be a serious miscalculation on his part.

Although initially in shock over the attack, the colony regained its composure and a plan of action was established for both defense and aggression against the Indians. John Smith, who was in England at the time of the massacre, did not believe that the colonists would leave their plantations to march against the Algonquin, so he planned to return to Virginia with a ship filled with soldiers, sailors and ammunition so that he could establish a "running army" to deal with the natives. For whatever reason, though, Smith never returned to Virginia.

The colonists did mount a savage campaign that was designed to drive the Indians from the region. A shipment of weapons arrived from England soon after the massacre and these the settlers used in this new war. They sought revenge against the Indians by surprise attacks, burning of villages and crops, destroying boats and canoes and slaughtering women and children. It is unclear how many, if any, Indians died in the initial massacre at Jamestown in 1622, but many hundreds died in the colonists' counterattack. After a decade of war, disease and famine, a peace treaty was signed in 1632, officially separating the English and Native American lands.

Peace lasted for a dozen years and by 1644, the English and the Algonquin were at war once again. Nearly five hundred colonists perished in the fighting, along with scores of Native Americans. Opechancanough, who was quite old by this time and had to be transported by litter, was captured and imprisoned at Jamestown, where he was killed by one of the colonists appointed to guard him. His death marked the decline of the Indian confederacy and eventually, its destruction.

The Jamestown Massacre also brought about the demise of the Virginia Company of London, which had held the colony's charter. Criticized for continuing to enlist new colonists in England in spite of food shortages and disease, the company was disbanded when Virginia became the first royal colony in 1624. The massacre also led to a change in policy over how Native Americans were treated by the English in America. The natives could no longer be trusted to live peacefully with the colonists. News of what happened in Jamestown traveled north to Plymouth and, after its establishment in 1630, the Massachusetts Bay Colony became very cautious about its dealings with the local Indians. After the massacre, the Indians began to be seen as the enemy, establishing a pattern for English-Indian relations that continued for centuries.

The massacre also had an effect on the people of Jamestown that was not as tangible as starvation and disease. The people were terrified in the days and weeks after the attack, fearing that the Indians would return and again find the colony unprepared. Stories began to circulate, not only of Indians in the forests and in the shadows but of the ghosts of massacre victims, who returned to warn the living of an imminent attack.

"Stories of signs and omens have spread," one colonist wrote, "and they tell of spirits that have been heard, predicting of more bloodshed."

Were the stories true? Did some of the colonists actually encounter the ghosts of slain friends and relatives in the homes where they once lived? Or were the stories merely tales created to frighten children into being careful, or warnings that were spread to try and get the settlers to prepare for the worse?

We will likely never know for sure but if sudden death, terror and trauma can cause a place to become haunted, then Jamestown in 1622 was certainly a fitting location for an unearthly visitation or two.

# 1811: WHEN THE MISSISSIPPI RIVER RAN BACKWARD

Strange things began to happen in the Missouri Territory in 1811. Residents along the Mississippi River, near the settlement of New Madrid, began reporting all manner of weird happenings. First, it was the animals. Livestock began to act nervous and excited. Dogs began to bark and howl and even the most domesticated of animals turned vicious. Wild animals began to act tame. Deer wandered out of the woods and up to the doors of cabins. Flocks of ducks and geese landed near people. It was unlike anything the local residents had ever seen before.

Soon, stories spread of eerie lights that were seen in the woods and in the hills. Strange, bluish white flashes and balls of light were seen floating in the trees and cresting the nearby ridges.

Perhaps strangest of all, especially to the more superstitious among the settlers, was the comet that had been seen in the sky for months. In the fall of 1811, it was at its brightest and in September of that year, this anomaly in the sky was joined by a solar eclipse that led some to believe that a dire event was coming soon. And they were right.

During the winter of 1811-1812, a series of devastating earthquakes shook the nation from southeastern Missouri to Boston, New Orleans and Washington. Centered in the Mississippi Valley region, they were the strongest known seismic events in North America, east of the Rocky Mountains. They are known today as the New Madrid earthquakes due to their horrible effects on the small town of New Madrid, Missouri. They caused destruction like   never seen, before or since, and gave rise to incredible accounts of bizarre events. There was even a tale of a supernatural prediction that seems to defy all logic.

The New Madrid earthquakes began at about 2:00 a.m. on the morning of December 16, 1811. The ground shook and heaved like waves on the ocean and the violent shock was accompanied by a loud sound like distant thunder, but more hoarse and vibrating, witnesses said. One eyewitness later wrote that the thundering sound was "followed in a few minutes by the complete saturation of the atmosphere, with sulphurous vapor, causing total darkness. The screams of the affrighted inhabitants running to and fro, not knowing where to go, or what to do - the cries of the fowls and beasts of every species - the cracking of trees falling, and the roaring of the Mississippi formed a scene truly horrible."

The violent trembling caused roofs to collapse, chimneys to fall, items in homes to be thrown about and numerous injuries. Rocks and dirt collapsed along the bluffs of the Mississippi and in some places, sand and water were forced to the surface in frightening eruptions. In the darkness before dawn, no one had any idea just how much damage was being done.

Between the initial earthquake and sunrise, a number of lighter shocks occurred, followed by another violent shaking just as the sun as coming up. The terror that had taken over the local populace, as well as the animals in the region, was now, if possible, doubled. People began to flee in every direction, perhaps believing that there was less danger if they could get away from the river. Many were injured, not only from the shock of the earthquakes, but in their haste in trying to escape.

**Two Photos taken in the early 1900s that still show some of the damage from the 1811-1812 earthquakes.**
**(Left) Landslide trench and ridge in the Chickasaw Bluffs east of Reelfoot Lake, Tennessee, resulting from the New Madrid earthquake.**
**(Right) Taken in 1904, this photo shows earthquake damage and one side of fault trench or "fissure" near banks of St. Francis River, Clay County, Arkansas**

Thousands of minor shocks and occasional stronger earthquakes were experienced during the following days and weeks. On January 23, 1812, at about 9:00 a.m., an earthquake comparable to the one in December took place. It was reportedly felt as far away as Boston. According to many accounts, the earth remained in continual agitation until February 4, when another strong quake occurred. Four events took place over the course of the next few days and then on February 7, around 4:00 a.m., another violent concussion shook the region. One witness, Eliza Bryan wrote: "The awful darkness of the atmosphere, and the violence of the tempestuous thundering noise that accompanied it, together with all of the other phenomena mentioned as attending the former ones, formed a scene, the description of which would require the most sublimely fanciful imagination."

It was as if the gates of hell had opened in southeastern Missouri.

The earthquake caused two waterfalls to form on the Mississippi River near New Madrid and, for a short while, the Mississippi River ran backward until the mighty force of the water caused the falls to collapse. At first, the river had seemed to recede from its banks, and its waters gathered up in the center, leaving many boats stranded on bare sand. The water then rose fifteen to twenty feet in the air and then expanded, causing it to rapidly rush toward the shore and overflow the river's banks. The boats that had been left on the sand were torn from their moorings and driven more than one-quarter mile up a small creek. The river fell rapidly, as quickly as it had risen, and receded from the banks in such a torrent that it ripped away whole groves of cottonwood trees that had been growing along the shore. They were broken off with such precision that in some instances, people who had not witnessed the event, refused to believe they had not been cut. Thousands of fish were stranded on the banks, left behind by the surging water. The river drowned the inhabitants of a Native American village, devastated thousands of acres of forest and created Reelfoot Lake, about fifteen miles south of New Madrid.

During the hard shocks, the earth was torn to pieces. Hundreds of acres were covered over, in various depths, by the sand that came out of the fissures, great, yawning gaps that opened up all over the countryside. Some of them closed immediately after vomiting up sand and water, but others remained as open wounds in fields, pastures and forests.

After the February 7 earthquake, only weaker aftershocks took place, which still occur today.

No non-Native Americans were reported killed during the earthquakes of 1811-1812, but many towns and cities experienced damage from the shaking ground. It is believed that the damage and death toll would have been much higher, perhaps at catastrophic levels, if the region had been more heavily populated at the time. In 1811, that portion of the Mississippi Valley was still sparsely inhabited frontier. If the area had been as populated as it is today, the New Madrid earthquakes would have been one of the worst disasters in American history.

**Tecumseh**

Terrifyingly, there is still a chance of this happening. Minor tremors still occur along what is known as the New Madrid Fault Line on an almost daily basis and scientists believe that another major quake is inevitable. When it might happen is anyone's guess.

The New Madrid earthquakes had a major effect not only on the Mississippi Valley but on American history. They were also connected to an intriguing supernatural prediction allegedly made by the Shawnee Indian leader, Tecumseh.

Tecumseh (whose name meant "Shooting Star" or "Panther Across the Sky") was born in March 1768, just north of present-day Xenia, Ohio. His father was Pucksinwah, a minor Shawnee war chief of the Kispoko or "Panther" branch of the tribe. His mother, Methoataske, belonged to the tribe's Pekowi branch. The tribe was living somewhere near present-day Tuscaloosa, Alabama, at the time of his parent's marriage, having been in that region among the Creek Indians after being driven from their homes by the Iroquois. Around 1759, the Pekowi branch of the tribe decided to move north into the Ohio country. Rather than force his wife to be separated from her family, Pucksinwah decided they would also move north. The Pekowi settled in the area where Tecumseh was later born. Not long after his birth, the family moved again and during the 1760s, Pucksinwah fought in the French and Indian War. He was killed during the conflict known as Lord Dunmore's War, at the Battle of Point Pleasant, in 1774.

In the eight years after his father's death, Tecumseh's village was attacked at least five times by colonials and later by American armies, since the Shawnee allied with the British during the Revolutionary War. Tecumseh's family moved to Chief Blackfish's nearby village of Chillicothe but the town was destroyed in 1779 by Kentucky militia as a reprisal for Blackfish's attack on Boonesburough. Tecumseh's family fled again, this time moving to another nearby Kispoko village, which was destroyed the following year by soldiers under the command of George Rogers Clark. The family moved a third time to the village of Sanding Stone, which was attacked by Clark in November 1782. They fled once more, this time to a new settlement near present-day Bellefontaine, Ohio.

Violence and bloodshed continued across what was then the Northwest Territory after the American Revolution. The Wabash Confederacy formed and included all of the major tribes of the Ohio and Illinois country. They joined together in an attempt to keep American settlers out of the region. As the war between the confederacy and the Americans intensified, Tecumseh took an active role, fighting alongside his older brother, Cheeseekua. Tecumseh took part in several battles, including the Battle of Fallen Timbers in 1794, which ended the war in favor of the Americans.

Tecumseh settled in what is now Greenville, Ohio, the home of his younger brother, Lowawluwaysica ("One With Open Mouth") who would later take the new name of Tenskwatawa ("The Open Door") and achieve widespread fame as "The Shawnee Prophet." Tenskwatawa began a religious revival among the Shawnee in 1805 when he rooted out the "cause" of a smallpox outbreak by hunting down a witch. His beliefs were based on the teachings of early tribal prophets, who had predicted a coming apocalypse that would destroy the European settlers. A revival of the prophecies became very popular at a time when it seemed the flood of white settlers was going to engulf the Indian lands. Tenskwatawa urged his people to reject the ways of the Europeans, give up firearms, liquor and European- style clothing. He called on them to only pay traders half the value of their debts, and to refrain from giving over any more land to the United States. These teachings created great tension between the settlers and Tenskwatawa's followers and were openly opposed by Shawnee leader Black Hoof, who was trying to maintain peace with the Americans.

The first record of Tecumseh's peacetime interactions with Americans was in 1807, when Indian agent William Wells met with Blue Jacket and other Shawnee leaders to determine their intentions after the murder of a settler. Wells was highly respected by the Indians on the frontier Tecumseh was among those who spoke with Wells and assured him that his band of Shawnee intended to remain at peace. He explained to Wells that his people intended to follow the will of the Great Spirit and the teachings of his prophet, Tenskwatawa. They planned to move to a new village, deeper in the frontier and farther away from the newly arriving settlers.

But Tenskwatawa and Tecumseh did not leave the region. In fact, Tenskwatawa continued to attract new followers. By 1808, tensions between the settlers and the Shawnee escalated to the point that Black Hoof demanded that Tenskwatawa and his people leave the area. Tecumseh was among the leaders of the group and he helped to decide to move them farther northwest and establish the village of Prophets Town near the confluence of the Wabash and Tippecanoe rivers. The site was in territory that belonged to the Miami Indians and Chief Little Turtle of that tribe warned them not to settle there. Despite the threat, they moved into the region. The Miami did not take action against them and it is believed that Tecumseh may have already been holding council with them to build a large tribal confederacy to counter the American expansion into Indian lands.

Within a short time, Tenskwatawa's religious teachings became more widely known, as did his predictions of coming doom for the Americans. He attracted numerous members of other tribes to Prophets Town and this formed the basis for the confederacy of southwestern Great Lakes tribes that Tecumseh envisioned. He eventually emerged as the leader of this confederation, although it was largely built on the religious appeal of his younger brother. Relatively few in the confederation were Shawnee. Although Tecumseh is often portrayed as the leader of the Shawnee, the confederacy was primarily made up of other tribes.

**William Henry Harrison**

In September 1809, William Henry Harrison, at that time governor of the newly formed Indiana Territory, negotiated the Treaty of Fort Wayne in which a delegation of Indians ceded three million acres of Native American lands to the United States. The treaty is largely regarded as a farce. It was not authorized by President Thomas Jefferson and the Indians were not only bribed with large subsidies but were given liberal doses of alcohol before the negotiations began.

Tecumseh's strong opposition to the treaty marked his emergence as a prominent leader. Although Tecumseh and the Shawnee did not lay claim to any of the land that was sold, he was shocked by the sale since many of the followers at Prophets Town, including the Piankeshaw, Kickapoo, and Wea, were the primary inhabitants of the lands in question. Tecumseh reminded the Native Americans of an idea first advanced by the Shawnee leader Blue Jacket years before: that Indian land was owned in common by all tribes and could not be sold without agreement by all.

Tecumseh was not ready to confront the United States directly, so he instead spoke out against the Indian leaders who had signed the treaty. He began to travel widely, making impassioned speeches in which he urged warriors to abandon the chiefs who had betrayed them and join him in a resistance to the treaty. It was illegal, he insisted, and asked Governor Harrison to nullify it. He warned him that whites should not attempt to settle on the lands that were stolen by the treaty. Tecumseh was quoted as saying, "No tribe has the right to sell [land], even to each other, much less to strangers.... Why not sell the air, the great sea, as well as the earth? Didn't the Great Spirit make them all for the use of his children?" He concluded, "The only way to stop this evil [loss of land] is for the red man to unite in claiming a common and equal right in the land, as it was first, and should be now, for it was never divided."

In August of 1810, Tecumseh led four hundred warriors from Prophets Town to confront Harrison at his home in Vincennes. Their appearance terrified the townspeople and the situation turned heated when Harrison rejected Tecumseh's demand. The governor argued that individual tribes could have relations with the United States and added that Tecumseh's interference had angered the tribes who had sold the land.

Tecumseh replied to Harrison, "You have the liberty to return to your own country ... you wish to prevent the Indians from doing as we wish them, to unite and let them consider their lands as common property of the whole ... You never see an Indian endeavor to make the white people do this ..."

His anger boiled over and he ordered his men to kill Harrison on the spot. The governor bravely drew his sword, determined to go down fighting. The small garrison that defended the town quickly moved to protect Harrison. Before fighting began, Pottawatomi chief Winnemac stepped forward and urged the warriors to leave in peace. He explained to Tecumseh that violence was not the way to handle the situation and Tecumseh reluctantly agreed. Before he left, however, he told Harrison that unless he rescinded the treaty, he would seek an alliance with the British, who were already at work on the frontier trying to incite the Indians to rise up against the American settlers. As early as 1810, British agents had sought to secure an alliance with the Native Americans tribes to assist in the defense of Canada should war with the United States break out. The Indians had been reluctant to accept, fearing there was no benefit to the alliance. Following the confrontation with Harrison, Tecumseh secretly accepted the offer of alliance and the British began to supply his confederacy with firearms and ammunition.

Tecumseh had already attracted a great following but he and his brother, Tenskwatawa, were soon able to rally even more. It was said that Tecumseh claimed that the Great Spirit would send a "sign" to the Native Americans to show that he had been chosen to lead them and in March 1811, a great comet began to appear in the night sky. Tecumseh, whose name meant "Shooting Star," told his people that the comet signaled his rise to power. The confederacy accepted it as the sign they had been waiting for.

A short time later, Tecumseh again met with William Henry Harrison after being summoned following the murder of settlers on the frontier. Tecumseh told Harrison that the Shawnee and their Native American brothers wanted to remain at peace with the United States but the differences between them had to be resolved. The meeting was likely a ploy to buy time while he built a stronger confederacy. Harrison was not fooled by Tecumseh's claim of wanting peace. He was more convinced than ever that hostilities were imminent.

After the meeting with Harrison, Tecumseh traveled south on a mission to recruit allies among the Cherokee, Choctaw, Creek, Chickasaw and Seminole. Most of the southern nations rejected his appeals, but a faction of the Creeks, who became known as the Red Sticks, answered his call to arms against the white men, leading to the Creek War. They were eventually defeated by General Andrew Jackson in 1814.

While Tecumseh was away in the south, another "miraculous" event occurred that convinced his followers that a war with the Americans was the right course of action. On September 17, 1811, a solar eclipse occurred – a "Black Sun" that was allegedly predicted by the prophet Tenskwatawa. A "Black Sun" was said to predict a future war and Tenskwatawa was believed to have prophesied the coming of the eclipse many weeks before. It is widely believed today that he consulted with an astronomer about the eclipse, but no one knew this at the time. The prediction seemed to be a supernatural one – but it was nothing compared to the one that Tecumseh would make a short time later.

Harrison left the territory for business in Kentucky shortly after the meeting with Tecumseh, leaving John Gibson as acting-governor. Gibson, who had lived among the Miami tribe for many years, was given word about Tecumseh's plans for war. He immediately called out the militia and sent an emergency letter to Harrison, asking him to return. The militia soon formed and Harrison returned with a small force of army regulars. He had received word from Washington, which authorized him to march up the Wabash River from Vincennes on a preemptive expedition to intimidate Tenskwatawa and his followers and force them to make peace. Tecumseh was still in the south, lobbying tribes to join his confederation.

Harrison gathered the militia companies near a settlement north of Vincennes and was joined by a sixty-man company from Croydon, Indiana, called the Yellow Jackets, so named for their bright yellow coats, and two companies of Indiana Rangers. His entire force of about one thousand men set out toward Prophets Town. The army reached the site of present-day Terre Haute on October 3. They camped and built Fort Harrison while they waited for supplies to be delivered. On October 10, Indians ambushed a scouting party of Yellow Jackets and prevented the soldiers from hunting in the nearby woods. Supplies began to run low and on October 19, rations were cut. Finally, nine days later, a shipment of food and ammunition arrived and an encampment was set up near the confluence of the Wabash and Tippecanoe rivers.

During the early morning hours of November 7, the Native Americans attacked.

Many years later, Tenskwatawa denied that he ordered his warriors to attack Harrison. He blamed the Winnebagos in his camp for launching the attack, or at least encouraging it. Without Tecumseh's military leadership, his brother was unable to control his followers. The people of Prophets Town were worried by the nearby army and feared being overwhelmed by the white soldiers. They had begun to fortify the town, but the defenses had not been completed. During the evening, Tenskwatawa consulted with the spirits and decided that sending a party to murder Harrison in his tent was the best way to avoid a battle. He assured the warriors that he would cast spells that would prevent them from being harmed and confuse the Americans so they would not resist. The warriors began looking for a way to sneak into the camp but the attack on Harrison failed.

Around 4:30 a.m., Harrison's sentinels were shocked to find warriors advancing on them from the early morning fog. Soldiers awoke to scattered gunshots and discovered themselves almost encircled by Tenskwatawa's forces. First contact was made on the north side of the camp, but this was likely a diversion since fierce fighting broke out moments later as Indians charged the southern corner of the line. The attack took the army by surprise as the warriors shouted and rushed at the defenders. Yellow Jacket commander Captain Speir Spencer was among the first to be killed. Lieutenants McMahan and Berry, the other two Yellow Jacket commanding officers, were also soon wounded and killed. Without leadership, the Yellow Jackets began to fall back from the main line, retreating with scores of militia soldiers. The warriors rushed after them and entered the camp. The soldiers

# THE TIPPECANOE CURSE?

According to legend, the Tippecanoe Curse was placed on William Henry Harrison after the Battle of Tippecanoe by Tecumseh's prophet brother Tenskwatawa, who allegedly possessed supernatural powers. The curse is sometimes used to describe the pattern where from 1840 to 1960 each American President who had won election in a year ending in zero died in office. It was "broken" by Ronald Reagan, who survived being wounded in a March 1981 shooting.

The curse, which gained popularity after being published in a *Ripley's Believe it or Not* book in 1931, began with William Henry Harrison, who died in 1841 after being elected to office in 1840. For the next one hundred and twenty years, presidents elected during years ending in a zero ultimately died while serving in office, from Harrison to John F. Kennedy.

Presidents elected in "zero years," and who died in office, included Harrison, who died of pneumonia; Abraham Lincoln (assassinated); James Garfield (assassinated); William McKinley (assassinated); Warren G. Harding (cause of death unknown – possibly heart attack, stroke or poison); Franklin D. Roosevelt (cerebral hemorrhage); and John F. Kennedy (assassinated).

It was not until Ronald Reagan in 1980 that a president's election on a "zero year" was not followed by his death in office. Reagan survived eight years in two terms, despite being seriously wounded in an assassination attempt within months of his inauguration. It is believed by a few that the curse was broken when Reagan survived the assassination attempt and left office alive to ultimately suffer from Alzheimer's Disease for almost a decade before succumbing to pneumonia on June 5, 2004. The next president in the line of the curse, 2000 electoral victor George W. Bush, successfully finished out his second and final term on January 20, 2009.

regrouped under the command of Ensign John Tipton, a future U.S. Senator, and with the help of two reserve companies under the command of Captain Rodd, repulsed the warriors and sealed the breach in the line.

The second charge by the Native Americans hit both the north and south ends of the camp, with the southern end being attacked the hardest. The regulars were able to reinforce the line and hold their position as the assaults continued. On the northern end of the camp, Major Joseph Daviess led his men in a counter charge that punched through the Indian lines before being repulsed. Most of the men made it back to Harrison's line but Daviess was killed. Throughout the next hour, the troops fought off several more brutal charges. When the Indians began to run low on ammunition and the sun rose, revealing the small size of Tenskwatawa's army, they finally began to withdraw. A rallying charge by the regulars forced the remaining Native Americans to flee. The Battle of Tippecanoe had lasted just over two hours.

The Indians retreated to Prophets Town where, according to one chief's account, the warriors confronted Tenskwatawa and accused him of deceit because of the many deaths, which his spells were supposed to have prevented. He blamed his wife for desecrating his magic medicine and offered to cast a new spell. He insisted that the warriors launch a second attack, but they refused.

Fearing that Tecumseh was on his way with reinforcements, Harrison ordered his men to fortify the camp with earthworks. As the sentries moved back into position, they discovered – and scalped – the bodies of 36 warriors. The following day, November 8, Harrison sent men to inspect the town and found that it was deserted, except for one elderly woman who was too sick to leave. The rest of the defeated Indian forces had left during the night. Harrison ordered the troops to spare the old woman but to burn down Prophets Town and to destroy the Indians' cooking implements, which would make it hard for the confederacy to survive the winter. Everything of value was taken, including five thousand bushels of corn and beans. Some of the soldiers dug up bodies from the burial grounds and scalped them. Harrison's troops buried their own dead on the site of their camp and then built large fires over the mass grave in an attempt to conceal it. However, after Harrison's troops had departed, the Indians dug up the corpses and scattered the remains in retaliation.

After the battle, the wounded soldiers were loaded into wagons and taken to Fort Harrison to recuperate.

Most of the militia was released from duty and returned home. In his initial report to Washington, Harrison told of the battle at Tippecanoe and stated that he feared reprisals from the Indians. The first dispatch did not make it clear who had won the engagement and Secretary of War William Eustis at first interpreted it as a defeat. The next dispatch made the American victory clear and spoke of the defeat of Tecumseh's confederation since no second attack materialized. Eustis replied with a lengthy note demanding to know why Harrison had not taken adequate precautions in fortifying his camp. Harrison responded that he considered the position strong enough to not require fortification. The dispute was the start of a disagreement between Harrison and the Department of War that later caused him to resign from the army in 1814. But the battle certainly did not damage his reputation. When he ran for President of the United States during the election of 1840, he used the slogan "Tippecanoe and Tyler Too" to remind people of his heroism during the battle.

At first, the newspapers carried little information about the battle. One Louisville paper even printed a copy of the original report calling the battle an American defeat. However, by December, most of the major American papers began to carry stories about the incident, outraging the public. Many Americans blamed the British for inciting the tribes to violence and supplying them with weapons and ammunition. Andrew Jackson was at the forefront of those calling for war, claiming that Tecumseh and his allies were "excited by secret British agents." Western governors began calling for the expulsion of Native Americans from their territories and the War Hawks in Congress passed resolutions condemning the British for interfering in American domestic affairs. The Battle of Tippecanoe inflamed tensions with Britain, which would result in a declaration of war a few months later.

Accounts vary as to the immediate effect the loss had on Tenskwatawa. Some reports claimed that he lost much of his prestige after the battle because his claims that the warriors could not be hurt proved to be untrue. During meetings with Harrison after the battle, several tribal leaders claimed that his influence was destroyed. However, some historians believe that this was likely an attempt to mislead Harrison and calm the situation and that Tenskwatawa actually continued to play an important role in the confederacy.

Massacres of settlers became commonplace in the aftermath of the battle. Numerous homes and settlements in the Indiana and Illinois territories were attacked, leading to the deaths of many residents. Prophets Town was partially rebuilt over the next year, but was again destroyed in another campaign against the Indians in 1812. The Battle of Tippecanoe was a serious blow to Tecumseh's dream of a confederacy. When he returned from his travels, Tecumseh was angry with his brother, whom he had instructed to keep peace.

Tecumseh continued to play a major role in military operations on the frontier, however, and by 1812 the confederacy and Tecumseh had regained some of their former strength. Many believe that this resurgence in power was in large part thanks to the events that occurred along the Mississippi River in the winter of 1811-1812.

In the spring and summer of 1811, Tecumseh began traveling to villages in the Midwest and the South, urging the tribes to join his confederacy. Many warriors joined him, although others ignored his pleas, doubting that he would succeed. One Alabama tribe, whose camp along the Mississippi River Tecumseh visited in November, even treated him with contempt. This angered Tecumseh so much that he told them that when he returned to his home, he would stomp on the ground and cause their village to fall down. They laughed at him – but it seemed that Tecumseh's threat was fulfilled a few weeks later.

On December 16, the devastating New Madrid Earthquake shook the South and the Midwest. Some of the Alabama tribe believed that Tecumseh's supernatural power actually caused the earth to shake while others believed he prophesied that the event would occur. While the interpretation of this event varied from tribe to tribe, one consensus was universally accepted: the powerful earthquake had to have meant something. For many tribes it meant that Tecumseh was a powerful leader and must be supported.

When the earthquakes began, Tecumseh was at the Shawnee and Delaware Indian villages near Cape Girardeau, Missouri, fifty miles north of the epicenter at New Madrid. The earthquakes continued as he traveled back to Prophets Town. He arrived there in February 1812 and by that time, word of his mysterious prediction had spread and more allies had flocked to his cause. Despite the setback of the battle, Tecumseh began to rebuild the confederacy.

He soon led his forces to join the British army as they invaded northwest from Canada. Tecumseh joined British Major-General Sir Isaac Brock in the siege of Detroit and forced its surrender in August 1812. This victory was reversed a little over a year later, as Commodore Oliver Hazard Perry's victory on Lake Erie, late in the summer of 1813, cut British supply lines and forced them to withdraw. The British burned all public buildings in Detroit and retreated into Upper Canada along the Thames Valley. Tecumseh and his men followed fighting rearguard actions to slow the American advance.

A second British commander, Major-General Henry Proctor, did not fare as well with Tecumseh as his predecessor did and the two disagreed over tactics. Proctor favored withdrawing into Canada when the Americans faced a harsh winter. Tecumseh, however, was eager to launch an offensive that would ravage the American army and allow his warriors to return home to the northwest regions. Proctor failed to appear at Chatham, Ontario, though he promised Tecumseh that he would attack the Americans there. Tecumseh moved his men to meet Proctor and told him that he would withdraw no further. If the British continued to want his help, then fighting needed to be carried out. William Henry Harrison crossed into upper Canada on October 5, 1813 and won a victory against the British and their Native American allies at the Battle of Thames. Tecumseh was killed, and shortly after the battle the tribes of his confederacy surrendered to Harrison at Detroit.

Tecumseh remains an enigmatic figure today. He is seen as a hero to many, refusing to give in to the overwhelming wave of white settlement. But in his time, he was greatly feared as a killer of innocents and a hindrance to the development of the country. What he actually was remains in the eye of the beholder.

But one question still baffles us: did Tecumseh predict the New Madrid Earthquake or did he cause it? Or was it merely a coincidence that he threatened to "shake the earth" and it actually happened a short time later? Or was the story of his eerie prophecy invented after the fact to add credence to his claim that the Great Spirit wanted him to lead the Native American confederacy in its fight against white expansion?

We may never really know.

# 1812: THE MASSACRE AT FORT DEARBORN

It may not have been a cold morning in April 1803, when Captain John Whistler climbed a sand dune around which the sluggish Chicago River tried to reach Lake Michigan but chances are it was. A chilling wind would have been a characteristic greeting from the landscape that Whistler had come to change. His orders had been to take six soldiers from the 1st U.S. Infantry, survey a road from Detroit to the mouth of the river, and draw up plans for a fort at this location. The British had also planned to build a fort at the entrance to the Chicago River but Whistler managed to beat them to the site. One has to wonder how the city might be different today if the British had managed to show up first.

After claiming the site, Captain Whistler returned to Detroit to get his garrison and his family. He was 45 years old and neither his poor Army pay nor the dangers of the frontier stopped him from living a full domestic life. Eventually, he fathered fifteen children.

Captain Whistler's family was spared the arduous trek over erratic Indian trails to the Chicago River. While the troops marched on foot, the captain and his brood boarded the U.S. schooner *Tracy*, which also carried artillery and camp equipment. It sailed to the mouth of the St. Joseph River, where it met the troops. The Whistler family took one of the *Tracy's* rowboats to the Chicago River, while the troops marched around the lake.

There were 69 officers and men in the contingent that had the task of building Fort Dearborn, which was named in honor of Secretary of War Henry Dearborn, a man who would go on to be considered one of the most inept leaders in American history. During the War of 1812, Dearborn was placed in command of all the American troops between Lake Erie and the Atlantic. He tried to capture Montreal, but his troops were so disorganized that they never even made it across the Canadian border. Dearborn was finally relieved of his command by President James Madison in 1813 after he narrowly avoided being court-martialed. In spite of this, a number of Chicago parks and developments were named in his honor, leading author Norman Mark to refer to him as "an example of one of history's most successful failures."

The hill on which Fort Dearborn was built was eight feet above the Chicago River. The water curved around it and, stopped from flowing into a lake by a sandbar, ran south until it found an outlet. To this spot, the soldiers hauled the wood that had been cut along the north bank. The fort was a simple stockade built of logs, which were placed in the ground and then sharpened along the upper end to discourage attackers. The outer stockade was a solid wall with an entrance in the southern section blocked with heavy gates. An underground exit was located on the north side. As time went on, the soldiers built barracks, officers' quarters, a guardhouse and a small powder magazine made from brick. West of the fort, they constructed a two-story log building, with split-oak siding, to serve as an Indian agency, and between this structure and the fort they placed root cellars. South of the fort, the land was enclosed for a garden. Blockhouses were added at two corners of the fort and

**Fort Dearborn in 1803**

three pieces of light artillery were mounted at the walls. The fort offered substantial protection for the soldiers garrisoned there but they would later learn that it was not enough.

When the War of 1812 unleashed the fury of the Native Americans on the western frontier, the city of Chicago almost ceased to exist before it got a chance to get started. On August 15, 1812, the garrison at Fort Dearborn evacuated its post and, with women in children in tow, attempted to march to safety. But it was overwhelmed and wiped out, in a wave of bloodshed and fire, after traveling less than a mile. The story of the massacre will be repeated for as long as Chicago continues to stand and marks not only the deadliest event in the history of the city but also serves as one of American history's great disasters.

At the start of the War of 1812, tensions in the wilderness began to rise. British troops came to the American frontier, spreading liquor and discontent among the Indian tribes, especially the Potawatomi, the Wyandot and the Winnebago, near Fort Dearborn. In April, an Indian raid occurred on the Lee farm, near the bend in the river (where present-day Racine Avenue meets the river) and two men were killed. After that, the fort became a refuge for many of the settlers and a growing cause of unrest for the local Indians. When war was declared that summer, and the British captured the American garrison at Mackinac, it was decided that Fort Dearborn could not be held and that it should be evacuated.

General William Hull, the American commander in the Northwest, issued orders to Captain Nathan Heald through Indian agent officers. He was told that the fort was to be abandoned; arms and ammunition destroyed and all goods were to be distributed to friendly Indians. Hull also sent a message to Fort Wayne, which sent Captain William Wells and a contingent of allied Miami Indians toward Fort Dearborn to assist with the evacuation.

There is no dispute about whether or not General Hull gave the order, nor that Captain Heald received it, but some have wondered if perhaps Hull's instruction, or his handwriting, was not clear because Heald waited eight days before acting on it. During that time, Heald argued with his officers, with John Kinzie, a settlement trader who opposed the evacuation, and with local Indians, one of whom fired off a rifle in the commanding officer's quarters.

The delay managed to give the hostile Indians time to gather outside the fort. They assembled there in an almost siege-like state and Heald realized that he was going to have to bargain with them if the occupants of Fort Dearborn were going to safely reach Fort Wayne. On August 13, all of the blankets, trading items and calico cloth were given out and Heald held several councils with Indian leaders, which his junior officers refused to attend.

Eventually, an agreement was reached that had the Indians allowing safe conduct for the soldiers and settlers to Fort Wayne in Indiana. Part of the agreement was that Heald would leave the arms and ammunition in the fort for the Indians, but his officers disagreed. Alarmed, they questioned the wisdom of handing out guns and ammunition that could easily be turned against them. Heald reluctantly went along with them and the extra weapons and ammunition were broken apart and dumped into an abandoned well. Only 25 rounds of ammunition were saved for each man. As an added bit of insurance, all of the liquor barrels were smashed and the contents were poured into the river during the night. Some would later claim that Heald's broken promise was what prompted the massacre that followed.

On August 14, Captain William Wells and his Miami allies arrived at the fort. Wells has largely been forgotten today (aside from the Chicago street that bears his name) but at the time, he was a frontier legend among soldiers, Native Americans and settlers in the Northwest Territory. Born in 1770, he was living in Kentucky in 1784 when he was kidnapped by a raiding party of Miami Indians. Wells was adopted into the tribe, took a Miami name – Apekonit, or "Carrot Top" for his red hair – and earned a reputation as a fierce warrior. He married into the tribe and his wife, Wakapanke ("Sweet Breeze") was the daughter of the great Miami leader, Little Turtle. The couple eventually had four children and remained together even after Wells left the Miami and settled at Fort Wayne as the government's Indian agent.

When Wells received word from General Hull about the evacuation of Fort Dearborn, he went straight to Chicago. His niece, Rebekah, was married to the fort's commander, Captain Heald. But even the arrival of the frontiersman and his loyal Miami warriors would not save the lives of those trapped inside Fort Dearborn.

Throughout the night of August 14, wagons were loaded for travel and the reserve ammunition was distributed. Late in the evening, Captain Heald received a visitor, a Potawatomi named Mucktypoke ("Black Partridge"), who had long been an ally to the Americans. He knew that he could no longer hold back the anger of his fellow tribesmen and he sadly gave back to Heald the medal of friendship that had been given to him by the U.S. government. He explained to Heald, "I will not wear a token of peace while I am compelled to act as an enemy."

Heald had fair warning that the occupants of Fort Dearborn were in great danger.

Early the next day, a hot and sunny Saturday morning, the procession of soldiers, civilians, women, and children left the fort. Leading the way was William Wells, riding a thoroughbred horse. Wells, in honor of his Miami heritage, had painted his face black. He was now a warrior prepared for battle – and for death.

A group of fifteen Miami warriors trailed behind him and they were followed the infantry soldiers, a caravan of wagons and mounted men. More of the Miami Indians guarded the rear of the column. The procession included 55 soldiers, twelve militiamen, nine women and eighteen children. Some of the women were on horseback and most of the children rode in two wagons. Two fife players and two drummers played a tune that history has since forgotten, perhaps marching music to inspire the exodus.

The column of soldiers and settlers was escorted by nearly five hundred Potawatomi and Winnebago Indians. In 1812, the main branch of the Chicago River did not follow a straight course into Lake Michigan. Instead, just east of the fort, it curved to the south, struggled around the sand dunes, and then emptied into the lake. The shoreline of the lake was then much closer to the present-day line of Michigan Avenue. The column from Fort Dearborn marched southward and into a low range of sand hills (near what is now Roosevelt Road) that separated the beaches of Lake Michigan from the prairie. As they did so, the Potawatomi moved to the right, placing an elevation of sand between them and the column. They were now mainly hidden from view.

The procession traveled to an area where 16th Street and Indiana Avenue are now located. There was a sudden milling about of the scouts at the front of the line and suddenly a shout came back from Captain Wells that the Indians were attacking. Captain Heald ordered his troops to charge and the soldiers scurried up the dunes with   bayonets fixed, breaking the Potawatomi line. The Indians fell back, allowed the soldiers in, and then enveloped them. Soldiers fell immediately and the line collapsed. Eventually, the remaining men retreated to the shoreline, making a defensive stand on a high piece of ground, but the Potawatomi overwhelmed them with sheer numbers.

The soldier's charge led them away from the wagons, leaving only the twelve-man militia to defend the women and children. Desperate to protect the families, the men fired their rifles until they were out of ammunition and then swung them like clubs before they were all slain. What followed was butchery. A Potawatomi climbed into the wagon with the children and bludgeoned them to death with his tomahawk. The fort's surgeon was cut down by gunfire and then literally chopped into pieces. Rebekah Heald was wounded seven times but was spared when she was captured by a sympathetic Indian chief. The wife of one soldier fought so bravely and savagely that she was hacked into pieces before she fell.

Aware of the slaughter taking place at the wagons, William Wells rushed to the aid of the women and children. Overcome by the massive number of Potawatomi, he never made it. Wells was said to have fought more than one hundred Indians, single-handed and on horseback. He shot and hacked at them until his horse fell beneath him. Indians pounced on him and killed him in the sand. One Potawatomi took Wells' scalp, while another cut out his heart, divided it into small pieces and gave them to other warriors. Honoring the slain hero, and hoping to gain a small amount of his great courage, they ate the heart of William Wells.

Then a Potawatomi attacked Margaret Helm, the wife of the fort's lieutenant. As the two fought, a second Potawatomi joined the fight, seized Mrs. Helm, and dragged her into the lake, where he proceeded to drown her – or that was how it appeared. The second warrior was Black Partridge, a close friend of Lieutenant Helm. The pretend drowning was actually a ruse to save her life.

Although it must have seemed much longer, the battle was over in less than fifteen minutes. Captain Heald, who had been wounded twice in the fighting and would walk with a cane for the rest of his life, agreed to parlay with Potawatomi chief Black Bird. After receiving assurances that the survivors would be spared, Heald agreed to surrender. Sixty-seven people had lost their lives in the massacre: William Wells, 25 army regulars, all twelve militiamen, twelve children, two women and fifteen Potawatomi.

The surrender that was arranged by Captain Heald did not apply to the wounded and it is said that the Indians tortured them throughout the night and then left their bodies on the sand next to those who had already fallen.

Many of the other survivors suffered terribly. The Potawatomi divided up the prisoners and most were eventually ransomed and returned to their families. Others did not fare so well. One man was tomahawked when he could not keep pace with the rest of the group being marched away from the massacre site. A baby who cried too much during the march was tied to a tree and left to starve. Mrs. Isabella Cooper was scalped before being rescued by an Indian woman. She had a small bald spot on her head for the rest of her life. Another man froze to death that winter, while Mrs. John Simmons and her daughter were forced to run a gauntlet, which both survived. In fact, the girl turned out to be the last survivor of the massacre, dying in 1900.

Captain Heald, along with his wife, was also taken prisoner. He and Rebekah were taken to Fort Mackinac and were turned over to the British commander there. He sent them to Detroit, where they were exchanged with the American authorities.

After the carnage, the victorious Indians burned Fort Dearborn to the ground and the bodies of the massacre victims were left where they had fallen, scattered to decay on the sand dunes of Lake Michigan. When replacement troops arrived at the site a year later, they were greeted with not only the burned-out shell of the fort, but also the grinning skeletons of their predecessors. In 1816, the bodies were finally given a proper burial, likely around present-day Prairie Avenue and 17th Street, and the fort was rebuilt. Twenty years later, it was finally abandoned when the city of Chicago was able to fend for itself.

The horrific Fort Dearborn Massacre is believed to have spawned its share of ghostly tales. The actual site of the massacre was quiet for many years, long after Chicago grew into a sizable city. However, construction in the early 1980s unearthed a number of human bones around 16th Street and Indiana Avenue. First thought to be victims of a cholera epidemic in the 1840s, the remains were later dated more closely to the early 1800s. Due to their location, they were believed to be the bones of the massacre victims.

The remains were reburied elsewhere but within a few weeks, people began to report the semi-transparent figures of people wearing pioneer clothing and outdated military uniforms wandering around an empty lot that was just north of 16th Street. The apparitions reportedly ran about in terror, silently screaming. The most frequent witnesses to these nocturnal wanderings were bus drivers who returned their vehicles to a garage that was located nearby, prompting rumors to spread throughout the city.

In recent times, the area has been largely filled with new homes and condominiums and the once-empty lot where the remains were discovered is no longer vacant. But this does not seem to keep the victims of the massacre in their graves. Current paranormal reports from the immediate area often tell of specters dressed in period clothing, suggesting that the unlucky settlers of early Chicago do not rest in peace.

# 1856: THE PICNIC TRAIN TRAGEDY

Railroads provided the first means of mechanical transportation in America and ushered in an era of swift and relatively comfortable travel. For nearly two decades, the railroads were mostly free from serious mishaps, but by the 1850s, the primitive signals, unpredictable locomotives and hurriedly laid lines conspired to bring about accidents, disasters and death.

In 1856, a horrific accident occurred when two trains collided near Camp Hill, Pennsylvania. One of the trains carried hundreds of children on their way to a picnic. This terrifying disaster left a permanent mark on the hearts, minds and spirits of the region where it occurred.

Railroads in America were remarkably free from accidents during the first twenty years or so of their existence. From 1829 to 1853, there were no disastrous wrecks and while a few passengers were killed in those early days, the number of fatalities was few compared to the years after the Civil War when the death rate from railroad wrecks went up alarmingly. Up until 1853, no more than a half dozen people were killed in any single accident. In late April and early May 1853, however, the early safety record of American railroading came to a sudden halt when 67 people were killed in two separate accidents.

Those would not be the only wrecks to occur that year. There were actually a number of frightening accidents that took place – deadly collisions, derailments and explosions. The reason behind the sudden change from safe, reliable travel to frequent calamities was mostly due to cheap construction. American railroads were very cheaply built. After 1850, the railroads expanded rapidly, often ahead of adequate capital. One solution for the finance problem was for speculators and developers to build as cheaply as possible. As a result, many rail lines had sharp curves, steep, bumpy grades, wooden rather than stone or metal bridges, and light rolling stock. Often the tracks were laid with little ballast under the ties and no time or money existed for maintenance and upkeep. Once the tracks were laid, they were seldom looked at again. In winter, the track bent high from the frost, and in the spring, lines with often buried with mud on top of the rails.

The federal government actually encouraged questionable railroad construction through its land grant policy, which gave railroads land and loans only as mileage was completed on their lines. As a result, the government

placed a premium on speed in construction and length, not quality, of track. In the end, almost all of the government-subsidized lines were poorly built.

The first railroad accident of 1853 cannot be classified as a disaster since only three people were killed, but it did introduce a new era in railroad history. On January 6, 1853, the Boston and Maine's noon express out of Boston heading for Lawrence, Massachusetts, was derailed at Andover with a broken axle. There were between sixty and seventy people on board. The train had been traveling at a dizzying forty miles per hour when it fell down a steep embankment and smashed apart. The only passenger killed outright was Benjamin Pierce, the eleven-year-old son and only surviving child of President-elect Franklin Pierce. General Pierce was badly bruised in the incident but it was reported by telegraph that he had been killed in the wreck. Newspapers all over the country headlined his death and in Washington, Congress adjourned out of respect. The first wreck of 1853, although a minor one, turned out to be highly publicized.

Another accident occurred on March 4. A rear-end collision occurred in the Allegheny Mountains near Mt. Union, Pennsylvania, killing seven people. This was the highest death toll in American railroad history at that point. An emigrant train had stopped because of a mechanical problem and a mail train ran into it at full speed from behind. The locomotive tore into the emigrant train and as its boiler burst open, searing steam poured over the emigrants, scalding and disfiguring many of them. The cause of the accident was gross carelessness. The brakeman, sent to the rear to signal any approaching trains, had fallen asleep.

And then came the disasters.

Two accidents occurred only a few days apart, stunning the nation. On April 25, 1853, an express and emigrant train collided near Chicago, killing 21 people. The express train, which was headed for Toledo, rammed the emigrant train broadside at a crossing. According to one eyewitness, the wrecked cars lay piled up in a swamp that flanked the tracks. The scene was described as, "An immense heap of iron, splinters, doors, and baggage with the crushed locomotive of the express train hissing steam from its ruptured boiler. Groans and cries assailed the ears of those who hastened from the first class cars. Time will not efface the memory of that terrible and heart-rending spectacle from the mind of the unwilling beholder. A heap of ruins, from which shrieked out upon the midnight air cries for help, mingled in strong discord with the deeper groans of the dying."

The accident had been caused by carelessness and ignorant rivalry between the crews of both trains. Evidence showed that the engineer of the emigrant train (which was running without a headlight) could have avoided the collision by either stopping or moving faster through the crossing. However, since he had the right-of-way, he took his time going through the intersection – a delay that cost 21 lives.

On May 6, before the public had recovered from the horror in Chicago, 46 passengers were killed at Norwalk,

Connecticut, when a train ran through an open drawbridge and plunged into the river. When the new Haven Railroad, which ran between New York and New Haven, was built, it bridged a number of rivers that emptied into the Long Island Sound. One of these was the drawbridge over the Norwalk River at South Norwalk, Connecticut. It was located about three hundred yards from the Norwalk depot, around a sharp curve. Before the bridge tender opened this bridge for a ship, he would signal by lowering a red ball from a pole by the tracks.

At 10:15 a.m. on the morning of May 6, 1853, the steamboat *Pacific* whistled to pass the closed bridge. Shortly after the steamer had passed through, and as the tender was getting ready to close the bridge, he saw a Boston-bound passenger train speed around the curve and plunge into the river. The speed of the train carried the engine all the way across the channel and into the central pier of the bridge. A baggage car, two mail cars, and two passenger cars fell into the river. A third passenger coach teetered on the edge, and then broke in two. Forty-six lives were lost either from drowning or being crushed. A coroner's inquest found the engineer guilty of gross negligence and blamed him for the accident.

On May 8, just two days after the drawbridge tragedy at Norwalk, two trains collided in a cornfield at Secaucus, New Jersey. A Paterson & Hudson River Railroad emigrant train from Jersey City and an eastbound Erie express crashed head-on, killing two brakemen. No passengers died.

Another serious collision occurred later in that year of disasters on August 12, 1853, on the Providence & Worcester Railroad at Valley Falls, Rhode Island. On that morning, an excursion train with seven passenger cars loaded with 475 holiday travelers was en route to Narragansett Bay via Providence. On the same morning, a train with two passenger cars left Providence, bound for Worcester. These trains, going in opposite directions, were set to pass each other on a double track siding near Pawtucket. The train out of Providence was on time and, on reaching Pawtucket, stopped for five minutes, according to company regulations. It then slowly proceeded toward the single track. As it rounded a sharp curve, suddenly, the train bound for Providence came down on it at full speed, which was about forty miles an hour. The two trains collided head-on at Valley Falls Station, killing thirteen people and injuring thirty others.

The first car of the excursion train was shattered and nearly everyone in it was either killed or injured. The second car was much less damaged but was somehow driven back into the third car, where casualties were much heavier. A survivor later wrote, "I was in the sixth car of the train. The first intimation that anything was wrong was three violent jerks succeeded by a crash and, what we supposed, the explosion of the boiler. There was, of course, a general rush for the doors, and passengers ran in confusion. It seemed as though the cars had not more than come together before a man was at work with an axe cutting into one of the windows of the second car to take out the body of a woman who had been instantly killed while attempting to escape. Two men were hanging between the roof of the second and third cars, lifeless, and another poor fellow caught while attempting to get out of a window, was imploring for help. The wounded were taken to a grove nearby. The dead were laid upon the grass. One young man presented a piteous sight. His arm was torn off near the shoulder, and he was left upon the grass, where he held up his lacerated stump and begged for help."

The disaster was caused by bad judgment on the part of Edwin Gates, the engineer of the Worcester-bound train. Gates thought that since the excursion train would be scheduled to wait five minutes at the siding, he would be able to make it to the double track before the other train finished waiting and started off again. His mistake proved to be a fatal one. Even though Gates raced at full speed to make up time, he was caught on the single track with the excursion train approaching around a sharp curve. A New York newspaper editor later wrote about the Valley Falls crash, "A vast majority of railroad disasters are directly owing to the stupidity and neglect of the employees and the apathy and avarice of the railroad owners."

The year 1853 was just the beginning of railroad disasters. With each passing year, the railroads reached farther points and the traffic on the rails steadily increased. And, year after year, the death toll rose. Calamites and fatalities continued for more than a half-century before mechanical improvements and safety devices began to lower the accident rate --- many years too late for scores of unlucky passengers.

One of the most tragic accidents during the middle nineteenth century occurred in 1856 between Camp Hill and Fort Washington, Pennsylvania. Two trains, traveling on the same track in opposite directions, collided and killed between 59 and 67 people (records are unclear) and injured more than one hundred. The incident was referred to as "The Great Train Wreck of 1856," "The Camp Hill Disaster" and "The Picnic Train Tragedy" and managed to shock all of America. It became one of the signature events of the era.

The disaster occurred on July 17, 1856, one of the hottest days of the year. An excursion train that was operated by the North Pennsylvania Railroad, known as the "Picnic Special," had been rented by St. Michael's Roman Catholic Church in Philadelphia to send their Sunday School children on a picnic in Shaeff's Woods, a shady grove near the

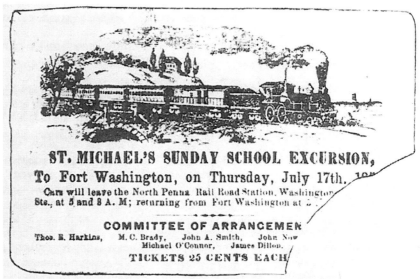

**ST. MICHAEL'S SUNDAY SCHOOL EXCURSION,**
To Fort Washington, on Thursday, July 17th.
Cars will leave the North Penna Rail Road Station, Washington Sts., at 5 and 8 A. M; returning from Fort Washington at 2.

**COMMITTEE OF ARRANGEMEN**
Thos. B. Harkins,    M. C. Brady,    John A. Smith,    John Now
        Michael O'Connor,    James Dillon.
**TICKETS 25 CENTS EACH**

**The remains of a ticket for the St. Michael's "Picnic Special" excursion**

railroad's Wissahickon station. The train, which was reported by the *New York Times* to have been carrying eleven hundred people (although there may have been as many as fifteen hundred passengers) was due to arrive at Wissahickon at 6:00 a.m. It left the depot at Master Street and Germantown Avenue in Philadelphia at 5:10 a.m., 23 minutes late, partly due to the large number of passengers that were on board.

The train was operated by engineer Henry Harris. The engine, known for having low steam pressure, was struggling with the twelve cars that were overloaded with passengers. A priest, Daniel Sheridan, was in the lead car with the older children. The rear cars carried women and the younger children. The train fell even more behind schedule as the engine was forced to make periodic stops to regain enough pressure to continue.

At the Wissahickon station, another train, engineered by William Vanstavoren, waited for the excursion train to pass on the single track. The train from Philadelphia was running late but the conductor did not try and telegraph Philadelphia, so no one had any idea when the train had departed. There was a customary fifteen-minute waiting period for regularly scheduled trains, but the "Picnic Special" was an excursion train, which confused the situation. At 6:15 a.m., Vanstavoren's train, carrying twenty passengers, pulled out of the station.

Vanstavoren was confident that he could make up the time he had lost while sitting in the station. He knew that the "Picnic Special" was due in the opposite direction on the same single track, but he calculated that they could use the siding at Edge Hill to safely pass each other. As he neared the blind curve just past Camp Hill Station, the train was traveling slightly downhill. Unfortunately, the excursion train was rounding the same curve with the same blind spot. Although engineer Harris blew his whistle almost continuously, the Doppler effect was not clearly understood at the time and, as a result, neither engineer knew where the other one was.

As each locomotive rounded the curve, they finally saw one another – but it was too late. To the sound of a horrendous screeching of brakes, the two trains collided at 6:18 a.m. The boilers made direct contact and caused an explosion that could be heard five miles away. The sounds of crashing metal, splintering wood, hissing steam and the screams of the passengers followed in the wake of the deafening explosion. The three front cars of the "Picnic Special" were utterly destroyed and a fire rapidly spread backward to the rest of the wooden cars. The initial impact did not claim most of the victims; rather most were burned to death – trapped in the derailed cars, which now lay on their sides. The women and children who occupied the rear coaches escaped serious injury and jumped from the train, wailing in a frenzy of terror and grief.

The blaze from the collision could be seen for several miles and a crowd began to gather from neighboring towns. It was later said that an unknown man rode on horseback through the countryside, shouting to residents, "Bring your camphor bottles, balsam and lint; there's been a horrible accident!" But the heat from the burning wreckage was so intense that it was impossible to get close enough to try and rescue those trapped inside the trains. Witnesses later reported seeing hands and arms that protruded from the cars, grasping blindly for help, but none could be offered.

A later report stated, "The most horrible sight of all was that of the burning cars; in a few minutes after the collision, the fire spread rapidly through the broken remnants, burning and roasting to death many men, women and children. The groans and shouts of wounded and those held by the rescuers were of a character to appall the bravest heart."

A bucket brigade, equipped with tubs, pails, kettles and other utensils, formed along the Sandy Run creek, which ran about 25 feet below the level of the tracks. The onlookers valiantly threw as much water at the wreckage as they could, but the brave effort yielded little in the way of results. The Congress Engine and Hose Company of Chestnut Hill finally reached the scene and, in a short time, managed to dampen the flames and pull the victims from the smoldering tangle of wood and steel.

A Camp Hill man named John Spencer, who lived within sight of the disaster, gave an account of what occurred during a coroner's investigation: "I was looking out of my shop window and saw the train approaching. I saw the down train first, just coming through the cut above Camp Hill station. It was slacking off as much as it could when it came through there. I had just time enough to turn around and saw the up train coming under the bridge at Camp Hill station. It was pretty smart. They were running about as they cleverly could. I heard the whistle on the train coming up before it reached the bridge... I could not see that the speed of the up train diminished between the time I first saw it and the time of the collision....eleven of the bodies of the dead were carried to my shop."

Mary Johnson Ambler, a Quaker woman who lived near the Wissahickon station, quickly gathered first aid materials and ran the two-mile distance between her home and the accident site. The care that she gave to the injured made such an impression that after her death in 1868, the North Pennsylvania Railroad changed the name of the station from Wissahickon to Ambler. Eventually, the town itself was named in her honor.

The horrifying news of the tragedy soon reached Philadelphia and St. Michael's parish. Men rushed from the factories and women ran weeping through the streets. At the railroad station where the train had departed, parents had to be restrained by the police when they attempted to use handcars to reach the disaster scene. As quickly as possible, coaches were attached to an idle locomotive in the station, but they were almost completely filled with nurses, doctors and nuns from the Sisters of Charity.

Henry Harris, engineer of the "Picnic Special," died in the accident, as did Father Sheridan. The destruction of the front cars was so extreme that many of the bodies were never found. Others were so badly burned that they could not be identified.

The other engineer, William Vanstavoren, managed to escape uninjured from the accident. He suffered from unimaginable guilt, for even though he was not actually to blame he could not be convinced otherwise. After returning to Philadelphia and officially reporting the accident, he went to his home on Buttonwood Street and committed suicide by taking arsenic. He was later absolved of any blame. A jury convicted the engineer of the "Picnic Special" for "gross carelessness."

The North Pennsylvania Railroad was shattered by the accident. Company owners took steps to provide financial benefits for the injured and the survivors of the victims. They issued shares of stock to those who would accept it and payments to those who would not. As it turned out, the shares eventually paid worthwhile dividends. The railroad also closed operations on the following Sunday to honor the victims.

In St. Michael's parish in Philadelphia, the dead have never been forgotten.

# 1869: THE AVONDALE MINE DISASTER

The greatest mine disaster in American history, up until that point, occurred in Avondale, Pennsylvania, on September 6, 1869. The deadly fire that broke out that morning in the Steuben Shaft of the Avondale mine trapped and killed more than one hundred miners. In those days, Americans were not used to a calamity of that magnitude and the disaster gained the attention of the entire nation. Tragically, it would not be the last such catastrophe to occur – nor would it be the last to leave stories of ghosts behind.

In nineteenth century America, almost every kind of industrial work had the possibility of being fatal, but mining was perhaps the most dangerous occupation of all. By the 1860s, some anthracite coal mines in Pennsylvania had reached depths of more than fifteen hundred feet, using techniques that are now considered unbelievably primitive. The problems came with the sinking of such shafts, largely due to the fact that there were few Americans with the expertise needed for deep mining. There were no professional engineers at that time and so coal mine owners depended on skilled miners from England, Scotland, Ireland and Wales for assistance. These men had a practical knowledge of mining and helped to construct the deep mines. Even with this knowledge there remained a number of problems with working so deep underground, including methods to drain water out of the mine and also to a system to ventilate the mine and provide fresh air for the miners. A particular problem to coal mines was the methane gas that sometimes accompanied the coal and could -- and often did -- catch fire and explode.

These problems, along with falling rock, dangerous equipment, cave-ins, runaway mine cars and general accidents, posed a horrible threat to miners. Fires that broke out in the deep recesses would consume the available oxygen in the mine and even men who were not close to the fire could be suffocated and killed. This is exactly what happened at the Avondale Mine disaster in 1869, the greatest early industrial accident in history.

Avondale was located in Luzerne County in northeastern Pennsylvania. The mine was on the banks of the Susquehanna River, four miles from Plymouth, a mining town in the Wilkes-Barre area, in the heart of the anthracite coal regions of Pennsylvania. Anthracite coal was extremely valued in home heating at the time and virtually all of this "hard coal" in America was mined in a relatively small area of Pennsylvania that stretched roughly from Scranton to Pottsville.

The Avondale disaster occurred on the morning of September 6, 1869, the first day after a lengthy labor strike had come to an end. The mine opened early that morning and scores of young men and boys had gone down into the shaft, determined to make up for the losses caused by the strike. Unknown to the men, a fire has started during the early morning hours when the ventilation fans had been turned on. The ventilating furnace let off some sparks and they ignited a wooden coal breaker, a device that chopped chunks of coal into various sizes and eliminated slate. Coal was sold in sizes such as pea, nut and stove.

Disaster at the Avondale Mine (*Harper's Weekly*)

Home furnaces required certain types of coal, which made coal breakers an essential part of every operation.

The blaze was discovered around 9:00 a.m. by the stable boss of the mine, who had gone down into the pit to bring a load of hay for the hauling mules. He immediately gave an alarm but moments later, a cloud of smoke, followed by a wall of flames, rose through the upcast compartment of the mine. The flames set fire to the engine house and the equipment at the top of the shaft, sending everyone into a panic and driving the engineer from his post. Because of the smoke and the intense heat at the mouth of the mine, there was no way to get to the miners trapped inside.

Dispatches were sent to all the neighboring cities and in a short time the fire departments of Wilkes-Barre, Scranton, Kingston, and adjoining towns were on their way to the scene. The news of the accident spread quickly and people rushed to the burning mine, hoping to rescue the miners, but they were powerless against the searing heat. Thousands of people flocked to the shaft within hours and their arrival added to the confusion and hampered the delivery of rescue equipment.

The flames swept up and engulfed the immense wooden structures that covered and surrounded the mineshaft, sending flames hundreds of feet into the air. The great clouds of smoke from the fire could be seen for miles around. As the wooden buildings burned, the pulley wheels, chains and all matter of steel material that was spread through the engine house collapsed down into the mine, following by burning timbers and flaming debris.

As the fire engines began to arrive, they pumped a feeble stream of water onto the inferno that did little to slow the spread of the flames. The fire continued to devour the buildings around the mine, raging for several hours. By almost nightfall, the fire had been subdued and a band of fifty volunteers, made up of other miners, superintendents and firemen, offered to go down into the mine. They vowed to rescue the trapped miners --- or die trying to do so. The set off on their quest, but with the shaft choked for nearly forty feet with fallen debris, darkness had come before they could gain entry into the mine itself.

A dog and a lamp were first let down as far as possible into the shaft. This would allow the rescue party to see if the air was breathable down in the mine. They pulled them both back up and found that the dog was still alive and the lamp was still burning. An hour later, a miner was lowered down the shaft and he returned in a few minutes, nearly exhausted. It took a large group of men to move all of the charred timbers and ruined equipment

**Reviving the rescue workers, who were overcome with gases while searching for survivors in the mine (*Harper's Weekly*)**

out of the way so that passage could be gained by the rest. They opened a landing at the bottom and they advanced about sixty yards into the main gallery of the mine. Their boots echoed hollowly in the silent chamber. No sounds came from within.

They soon made an unsettling discovery. The stables were filled with dead animals. The mules that had been used for hauling in the mine were lying lifeless on the floors of their stalls.

Just beyond the stables was the main door into the mine. Under normal conditions, the door would remain open for ventilation. Now, it had been sealed shut. The rescue party, starting to fall ill from the smoke and gases in the mine, began pounding on the door with a club and shouting as loud as they could to the men still trapped on the other side. They received no response and nearly overcome, they returned to the bottom

**Two images of bringing out the dead from the Avondale Mine (*Harper's Weekly*)**

of the shaft and were drawn back up to the surface.

A second rescue party had already been assembled and they went down into the mine, only to return a short time later, unable to withstand the gases. A large ventilating fan was put together at the surface and a canvas hose was dropped down into the shaft to provide fresh air. A third team was sent down and they penetrated deeper into the mine. They found that the ventilation furnace was still burning and that gases from the original fire were being drawn into the rest of the mine. This fire had to be put out before the men could venture any deeper and so water was sent down from the surface. Unbelievably, the hoses were too short and only a small stream of water could be applied to the blaze. Efforts continued throughout the night and by morning, the furnace fire had finally started to die out on its own.

During the second day, several attempts were made to reach the trapped miners but the accumulated gases prevented any extended search. By the early morning hours of the third day, the air had greatly improved and another team entered the depths of the mine. Within two hours, they came upon two corpses, who could not be recognized because of their blackened and burned features. They were the only two bodies that were found to be burned, leading the search party to believe that they had been separated from the rest of the miners when the fire broke out.

A message was sent to the surface stating that two casualties had been discovered and several more bands of would-be rescuers descended into the mine to assist with the search. A few hours later, a search party that had entered the eastern tunnels of the mine discovered the entire work force of the mine, huddled together behind an embankment that had been erected to seal off the deadly gases from the fire.

All one hundred and eight of them were dead.

Fathers and sons were found clasped in one another's arms. Some of the dead were kneeling, as if in prayer, while others lay on the ground with their faces downwards, as though trying to extract a mouthful of fresh air from the floor of the mine. Some sat holding hands with one another, as if seeking comfort in the face of death, while others appeared to have fallen while still walking. Death had not come from the fire --- at least in that they had not been burned to death --- but from the sudden loss of oxygen caused by the fire. With no ventilation, and no alternate air source, the fresh oxygen in the mine had been sucked out and consumed by the flames. The gas from the fire had seeped into the mine and killed everyone who came into contact with it.

Two hours after this grim discovery, sixty of the bodies had been taken to the surface and the last of the

A *Harper's Weekly* illustration of the dead men that were discovered by the rescue party in the mine.

unfortunates followed a short time later.

The miners simply had no way to escape. Investigators would come to believe that if a second or exit shaft had existed, nearly all of the deaths could have been avoided. Pennsylvania Governor John Geary blamed the disaster on "grossly negligent operations." Most agreed, although not everyone did. Some believed the disaster had been arranged on purpose.

The tragedy occurred just after a three-month strike that had caused tensions to run high all summer between Welsh and Irish miners. The largely Protestant Welsh tended to be the skilled miners, and favored ending the strike, while the Irish, predominately Catholic, were overwhelmingly laborers and were less enthusiastic about settling quickly. At the official inquest, which was held just two days after the disaster, a number of Welsh workers claimed that the Irish had sabotaged the mine because of the ethnic feud. One six of the one hundred and ten men that died were Irish, a fact that fueled the claims of a conspiracy.

In truth, many of the Irish workers did not come to work that day because they were attending the funeral of a prominent Irish civic leader. Their absence had nothing to do with sabotage and no credible evidence ever emerged to prove the conspiracy claims – but this didn't stop the rumors from spreading.

The conspiracy theories were further exacerbated by the belief that a secret Irish order called the Molly Maguires was operating in the area. The Molly Maguires were allegedly present in the anthracite coal fields of Pennsylvania from approximately the time of the Civil War until a series of sensational arrests and trials that occurred in the late 1870s. Evidence that the Molly Maguires were responsible for coal field crimes and labor unrest came largely from allegations made by powerful industrialist Franklin B. Gowen and the testimony of a single Pinkerton detective. There is little doubt that some Irish miners conspired to resist the terrible working conditions of the mines, but whether or not this "secret society" had anything to do with mine violence and

# 10 MOST DEADLY AMERICAN MINING DISASTERS

1. Killed: 361 - Dec. 6, 1907 - Monongah No. 6 & No. 8 Coal Mine explosion, Monongah, WV
2. Killed: 263 - Oct. 22, 1913 - Stag Canon No. 2 Coal Mine explosion, Dawson, NM
3. Killed: 259 - Nov. 13, 1909 - Cherry Coal Mine fire - Cherry, IL
4. Killed: 239 - Dec. 10, 1907 - Darr Coal Mine explosion - Jacobs Creek/Van Meter, PA
5. Killed: 200 - May 1, 1900 - Winter Quarters No. 1 & No. 4 Coal Mine explosion, Scofield, UT
6. Killed: 195 - May 19, 1928 - Mather No. 1 Coal Mine explosion - Mather, PA
7. Killed: 184 - May 19, 1902 - Fraterville Coal Mine explosion - Coal Creek, TN
8. Killed: 181 - Apr. 28, 1914 - Eccles No. 5 & No. 6 Coal Mine explosion - Eccles, WV
9. Killed: 179 - Jan. 25, 1904 - Harwick Coal Mine explosion - Cheswick, PA
10. Killed: 172 - Mar. 8, 1924 - Castle Gate No. 2 Coal Mine explosion - Castle Gate, UT

sabotage is open for debate. The only thing that remains certain is that the Molly Maguires left virtually no evidence of their existence, and nearly everything that was known about them was written by biased contemporary observers. There is nothing to suggest that any Irish saboteurs were responsible for the Avondale disaster. It was simply, as stated by Governor Geary, a case of negligent operations by the owners of the mine.

The story of the Avondale Mine Disaster spread all over the country. Papers throughout America, including the widely read *Harper's Weekly* and *Leslie's Illustrated Newspaper*, covered the tragedy. A popular ballad was written that told the story of the disaster and through word of mouth, it gained great fame.

Not surprisingly, the calamity provided a source of ghost stories shortly after the mine's re-opening. Rumors began to spread that the ghosts of the disaster victims were still lingering in the depths of the Steuben Shaft. For several weeks, workers refused to enter the mine until the management found a way to remove the ghosts. Needless to say, mine company officials were quick to dispel the rumors. According to one of the managers, the story of ghosts came about when a miner had tried to light a match on his wet clothing. The resulting weird flashes, which were seen in the blackness of the mine, were mistaken for ghosts by another miner.

What about the voices, whispers and strange sounds that had been heard in the mine? Officials had an answer for that one, too. They claimed the sounds were being caused by ground water that seeped into the earth and then dripped into the mine. The sounds varied depending on what objects the water dripped on and they were apparently being mistaken for spectral voices. A man working by himself in the darkness was prone to hearing things, they said, especially in a place where so many of his fellow workers had recently died.

There were no ghosts, officials announced, just superstitious miners who told tall tales. But not everyone was convinced. If the ghosts were merely wet matches and a dripping ceiling, then why had the experienced miners never encountered these natural occurrences before? Why did they not begin to happen until after the deaths of the unlucky workers? No answers were ever provided and perhaps because of this, the rumors of ghosts in the Avondale mine persisted until it closed many years later.

# IMAGES OF AVONDALE TODAY

**Abandoned buildings at the site today**

**Entrance to the shaft where the minders died**

# 1871: HORROR ON THE RAILS
# THE REVERE RAILROAD ACCIDENT

Following the Civil War, railroad travel in America reached its peak of popularity. The major lines battled to build a coast-to-coast track that would connect the farthest reaches of the country. The rush to build bigger and faster caused accidents and disasters to occur.

In 1871, a catastrophic rear-end collision near Revere, Massachusetts, still holds a chilling place in railroad history. Although only 32 people were killed, the accident made an impression on the lives of mid-Victorian Americans. It remains today as one of the best-known American railroad disasters.

The Revere disaster happened on the Eastern Railroad line on August 26, 1871. It was a Saturday evening and rail traffic was especially heavy that weekend. The Eastern Railroad Company had been forced to run an extra "accommodation" train on Saturday evening to handle the demand. Weekend events, including two large camp meetings and a military muster, had sent the railroad scrambling to keep up with the passenger load. This turned out to be one of the reasons for the accident.

Because of the many travelers, 192 trains left Eastern's Boston station on each day of that weekend. A normal number would have been 152. Four trains had been scheduled to depart from Boston between 6:30 p.m. and 8:00 p.m. Three headed for Lynn, eleven miles to the north, and the fourth to Portland, Maine. But the 6:30 train and the two that followed it, including the accommodation train, left the station behind schedule. The Portland express set out a few minutes after its scheduled 8:00 p.m. departure. Already behind schedule, the accommodation train lost more time on account of the delay of a southbound train from Lynn.

The snag halted traffic at the Everett Junction, which lay between Boston and Revere, until the track cleared. Normally, a flagman kept traffic flowing by directing waiting trains to tracks that were not in use. On August 26, however, the usual flagman was sick. His replacement held the accommodation train in place rather than coordinate a maneuver that would allow it to continue traveling northward. The delay allowed the Portland express to draw closer to the lagging accommodation train.

**A contemporary illustration of the deadly Revere, Mass. crash in 1871**

A telegraph message could have easily warned the engineers of the narrowing distance between trains and automatic signals could have provided further information of the interval between them. However, Eastern had failed to invest in these new devices. In addition, the accommodation train, which had stopped at the Revere station, did not have effective rear lights that would have signaled the engineer of the approaching train that another train was on the tracks ahead of him. These problems, combined with darkness and a light mist that had drifted in from the ocean and made the rails slippery, were a recipe for disaster.

The express train was traveling at about thirty miles an hour when it approached Revere. It was already dark at 8:30 p.m. (America had not yet adopted daylight savings time) and the accommodation train had no illumination. The engineer looked away to check on a signal pole that controlled a switch to a siding as he rounded the curve in the approach to Revere station. He didn't see the train ahead of him until it was too late. As the headlight of the express train flashed across the rear car of the train ahead, the engineer sounded the whistle that instructed trainmen to set the brakes manually. Moist from the mist, the rails were slippery and the express slammed into the back of the other train.

On impact, the engine forced itself two-thirds of the way into the rear car of the accommodation train, which was packed with people. The force of the collision ruptured the locomotive's steam valves, searing the victims with hot vapors. Coals from the firebox mixed with oil from broken kerosene car lamps and burst into flames. The flames spread quickly and soon, all of the cars of the accommodation train were on fire. "Crushing, scalding and burning did their work together," wrote Charles Francis Adams, grandson of president John Quincy Adams and the member of the Massachusetts Board of Railroad Commissioners who reported on the accident. Half of the occupants of the rear car were killed – either crushed to death by the impact or burned in the fire that followed. Another 57 people were seriously injured.

The public was outraged by the accident and meetings were held in Boston to condemn the railroad. Headlines of "Deliberate Murder" appeared in some newspapers. Charles Francis Adams used the disaster to push for railroad safety improvements and convinced rail managers in Massachusetts to endorse a variety of reforms, including telegraph communications, sturdier passenger cars and the installation of automatic signals. Adams also urged the introduction of Westinghouse air brakes, which allowed the train engineer to set the brakes for the entire train, rather than continue the old method of having the brakeman react to the train whistle and set the brakes by hand. Federal legislation required all trains to install the system in 1893. In addition, the use of kerosene lights in trains was banned starting in 1887, when all trains had to install electric lights.

The Eastern Railroad Company adopted some of these improvements after the accident, but the cost of the reforms added to the company's growing debt, a financial burden that resulted in part from all of the lawsuits and liability settlements from the crash. The railroad barely dodged bankruptcy but it managed to limp along until 1882, when it was taken over by the Boston and Maine Railroad.

Railroad lore tells of at least one ghost story connected to this horrible accident, a phantom signalman who warned oncoming trains near the last curve before the Revere station. In the weeks, months and years following the crash, railroad engineers often told of seeing a waving signal light as they approached the station. The light appeared to be in someone's hands, although none of them ever got close enough to see who was holding it. As the train slowed down at the curve, the light always disappeared. Word spread up and down the line that the signalman was a ghost.

But who was this mysterious figure? Railroad workers wanted to believe that it was one of their own, perhaps a victim of the crash who now warned his living co-workers of possible danger. Others claimed that the ghostly man was a passenger on the accommodation train who had been killed in the collision. He was now trying to warn

## 10 MOST DEADLY AMERICAN TRAIN WRECKS

1. Killed: 101 - July 9, 1918 – Two-train collision - Nashville, TN
2. Killed: 96 - Aug. 7, 1904 - Train derailed on a bridge due to a flash flood - Eden, CO
3. Killed: 96 - Mar. 1, 1910 - Two trains swept into a canyon by an avalanche - Wellington, WA
4. Killed: 92 - Dec. 29, 1876 - Lake Shore train fell due to a bridge collapse - Ashtabula, OH
5. Killed: 92 - Nov. 1, 1918 - Subway train derailed in Melborne St. Tunnel, Brooklyn.
6. Killed: 85 - Feb. 6, 1951 - Pennsylvania RR train plunged through a temporary overpass - Woodbridge, NJ
7. Killed: 81, Injured: 372 - Aug. 10, 1887 - Train crashed due to a burning train trestle - Chatsworth, IL
8. Killed: 79 - Nov. 22, 1950 - Rear-end Collision - Richmond Hill, NY
9. Killed: 72 - Dec. 16, 1943 - Collision of two Atlantic Coast Line trains - Rennert, NC
10. Killed: 50 to 60 - July 17, 1856 - Two trains collided - Camp Hill near Ft. Washington, PA

oncoming engineers so that what happened to him would not befall anyone else.

The story of the Revere ghost light continued for many years, long after Boston and Maine took over Eastern's line. But reforms brought changes to the railroad and construction and refurbishments along the old line brought an end to the haunting for good. The ghost has since been largely forgotten, much like the disaster itself, and is only recalled in the pages of old books and in the half-remembered tales of railroad buffs with a penchant for the unusual.

## 1876: HORROR FOR THE HOLIDAYS
## GHOSTS OF THE ASHTABULA BRIDGE DISASTER

The holiday season of 1876 should have been a joyous time for those in northern Ohio. Christmas Day had just passed and America's Centennial Year was coming to an end with a New Year's Celebration that was only days away. However, on December 27, the region was blanketed by an intense winter storm that showed no signs of letting up. This could have been taken for an ominous sign that dark days were ahead but no one had any idea just how dark those days would become.

On Friday, December 29, the small town of Ashtabula, located in the northeast corner of Ohio, was a white wasteland of snow and ice. A blizzard had hammered the little town with more than twenty inches of snow and wind that whipped along at more than fifty miles an hour. Despite the weather, the town train depot was bustling. Anxious passengers, many leaving town for the holidays or waiting for trains to arrive, crowded into the station. Many of them awaited the arrival of the No. 5 Pacific Express that was running more than two hours late from Erie, Pennsylvania. Weather delays had kept it in the Erie station until after 6:00 p.m. Many of those waiting in the depot had friends and family on the train or needed to make the connection to continue their own journey.

While things may have been anxious in the station, the scene was much more relaxed and festive aboard the No. 5 train. The warm and snug passengers were seemingly oblivious to the frigid conditions outside as two locomotives pulled two express cars, two baggage cars, one smoking car, two passenger cars and three sleeping cars along at a steady ten miles per hour. The passengers ate and chatted, played cards or slept peacefully in their berths. Others prepared to leave the train at Ashtabula or warmed themselves near the coal-fired heaters that provided heat for all of the cars, except for the smoking car, which had an old-fashioned wood stove. All of the cars were cozily lit by oil lamps, providing the illusion of being completely separated from the storm outside. The exact number of passengers aboard the train remains a mystery to this day, but it is believed that there were at least 128 passengers and nineteen crew members on the No. 5 as it steamed onto the railway bridge that spanned Ashtabula Creek.

Daniel McGuire, the engineer of the first locomotive, the "Socrates," was the first to realize that there was a problem. As the engine crossed onto the bridge, he pulled the throttle out and increased the speed of the train. They needed the extra power to drive the train through the two feet of snow on the tracks and to push against the gale force winds that buffeted the train on the open bridge. But as the "Socrates" approached the western abutment of the bridge, McGuire had the sudden sensation that the engine was "running uphill." He looked back and was stunned with horror as he saw the rest of the train -- the second engine, the "Columbia," and eleven cars -- collapsing with the bridge as it plunged more than eighty feet downward to the creek below. McGuire pulled the

**(Left) A _Harper's Weekly_ illustration of the aftermath of the crash.**
**(Right) A photograph of the bridge over the Ashtabula River, taken after the disaster.**

throttle out all the way and the "Socrates" surged ahead. He broke the coupling with the second engine, the "Columbia," and somehow coaxed the locomotive to safety. As he pulled the brakes on the other side, McGuire heard the chilling sounds of crashing and twisting steel coming from the swirling darkness of the storm.

The Ashtabula depot lay just one thousand feet beyond the bridge and William Alsell, a telegraph operator, was the first person at the station to realize what had happened. He had hoped to hitch a ride through town on the train when it left the station and he had heard the whistle of the No. 5 as it approached the bridge. He was actually walking toward it when it started across the bridge. When he caught a glimpse of its lights, he turned to head back to the depot and gather his belongings when he heard the horrific crash. He spun around just in time to see the lights from the sleeping cars as they fell and then vanished into the darkness. He immediately began running to the bridge, only to discover that the structure was no longer there.

The experiences of the passengers and crew aboard the train were even more horrifying. Miss Marian Shepherd, a survivor of the disaster, was in her sleeper berth and later recalled that she knew something was wrong when the bell rope snapped in two, with one piece smashing an oil lamp and the other knocking over a burning candle. A moment later, she heard a thudding noise that sounded as though the train wheels had jumped the track and were now riding on the wooden ties. This was followed by a tremendous shattering sound as if all of the glass in the entire train had suddenly broken at once. The train car plunged downward and Miss Shepherd distinctly remembered the cry of someone in the car as he wailed, "We are going down!" The scream was followed by the sickening sensation of falling and she desperately braced herself. Outside the sleeping berth, the air was filled with seats, lamps and human bodies as the car pitched into space. Seconds later, the sleeper hit the rest of the No. 5 cars and all of them crashed into the freezing waters of the creek.

Surrounded by the broken bodies of those who did not survive the fall, Marian struggled to get out of her berth and fight her way to safety. She was in shock and terrified by the screams of the injured around her in the darkness. Those who were alive also tried to get out and cries were mixed with the terror of drowning in the icy water. As it happened, the fear of drowning was second only to the danger of being burned alive. The cars had fallen in an upright position and were now stacked and smashed upon one another, with the bottom layer below the surface of Ashtabula Creek. Within five minutes of the wreck, the last car, with its heater still burning, caught on fire. People like Marian, both dazed and bleeding, managed to stumble out of the cars and saw the winter night illuminated by flames as the cars caught fire one at a time. Within just a few minutes, the remains of the cars and single locomotive had turned into a blazing inferno. The heaters, lamps and the heavily varnished woodwork of the cars combined to engulf the mass of twisted wood and metal into a tower of flames.

The survivors of the disaster would never forget what they saw that night. Most of them worked frantically alongside a rescue crew from town as they tried to pull the wounded and the dead from the burning cars. Finally, the heat grew so intense that they were driven back, unaware that many of those who had been already rescued

**A picture postcard of the Ashtabula Bridge Disaster from the late 1800s**

were now sinking into the waters of the creek. The heat from the fire had melted the ice on the river's surface and now the water was surging up towards the bloody and burning debris. As they cried for help, the cold water washed into the wreck, drowning many of those still trapped there -- perhaps mercifully when faced with burning to death. One woman, later recalled by engineer Daniel McGuire, was trapped in the wreckage as the fire burned toward her and she begged with someone to cut off her legs and pull her out before the flames reached her. Tragically, no one made it to her in time and McGuire could only watch helplessly as she burned to death. McGuire's friend, "Columbia" engineer, Peter Levenbroe, had been crushed in the engine when it fell. He died on the way to the hospital in Cleveland.

William Alsell, the telegraph operator, had fallen and stumbled down the snow-covered hill to the wreck just moments after seeing the train plunge to its doom. Kicking out windows, he pulled wounded and unconscious passengers to safety and fought bravely to keep them from the fire and icy waters. Meanwhile, Daniel McGuire, after bringing the "Socrates" to a halt, sprinted to the depot with the terrible news before returning to the scene. A minute later, brakeman A.L. Stone, who had escaped from the last car, limped into the station. He was badly hurt and bleeding but managed to send a telegram to Erie in case another train was following behind the No. 5. Within minutes, every bell in Ashtabula was sounding the alarm for firemen and volunteers.

The situation surrounding the fire, which killed more people than the initial wreck, has been a subject of mystery and debate since 1876. Although the Ashtabula fire department managed to get one engine down to the fire, no hoses were ever connected and no water, save for a few buckets of melted snow, was ever directed at the burning debris. It was rumored afterwards that officials from the Lake Shore & Michigan Southern Railroad forbade anyone to put out the fire. The reason, according to rumors, was that the company's insurance liability would be less if the passengers were not only dead, but burned beyond recognition, as well. There was no truth to this but it added to the finger-pointing and blame that followed.

The less dramatic reasons were the confusing conditions at the scene. No one had ever seen anything like it before and when Ashtabula fire chief G.A. Knapp arrived on the scene 45 minutes after the crash (possibly intoxicated), he found a scene of total pandemonium. There was no organized effort to do anything. Passengers and rescuers were simply trying to save anyone they could and were hampered by the fire, the water, smoke, snow and treacherous terrain. Efforts were further impeded by the hundreds of spectators who had gathered and by the activities of thieves, who boldly robbed the wounded and helpless passengers. The terror at the scene was increased by the terrible snapping noise created by the paint on the train cars as it ignited.

Fire Chief Knapp gazed in bewilderment at the wreck and asked train station agent George Strong which side of the burning mass he and his men should put water on. Strong, more concerned about the advancing flames killing people than where the fire department should direct their water, told him to worry about getting the people out instead. This was likely the right decision, but it never mattered for no actual orders were given by Knapp, Strong or any Ashtabula officials that night. The firemen simply pitched into the efforts of the rescue workers and concentrated their efforts on pulling the wounded from their fiery and watery fates. The fire eventually burned itself out and by daybreak the train was a blackened pile of burned metal, scorched debris and roasted human flesh.

It took more than a week to clean it all up. Although one hundred and fifty men were eventually sent to the scene by the railroad, they never found all of those who were missing – nor did they identify all of the dead. The main problem was that no one had any idea just how many passengers had been on the train. The conductor's records showed 128 passengers but others claimed upwards of two hundred were on board when the wreck occurred. The best estimate is that 89 were killed and 63 were injured, five of whom died later. There were nineteen corpses, or parts of corpses, that were never identified. A temporary morgue was set up in the Lake Shore & Michigan Southern freight depot and weeping loved ones searched through the boxes of remains for weeks afterward. Many of them were identified only by jewelry that somehow managed to escape the notice of thieves at the disaster site. After funeral services at two Ashtabula churches were conducted on January 19, 1877, the unidentified dead were buried in nearby Chestnut Grove Cemetery. A monument was created for them in the 1890s, largely funded by Governor William McKinley and Lucretia Garfield, widow of the late president.

The investigations into the disaster began as the fires were still smoldering. At 9:00 a.m. on the day after the accident, an inquest was convened under the authority of Justice of the Peace Edward W. Richards. It lasted for 68 days and dozens of witnesses were heard. The jury in the case reached a series of eight verdicts, all highly critical of the Lake Shore & Michigan Southern railroad and the rescuers at the scene. The verdicts are still considered controversial today.

They ruled that the railroad was entirely responsible for the accident and the deaths and injuries resulting from it. The jury stated that the company had willfully designed, constructed and erected a fatally flawed bridge and then had failed to adequately inspect it for the next eleven years, leading up to the disaster. Additionally, they also found that the railroad, in violation of Ohio law, had failed to warm the passenger cars with a "heating apparatus so constructed that the fire in it will be immediately extinguished whenever the cars are thrown from the track." Finally, the jury blamed the fire department and the railroad officials at the disaster scene for many of the fire deaths, claiming that they should have put out the fire rather than try to rescue trapped victims.

None of those accused by the jury took it lightly. The Lake Shore & Michigan Southern Railroad eventually paid off about $500,000 in damage claims with little dispute. However, the company refused to admit responsibility for the bridge failure, arguing that the wreck was caused by either the "Columbia" leaving the track, a broken rail or incredibly, a tornado that swept down and wiped out the bridge. The most vocal in rejecting blame was Amasa B. Stone, Jr., a Cleveland millionaire and railroad mogul who had designed and built the bridge. Until the day he died, he insisted the bridge had been sound and that it had to be human error or an act of God that caused the disaster.

Stone was wrong but the truth was more complex than either side would ever have allowed. The original railroad bridge over Ashtabula Creek had been a wooden one. In 1863, Amasa Stone made plans to replace it with a design of his own. The key section was the middle span, a 154-foot piece that sat on two stone abutments that were put up after an extensive fill had narrowed the river valley. It was a variation on the long-used wood and iron truss but Stone's new design used an all-iron structure, a type that had never been tried and as it turned out, would never be replicated. The new structure was installed in the fall of 1865 and was a series of fourteen panels that were protected against the force produced by the weight of the trains by enormous diagonal I-beams. All of the steel in the bridge was produced at the Cleveland Rolling Mills, which was owned by Stone's brother, Andros. The crew installing the bridge ran into many problems and at one point, it had to be entirely taken down and then put back up again at great expense. When Joseph Tomlinson, an engineer on the project, warned Stone about the stress on the trusses, Stone fired him. When completed, the bridge was tested by the weight of six locomotives and pronounced safe.

After the disaster, many would remark that it was not so surprising that the bridge fell but that it managed to stay up for eleven years without mishap. It was inspected four times each year by railroad officials, who reported no problems -- except for the suspicious "snapping" noise that train engineers sometimes heard as they traveled over the bridge. Also, among the details missed by inspectors was the fact that the metal on the ends of the beams had been crudely filed down to make them fit. If inspector Charles Collins, who looked at the bridge just ten days before the calamity and found no problems, had gotten down among the I-beams and had seen what many others saw when the ruined bridge was on the ground two months later, he would have shut it down immediately. Several of the I-beams were as much as three inches out of alignment at their juncture with the bearing blocks. Given that the essence of the design was the connection of all of the parts, the displacement of the I-beams meant that it was just a matter of time before something horrible occurred.

Amasa Stone refused to admit guilt, though, and was especially arrogant when questioned by a special investigative committee of the Ohio legislature on January 18, 1877. Not only had the bridge been safe, he insisted, but it had been designed to be stronger than it needed to be. As for the stoves that set the cars on fire, he insisted that he had examined every other type of stove that was available and had dismissed them as unsuitable. The stoves that he had used, manufactured by Baker, had simply been the best. No stove could be designed to extinguish itself in case of an accident. In his final opinion, he stated that the train had jumped the tracks and in turn, had demolished the bridge.

Inspector Charles Collins was the mirror opposite of Stone. The man who had recently inspected the bridge reportedly "wept like a baby" when he saw the wreckage and loss of life in the Ashtabula valley. Although he testified in public that he always thought the bridge was safe, there were whispers that he told a different story to those who were close to him. Some maintained that he had been forced to give favorable reports about the bridge by the company and that he often said that he prayed "it will be a freight and not a passenger train" that fell when the bridge finally went down. Collins took most of the blame for the company after the disaster and there was no question that he blamed himself for the accident. Three days after he testified to the special committee, he was found dead in his bed at his home on Seneca Street in Cleveland. He had blown his brains out with a pistol hours after he completed his testimony.

Fate eventually caught up with Amasa Stone, as well. Although he never accepted any responsibility for the accident and avoided personal legal consequences for it, there is no question that he was hurt by the public perception of him as a "murderer." His temperament, never a happy one to begin with, became even darker after business reverses and then ill health followed in the wake of the Ashtabula disaster. His only son had drowned while he was a student at Yale and Stone had been plagued with stomach pains and insomnia, sleeping as little as two hours a night. By 1883, he had endured all that he could stand and on the afternoon of May 11, he locked himself in his bathroom and fired a bullet through his heart. When Stone's wife discovered the bathroom door locked and no response when she knocked, she had the butler climb through the transom. Stone was discovered lying in the bathtub, half-dressed, a silver-plated Smith & Wesson revolver by his side.

There is little to be seen today where the terrible events of December 1876 took place. The river now flows beneath an ordinary viaduct and it is impossible now to imagine the horror, fear and death that took place there. In spite of this, some mysteries do remain. According to some, the No. 5 train was said to have been carrying as much as $2 million in gold bullion on that cold December night. If it was, all of it was lost in the valley below and remains there today, still waiting for someone to find it.

Whether there is lost treasure in the valley or not, there are no ghosts there. Those who lost their lives have strangely not been found at the place where their lives ended so tragically but rather at the Chestnut Grove Cemetery, where the remains of the unidentified were laid to rest. It is there, near the stark, granite obelisk that marks the common grave, where visitors to the graveyard have reported seeing specters walk about. The wraiths, often seen in period warm weather clothing, wander about carrying carpetbags and baskets. Screams are sometimes heard in the darkness and some claim that a burning smell often sweeps through the air nearby.

Just a short distance away from the mass grave is the ornate gothic mausoleum of Charles Collins, the luckless inspector who had missed the fatal flaws in the Ashtabula Bridge. It is ironic that he would be entombed to close to the graves of those who death he inadvertently caused and not surprisingly, his ghost is said to haunt this place, too. According to the stories, the spectral figure of a man has been seen near the tomb. He often appears with his face in his hands, weeping bitterly. "I'm sorry -- I'm so very sorry," he cries, wringing his hands in torment and then he vanishes, never finding the forgiveness that he so desperately craves.

# 1906: 'THE DAMNDEST FINEST RUINS'
# THE GREAT SAN FRANCISCO EARTHQUAKE

*"Our fine city lies in ruins, but those are the damndest, finest ruins the world has ever seen."*
**Eugene Schmitz, San Francisco Mayor, 1906**

In 1906, San Francisco was regarded as one of the world's great cities. From its start as a rough-and-tumble mining town during the gold rush of 1849, it became a cosmopolitan destination of nearly a half-million people that many considered the "Paris of the West." There were fashionable department stores, luxury hotels, widely read newspapers, and an opera house that hosted the greatest tenor of the time, Enrico Caruso.

But San Francisco's standing as one of America's great cities was shattered on April 18, 1906.

The sun rose as usual on the morning of April 18. The brilliant California sunshine began to chase away the fog and the mist that surrounded the city after dark and a fresh wind promised a delightful day. Unlike hurricanes, earthquakes give no warning to those they are about to destroy. There is no such thing as "earthquake weather" – no change in temperature, no wind, no thunder. There is nothing to cause feelings of suspense or alarm before the actual shock occurs.

At 5:00 a.m., the streets of San Francisco were quiet and nearly empty. The only people out there a handful of policemen, a few journalists leaving their offices after a long night at a desk, workmen heading to early work and the wagon drivers who delivered the morning's milk to the city. And, of course, in San Francisco, there were also parties of revelers who had been out all night enjoying themselves, still in evening dress as they journeyed home.

Earlier the previous night, some of these same revelers had attended a performance of *Carmen* at the Grand Opera House in which Enrico Caruso had taken the part of Don Jose. The legendary tenor was on a nationwide tour but the following morning, he would be found collapsed on the ground, weeping in fear, among a crowd of shocked survivors in a downtown square. He vowed never to come back to San Francisco -- and he never did.

At 5:12 a.m., the city began to shake. A terrible noise roared across the landscape and the ground began to move. A powerful earthquake, centered just off the coast, shook the city to limits beyond imagination. The quake arrived in two shuddering movements, the second more powerful than the first. Emma Burke, the wife of a local attorney, wrote, "[It] hurled my bed against an opposite wall. It grew constantly worse, the noise deafening; the crash of dishes, falling pictures, the rattle of the flat tin roof, bookcases being overturned, the piano hurled across the parlor, the groaning and straining of the building itself, broken glass and falling plaster, made such a roar that no one noise could be distinguished."

Ship captains said it felt as though their vessels had been washed onto a sea of rocks. Wooden, frame structures snapped, splintered and collapsed, while brick buildings that had not been strongly reinforced tumbled to the ground. Stunned and sleepy residents ran out into the streets, many of which had opened up with yawning fissures. Trees whipped over, telephone poles snapped and the streetcar rails buckled and bent. Amidst all of the noise, all of the church bells of San Francisco, tolled out an eerie alarm, swayed by the quake, that lasted several minutes after the shaking came to an end.

One eyewitness account by P. Barrett described it this way: "We could not get to our feet. Big buildings were crumbling as one might crush a biscuit in one's hand. Ahead of me a great cornice crushed a man as if he were a

**Photographs of just a fraction of the damage that was done to San Francisco during the 1906 Earthquake and Fire**

maggot." A policeman on duty the morning of the quake likened the ground's movement to a wave in a rough sea rolling down the street. He later stated, "I could see it actually coming. The whole street was undulating. It was as if the waves of the ocean were coming toward me."

The center of the earthquake may have been out to sea, but the damage, thanks to the extensive use of unreinforced brick masonry, was centered on Chinatown, the waterfront working-class neighborhood south of Market Street. When the tremors tore through this reclaimed swampland, the earth literally tore itself apart, causing businesses, homes and hotels to collapse. Many structures were destroyed, including the four-story Valencia Street Hotel, which completely fell down upon itself. The night clerk ran from the building and gave this account: "The hotel lurched forward as if the foundation were dragged backward from under it, and crumpled down over Valencia Street. It did not fall to pieces and spray itself all over the place, but telescoped down on itself like a concertina." Surviving guests in top floor rooms merely had to step outside to escape the fallen building. Those who were staying in rooms on the floors below were crushed. One hundred people may have died in the hotel.

In the quiet of the city after the shaking stopped, even more destructive forces were at work. Much of the water supply to the city came in rigid iron pipes and about thirty thousand of them ruptured with the intense tremors. This would be a significant problem once the fires began and they began almost immediately, fed by escaping gas. The quakes had broken the city's fire alarm system, but the billowing smoke directed firefighters where to go. They hooked hoses to the hydrants but when they opened the valves, no water gushed forth. The lines had all been broken.

For the next three days, residents struggled to contain what became a firestorm. The tight, wooden-frame construction made fast fuel for the blaze as it jumped from building to building and devoured block after block. It swept east, destroying a local college, the Hall of Records and San Francisco's massive City Hall. Walls of fire came from every direction and smoke filled the sky.

Author Jack London, who rode to San Francisco from his ranch in Glen Ellen, wrote about the earthquake and fire for newspaper readers across the country who were eager for news. He wrote, "Within an hour after the earthquake shock, the smoke of San Francisco's burning was a lurid tower visible a hundred miles away. And for three days and nights this lurid tower swayed in the sky, reddening the sun, darkening the day, and filling the land with smoke."

**Famous adventure author Jack London went to San Francisco after the disaster to report on what he saw there.**

Residents fled from the city, taking away what possessions they could. Navy boats and local firefighters had saved the wharf, which allowed tens of thousands to escape by water. Others fled to high ground at Telegraph Hill and at Lafayette Square.

The fate of those still trapped in the earthquake rubble was a horrific one. At places like the Valencia Street Hotel, rescuers worked feverishly to free survivors that were pinned beneath the stone and metal, but they were forced to retreat as the fire descended. Those not crushed to death were burned alive.

The blaze was so intense that it created its own weather pattern, drawing storm-force winds to feed itself with oxygen. "Near the flames, the wind was often half a gale, so mighty was the suck," wrote Jack London. With the water lines broken and the fire hydrants useless, firefighters tried to pump water from the sewer lines beneath the streets. The small trickle that resulted was useless against the inferno.

Dennis Sullivan, the city's fire chief, had warned against the hazard of a city that was tightly clustered with wooden buildings and was aware of the devastation that a large fire could cause. He had introduced a plan to dynamite buildings to create firebreaks in the event of a massive fire. But Chief Sullivan was killed in the first minutes of the earthquake when a brick chimney fell on him. With his death, any semblance of a plan was lost.

Sullivan's successor, John Doughtery, had no expertise with dynamite and no idea what to do to

Dynamite was used to try and stop the spread of the fire that began after the earthquake. Unfortunately, the explosives doomed much of the city that was not already burned.

try and stop the spread of the fire. Grasping at what he could from Sullivan's plan, he contacted the military base at the Presidio and asked for the Army's help. General Frederick Funston, the post commander, assisted by ordering his troops into the streets to maintain order, help fight the fires and coordinate the demolition work needed to create a fire break. In the July 1906 issue of *Cosmopolitan* magazine, Funston wrote, "I doubt if anyone will ever know the amount of dynamite and gun cotton used in blowing up buildings, but it must have been tremendous, as there were times when the explosions were so continuous as to resemble a bombardment."

As it turned out, the dynamite doomed much of the city that wasn't already burned, starting additional fires and helping some of them to spread. In Chinatown, an estimated sixty fires were started from the demolition alone. Worsening this misguided strategy, the soldiers often used gunpowder instead of dynamite, which simply set buildings on fire rather than knocking them down. According to the *San Francisco Chronicle,* at one point the troops actually shelled buildings with artillery fire. When they did use actual dynamite, the ineptness of those in charge allowed flaming debris from the buildings to ignite ruptured gas lines and to set surrounding buildings on fire.

Late on the night of the earthquakes, Jack London found himself standing in Union Square, the heart of the city. He wrote, "It was packed with refugees. Thousands of them had gone to bed on the grass. Government tents had been set up, supper was being cooked, and the refugees were lining up for free meals." By the early morning hours of April 19, the square was deserted and burning on three sides. The refugees had moved on fled.

The fire – and the dynamiting – continued the next day. By Friday, the center of the city was smoldering and firefighters mounted a final, total-destruction campaign to stop the fire at Van Ness Avenue. Unbelievably, the firebreak worked – but San Francisco was in ruins. Four square miles of city and 522 blocks had been destroyed. More than twenty-eight thousand buildings were now rubble.

Rumors spread that looting in the days after the quake was rampant, but this seems to have been more legend than truth. In spite of this, Mayor Eugene Schmitz issued an illegal "shoot to kill" order and the military pressed citizens into work crews at gunpoint. Word spread and newspapers across the country damned San Francisco officials for these questionable acts.

Fearing more bad press, the city's leaders reported the official death toll from the quakes and the fires to be less than five hundred. Historians have since argued that anywhere from three thousand to six thousand people were likely killed in the devastation. More than three hundred thousand fled the city in the hours after the initial quakes.

"San Francisco is gone," Jack London wrote in one of his newspaper dispatches. "Its industrial section is wiped out. Its business section is wiped out. Its social and residential section is wiped out. The factories and warehouses, the great stores and newspaper buildings, the hotels and the palaces of the nabobs, are all gone."

Property losses from the disaster have been estimated at more than $400 million (which would be over $5 billion in today's dollars), however political and business leaders strongly downplayed the effects of the

## MOST DEADLY AMERICAN EARTHQUAKES

1. Killed: 700 to 3,000 - Apr. 18, 1906 - Caused fire that burned 4 sq. miles - San Francisco, CA
2. Killed: 117 - Mar. 10, 1933 - Long Beach, CA
3. Killed: 117 - Mar. 28, 1964 - Strongest recorded in North America with a magnitude of 9.2 – Alaska
4. Killed: 67, Injured 3,000 - Oct. 17, 1989 - San Francisco Bay area, CA
5. Killed: 60 - Aug. 31, 1886 - 7.3 Magnitude - Charleston, SC
6. Killed: Unknown - Dec. 16, 1811 - Largest series of North American quakes - New Madrid, MO

earthquake, fearing the loss of outside investment in a city that badly needed to be rebuilt. Now, both the fatality and the monetary damage estimates had been manipulated.

In his first public statement after the disaster, California Governor George C. Pardee immediately spoke of rebuilding. He said, "This is not the first time that San Francisco has been destroyed by fire, I have not the slightest doubt that the City by the Golden Gate will be speedily rebuilt, and will, almost before we know it, resume her former great activity." The earthquake – which had caused the fire in the first place – was not even mentioned.

Almost as the dust was still settling after the earthquake, planning and reconstruction ideas began to be hatched to rebuild the city. Funds were tied up, though, mostly due to the fact that all of the major banks had burned in the fire, requiring a wait of more than a week before their fire-proof vaults were sufficiently cool enough to be opened without risk of the items inside spontaneous combusting.

The grand scheme of citywide reconstruction required investment from sources in the East, hence the political whitewash and dismissal of the earthquake, claims of tougher building codes and a playing down of the death toll from the disaster. Potential investors called for ambitious plans and one of the most famous came from famed urban planner Daniel Burnham, who had designed the 1893 World's Columbian Exposition in Chicago. His plan called for, among other things, Haussmann-style avenues (one-way cross streets between avenues), boulevards, main thoroughfares that radiated across the city, a massive civic center complex with classical structures and what would have been the largest public park in the world. The plan was dismissed as impractical and unrealistic. While the original street grid was restored, many of Burnham's proposals inadvertently saw the light of day, such as a neoclassical civic center complex, wider streets, a preference of arterial thoroughfares, a subway under Market Street, a more people-friendly Fisherman's Wharf, and a monument to the city on Telegraph Hill, known as Coit Tower.

Work soon began. At first, building standards were much more stringent than they were before the disaster but within a year, with the rush to get the city back on its feet, they were nearly as shoddy as they were before. Building codes were actually taken off the city's books after thirteen months, largely due to impatience over the speed of new construction. Part of the rush to rebuild was the desire to be ready for the Pan-Pacific International Exposition, which was set to be hosted by San Francisco in 1915. And indeed, by that year, there was almost no visible damage to be seen in the city. San Francisco had truly "risen from the ashes" – or so it seemed on the surface.

Unfortunately, the disregard shown to earthquake safety during the rebuilding still plagues the city today. A majority of the buildings in San Francisco today were built during the first half of the twentieth century using the lax codes. Some scientists and historians have suggested that another earthquake as powerful as the one in 1906 would devastate the city and account for many thousands of deaths. With earthquakes still impossible to predict, we can only wonder when the next disaster will occur.

# 1907: THE DEADLIEST MONTH THE NAOMI, MONONGAH AND DARR MINE DISASTERS

Over the past few years, we have repeatedly borne witness to the extreme danger under which men toil for crabs in the Bering Sea. In fact, most people may have come to believe that this must be the most deadly civilian occupation. They would be wrong.

Historically, one particular job gave a man the greatest chance of never seeing home again after leaving for work. In America, more people have been killed in coal mines than in any other work place. The deadly statistics are astounding and yet they have gone relatively unnoticed. Nearly all of those killed were poor, hard working, and more often that not - foreign. A majority of early coal miners in this country did not even speak English. Today this sounds unusual, or even discriminatory, but in the past, that was indeed the norm and rampant discrimination did exist. Perhaps that is why so few of us are aware of just how bloody the coal with which we built our nation really was.

A majority of the coal miners in the eastern part of the United States had scrimped and saved to book passage across the Atlantic. Most came from Italy, Poland, Hungary, Russia or the Slavic nations before passing through Ellis Island, and into the dark and dangerous subterranean caverns of the coal mines. They came to America in search of a better life for themselves and their families. The terrible irony was that the working conditions in the American mines were so bad that these immigrants were three to four times more likely to be killed than the friends and family they left behind, working in European mines.

Officially, 26,434 coal miners died during a seventeen-year period between 1890 and 1907. Over a greater span of time 121,209 miners died between 1839 and 1977 - averaging nearly three people a day, seven days a week for 138 years. These deaths were the result of a variety of causes including slate falls, cave-ins, explosions, accidents and poisonous or asphyxiant gasses. They did not however, include those who died from diseases such as black lung (from years of breathing in coal dust), emphysema or pneumonia caused by working in freezing water when the tunnels flooded.

The bloodiest year was 1907 with 3,242 miners killed. But the horror of that year reached its peak when 702 miners perished in just one month - the deadliest month. During that December, explosions occurred in five mines - the Naomi and Darr mines in Pennsylvania, the Monongah Mine in West Virginia, the Yolanda Mine in Alabama (57 killed) and the Carthage Mine in New Mexico (11 killed). Naomi exploded on December 1st and Carthage exploded on December 31st.

Mine owners were routinely accused of suppressing the actual number of workmen killed in the mines. When "official" death tolls were published by the mine owners, they only recorded the number of whole bodies recovered and counted against the roll call performed as each miner entered the mine. Dozens of men or boys had mine support jobs that weren't counted in the roll. There were other reasons why additional people would be in the mines. Coal miners of old were not paid by the hour or the day, but by each ton of coal they blasted, picked and loaded into coal carts. Because of this method of payment, the miners developed a practice of taking other people in with them to help them load more coal in a shift. Most often, the additional help that accompanied the men into the mine were their own sons, some as young as nine years old. Some miners "subcontracted" with people passing through or family members just arrived in America who were not yet "on the roll" at the mine. The miner would pay these men a portion of their pay for their help. Because of this common practice, which was encouraged by mine management, often up to fifty percent as many people might be in the mine at any given time than the official number at roll call.

When major accidents occurred, miners insisted that the fatalities were much higher than the numbers released to the public, and experts today agree. The low end of the modern estimates suggests that at least half again as many miners died. Factoring in this estimate, the "unofficial" death toll for the same 138 years noted earlier rises from 121,209 to over 181,000, and instead of 702, more realistically - 1,100 men and boys breathed their last in December of 1907 - the deadliest month.

The following stories are accounts of what happened in three of the mines that exploded in that deadly month, and to those poor souls who were unlucky enough to be working deep in bowels of the mines when the blasts snuffed out their lives.

**A very young boy working as a 'trapper' in a coal mine. He was in charge of opening and closing the door to 'trap' a certain space so the ventilation system would be more efficient.**

## THE DEADLIEST MONTH BEGINS: THE NAOMI MINE EXPLOSION FAYETTE CITY, PENNSYLVANIA

"It was the blackdamp that got em......"

Coal mining towns in the late nineteenth century through the mid twentieth century, known as "patch towns," or more simply "patches," were unique to most other small towns in America. Patch towns were built up around mine entrances and were owned by the same company that owned the mine. When a mine was sold to another coal company, the patch town was sold along with the mine. Sometimes, there were two or more mine entrances near each other with the tunnels branching out in different directions. This arrangement made the patch town a more efficient investment for the coal companies. Everyone who lived in the patch either worked for the company, worked in the mine, or were families of those who did. The houses were simple and each patch had only two or three house designs - nearly all of them "half houses" - what might be considered duplexes today. Each design varied in the number of bedrooms and their placement on the hillside. The houses of mine managers and officials were larger, nicer and if possible, were positioned higher up on the hill in an area known as "bosses row," where they could look down on the miners' homes. With most coal companies, if you worked in the mine, you were required to live in company housing and your rent was deducted from your pay.

Every patch had a general store and usually a baseball field - if enough land was available to level out. The company not only owned the houses, it owned the stores as well. Most miners were not paid with money, but with "scrip." Each coal company printed its own scrip and it was not interchangeable with that of other companies. This system forced miners and their families to buy everything they needed, from clothing to soap to food, from the company stores at inflated prices. When they left the mine, they were guaranteed to be penniless as whatever scrip they might have saved would be worthless anywhere else. Credit was always available at the

**A row of miner's houses in a typical patch town.**

company store since the workers couldn't leave as long they were in debt to the store. This system kept the miners bound to the company and unable to leave. If a miner was so badly injured that he would no longer be able to work, or if he was killed, the family was usually required to evacuate their house by the next day. If a miner quit his job, or was fired, he and his family would have to be out by sundown.

The life of a coal miner and his family was a harsh one, without much hope for a better future. Tennessee Ernie Ford immortalized the plight of the coal miner when he sang Merle Travis' *Sixteen Tons*. Although most people have heard this song or could even sing along, few may really realized its true meaning. The chorus says it all:

*You load sixteen tons, what do you get?*
*Another day older and deeper in debt*
*Saint Peter don't you call me 'cause I can't go*
*I owe my soul to the company store*

And then there were the Iron and Coal Police. Coal companies employed men to act as a private police force to "keep the peace" in their patch towns. They often had cause to break up fights between men of feuding nationalities but as patches were private property, and the coal police were paid by the coal companies, the only laws enforced were those set down by the company. Thus, their duties also included activities such as forcibly throwing families from their homes or roughing up men who dared to utter the word "union," or making those who were deemed to be trouble-makers disappear. The coal police were generally feared by all. Children who were naughty or wouldn't go to bed were reminded that if they misbehaved, the coal police would get them.

Leaving for work each day meant walking great distances under ground. Sometimes the men had to travel for miles through the long, dark tunnels before finally reaching their work sites. The mines were divided up into "rooms" where they worked to force the coal out of the seams using blasting powder, picks and shovels. The rooms were connected by long tunnels, shafts and "crossings," where tunnels intersected. To ventilate out the poisonous or explosive gasses and bring in fresh air, long, vertical air shafts were sunk from the surface. These shafts were often the only thing separating the miners from certain death every time they entered the mines.

Even though powered engines hooked up the loaded cars of coal and pulled them out of the mines, the tunnels were also home to horses and mules, which helped with the heavy labor involved in getting the coal into the cars. Most coal mines operated seven days a week, but Sunday was kept a holy day - unless the miners needed the pay badly enough, then they would work on Sunday.

Of all the things these poor, hard working people had to fear, the thing they feared the most was when the earth moved. And only one thing could make the earth move - an explosion - deep down underground.

The Naomi mine, owned and operated by the United Coal Company, lay just outside tiny Fayette City, on the east bank of the Monongahela River in southwest Pennsylvania. Two hundred miners worked in Naomi on a regular basis. There had been an explosion in the mine earlier in the year. Though only a few miners were injured it was determined that a new air shaft should be sunk to clear out the excessive buildup of gasses, called "whitedamp" or "blackdamp," that had been collecting in the mine - but the work had not even been started.

On December 1, 1907, 43 men and boys made their way into Naomi's depths. It was a Sunday afternoon and those not afraid to break the Sabbath were starting the four to midnight shift. There was nothing special about that day, except that there were a few less people working than would be on the following morning.

The shift that evening was progressing as usual and Joseph Robish, known as Pumper Joe, was making his rounds. Pumper Joe was a waterman. His primary job was to spray water on the floors of the tunnels to keep the coal dust down. Nothing was more dangerous or explosive down deep than methane gas (blackdamp) and coal dust. There wasn't much coal dust built up so his first pass through the mine went rather quickly.

Pumper Joe had one real weakness - he dearly loved a good puff on his pipe. Although the other men had repeatedly begged him not to do so, in fear for their own lives, he had been known on occasion to light up a bowl before exiting the mine. On that day, he must have been particularly anxious for his first smoke break of the evening as he took a shortcut through an inactive part of the mine, making his way toward the entrance. It is supposed that as Joe headed out, he stopped and filled his pipe. He used the small flame in his head lamp to light it. Then he took off his cap and removed the cover of his sealed lamp --- and the earth moved.

At 7:26 p.m. a huge explosion blasted through the Naomi mine. Homes and churches all over Fayette City emptied. They instantly knew what had happened: their greatest fear come true. The streets filled with people as they ran to the mine. In a matter of minutes, a mass of people had gathered around the

**Twelve-year-old boy working the mines.**

mine entrance, their numbers so large that the first group of rescuers had to struggle to get to the mine. Many in the crowd did not speak English so they could not understand the pleas for them to get back. The air was filled with screams, sobs, moans and curses as friends and family pressed in close to the mine entrance, which had remained intact.

Monesson's *Daily Independent* described the event: "...entombed miners, who, like rats in a trap were caught where the tons of earth and rock were heaved into the passage completely blocking any possible chance of escape. Hope has been practically abandoned and the final list will, it is feared, include every man who was in the mine when the explosion occurred. The scenes around the mine are heartrending. Mothers, wives and sisters have flocked about the entrance to the veritable tomb since the first shock which told of the frightful disaster."

Henry Louttit, a state mine inspector, and J.D. O'Neill, Naomi's superintendent took charge of the rescue efforts. Almost from the start, they had opposing views of how the work should proceed. Word of the explosion spread quickly and miners from other mines flooded in from all directions. Unfortunately, sightseers and morbidly curious spectators also flocked to the area. The crowd around the mine grew so rapidly that United Mines had to call in thirty of their "special police" to help rope off the area and control the mass of people so that rescuers could do their work. The prevailing opinion of the company was that the "agitated foreigners" might riot or just rush the mine in an attempt to enter and find the men themselves. Others believed that this was an extreme overreaction and was just more evidence of the company's bias against its non-English speaking employees and its heartless behaviors towards their families.

Only one man had made it out of the mine alive, having been near the entrance when the explosion occurred. He stumbled out of the smoke and into the night air then collapsed, dying soon after from the poison gas he had breathed during his escape.

The first group of nine rescuers to enter the mine were quickly overcome by the thick smoke and blackdamp. They, in turn were pulled from the mine "in the nick of time" by the second rescue party. For several hours after the initial blast, rock falls continued throughout the tunnels, slowing rescue efforts and increasing the danger that the rescuers, too, might become trapped. The greatest threat the rescuers faced, however, was from the blackdamp, or afterdamp: poison gasses, mostly carbon dioxide and nitrogen, resulting from the explosion and fire. Blackdamp would cause lung congestion, choking and then death. Rescue soon became recovery.

The searchers were divided into groups of 30 to cover three shifts. The blackdamp was so bad that the men in each shift were only allowed in the mine for thirty minutes at a time and were rotated in and out. Believing that the crowd would disperse and go home if they were given no reason to hope, Thurston Wright, an official from United Coal, announced that there was no possibility that anyone could still be alive inside the mine. Anyone who had survived the explosion could not have survived the extended exposure to the blackdamp. This statement had the opposite effect on the crowd. Families refused to leave until their men were brought to the surface and outsiders, who had come out of curiosity, stayed with the ghoulish intent to witness the mangled corpses as they were recovered.

Louttit and O'Neill argued over where to put the greatest effort into opening the mine up and where they were most likely to find survivors or bodies. O'Neill, the company man, believed they should stay away from the main entrance, fearing continued rock falls. He pushed for exploring the depths by entering through air shafts. Louttit argued that they should start at the main entrance, opining that everyone who might have survived the explosion would have made their way to the entrance as quickly as they could and would have been stopped by the rock fall blocking their exit.

The recovery teams found that the explosion itself had killed only about half of the victims. The remaining men had died from the blackdamp. The men working farthest from the explosion had tried to walk out after hearing the blast. Many of these men were found where they had fallen, in the "haul way" leading toward the entrance. Others were discovered sitting on the floor, leaning against the tunnel wall with lunch pails in their laps. A few had been kneeling in prayer when overtaken by the blackdamp. The bodies were sooty and smudged with coal dust, but otherwise looked as if they had stopped to take a nap.

Fifteen men were found to have perished just inside the rockfall at the main entrance. Some wondered if they might have been saved had the rescuers started at that spot.

The men who were taken by the explosion didn't fare so well. Their bodies were charred, crushed or blown apart. None were recognizable. In some cases, it was difficult to determine which scattered body parts belonged together. The rockfall was so vast that some men were covered with many tons of rock. It was only a guess as to how long it would take to get everyone out. O'Neill capitalized on this as he reported an exaggerated, over-estimation of the time it would take to complete the recovery operation, again in the hope that the crowds would disperse - but to no avail.

It was decided that the bodies would be held underground and a temporary morgue was set up in the powerhouse. The exact reason for this was hard to determine. O'Neill was quoted that he didn't want anyone brought to the surface until everyone had been recovered and they would be carried out together. Many believed that he didn't want the crowd to discover how deadly the explosion had been and planned to sneak the bodies out later. However, S.A. Hagan, the Fayette County Coroner, stated that he and his assistants wanted to make the bodies more "presentable" before bringing them out, to ease their families' pain. Regardless of the reason, the victims' families had to wait three days to get their loved ones' remains. The miners who had stayed in the mine for so long were finally brought to the surface. The men who had been identified were buried on December 5. The company allotted $40 per person for burial.

The recovery effort continued and eight days after the explosion, Naomi gave up her last body, crushed and horribly decayed. The United Coal Company placed its official death count at 32, even though 43 men and boys went into the mine that afternoon and only one made it out - just before he died.

The investigation following the explosion determined the official cause as "unknown" but believed that it was from an opened flame used to light a pipe or shorted-out wiring. The United Coal Company's only reprimand was for trying to use electricity inside the mine. No mention was made of the previous explosion, the necessity for a new air shaft or the fact that a shaft had not been put in.

There were no officials who knew for sure what had happened inside Naomi that cold December evening, and certainly, there were no miners working the mine that night left to tell the tale. But quite possibly there was one person who knew the truth of what had happened and for many years he did his best to keep it from happening again.

Pumper Joe, that notorious pipe smoker, was seen for years wandering Naomi's tunnels and crossings, looking gloomy and miserable. He had also apparently given up the smoking habit. In life, he kept his pipe firmly clenched between his teeth, even when not lit, but in death, his ghost no longer has a pipe. And until Naomi was closed for good, he seemed to be busy protecting the men in another way. As miners walked home from a long, back-breaking shift loading coal, they might feel like having a smoke as they strolled. They would reach into their pockets for their pipe tobacco or maybe a stub of a cigar and find nothing there. Some superstitious miners took to promising Pumper Joe that they would never smoke in the mine if only he would stop taking their tobacco, but the tobacco continued to disappear. Evidently Pumper Joe was not the trusting sort, or maybe he just wanted to remove the temptation. Either way, tobacco frequently went missing from pockets as long as men worked the Naomi mine.

In the wake of the disaster, the Naomi mine needed to be cleared and rebuilt to working condition. Far fewer miners were needed for the restoration effort so many men were out of work. Several decided to move on to work another mine - and so they left for Jacob's Creek and the Darr mine.....

# THE DEADLIEST MONTH: THE MOST DEADLY COAL MINE DISASTER IN AMERICAN HISTORY MONONGAH, WEST VIRGINIA

Coal fields in Pennsylvania, Ohio and West Virginia were so prevalent that they were given names to tell them apart and the individual mines within the fields were numbered. Some mines were simply named after their locations. Others claimed names that represented strength or a sort of patriotism, such as the Vigilant mines. Still others carried the names of their owners or managers, who named several others after their wives and daughters,

giving us seven Vestas, a Naomi and the charming Rachel and Agnes, for example. The Monongah mines and Monongah, the adjoining patch town supplying the mines with workers, were named after the Monongahela River that flowed through some of the richest coal fields in the world.

The Monongah patch town was built almost on top of mines No. 6 and No. 8. As with all patches, the six thousand residents of Monongah either worked in the mines, for the coal company, or were families of those who did. The patch and the mines were located on the West Fork of the Monongahela River, just six miles from Fairmont, West Virginia. Mine No. 6 and No. 8 were on the west side of the river and mine Nos. One, Two, Three, Four, Five and Seven were on the east side, connected by a simple iron bridge. This was a very busy place.

The Monongah mines, eight of them in all, had been previously owned and operated by the Fairmont Coal Company, but were now a

The Monongah patch. The entrances to No. 6 and No. 8 were across the river from the patch but the mines themselves extended underneath. The highest level of houses formed "bosses row."

(Left) A group of miners gather for a photo outside of a Monongah mine. The tipple is clearly visible behind the men on the upper right. (Right) Monongah miners posing on an electric dynamo motor with a loaded trip. Each car held approximately two tons of coal.

part of the even larger Consolidated Coal Corporation. No. 6 and No. 8 were huge mines covering roughly seven hundred acres, of which over two hundred thirty acres had already been exhausted or were currently being mined. Both mines had slope entrances that dropped at about sixty degrees. Their entrances were one and one-quarter miles apart and they extended out in opposite directions but were connected by a passage at about three thousand feet. Even though they were joined at one point, they were ventilated separately.

These were good places to work as far as mines went. No. 6 had been opened in 1899 and No. 8 two years earlier in 1905. Both mines had the most modern equipment and ventilation systems, each having fans that were so massive that on occasion, air moved at nearly forty miles per hour, sometimes blowing out miners' head lamps. This was a tolerable nuisance considering the fans kept the mines nearly free of whitedamp and blackdamp, poisonous and explosive gasses. The fans also kept the mine at a comfortable working temperature of sixty degrees.

Although horses and mules were still used down deep, most of the heavy work was done with electric dynamo motors. The motor was akin to a locomotive, but only about three feet high, enabling it to pass through the tunnels without striking the roof timbers or props holding up the ceiling. They were used to pull each trip up the long slope and out of the mine to the tipple, the building where the cars were "tipped" to empty their loads onto barges or train cars. A "trip" was a train of up to fifty coal cars carrying two tons of coal each. There were six hundred coal cars within these two mines, and all had to be filled by hand.

Friday, December 6, 1907, dawned cold and crisp as hundreds of men and boys left their homes in and around Monongah and walked to work. They were all mine workers heading toward their respective mines. There were miners, pumpers, motormen, trappers, slag pickers, tipplemen, blacksmiths, mechanics, mule drivers and other support workers. Over six hundred of them were headed into No. 8 and No. 6. This would have been just another day in the mine except that the men were actually looking forward to working. The mine had been closed down the previous day and Christmas was coming. Word had spread that the mine had been closed because it was gassy and needed to be ventilated but the miners believed that they were being punished for recent talk of organizing. But now they were going back to work so everything would be all right. The fans had run all the previous day so there would be no gasses and the mines would be dry.

The only dark spot on the horizon was a fresh worry about the possibility of an explosion. As the men walked to work, most were discussing a story they had been following closely: the deadly explosion in the Naomi Mine in Pennsylvania just five days earlier. Over forty men had been killed in that one. It was certainly not the worst accident they had heard of but it had been nearby and some of these men might have known a Naomi miner or two. Every man who entered a mine knew that he might not make it back out, but he tried not to dwell on it. Even so, when there was an explosion somewhere, every miner felt the loss and the possibility of meeting the same fate came to the forefront of his thoughts.

As each miner approached his mine entrance, his name called out from a roll sheet. As was usual, the prepared roll was only for the actual miners listed as employees "on the books." The count did not include most of the support workers or anyone the miners may have brought along to assist them, such as sons, relatives or paid helpers. It was impossible to know how many people were in the mines at any given time but educated estimates were possible. The roll on December 6 placed 478 men in the two mines but the more reasonable estimate had the number between 650 and 700 men.

After being called off the roll, each miner collected an open air, lard oil head lamp for their caps and a ration of black powder and a length of fuse. Then, with their lunch pail in one hand and carrying their pick and shovel over their shoulders, they started down the long slope into the dark depths till they reached the "room" they were working.

**Two coal mule drivers. Open air head lamps were still in general use in many mines as shown in this 1908 photo.**

The coal lay in seams along the walls of the rooms. The days of swinging a pick all day long, chipping away at the wall of coal were long past. By 1907, miners were blasting with shots to dislodge the coal so they could load their cars. They drilled deep into the wall, loaded the hole with black powder and fuse, then tamped it down with material such as clay, dirt or even coal dust to contain the blast within the coal seam. If everything was done properly, the ignited shot would break loose or crumble enough coal for the miner to load for several hours before setting off another shot. If the shot had not been prepared properly, the result was a completely different story. For instance, a "blown shot" would occur if it hadn't been tamped well enough or without enough tamping material. A sheet of fire would shoot out of the hole without breaking any coal loose. If the shot contained too much black powder, the resulting oversized explosion could blast chunks of coal across the room, injuring or even killing nearby miners.

On that fateful Friday, the men were in a hurry to start loading. They wanted to make up for the wages they had lost when the mine was closed the day before. Within a few minutes of starting the shift, hundreds of shots were fired off in rapid succession. The blasts were so frequent that at times, it sounded almost like a drum roll, echoing through the rooms and down the long tunnels. Not everyone was experienced at handling black powder and with the almost frenzied pace of the shots, an accident was bound to happen. And as the miners worked increasingly faster, sometimes they got sloppy.

As a standard safety precaution, pumper carts routinely passed along the haul-ways (tunnels used for transporting loads of coal) and crossings (tunnel intersections) spraying down the floors with water to abate the coal dust, but it still tended to build up if they weren't careful. Most miners had developed a healthy respect for the explosive hazards resulting from of a buildup of coal dust in the air. They took care to sweep up before firing off a   shot, but the dust continued to increase. The fans had been running all the day before without anyone in the mine so everything was very dry, creating a comfortable working environment but also a higher level of dust than usual.  Men, horses and mules walking up and down the haul-ways with thousands of footfalls and the pounding of hooves broke up the small pieces of coal on the floor into even more dust. One of the miners who had left the mine just before the explosion to get his head lamp repaired, said that in some places, the floating dust was so thick that day it was hovering hip-high.

The morning continued as usual, with a cacophony of shots signaling a productive day in progress. The tunnels were filled with music as well as dust. The men sang or whistled as they worked, in Italian, Polish, Russian and even some in English. William Jenkins, the blacksmith for the mines, was working in his shop when he looked up to see a motor and loaded trip move slowly up the slope from No. 6 toward the tipple. It was a common enough sight, since his shop was just up from the No. 6 entrance. But this trip was not destined to make it to the tipple. Jenkins heard a metallic snap and saw the eighteen-car trip speeding past his shop again, this time in the wrong direction. He ran outside to hit the lever that would switch the rail to a siding but the trip was moving too fast and he didn't make it in time. The heavily loaded trip picked up speed as it re-entered No. 6 and began its seven hundred forty-foot journey to the bottom of the slope. It would be moving very fast by the time it slammed into the bottom and there was no way to warn the men inside of what was coming. At about that same time, a group of inexperienced miners were preparing to set off an extra-large shot, large enough to drop enough coal to last them for rest of the day. They drilled the shot hole deeper than normal and loaded in an extra-large charge of black powder --- and the earth moved again, and then again.

At 10:28 on the morning of December 6, a massive explosion shook the ground so violently that people felt it over eight miles away. Thick smoke and dust burst forth from No. 8 as the entrance completely disintegrated, tossing massive timbers and heavy concrete chunks into the air. The boiler house and fan house were both completely demolished, killing everyone inside. A large part of the fan itself was blown across the river and became lodged in the mud along the far bank. The concrete roof of the engine house was blown into many pieces. One chunk, weighing over a hundred pounds, was thrown nearly five hundred yards. Almost immediately, a second explosion was heard and felt as a dirty white smoke poured from the mouth of No. 6, though the entrance remained largely intact.

Everyone in an eight-mile radius knew instantly what had happened. The violent surge in the earth wreaked havoc on the surface as well as in the depths of the mines. In Monongah, sidewalks heaved and buckled, streets split and separated, people and horses were tossed savagely to the ground, streetcars were knocked from their rails, buildings shook and some smaller ones collapsed. A thick, sooty ash spread over everything - even in Fairmont, six miles distant. Fairmont didn't escape damage from the blast, either. A trolley pole on a streetcar was broken into two pieces and hundreds of windows in houses and stores were shattered. Not a single piece of window glass remained whole in one particular Fairmont neighborhood.

Many witnesses saw the results of the explosions from outside the mine but only one person inside the mine survived to tell his tale. Christina Ceredili was sweeping dust from her patch house porch when she heard and felt the explosion. At first, she shrugged it off as coming from the men who were trying to blow away an old bridge

**Two photos of the No. 8 entrance taken after the explosion.**

pier when she noticed the smoke blossoming out of No. 6, then seconds later, from No. 8. Mr. Sloan, a tippleman for No. 2, also saw the smoke issuing from the two entrances but he felt that No. 6 had blown first. Luther Toothman, a carpenter for No. 6, survived the explosion because he was on temporary loan to No. 2 so he wasn't inside the mine when it blew.

Joe Newton happened to be standing just fifty feet from the No. 8 entrance when the explosion occurred. He was blown off his feet and into the air. He lost an eye and two fingers but survived the ordeal. He was one of only two people directly impacted by the explosion and lived.

**Some families anxiously waited for days behind ropes for any word about their loved ones.**

Within minutes, the area around the mine entrances was clogged with people. Family members had fled their homes and rushed to the scene in the hopes of finding their father, brother, son, or friend. Being largely of Italian or Polish descent, along with Turkish, Austrian and Russian, few of these families spoke English so it was difficult at first to communicate the necessity of moving away from the mines so that rescuers could get through. Eventually, stakes and ropes were put up to help keep the crowds back and so the rescue efforts could begin.

Lee Malone, Monongah's General Manager, speaking on behalf of the Consolidated Coal Corp. announced that 478 men had checked in for work that morning. He added that the actual number of men in the mine was much higher and added another one hundred people to his estimate. A few hours later, after communicating with his employers, he "drastically revised downward these initial figures." The death toll figures would be lowered many times over the next week.

A writer for the *Pittsburgh Dispatch* described what he saw when he arrived at the site of the explosion, "What had first seemed like distant thunder, in a few seconds was transformed into a roar of a thousand Niagaras. Like an eruption of a volcano the blazing gas rushed to the surface, and vomited tongues of red flame and clouds of dust through the slopes. The thirty-foot fan [at No. 8] which supplied the fresh air was lifted like a toy and wafted across the river. Poor little Charles Honaker, fifteen years old, a trapper, with clothing ablaze, literally a human torch, was enveloped in the fiery torrent. Several men who were in the mine near the entrance were likewise carried in the claws of death and strewn in the pit's mouth. Monongah mines have blown up a thousand men... The words were repeated from mouth to mouth - - but everyone knew it was useless to burden human tongues with the message of the tragedy."

At first, women and families waited anxiously to hear of their family's plight. The mines were so vast that they felt it would be nearly impossible for the explosions to have killed everyone. However, they eventually came to grips with the reality of the situation soon after they arrived at the entrances and saw the damage. Nevertheless, guards had to be placed around the work areas to keep frantic family members from rushing the entrance in the hopes of finding their men themselves - a complete and utter impossibility.

The first group to attempt entry into the mines was soon driven back by the smoke and afterdamp - the poisonous gasses created by the explosion and fire. Several of them had to be hauled from the mine after they were overcome. Rescue workers were forced to work in shifts, and were only allowed inside for fifteen minute at a time. The exploration of the interiors continued despite the hardships.

Amid all this hopelessness was a single moment of hope. There was another reason to be concerned for the safety of the waiting public. Natural sinkholes, or depressions in the earth, could be found around the areas of the mines. A few of these sinkholes, known to the miners as "toadholes," were very deep and opened up into one of the mines. It wasn't uncommon for unsuspecting children or animals to fall into a toadhole and find themselves to have dropped into the No. 8 headings (the area over the slope). That is, if they survived the fall. Officials feared that grieving family or friends might try to enter the mine through a toadhole in an attempt to rescue their men and would be killed.

Late in the afternoon, near 4:00 p.m., the men guarding one of the toadholes began hearing loud groans drifting out of the hole. Tom Weeks volunteered to go in. After tying a wet cloth over his mouth and nose, he was lowered down the hole and into No. 8. He quickly found a confounded man on the tracks, about one hundred feet beyond the opening, rambling rapidly in Polish. His name was Peter Urban and he had been working with his brother Stanislaus at the time of the explosion. His brother was killed but somehow Peter had survived. He was taken to the hospital and was later released. Other than being shaken up, and likely in shock, he was only mildly physically harmed. Peter Urban was the only survivor to be taken from either mine.

After Peter Urban's miraculous discovery and rescue, the press was rife with stories of sensational discoveries of more survivors and fantastic rescues and recoveries. Sadly, none of these stories proved to be true, but they did have a profound effect on the waiting crowds. Families and friends of the trapped miners continued to cling to any hope they could muster, and stayed rooted to their spots for days on end. It was a cruel joke on them.

The rescue efforts quickly became more organized. Miners from other shifts and from the other six Monongah mines in operation were called in to lend aid - but only as many as could be spared by the other mines. The work in those mines had to go on. These men worked in shifts, spending no more than fifteen minutes in the mine at a time. At first, it was extremely difficult going without any sort of safety respirator. The volunteers-turned-heroes, who were among the first to enter the mine, were forced to breathe the toxic gasses and foul air. Despite the precaution of severely limiting the amount of time these men spent in the mine and were exposed to the afterdamp, several of them were hauled from the mine, delirious from the gasses, and taken to the hospital for treatment. Three of the first brave men who volunteered to enter the mine died from breathing the afterdamp. They had entered, in hopes of rescuing their fellow miners, soon after the explosion but before the gasses could be ventilated out of the mine.

In No. 6, the entrance was relatively undamaged but an eighteen-car trip had crashed at the bottom of the slope, slamming into the wall and become tangled together. The trip cars and the 36 tons of coal they carried had to be pulled apart and cleared away before the rescuers could advance farther into the mine. The men who had been in the shack at the bottom of the slope were killed without any warning. One man was found sitting on a bench, still holding a cup of coffee in his hand, his head tipped back against the wall of the shack. When a rescuer tipped his head forward, coffee poured from his mouth.

The massive ventilation fan in No. 8 had been destroyed but by midnight, a smaller temporary fan was installed and put into service. The fan in No. 6 was only damaged. The repair was fairly simple so it, too, was put back into service. Unfortunately, the brick blocking walls used to seal off the unused and inactive areas were all blown out. The result was that the fans were blowing randomly through the entire mine and the ventilation process had become terribly inefficient. The men had to construct temporary blocking walls using large sheets of canvas to redirect the ventilation through areas where the gasses and extreme heat were trapped. This was slow going as they sometimes had to drag the blocking materials, as well as the bodies of dead miners, for thousands of feet and had to traverse huge mounds of rock falls, wrecked machinery, smashed coal cars and fallen timbers and props.

According to the *Fairmont Times*: "A dozen physicians stood about the opening of the two mines all day, but their services were but slightly needed. Those who went to their work undreaming of the calamity awaiting them have no need for physicians. When the shock came they died suddenly. It is not believed there was any suffering in that pit of horror. The end came in an instant and out of the four hundred few knew what had happened. Some men died without changing their positions. One man was found sitting in repose on a bench, his dead body sitting upright in the same attitude as when he sat down. To others the death was more horrible. One man was blown almost to pieces, but in the pocket of his vest his watch was still ticking."

And so it was on the inside. As recovery teams worked their way through the mines, there were gruesome discoveries around nearly every corner. They found that the bodies of those who were working inside the rooms were left nearly unscathed and many lay on the floor just as they fell when the concussion struck them. The most damaged bodies were found in the haulways, headings and crossings. Evidently, the most powerful part of the explosion traveled along these channels, blasting apart everything in the way, be it man or beast. It appeared that a vast majority of the victims died almost instantly, rather than lingering and eventually dying from the afterdamp.

To add to the horror of those scenes, the volunteers found the conditions inside the mine were nearly unbearable. The trapped heat was fierce and the afterdamp caused headaches and nausea. The stench of death was intolerable, and it had been intensified by the heat.

Outside, the crowd continued to grow. As with all disasters, a certain number of the morbidly curious had descend upon the site, but for the most part the crowd at the Monongah disaster was made up of mourners who continued their vigil around the clock. Frequently, the air was shattered with the screams and sobs of someone suddenly overcome with the immensity of what had happened. These occasional outbursts came from frantic women, worn down from exhaustion, worry and sorrow. Some were said to cry out with shrieks of agony. An Italian woman, awaiting word of the fate of her husband, son and brother, lost control and "tore out her hair and with her nails cut gashes in her face," according to a newspaper report. Unable to calm her, friends eventually carried her home. A Polish woman worked her way past the barriers and, running wildly down toward the slope, broke past the guards in an attempt to breach the mine entrance and find her men herself. She was overtaken just in time and carried back behind the barrier by "two stout men." Another woman tried to end her suffering by throwing herself into the river, but she was pulled from the frigid waters by several bystanders. One young woman laid down on the frozen ground and cried herself to sleep before being carried home by her sisters.

The people in the crowd were so desperate for news of their missing loved ones that any passing official or rescue worker was mobbed with women begging and pleading for information. There was nothing anyone could say to them to ease their pain; there was no news to tell. When the first few bodies were removed from No. 6, there was a near riot as people pressed in to see if they could find one of their family among the dead.

On December 7, the work continued but was growing a little easier as the ventilation system became more efficient. Dozens more bodies had been found and removed. Company officials lowered the estimated dead to less than 400.

Monongah was completely unprepared for such a disaster. But a mine disaster of this magnitude had never happened before so that was not surprising. Three hundred coffins were called for from Pittsburgh and Zanesville, Ohio. A temporary morgue was set up in a partially completed bank building to house and display the victims for possible identification. Many distraught family members chose to wait outside the morgue as bodies began to arrive. At first, the numbers grew very slowly, with only a handful carried out every few hours but as the headings were cleared and more of the mine ventilated, the recovery proceed at a much faster pace. Some individuals roamed up and down the long aisles almost continuously, hoping to catch sight of something - anything - that would help them identify their loved ones. Inevitably, there were disagreements over some of the identifications, with two families laying claim to a single body. Occasional punches

**Bodies carried from the mines, across the bridge and through the waiting crowd to the temporary morgue.**

(Left) Stacks and stacks of coffins lining the streets of Monongah.
(Right) The overflow of bodies was moved into the street. Family and friends walked along the rows, trying to identify their men.

were thrown but most disputes were settled.

Trouble arrived with the dawning of December 8. Fires had broken out first in No. 8 and then in No. 6. After a short time, flames could be seen shooting out of several toadholes. A reporter for the *Pittsburgh Dispatch* wrote: "The guards announced that another explosion was liable to happen at any minute. Instantly, the crowd scattered along the trolley tracks, and over the fields, and across the bridge, and some ran pell-mell into town. There were some in the throng about the mine entrance, however, who did not join in the mine panic. These were men and women who had dear ones in the smoking entries." After several hours, both fires were extinguished and the recovery was resumed.

By December 10, company officials announced that they had lowered the expected death toll to no more than two hundred. They did this even though 175 bodies had been already removed and less than one-forth of the mine had been explored. Families railed against the company, as it was accused of misleading them and the rest of the country about the severity of the accident while trying to protect its own image. However, the company stood by its numbers.

Dozens of men went to work digging rows and rows of graves in the half-frozen earth. The rain and melting snow made digging even more difficult. Graves dug the night before were half-full of water by the next morning and had to be bailed out. Embalmers arrived from every town in that part of West Virginia. Three undertakers and thirty embalmers worked around the clock in shifts, preparing bodies for identification and eventual burial. The first person brought in to identify the bodies was the payroll clerk, although many of the corpses were so badly damaged that it would be impossible for anyone to recognize them.

Coffins began arriving by train. The simple, unlined wooden boxes were stacked up in long lines in the street outside the morgue. Families objected to the crudeness of the coffins so men were hired to tack black cloth to the insides of the boxes so the "occupant would not be facing bare wood," as one newspaper wrote. When the morgue was filled, the overflow of bodies in coffins were lined up outside on the street. There was simply no more room for those that had already been prepared for burial and the flow of bodies out of the mine continued.

Graves were dug in long rows. Mine officials had originally decided to have long trenches dug and have the coffins placed in the trenches side by side. This plan was met with violent reactions from the families of the dead mine workers. They could not tolerate the idea that their loved one might be buried alongside an unacceptable person: an Italian next to a Pole, a Protestant next to a Catholic, and so on. The idea was quickly abandoned and individual graves were dug.

Even in death, the men were treated with racial or national bias. Upon identification, Americans were taken to their homes, while Italians were taken directly to the Monongah Cemetery, where a tent had been set up to shelter the bodies awaiting burial. Those of Slavic heritage were taken to the Polish Catholic Church. The Monongah Cemetery was essentially Catholic with a fence dividing the cemetery in two. The Italian Catholics were buried on one side and the Polish Catholics were buried on the other.

A new cemetery was started on a desolate hillside near town in which to bury the Protestants and the unidentifiable remains. A section of this cemetery became a potter's field for the burial of paupers. The grave diggers believed that there were likely many people buried there as unknowns who were really known to their families but who couldn't afford a decent burial. Each morning, sticks or patterns of stones would be found over some of the graves. They would be removed but would reappear the next day. After a few days, this would stop happening. The grave diggers believed the crude markers were no longer needed after the positions were memorized by the families.

After all the dead had supposedly been removed from the mines, the company announced that the final death toll was 361, making this the most deadly mining disaster in U.S. history. That total continues to be disputed even today. One of the most compelling pieces of evidence is that the gravediggers reported that six hundred and twenty graves had been dug and filled, even before all the bodies had been recovered. Many people believe that even that number is low as there were believed to be many bodies that were never recovered, having been left buried under mountains of slate that were not removed, or those who were caught directly in the path of the explosion, causing their bodies to be vaporized. Additionally, there were many graves dug in the new potter's field section during that week, but there were no paupers yet buried there. One reporter made note of the fact that the company officials never really knew how many men had been in the mine or how many had been lost, and yet they knew the exact number of horses and mules lost within hours of the explosion.

Many heart-rending stories became known in the days and weeks following the tragic explosion. The body of John Hearmans was carried into the first floor of his house as his wife lay in an upstairs bedroom, giving birth to their fifth child. Many women were not lucky enough to recover their husbands' bodies. One such widow, Mrs. G. L. Davis, collected a small bag of coal every day from the entrance to No. 6. She would carry it up the mountain and add it to a pile next to her home, never burning any or allowing anyone else to burn it. She continued this ritual for several years, until her death. When she died, the pile of coal had gotten very large and her family donated it to the local churches. Several women, fearing their eminent destitution, went to the company demanding death certificates for their husbands. They hoped to be able to marry as quickly as possible, at least before they were turned out of their houses and left homeless with their young children.

The exact cause of the explosion could not be determined and no witnesses survived the blast. Some suggested that there may have been an isolated pocket of blackdamp that flashed over or that someone had been careless with the flame in his open-air head lamp. Others wondered if the runaway trip might have somehow been the cause, but it was later determined that the explosion occurred before the trip had reached the bottom of the slope. Chief Mine Inspector James Paul proffered the most dominant and logical theory that the large quantity of coal dust floating through the mine had been ignited by a blown-out shot, resulting in the catastrophic explosion. The coroner's jury agreed.

Today, people might expect that there would have been sweeping changes following that devastating accident. Sadly, this was not to be. There were some token efforts made to force change. The federal government established the U.S. Bureau of Mines within the Department of the Interior to study safety issues and problems but gave them no power to enforce their guidelines. The Progressive Movement, a private organization of citizens concerned about the safety of the American worker, pushed for government regulations and improved working conditions in the coal mines but seemed to be appeased with the creation of the bureau and moved on to other issues. Men and boys continued pulling coal from hundreds of unsafe mines and they continued to die doing so.

The explosion left over four hundred widows and more than one thousand orphans. A call for aid went out all over West Virginia and throughout the country. Many people were very generous and dollars poured into Monongah. The Consolidated Coal Corporation settled $150 on each widow and $75 on each child under the age

Peter Urban, the sole survivor of the explosion, went back to work in the mine after he recovered from his injuries.

of sixteen. They also allowed the families to continue living in their patch houses for a limited amount of time, two weeks in most cases. No. 6 and No. 8 were reconstructed and reopened within a few months and the men continued to mine Monongah's coal by the light of open-air head lamps.

Peter Urban, the sole survivor of the Monongah Mine explosion, spent the next three months recovering from his ordeal and then returned to work in No. 8. Urban remained in Monongah with his wife and family and fathered two more children. He was injured a few times over the next few years, including a broken leg and a sprained back, but each time, he went back into No. 8, "his mine," to work. Just nine years after narrowly avoiding death in the explosion, a large chunk of ceiling collapsed in the room where Urban was working and he was killed on the spot. No. 8 had finally claimed the only one that got away.

Providence alone saved three other lives that day. The morning had been going well for most of the men but three miners, two Italians and an American, decided to climb the slope into the sunshine for three very different reasons. One Italian had discovered he had left his chewing tobacco in his jacket outside and, unable to complete an entire shift without a chew, he left to get the tobacco. The other Italian was loading away when his head lamp suddenly went out, and he decided to go to the smithy to get it repaired immediately, intending to return to work. The American had been out drinking and gambling the night before and was feeling a bit under the weather. Finding an unexpected roll of money in his pocket, he decided that if he had money to spend, he might as well be drinking. He was headed for the saloon, where he was found much later that night, and his name was taken off the list of expected dead.

Jimmie Rogers, an old Scottish immigrant miner, said that a "voice" had told him not to go into work that morning, so he stayed home. He didn't understand why he had received the warning until he felt the earth shudder and knew at once that the voice had saved his life. Rogers had paid attention to the voice because it had saved his life once before. In 1886, he was working in West Virginia in the Newburg Mine. On a cold day in January, a voice had told him to stay home. He was unsure what was wrong, but he heeded the warning. That day, the Newburg mine exploded, trapping and killing all thirty-seven men inside the mine.

Monongah Mine No. 6 and No. 8 were not only very bloody mines, they were also very haunted - even today, decades after they were closed down and sealed. Some men, who had worked No. 8 or No. 6 for years, or others who were transferred from one of the six other Monongah mines found reasons to stay out of the mines or just quit and moved onto mines in other coal fields. "Too many dead miners still roaming the older sections," they said.

Men working in a room that had been opened before the explosion would hear their names being called out, and when they turned, no one would be there. Miners would on occasion walk past older inactive rooms and hear sounds of arguing, laughing or sometimes even singing. When they stopped and checked the room, it would be empty. Some went home and told their families of following a small group of three or four miners down a haul-way or through an old crossing. They saw the men in front of them walk right through a large pile of slate from a ceiling collapse caused by the explosion, a pile of slate that was now blocking an old access tunnel. These phantom miners would be lost from sight as they melted through stone, on their way to dig coal.

A large number of men started avoiding the older sections of No. 8 and No. 6, preferring to work in the new cuts, where the only voices they heard were those of their friends, and the only miners they met with were alive and breathing. Over time, men slowly stopped looking over their shoulders and watching for vanishing miners. This was more likely because the older sections were "worked out'" rather than a cessation of the hauntings. Right up until the mines were sealed, stories of ghost miners wandering the old deserted sections, in search of black gold continued to be told.

Men lost in the explosion were not the only ones haunting the mines. Coal mines made great use of horses, mules and in some cases even donkeys. Mule drivers led their animals from room to room, picking up individual loaded coal cars and pulling them to the haul-ways where they were added to a trip. In mines that did not yet use the electric dynamo motors to haul the trips, horses or mules hauled the cars up the slope and out to the tipple, then return for the next load. The horses made the round trip in and out of the mine many hundreds of times every week. But this was better than the life led by the mine horses and mules that hauled the cars to the dynamo motors. They entered the mine early every morning and didn't breathe fresh air again until late that night. Some mines even had a stable area set up inside the mines so the horses lived out their working lives underground, never again to see the sunshine once they entered that dark hole.

The Monongah mine horses did stable outside at night but they worked the entire day underground, hauling loaded and empty coal cars to and from the motor. When they weren't needed, they were kept in

groups in the larger crossings, waiting for more cars to be filled. When the mine exploded, it killed everything in its path, be it man, boy or horse.

No. 6 was made of eight, one-mile square sections with a crosscut, or intersection, forming the corners of each. In one of these sections about half way up on the "Third Right," a dozen or more horses were slaughtered by the blast. They had been put there while waiting for loaders to fill their carts. The recovery team that first came upon this crossing were horrified by what they saw. Apparently, as the blast moved through the mine, the resulting pressure from both ends of the crosscut "pressed and squeezed the horses into one solid mass of flesh and bone."

The recovery and cleanup teams moving through the mine were there for one overriding purpose: to find and haul out all of the human bodies and body parts. This in itself was an overwhelming task and they didn't have time or energy to deal with the removal of these poor creatures. And yet - something had to be done. They decided that the quickest solution was to dispose of the rotting mass of flesh right there in the mine. They would "gob" the carcasses into a small worked-out room and seal it off from the rest of the mine. So there the horses remained, in almost the exact spot where they fell.

But did the unfortunate horses really remain in their makeshift tomb? Many said no. A few years after the disaster, a group of men were working in the part of the mine were the horses had been found dead. At lunchtime, the mine became quite silent, one of the only times that anyone could hear much of anything at all. As they sat along the wall, eating their meager meals, they began to hear the unmistakable sound of horses galloping down the heading of Third North. Slowly, the sounds grew louder and louder until the hooves, striking the hard stone floor of the tunnel, seemed to be upon them. They pressed themselves tightly against the tunnel wall, until the hoofbeats seemed to be passing them, eventually growing softer and softer till they faded away altogether.

Every man working in that section that day heard the horses. None doubted that the horses were really there, even though they couldn't see them, because they heard the galloping through that section again. They heard them many more times. The horses continued to run through their section once or twice, or even three times a week for a very long time. Miners will never again have the opportunity to experience the running of the Monongah horses as the mine has been sealed up for decades - but you never can tell - they may be running down there still.

# THE DEADLIEST MONTH:
# ANOTHER ONE BLOWS:
# THE DARR MINE EXPLOSION
# JACOB'S CREEK & VAN METER, PENNSYLVANIA

Backing into the foothills reaching east into the Allegheny Mountain range, and facing a lovely, swift river, sat the Darr Mine. The mine was owned and operated by the Pittsburgh Coal Company and was one of a cluster of mines in the area. Banning No. 3 was just downriver from Darr and Banning No. 1 was just beyond that. The old Port Royal mine had been worked out years ago and now sat dormant, not far upriver from Darr. The other mines were all deep mines, reaching far underground, while Darr was higher, much higher, in some places. Over four hundred and fifty people worked in Darr, most of them during the daytime since Darr only worked one shift.

Van Meter had been built on the same side of the river as the patch town for Darr. The company store was right at the leading edge of town with the company offices next door. Just behind the company office building was the "man-way" for the mine. This was not the main entrance and slope where the coal was hauled out, but the entry for the men and mules. It was company policy to keep a close eye on the men as they entered and left the mine and this was the perfect place to do just that.

Many of the miners working in Darr lived in company houses in Van Meter and the bosses' row was also there. There was a slightly uncommon set up however, because many other Darr miners also lived in the tiny village of Jacob's Creek. There were company houses in Jacob's Creek, just as in Van Meter, but some of the miners were allowed to own their own homes. All the privately owned miner homes were in Jacob's Creek. The miners' houses were simple wood framed double houses with gable roofs and a central chimney, one for each side. The bosses' dwellings were larger and nicer T-shaped double houses that looked out onto the river.

The most unique aspect of these two patches was that they were divided by the Youghiogheny River, more commonly called the Yough River, a tributary to the Monongahela. Jacob's Creek was located on the opposite bank from the mine itself. The nearest bridge was over two miles away, much too far to travel on

**The Darr company store in Van Meter. The man-way entrance to the mine was behind the store and company offices.**

foot to work. This created a dilemma: how to get the Jacob's Creek men to work on time. The solution was to build a ferry. Since the river currents were too raped and wild, it was impossible to build a water ferry so the company built a crude cable car, known as the "sky ferry."

The sky ferry was a simple box, strung on strong cables that crossed the river and landed in one of Darr's buildings. The box held six men at a time. They would glide to about half way and then pull themselves the rest of the way across the river by cranking on a cable. Once unloaded, the men on the other side would pull the box back for the next six men. In this fashion, a good number of men were able to work in Darr while living across the river.

William Campbell had been worried

Photo of the Darr Mine taken from the Jacob's Creek patch at the location of the sky ferry. The sky ferry 'car' is crossing the river in this photo. The car is visible about half up from the bottom and a third of the way from the right. It is hard to believe that six grown men with their mining equipment could fit in that tiny box.

about the gaseous conditions in the mine for months. It was his job to worry. He was the mine's foreman. The Darr mine had always been known as a gassy mine but it was getting worse. There was a huge fan for ventilation but it didn't seem to be clearing out the blackdamp (explosive methane gas). There were still too many pockets of the gas in too many places. The bad air just wasn't getting moved out as it should. It had gotten so bad that Mine Superintendent Archibald Black and David Wingrove, the former fire boss, had resigned their positions because of the "gassy nature" of the mine and the increased dangers to the miners. Campbell told his wife he had to get something done about the gas soon or one of these days he wasn't going be coming home.

He started badgering the management for a new air shaft, knowing that it was going to be a tough sell. He would have to take men away from loading coal to dig the shaft. He kept at them but wasn't making any headway. Finally, in his desperation, he dramatically announced to his bosses that he couldn't even think about Christmas because he doubted that he would ever see another one. That did the trick. He got permission to set some men to work sinking the new ventilation shaft. This was going to be a little complicated. To be effective, the shaft needed to be dug beyond the furthest end of the working tunnels. The plan was for the shaft to be sunk to the level of the tunnels about the same time that the tunnel would be dug out to meet the air shaft.

If all went well, they would meet up at the same time and the excess gas would be blown out and William Campbell would be able to sleep easy again. He hadn't had much sleep over the past few weeks. His worries about the blackdamp in his own mine were bad enough, but miners were dying - dying by the hundreds - and so many of them had died just this December. First there had been Naomi, less than ten miles away. Then just five days later there had been the big one, the worst one: Monongah down in West Virginia, but still close, only about sixty miles away. And it hadn't stopped there because another mine had exploded in Alabama!

Work was progressing well on the new air shaft and so far, they had been lucky, escaping injury or accident from all that blackdamp. On the morning of December 19, William Campbell kissed his wife goodbye and walked out of his home. He was feeling better and more confident than he had in a long while. Just forty more feet and the tunnel would connect with the air shaft. No problem, just twenty-four hours more and they would be through to the shaft. Christmas was going to be especially good this year.

William walked into the mine and down the slope with an almost-level two and a half percent grade, along with 225 other men and their helpers. He was going to be working off and on at the little office in the wooden shanty at the bottom of the slope. This was an especially easy walk, easier than most mines. Darr was a high mine, almost elevated. Instead of dropping down deep underground, it pushed back into the foothills as they rose up all around them.

Soon after work started that early morning, there was a problem. The fire boss had had to rope off a section of the mine because of large pockets of blackdamp. The men were still issued the outdated open air head lamps and it would not do for one of them to walk into one of the blackdamp pockets. As hundreds of men set off to work, the black powder shots started going off, echoing down the long, dark tunnels and into the various rooms. The men were settling into their routine. The coal was blasted out of the seam and the coal cars were being filled. The morning ran on as it always did and the men had started checking their pocket watches. It was nearly 11:30 - almost lunch time. A handful of men stepped over the cordoning rope put up earlier by the fire boss and walked into the restricted section --- and the earth moved once again.

The ground shook so violently that people felt the explosion miles away. The river, just a matter of feet from the main entrance, literally splashed straight up! Glass shattered in the windows of the tiny houses in Van Meter, just up the road, and in Jacob's Creek, directly across the river. A huge cloud of dirty white smoke and ash billowed out of the mouth of the mine, as it spat out broken timbers, stones and twisted pieces of iron. And to make things even more desperate, the mine was on fire somewhere deep inside. There was no doubt in anyone's mind what had happened. But how could there be another explosion so soon? The coal region, and indeed the entire country, was still reeling from three mine explosions already this month. The cruel irony was just about too much to bear.

The damage to human life was not limited to the men inside the mine. Many men who were working in the perimeter area around the entrance were injured. Frank Ballentine, the commissary operator, had his food shack positioned two hundred feet from the entrance. He already had several lunch customers in line when the mine blew. The concussion impact from the blast pulverized his shack and knocked Ballentine and the other men flat against a wall that crumbled behind them. John Lundway, the tipple operator, was also struck hard by the concussion. He was blown off the tipple and received several severe injuries. Lundway survived, but his father, who had been working in the mine that day, did not.

Four hundred men were believed to be trapped inside the Darr mine. In response, one hundred of the most experienced miners in the area converged on the site. They were all employees of the same company but worked in other mines such as the Bannings and Wickhaven. The men, upon hearing the explosion, rushed to the rescue before they were released by their supervisors. There was no time to ask - just to act as quickly as they could. As any miner and any miner's family knew, the first few minutes or hours were critical. Blackdamp and afterdamp were ruthless killers and they killed quickly. If those who had survived the explosion and subsequent fire were not pulled from the mine almost immediately, they would have little or no chance of surviving the afterdamp.

The rescuers at Darr were the first to use a breathing apparatus for the rescue and recovery efforts. Even with the air thick with afterdamp pouring from the mine entrance, the men wearing respirators were able to work a full two hours before being rotated out of the mine for fresh air. The danger to the rescue teams was so extreme that only unmarried men were allowed to enter the mine.

The debris and rock were cleared away from the entrance and the damage just

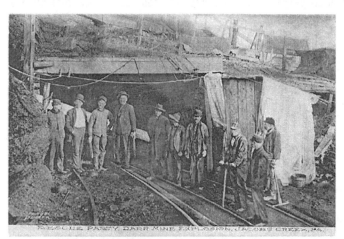

**A group of rescuers waiting for their shift to go into the Darr mine to search for survivors and recover bodies.**

inside the portal was not terribly extensive. The fire had extinguished itself but the gas and heat still emanating from the mine made it impossible to enter until late in the afternoon after the exhaust fan was repaired and restarted. They were also lucky that the brattice work, the heavy wooden timbers and props holding up the roof, with a few exceptions, was in unexpectedly good condition. This made their progress into the mine much faster and safer. About two hundred feet from the opening, the rescuers found something they would never have expected to find: a survivor!

Tom Williams had just re-entered the mine and was heading back down with his empty coal car when he heard the rumble rising up from deep in the mine. Without any time to think, he jumped into his coal car and curled up into a ball. Fortunately, much of the explosive energy had been spent by the time it reached him. He had been given a fighting chance, though there was little doubt that he would have been killed if not for the protection of his coal car, which was destroyed around him.

**Rare old newspaper photograph of Tom Williams, sitting on the destroyed coal car that saved his life.**

There was only one other survivor. Joseph Mapleton, a pumper who was found stunned and disoriented near the first air shaft. His injuries were minor and after his cuts and scrapes were bandaged, he joined the rescue effort.

The rescue team continued their descent along the slope, which was completely devoid of man, child or beast, living or dead. At about five thousand feet, they found the first victims. It was here where they came upon the pit boss' shanty. The first men who entered the tiny wooden structure were met with a startling and gruesome sight. The bodies of four men were huddled together on a makeshift bench along one wall. They were propped against each other, each body holding the next in place, eyes open wide in surprise. They appeared unscathed. The fifth member of their small group had not been so lucky. Mine foreman William Campbell lay dead, sprawled on the floor with his head blown off. He had almost made it to Christmas. Just six days short.

The team returned to the surface to be relieved by the next group and to report what they had witnessed. Five thousand feet in and only five bodies discovered. The recovery effort would have to go in much deeper than they had hoped. James Anderson, the general manager ordered that no bodies were to be brought to the surface and outside until the crowd was dispersed. The company released the expected death toll as no more than 200 dead.

The next team of rescuers entered the mine. This was to be a round-the-clock effort. Since they did not have to do any searching until after they reached the pit boss' shanty, they were able to move along much more quickly. After passing the shanty, the appearance of the mine began to change. The level of damage they saw was increased with nearly every step. They were able to make it another 2,000 feet and found a few more bodies. The dead were left where they had fallen and the teams pushed on ahead when they could; they were there to search for survivors. The dead could wait. Unable to explore much more because of heavy levels of afterdamp, they returned to the surface.

Teams continued to rotate through the mine but their efforts were continually hindered by the afterdamp. The respirators were of little help after a time and there were only a limited number to share. Additional gangs were sent in to board up rooms and tunnels that were found empty to re-direct the ventilation into the farther reaches of the mine. It would take time, but they would eventually be able to search the deepest areas. The prevailing theory was that a majority of the bodies would be recovered in an area called "the swamp," about three miles in.

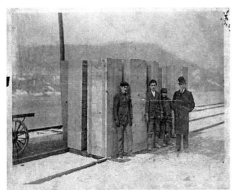

A shipment of coffins just arrived by train from Pittsburgh.

A group of families waiting behind ropes to learn of the fate of their loved ones.

By 11:00 a.m. on December 21, exactly two days after the explosion, only twelve bodies had been recovered and brought to just inside the entrance, where they were being held. No more bodies had been found but they had found a number of body parts: arms, legs, hands, feet...

As the recovery continued and more of the mine was ventilated sufficiently to make it safe for the men to search, many gruesome discoveries awaited them. One searcher found his best friend Andy Koslaski. His arm had been blown off and his head was horribly crushed. Four men had had time to take cover by jumping into a string of coal cars. The blast hit the cars and men with such force that some of their clothes were blasted through the wood of the car and particles of fabric became imbedded in the coal seam.

Two of the bodies found in "the swamp," a wet worked-out area frequently used as a toilet, were meshed tightly together. When the men lifted the first body in an attempt to separate them, they found that his suspenders were wrapped tightly around the neck of the second body. The explosion had ripped along the mine's roof, as it surged down one tunnel after another with such force that men standing upright had the tops of their heads sheared off where they stood. So many limbless and headless bodies were found and the shock to the rescuers so great that many of them became overwhelmed and had to be helped back to the surface.

The Pittsburgh Coal Company posted a notice that payday was being postponed for one week to reduce confusion. Many believed that they had an ulterior motive for this decision: they wished to be certain that they were not going to pay anyone who had died. Then they lowered the expected death toll again - this time to one hundred and fifty. The company owners also announced to the nation, through all the major newspapers, that they had ordered three hundred quality coffins from two Pittsburgh factories and had purchased a plot of land in Mount Olive Cemetery for burial of any unidentified remains. They also stated that they would pay the expenses of all the burials. This may have gone towards greatly improving their image but the reality was that the company required each of its regular employees to buy a $150 life insurance policy. When the policies were paid out, the company deducted the cost of their burial before turning the balance over to the named beneficiary.

At Darr, crowd control was not as big a problem as it had been after the other mine explosions. Darr's main slope opened up as it moved out of a very old, low-lying mountain. Running in front of the slope entrance was the Pittsburg and Lake Erie Railroad tracks and just a few feet beyond that was the Yough River. Since the mine fronted on this narrow strip of land, it was much more difficult for the crowds to gather around the entrance and it was easier to rope off and contain the crowds on both sides of the entrance. The crowd that formed out of Van Meter was generally quiet as they were being kept a good distance from the mine itself and there simply wasn't much space for them to gather. This was also to the benefit of their own safety as the mine continued to belch out poison blackdamp, long after the explosion and after the fire was extinguished.

The story on the Jacob's Creek side of the river was very different. Here, there was plenty of room for large groups of people to collect and excellent places from which to view the goings on across the raging waters. Along with friends and family of the men lost to the explosion, local newspapers estimated that the mass of people had swollen to nearly 25,000; most of whom fit into the category of morbidly curious. Additional police had to be called in to help control the growing crowd. Things were especially tense in the area where the sky ferry landed in Jacob's Creek. Frequent fights broke out as people tried to gain a coveted spot on the tiny six-person car and cross the river to get closer to the mine. This continued until a sizable portion of the police presence was positioned at the sky ferry.

Conrad Schuth and his family lived in Jacob's Creek. Schuth was a widower raising five children on his own. He had not been in the mine the morning of the explosion but his eldest son was. As a miner of old, deep inside he knew that his son had departed this earth and his despair was inconsolable. He felt that it should have been he instead of his son who had gone into the hole, never to return. He needed to get to Van Meter to be closer to his son so he waited at the sky ferry until he was able to gain a coveted spot. Halfway across to the opposite bank, Conrad Schuth found his own peace. He jumped into the raging river below, joining his son in death. He left behind four young children at home, now orphans all.

Mrs. Carino Petrano had the same idea, though she was not as successful. After waiting for nearly two days, she too secured a place on the sky ferry. Once over the water, she climbed onto the rim of the car and attempted to jump. The men on the ferry with her were able to catch onto her and they held her fast, while she continued to scream, "Let me go! Let me go! I want to die!"

In Jacob's Creek and Van Meter, police were met with rising animosity toward "foreigners." Many of them had either fled in fear or just decided that they had had enough. It was later reported that within the first two days following the disaster, four hundred miners and their families packed up and left, though many had not worked at Darr. Some headed back to the old country, where the rest of their family still lived, while others went to New Jersey to work in sweat shops in the textile industry where at least they would be above ground and in the daylight. This dramatic exit by so many may have explained the early overestimation of the death toll. As the exodus continued, there were cries of good riddance. "Let them go back to Italy, Poland and Hungary and bring bad luck to someone besides coal miners for a change," was the popular sentiment.

Dr. C.A. Wynn, the Westmorland County coroner, was very concerned and wanted to proceed with the utmost caution. He was well aware of the problems with body identification that arose following the Monongah mine explosion. Dr. Wynn believed that the percentage of unidentified bodies there was unacceptable and he wanted to make absolutely sure that as many bodies were identified at Darr as humanly possible. To this end, he developed a methodology that would increase the number of identifications. He also ordered that no bodies would be released until everything had been done to identify every single victim.

Dr. Wynn's plan included ordering detailed sketches made of each body or body part, indicating location and position where found. The victim's clothing was left on the body and a thorough record was taken of every distinguishing mark still visible and anything personal found on or with the body that could be used for identification purposes. This procedure was ahead of its time and proved to be very effective as they were able to identify many more victims than was typical, but it also proved to be very slow, much slower than at any other mine explosion.

The public protest was loud and persistent. Authorities were continually accosted by friends, families and townspeople wondering when they were to be allowed to give the victims a decent burial. "It is vulgar to postpone funerals in the name of identification," wrote a sympathetic reporter for a local newspaper. In spite of the public outcry, Dr. Wynn remained undeterred. He tried to explain his reasoning in his first public statement: "I intend that the people shall find out if possible the exact cause of this terrible death bearing catastrophe, and nothing will be suppressed. The coroner's jury (which had not yet been formed) will view the bodies and then release them for burial."

Within a few more days, a new problem arose for which Dr. Wynn was again blamed. With the accumulating mass of "undisposed bodies," the odor of decomposing flesh began to waft out of the mine's entrance. It was said that the stench of death could be smelled for a mile in any direction. Rescue workers began to drop out because of the odor. Complaints about the horrible smell were much written about in the press. According to the *Greensburg Daily Tribune*: "Others, used to such scenes and smells, braved it out. But there was not a man among the bravest who did not quelch. By the greatest efforts the bodies were tenderly picked up, but it is being proven imprudent to expose them to the air."

**Bodies were carried from the mine in coal carts pulled by mules and horses.**

**The tent that served as a temporary morgue. If one didn't know of the horrific contents of this tent, it might almost look festive and inviting.**

**Inside the morgue tent, the coffins containing unidentified bodies were lined up for viewing in the hopes that someone might recognize them, or something among their possessions.**

The *Greensburg Press* explained some of the complications caused by the stench: "Even horses this morning refused to go to the mine. When whipped, they dropped to the ground, and could not be forced to enter. The horses are needed by the rescuers to haul the bodies to the surface, and many of the men say they cannot continue the work without the help of the animals." There was one positive that came of the horrible smell: at times it seemed that the crowd was on the verge of rioting and rushing the mine entrance to search for themselves. However, the constant freezing drizzle and the smell of death seemed to keep them quiet and quell their hunger for answers.

But the work did continue somehow and a circus-like tent was set up alongside the company offices on the edge of Van Meter. The tent would serve as a temporary morgue and could hold up to one hundred bodies at a time. After detailed records of each body were taken, they were removed of their clothes and were swaddled in burial wrappings. Then they were placed in open coffins. Their clothes were tied in a bundle, which was placed on the foot of each coffin. Those still unidentified were laid out side by side in the tent while families paraded up and down the long rows, hoping against hope that they would be able to recognize something, anything that would allow them to rest easy knowing that their loved one had had a proper burial.

And there was evidence that Dr. Wynn's system was working. There were many stories of people recognizing not a face but a shirt, a belt, a pair of pants, a set of spectacles, special stitches mending a tear. Joe Simko had been brought to the holding area just inside the mouth of the entrance the day after the explosion. Then he lay in the morgue for two days. He remained unidentified, his family passing by his body several times without recognizing anything about him. Then a family member told a morgue worker that if a piece of cotton were found between the toes of any remaining leg, it would be Joe Simko. The wrappings were removed from the most likely body and a piece of cotton was found between two of the toes. It seems that Mrs. Simko had long worried about not being able to get her husband's body back if there were an explosion or a fire. To appease her, Simko had agreed to place the tiny piece of cotton between two toes of each foot every morning, never knowing

(Left) Mass grave site in the Mount Olive Cemetery. A single large pit was dug and the coffins were placed side by side and end to end.    (Right) Headstone marking the mass grave of Darr's unclaimed and unknowns in Mount Olive Cemetery.

that this would be the only reason he would be laid to rest under a stone that bore his own name.

Finally, on December 25, the bodies were released for burial, properly identified or not. By the end of December 27, the entire working portion of the mine had been explored and 228 bodies had been recovered. It was then that the real work of removing the large debris and the rock and roof falls would begin. They fully expected to find more bodies that had been covered up and they did: 19 more.

Day after day, funeral after funeral filled what should have been a joyous Christmas season and even those who had no direct association with the poor families affected by the Darr tragedy found themselves having difficulty celebrating in the face of such despair. Author Carlton Jackson described the sad irony: "A co-mingling of life and death was symbolized by Father Adam Bint of St. Timothy's Church in Jacob's Creek when on Christmas Day, he baptized ten orphaned infants and then said a requiem mass for their lost fathers."

The official death total was finalized at 239. Most of the dead were Hungarian and Italian, though they did not make up the majority of the Darr miners. The Mount Olive Cemetery plot purchased by the coal company was used as a mass grave for 71 miners, 32 who went unclaimed and 49 who remained unidentified but not forgotten. The company bought the plot and buried the unknown and unclaimed men, but never bothered to place a stone to mark the site or commemorate the event that took their lives. A headstone was placed two years later, in 1909, not by those responsible, but by the Hungarian-American Federation.

As was common after any mining disaster, there were many unanswered question and most pointed to a cover-up, if not out-and-out lies. According to the roll count, 375 men entered the mine that morning and that number did not include the helpers or many of the support workers. Why did the company order three hundred coffins the same day they lowered the expected death toll to two hundred lives lost? Why did the company again lower the expected death toll to 150 after 200 had already been recovered? Why did 45 Jacob's Creek houses in a row have funeral wreaths nailed to their doors? The questions continue to this day, though many believe that the answers are self- evident.

This might seem the logical place to conclude the retelling of this terrible tragedy, and it would be - except for the miracle, the "Intercession of St. Nicholas."

Bias based on ethnicity and nationality was as strong in this coal field as it was in most of the others. Newspapers reported the losses and survivors in two groups: Americans and foreigners. Many of the men and their families could not communicate with others as they spoke several different languages. The language barrier created other divisions: it caused the different nationalities and ethnic groups to band together and form fraternal organizations or clubs to aid and support their members. If a particular group had both Catholics and Protestants, they would form two separate clubs. Though these organizations did help their members, they also further isolated these groups from each other and from the "Americans" with whom they lived and worked. The result of this isolation was a growing animosity and distrust between the ethnic.

A majority of the "foreigners" working in the Darr and Banning mines were Southern and Eastern Europeans. They were Italians, Hungarians, Ukrainians, Slovaks, Belarusians, Serbs and Croats. There was also a sizable number of Rusyns, also called Carpatho-Rusyns, but because they were an ethnic group with no country or real homeland, it was difficult to understand just who they were. History has recorded their roll at the Darr and Banning mines with great confusion. They were a very religious people and their ancestors had joined with the Catholic Church many years earlier. However, since the Greek Catholic Church allowed them to follow their heritage and practice the Eastern Rite Orthodoxy, they generally chose to worship with them. Because of this, they sometimes answered to Greek Catholic when listing their ethnicity, and Rusyn was often confused with Russian. This group of Rusyns were alternately referred to as Greeks or Russians, of which they were neither, but the incorrect labels reappear throughout history.

There are but two days a year in which a devout Orthodox Greek Catholic would refuse to go to work in order to attend mass, no matter how poor or desperate they were. One of these days was the feast day of St. Nicholas the Wonderworker. There were no Greeks working the Darr mine but there were plenty of Rusyns.

St. Nicholas was the Bishop of Myra, now a part of Turkey. He was assigned the title of wonderworker because he was known for the many miracles he performed. He is the basis for our own St. Nick, the jolly old fellow who spreads Christmas cheer around the world. In Norway, St. Nicholas the Wonderworker is pronounced as "Sinter Claus" which has morphed into Santa Claus.

The original St. Nicholas was a saint of great import so the day he died became a feast day; a day of worship not to be confused with a festival. St. Nicholas died on December 6, so that became his feast day - that is, if you are following the Gregorian calendar. In the Sixteenth Century, Pope Gregory created a calendar intended to correct mistakes that had been made since the birth of Christ, which we still follow today. On the older Julian calendar, the Feast day of St. Nicholas was held on December 19. The Roman Catholic Church adopted the Gregorian calendar but the Greek Orthodox Catholic Church followed the older Julian calendar.

If anyone were to wonder what this has to do with hundreds of dead miners in 1907, they would only have to consider those two very important dates. In Monongah, there was no Greek Catholic church for the Ruysn miners to attend on such an important feast day. Instead, they attended the next closest thing: the Roman Catholic Church, which followed the Gregorian calendar and celebrated the Feast day of St. Nicholas on December 6. When the Monongah mine exploded, at least sixty miners who would otherwise have been in the mine, were saved because they had refused to work so that they might attend mass.

However, in Van Meter and Jacob's Creek, there was a large enough number of Ruysns that a Greek Catholic priest was assigned to their area. As the Greek Catholic Church followed the Julian calendar, they celebrated the Feast day of St. Nicholas on December 19. When the Darr mine exploded at 11:30 a.m., the mass was only about half over. Between two hundred and two hundred fifty miners had refused to go to work that day so they might attend their church. They were saved from an early death in the dark depths of the Darr mine.

The Roman Catholics, mostly Hungarians and Italians, had already celebrated St. Nicholas on December 6 so they were free to work the mine, and were killed in the explosion that morning. The Darr mine owners knew the devout Rusyns would not work on December 19, so they hired a group of outside miners to take their places for the day. They were in luck, a group of miners from the Naomi mine were available. These men were out of work while Naomi was being rebuilt following an explosion...

Orthodox and Byzantine (Greek) Catholic Churches use icons to tell their religious history. These icons are paintings depicting stories from the Bible or events in the life (or afterlife) of saints. The Miracle of the Intersession of St. Nicholas relates to the hundreds of miners who were saved because they were attending church to celebrate the feast day of St. Nicholas. This event is also sometimes called the Miracle of the Coal Miners. An icon was designed and painted to tell the story. Copies of the icon can be seen in several locations around the northeastern United States.

Over twenty years ago, a second icon was designed and painted in an attempt to ensure that this particular miracle would not be forgotten. This icon hangs in the Greek Catholic Church in tiny Jacob's Creek with copies hanging in several key churches around the area. The bottom of this icon shows scenes in a coal mining town with company houses, a tipple in the background and a mine entrance. We can see the dark, upraised faces of the poor trapped souls, peering out of the mine. St. Nicholas is reaching down from the heavens and lifts the miners up and away from danger and the explosion in his *rusknyk* or ritual towel, and embroidered cloth.

A coroner's inquiry was held after all the bodies had been removed and buried and investigators had checked out the entire mine. There was no argument about what had happened; there had been a single explosion with flaming detonation of coal dust traveling throughout the mine. Although the investigators could not agree about where the explosion had originated or what had caused it, the official results laid the blame squarely on the shoulders of the miners themselves because a few bodies had been found in an area that had been cordoned off as unsafe by the fire boss that morning. The Pittsburgh Coal Company was not held accountable in any way. Many people were outraged at these findings, believing that no matter what happened, the mine owners were so wealthy and powerful that they would never be held culpable and dead miners would always be blamed. The miners again realized that some things just never changed.

**The Miracle of Saving the Coal Miners icon depicting angels, a priest and a group of coal miners standing around an open coffin bearing St. Nicholas.**

A specific problem that had only been partially addressed during the inquiry was the most likely reason that Darr had always been an excessively gaseous mine. As claimed by the miners but flatly denied by the mine owners, deep underground, in various places, Darr was connected to the Banning No. 1, Banning No. 3 and Port Royal mines. This was considered a safety hazard even when safety seemed to be of little or no concern to any mine operators. If there was an explosion in one mine, there was a strong likelihood that the explosion would carry over into the attached mine, just as it had done in Monongah. The reason this was even more of a problem in this instance was that Darr sat very high in comparison so that gasses building up in the other three would filter into and collect in the Darr chambers. This problem was compounded by the fact that the old Port Royal mine had been worked out for years and had been allowed to fill up with water, creating even more dangerous gasses.

In 1957, a follow-up study was reported on by the *United Mine Workers Journal*. The study included an in-depth investigation of all five of the December 1907 mine explosions. They concluded that the main problem all five mines had in common was management neglect, and in some cases, brutal criminal neglect. They were all still using black powder to fire shots and all miners wore open flame head lamps. All five mines had problems with blackdamp (explosive gas) and were allowed to accumulate huge amounts of coal dust. It had

**St. Nicholas Saving the Coal Miners icon. This icon is in brilliant color but has a creepy aspect to it because the faces of the miners looking out of the mine are in black and gray.**

taken fifty years for the poor, hard working miners to be vindicated and the true blame laid at the feet of unscrupulous coal mine owners. Sadly no one involved in any of the explosions lived to read the report.

After the last body was buried and the last family member sent on his or her way, the Darr mine was cleaned up and in 1910, it was reopened, but the Darr name would never be used again. The old Darr entrance was now used as a second entrance for Banning No. 3. Heavy coal production continued for a few years and then started a steady decline until the Banning No. 3 and No. 1, including what had previously been the Darr mine, were closed down and sealed in 1919. These mines were left untouched until 1950, when they were rebuilt and reopened. The last of the coal reserves were removed and they were closed for that final time.

Although the mine was closed and sealed decades ago, the site is passed by thousands of people every year. The Pittsburgh and Lake Erie Railroad tracks that passed old mines and the Yough River have been dismantled and transformed into a lovely biking and walking path by the Rails to Trails program. There is no historical marker there to describe the horrific events of December 19, 1907. The state historical marker was placed instead at a corner of the Mount Olive Cemetery. A majority of those passing by the spot where so many men and boys lost their lives are totally unaware of the tragedy that happened there. All the Darr structures have been demolished except for a few foundations and retaining walls on the hillside, but they are lost in the trees that now cover the once-barren space. The "sky ferry," which made thousands of trips over the river carrying hundreds of thousands of miners, has not flown in over ninety years and nothing remains of it as well. Farther down the trail, moving away from Van Meter, there are still a few large concrete structures but they were part of the Banning No. 1 mine, and the are coming down one at a time. Soon, all but a few chunks of concrete will be gone, removing all evidence of what happened there a century ago.

Signs have been posted warning that the trail closes at dusk but there are plenty of folks out and about after dark; it's just that only a few of them are still alive. Intrepid searchers have found an old Darr air shaft part way up the hill from the trail and a few have ventured into the tunnel a short way before thinking better of it and retreating back to the safety of the surface. No one has seen anything while inside the tunnel but most have told of feeling extremely uncomfortable and anxious while inside and couldn't wait to get back out into the fresh air. This is not really unexpected, though. Climbing down an air shaft, in the dark, into a crumbling old mine tunnel that is still harboring pockets of poisonous and explosive gasses and was the site of hundreds of violent deaths, doesn't seem to be the sort of adventure where a person would feel comfortable and relaxed upon arrival!

The area itself does sometimes seem to have its own atmosphere. The air feels heavy and thick and there have been numerous reports of odd and unexplained things happening. Most often, what people experience are sounds: the sounds of men arguing. No one yet as been able to decipher what is being said but the voices are definitely angry and confrontational. The voices are clear but seem to come from nowhere and everywhere at once so listeners are unable to determine the source. "Gibberish" is the word most often used to describe what the voices are saying, but it is possible that since most of the miners were from eastern Europe, they could be speaking Slovic or Hungarian.

A young man, along with a few of his friends decided to camp out on the riverbank one summer evening. While gathering an armload of wood to start a riverside campfire, he heard a rustling in the trees behind him. Looking around, he expecting to see an animal but there was nothing there. When he turned back to his chore, someone whispered loudly into his ear, "Oh God!" The young men decided to camp elsewhere that night.

One evening around dusk, two women were casually walking along the trail, approaching Van Meter. One of the women stopped walking and said she was feeling uncomfortable. She began to cry, and very soon she was sobbing almost uncontrollably. Through her sobs, she kept repeating that she was "so embarrassed" and that she had no idea why she was crying. After a few minutes, she stopped crying as abruptly as she had started. The women were dumbfounded and decided to do some research. They learned of the disaster and of the men who died there. The woman who cried was especially moved when she learned that so many of the dead men were Hungarians: just like her father. She believes that there was some sort of connection through her own personal heritage, with the Hungarian women who stood on that same spot, sobbing at the loss of their husbands and sons nearly a century before.

## THE DEADLIEST MONTH: THE FINAL BLOW

The month of December in 1907 was a bloody one. Four catastrophic coal mine explosions had ripped across the eastern half of America, killing hundreds of coal miners. The month was finally drawing to a close. It was

December 31 and miners all over the country held their collective breaths -- and the earth moved one more time.

This time, death had crossed the country and landed in the New Mexico Territory to make its grudging farewell to 1907.

The mines at Carthage had been operating for a long time, having been the first to be opened in the New Mexico Territory. During the Civil War, Union soldiers worked the mines to provide coal for the blacksmiths in three local forts. Following the war, the mining operations were done almost exclusively by Mexican miners and the Carthage population had grown to nearly one thousand.

The Burnal Mine, owned by the Carthage Fuel Company, employed sixty miners, but on that last day of December only forty men had entered the mine. Work that morning had gone along as on any other morning. The noon bell clanged and many of the men came out into the sunshine to eat their mid-day meal. They had only just started to eat when the earth beneath their feet shook violently. Just as in Fayette City, Monongah, Van Meter and Yolanda, the men knew immediately what had happened.

At the time of the explosion, there were fourteen miners still inside the mine working. Eight men had been killed instantly and three died of their injuries soon after. Women in the community ran to the mine, ready to do their part to care for the dead and injured. The *Soccoro Chieftan* reported: "On every hand there were abundant evidences of the terrific force of the explosion. The bodies of some of the dead were blown against the walls of the mine with such great force as to flatten them almost beyond recognition. In one instance at least, a dead body was identified only by parts of clothing adhering to mangled flesh. The body of one miner who was coming out of the mouth of the mine when the explosion occurred, was shot a hundred yards into the air as from the mouth of a cannon, and nearly all the bones were broken by the fall."

Many of the dead and injured had small stones driven into their bodies as if they had been shot with a shotgun. The company surgeon, Dr. H. Bacon worked frantically trying to remove the stones but not everyone survived the procedure.

The mine was only mildly damaged and mining operations could have continued the next day, but instead, the company closed the mine to allow for the funerals. They re-opened on January 2, 1908 and went back to work.

The investigation that followed the explosion resulted in a familiar verdict. The explosion had been caused by a "windy shot," a shot that had dislodged a large quantity of coal but also caused a huge quantity of coal dust that was then ignited by another shot.

The month that seemed to have started so long ago had finally ended. The most deadly month, during the most deadly year was finally a part of history.

# 1910: "WHITE DEATH" THE WELLINGTON AVALANCHE AND RAILWAY DISASTER

As both explorers and railway builders attempted to conquer the Western mountains, they found that the Cascade Range in Washington was among the greatest challenges they would ever face. They were formidable mountains, shrouded in ice and snow for most of the year, and the steep cliffs and treacherous passes made travel nearly impossible. But they refused to be beaten by nature and the Great Northern Railway, headed by famed railroad magnate James J. Hill, began construction through Stevens Pass in the Cascades in 1891. Workers created a series of switchbacks to carry passengers and freight over the mountain route for several years.

In 1897, work began on the Cascade Tunnel, which would eliminate the switchbacks, reduce the avalanche risk and make the grades much easier to ascend and descend. The two-and-a-half-mile tunnel opened in 1900, although snow slides continued to block the entrances. In addition, the threat of avalanches increased after fire destroyed the timber that provided some protection for the track. But these minor problems were only a prelude to disaster.

During the early morning hours of March 1, 1910, an avalanche roared down Windy Mountain near Stevens

**The depot and bunkhouses at Wellington before the disaster occurred.**

Pass and swept two Great Northern trains into a ravine, sending 96 victims to their deaths. It was the deadliest snow slide in American history – and one that has left a haunting presence in its wake.

On February 24, 1910, after a snow delay at the east Cascade Mountains town of Leavenworth, two Great Northern trains, the Spokane Local passenger train No. 25 and Fast Mail train No. 27, traveled west through the mountains toward the coast. There were five or six steam and electric engines, fifteen boxcars, passenger cars, and sleepers. The trains had passed through the Cascade Tunnel from the east to the west side of the mountains, when snow and avalanches forced them to stop near Wellington, in King County. Wellington was a small town populated almost entirely with Great Northern railway employees.

The train stopped under the peak of Windy Mountain, above Tye Creek, where they were forced to wait for plows to clear the tracks. Meanwhile, the snow continued, piling up in five- to eight-foot-deep drifts. Four rotary plows – locomotives with rotating blades on the front that cut through snow and blew it aside – that were sent to clear the tracks ran into difficulty. The first hit a stump on February 25, knocking it out of commission. A second plow became stuck and couldn't refuel on February 27. Snow slides trapped the last two plows. The slides, which were strewn with rocks and timber, had to be cleared by shovel gangs before the plows could go back to work. Unfortunately, Mountain Division supervisor James H. O'Neil had fired the shovelers because of a wage dispute. This left both the rotary crews immobilized while trains No. 25 and No. 27 waited at the siding for six days. When the Wellington telegraph lines went down, cutting off all communication with the outside world, the agitation of the passengers reached its peak.

During the early morning hours of March 1, the snow that was falling from the sky turned to rain, accompanied by thunder and lightning. Thunder shook the mountains, stirring loose walls of snow and sending them hurtling down toward the tracks.

**Photographs of the Wellington Avalanche**

Shortly after midnight, Charles Andrews, a Great Northern employee, was walking towards the warmth of one of the Wellington's bunkhouses when he heard a rumble. He turned toward the sound and saw a horrific sight that he would never forget. He later described what he witnessed: "White Death moving down the mountainside above the trains. Relentlessly it advanced, exploding, roaring, rumbling, grinding, snapping -- a crescendo of sound that might have been the crashing of ten thousand freight trains. It descended to the ledge where the side tracks lay, picked up cars and equipment as though they were so many snow-draped toys, and swallowing them up, disappeared like a white, broad monster into the ravine below."

**Rescue and Recovery workers at the Site**

The wall of snow, which was ten feet high and a quarter of a mile wide, crashed down the mountainside. The avalanche swept the passenger train and the mail train into a gulch that was more than one hundred and fifty feet deep. Everyone – passengers, mail workers, Great Northern crew members – were all trapped inside. Some were killed instantly, while others suffocated, buried in the mounds of snow. A surviving train conductor sleeping in one of the mail train cars was thrown from the roof to the floor of the car several times as the train rolled down the slope before it disintegrated when the train slammed against a large tree.

**Bodies of the dead were taken away on toboggans.**

Wellington residents and crew members rushed to the crushed trains that lay far below and over the course of the next few hours, they dig out 23 survivors, many with injuries. As news slowly made its way out of the mountains, hundreds of volunteers and Great Northern employees converged on the scene to dig out the victims. The injured were sent to Wenatchee. The bodies of the dead were transported on toboggans down the west side of the Cascades to trains that carried them to Everett and Seattle. The death toll from the avalanche reached 96 people, including 35 passengers, 58 railroad employees sleeping on the trains and three railroad employees who were sleeping in cabins struck by the wall of snow.

An inquest that followed the disaster absolved Great Northern of negligence. Eventually, the courts ruled that the deaths had been caused by an act of God. The immediate cause of the

**Corpses stored for identification and burial**

**The site of the Wellington Avalanche today is only accessible by the Iron Goat Trail but it is a place that many believe is haunted.**

avalanche was the rain and thunder, but the conditions had been set by the earlier forest fire (started by locomotive sparks), which destroyed the shelter that had been provided for the tracks.

It took the Great Northern three weeks to repair the tracks before trains started running again over Stevens Pass. Because the name Wellington became associated with the disaster, the little town was renamed Tye. By 1913, to protect the trains from snow slides, the Great Northern had constructed snow-sheds over the nine miles of tracks between Scenic and Tye. The railroad also built a huge, double-track concrete snow shed in the area of the slide and, in later years, built a second tunnel through Windy Point at the trouble spot, where the slides had occurred. Still, Stevens Pass continued to pose problems for the line. In 1929, Great Northern rerouted its tracks through this troublesome section by constructing an eight-mile-long tunnel through the mountains – the longest railroad tunnel in America – and adding forty miles of tracks.

The old railroad line through Stevens Pass is now the Iron Goat Trail, a hiking trail through the forest with spectacular views of Cascade Mountains scenery. The trail travels past the old snow sheds, the remains of the original tunnel and the frightening ravine where pieces of the wreckage from the two trains still remain.

And if the stories are to be believed, it's not just twisted pieces of metal and remnants of railroad archaeology that remain at this place; some say the ghosts of the avalanche victims remain behind, as well.

Those who have the chance to visit the site of the Wellington disaster say that one can feel a very tangible history at the spot, despite the fact that everything that once existed as Wellington has long since vanished from the map. This is not an easy place to get to since the site is usually buried in snow from October to July in most years but there are many who come – hikers, history buffs, park rangers and ghost enthusiasts among them. And it's not just the ghost hunters who believe this place is haunted. Many of the park rangers won't go to the disaster site – or even into the nearby parking lot – after dark.

Many speak of uncomfortable and sometimes oppressive feelings as they navigate the hiking trail, walk through the old snow shed or brave the midday darkness of the crumbling railroad tunnel. But it's not just odd feelings and weird cold spots. Many claim they have heard and seen things here that should not exist – perhaps a little of the disaster victims who have remained behind. Inexplicable voices have sometimes been heard, echoing off the stone walls of the tunnel. On other occasions, these voices have even imprinted themselves on recording devices, offering chills to those who play them back later.

Some claim to have seen the victims of the avalanche. They report glimpses of people walking along the tracks near the site of Wellington where no people were walking before – and they say these mysterious figures vanish without explanation, as if they had never been there at all.

Has the sadness and tragedy of this terrible event left an impression on this place? Many who have visited here say that it has as it begs to be remembered as one of America's worst railroad disasters.

# 1918: THE CIRCUS TRAIN DISASTER

In the summer of 1918, one of the nation's largest circus companies, the Hagenbeck-Wallace Circus, was touring the Midwest. While this was still the heyday of the traveling circus, these were not good days for the company. World War I was in progress and governmental restrictions on the use of the railroads made moving two special trains filled with equipment, twenty-two tents, one thousand employees and almost four hundred animals a logistical nightmare. However, "the show must go on" and so plans were made, routes were mapped out, and then mapped out again, and the trains somehow managed to get from place to place, arriving in time to put on a great show.

However, in June 1918, a disaster near Hammond, Indiana, almost brought an end to

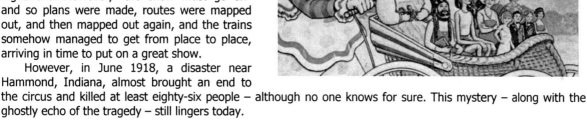

the circus and killed at least eighty-six people – although no one knows for sure. This mystery – along with the ghostly echo of the tragedy – still lingers today.

Based on a two-hundred-acre farm near Peru, Indiana, the Hagenbeck-Wallace Circus traveled across America in the early part of the twentieth century. At its peak, it was the second-largest circus in the country, just behind the Ringling Brothers and Barnum & Bailey Circus.

The circus had a bit of a tangled past. It began as the "Carl Hagenbeck Circus," formed by Carl Hagenbeck, an animal trainer who pioneered the use of rewards-based animal training as opposed to fear-based training.

Meanwhile, Benjamin Wallace, a livery stable owner from Peru, Indiana, and his business partner, James Anderson, bought a circus in 1884 and created "The Great Wallace Show." Wallace bought out his partner in 1890 and formed the "B. E. Wallace Circus."

In 1907, Wallace purchased the Carl Hagenbeck Circus and merged it with his own show. The circus became known as the Hagenbeck-Wallace Circus, even though Carl Hagenbeck protested. He sued to prohibit the use of his name but lost in court. Wallace sold out to Ed Ballard of French Lick, Indiana, in 1913.

By 1918, the circus boasted a show featuring "60 aerialists, 60 acrobats, 60 riders and 50 clowns." It also had a payroll of $7,500 per day and a nightmare on its hands as it tried to move the circus around the country during the days of wartime railroad restrictions.

In June, the circus was touring Indiana. After playing in Michigan City, the troupe packed up for its next stop in Hammond. By the time everything was loaded and the trains were underway, darkness had fallen. On board one of the trains, the exhausted performers caught up on their sleep as the train roared through the night. The next day, June 22, would mark their arrival in Hammond and a grand parade through town.

But there would be no circus parade in Hammond that afternoon.

The first section of the train, consisting of all of the animals and about half the performers, had departed at 9:00 p.m. By 2:00 a.m., the tents had all been taken down and the second section of the train was scheduled to depart. When engineer J.W. Johnson started the locomotive moving out of the Michigan City depot, his orders were simple. They called for the train to take the Michigan City tracks to Ivanhoe, a small station between Gary and Hammond, then switch onto the Michigan Central tracks and from there proceed to Hammond. Once he arrived in Hammond, he would move the locomotive onto a side rail that would take them to the lot where the circus would set up and perform.

The first hour of the journey was uneventful. However, just as the train neared the Michigan Central tracks, the fireman behind Johnson relayed a message that the brakeman had seen a small fire on one of the cars. This

**The scene of the Hagenbeck-Wallace crash the next morning.**

was a condition called a "hotbox," which was fairly common and usually manageable. It was more annoying to an engineer than alarming and Johnson reluctantly slowed the train to a stop. By the time it had halted completely, most of the train was already turned onto the Michigan Central tracks. Only the last five cars still rested on the main line. Regardless, this hardly represented a danger since the rear signals, as well as a flagman, would warn any oncoming train of their presence.

This should have been a routine stop on a casual journey – but fate did not work out that way.

Coming in fast and hard behind the Hagenbeck-Wallace train was engine No. 8485, pulling an empty troop train on its way to Chicago to pick up a load of soldiers destined for the front lines in France. The troop train was moving especially fast. In fact, the fireman in the Hagenbeck-Wallace coal car noted that the steam coming from the approaching train's smokestack didn't sound the way that it should. Instead of a series of puffs, it was a constant harsh, shrill shriek. From his years of experience, he knew what this meant. The engine was running at full throttle, in violation of the speed rules for this section of track. As he later testified, he was further alarmed when he saw that the engineer was ignoring all of the warning lights as the train approached Ivanhoe station. He later said, "I saw him pass those light and wondered what he was about – I wondered what in the world he was doing."

Engine No. 8485 never even slowed down. Its engineer, A.K. Sargent, had fallen asleep at the throttle. He would later claim that he was taking patent medicine pills and that he was overworked by the railroad for the war effort. He was later tried for manslaughter for his part in the accident but the trial ended in a hung jury.

The troop train slammed into the rear section of the Hagenbeck-Wallace train at thirty-five miles an hour. The force of the collision sent the engine careening four hundred feet, through the caboose and the last five cars of the train, which were mostly sleeping berths. The cars were crushed together or thrown from the tracks. The wreckage soon burst into flames. Many of the sleeping passengers never woke up and those who survived the crash were knocked unconscious in the jumble of debris. Many of them woke to find themselves trapped under heaps of broken wood and twisted steel. Broken gas lanterns caused the fire to spread even faster and many of the performers were burned alive. The night was quickly filled with the sounds of screams and cries for help.

Gary, Indiana, Mayor William Hodges visited the site and later told reporters, "It was one of the worst wrecks I have ever witnessed. The injured were lying in many different places. Bodes of the dead were strewn along the tracks. The cars were in flames. We saw several bodies in the ruins. Someone said there were twenty-five bodies in the remains of one car. Most of these were women."

Amazingly, though, the show business professionals of the Hagenbeck-Wallace Circus knew that the "show must go on." Against all odds, the circus continued on to fill its commitments, even though many of the performers were left behind to recuperate in area hospitals – and many others were left in morgues.

There has never been a complete count of how many circus performers died that morning in the horrific crash. The Hammond Historical Society, which has carefully researched the disaster, believes the most accurate death toll stands at eighty-six but no one will ever be able to say for sure. The problem was that, in many cases, no accurate lists were kept of those who traveled with the circus and many of the workers' names were not recorded at all. The last sleeping car contained the roustabouts, temporary employees who were hired for day labor. Many of these men were drifters, with no present or past, who used assumed names or nicknames to identify themselves. The wreckage added to the problem as bodies were torn into pieces or burned beyond recognition. Dismembered body parts were scattered along the tracks and after the fires had gone out, an unidentified charred head was found beneath the cowcatcher on the locomotive. The wreck is still remembered today as one of the greatest disasters in American circus history.

Cemetery marker for the Showmen's League of America, founded by Buffalo Bill Cody and headquartered in Chicago. Several dozen of the dead from the Circus Train crash were buried at Woodlawn Cemetery in Forest Park.

The Showmen's League of America, founded by Buffalo Bill Cody, retains its headquarters in Chicago today. In early 1918, this benevolent organization purchased a large plot called Showman's Rest at Woodlawn Cemetery in Forest Park, a Chicago suburb, to be used as a final resting place for many of its members. On June 27, just five days after the accident, the plot was the scene of a mass burial. On that day, fifty-six of those killed in the wreck were buried at the same time. Tragically, only thirteen of the bodies were positively identified. The unknown were all buried with dignity, not in a common grave. Each of them had his or her own coffin and headstone. Most of the stones were marked with the word "unknown" but others included clowns and inscriptions like "Baldy" and "4-Horse Driver."

Since those first burials, hundreds of other circus and carnival showman have been buried at Showman's Rest. Five stone elephants were installed to watch over the silent graves, their trunks lowered in mourning. These majestic statues pay tribute to those who lost their lives in the 1918 disaster and also to the legion of performers who have followed them to the grave.

Rumors and legends have surrounded Showman's Rest since it was started in 1918. In the early 1970s, locals began to report the sounds of wild animals roaring from within the confines of the cemetery grounds, particularly late at night. Stories spread that a number of circus animals had been killed in the wreck and had been buried in the cemetery next to their human companions. The cries, according to the stories, were the anguished sounds of the animal ghosts, calling out from beyond the grave. In time, these tales began to be accepted as fact and reports made their way into the media and into the folklore of Chicago.

Contrary to the popular story, though, there were no animals buried at Woodlawn Cemetery and no animals were killed in the train wreck. The "ghostly animal sounds" were simply carried on the wind at night from the nearby Brookfield Zoo!

But even though no ghosts are believed to linger at the cemetery, there are other bizarre tales that have emerged across the border in Indiana. Over the years, railroad workers and local residents have told of seeing a wreck at the site where the circus train disaster occurred in 1918. However, this wreck is not of physical wood and broken steel, but a phantom image of the tragedy that occurred that night. Others claim to see eerie specters who appear to be on fire and have heard the wailing and moaning of someone in terrible pain – but there is nothing there to be seen.

Do the ghosts of that terrible night still linger alongside the railroad tracks at what was once Ivanhoe station? Or are these merely memories of a tragic event that continue to repeat themselves over and over again, never allowing us to forget the lives that were taken on that dark night?

# 1918: 'DUTCHMAN'S CURVE'
# THE GREAT TRAIN WRECK OF NASHVILLE

"Because somebody blundered..." Those were the first words of a newspaper article that appeared in Nashville, Tennessee in the summer of 1918 that described the carnage that occurred after two passenger trains collided with one another on July 9, killing more than one hundred people. It was a calamity that has had a lasting effect on not only the history of the railroads in America, but the people of Nashville and on at least one location where the dead from the disaster have lingered behind.

The "Great Train Wreck of 1918," as it came to be called, occurred on July 9 when two passenger trains, operated by the Nashville, Chattanooga and St. Louis Railroad, collided head-on while traveling along a single track line known as "Dutchman's Curve," just west of downtown Nashville. Both trains were traveling at more than fifty miles an hour when they came together.

At 7:07 a.m. on that fateful morning, the Nashville, Chattanooga and St. Louis No. 4 train departed Nashville's Union Station, bound for Memphis. The train, pulled by the No. 282 locomotive, consisted of two mail and baggage cars and six wooden coaches. Engineer David C. Kennedy pulled out of the station and as he reached the signal tower in the railroad shops (the massive repair and refueling shops and roundhouse), he blew his whistle for a signal and was given a clear board. Before the train passed under the tower, however, the red board was dropped, signaling him to stop. It is believed that he never saw the signal, as both the tower man and the switch engineer tried in vain to attract his attention. No one knows why Kennedy continued on that day. He may not have seen the signal, but he was aware that another passenger train, the No. 1, had the right-of-way on the line and was approaching, even though it was behind schedule.

As the No. 4 train traversed the double-track section and prepared to enter the single line to Memphis, the conductor was busy taking tickets and mistook the sound off a passing switch engine for the No. 1 train. Without looking, he assumed that the other passenger train had safely passed. The rest of the crew either made the same error or were negligent in properly identifying the train.

Meanwhile, the No. 1 train, pulled by the No. 281 locomotive, was heading into Nashville from Memphis with one baggage car, six wooden coaches and two Pullman sleeping cars. The two trains were supposed to meet at Harding Station because the No. 1 was 35 minutes behind schedule, which further complicated the situation.

At 7:15 a.m., the two trains collided with bone-jarring force at Dutchman's Curve, near White Bridge Road and in the present-day Belle Meade neighborhood. Both trains were traveling at more than fifty miles per hour when they collided and it was said that the sound of the crash could be heard as far as two miles away. The wooden cars were crushed and hurled sideways and the steel of the locomotives and the sleeper cars wrenched apart with sounds like screams of pain.

Those who arrived in the minutes after the collision were greeted with a scene that could only be described as one of horror. Those escaping unhurt or with lesser injuries fled from the wreckage in a panic. The cornfields on both sides of the tracks were trampled and littered with pieces of iron and wood, hurled from the demolished trains. The dead were spread about the scene, grotesquely sprawled where they fell. The dying moaned for help or, unable to speak, rolled their heads from side to side, writhing in agony. Everywhere was blood, suffering and chaos.

Huge crowds, some seeking friends and loved ones thought to have been on the wrecked trains and others merely morbid curiosity-seekers, quickly flocked to the site. Police officers worked to hold back the onlookers, who crowded so close that it actually hindered the work of the rescue teams.

From the wreckage of the trains, shrieks and muffled cries were heard and soon, a steady stream of doctors and nurses rushed to the area. Ambulances, along with automobiles that had turned over by their owners to help in the rescue, began transporting the injured to local hospitals. Volunteers also pitched in to take the bodies of the dead to local undertakers.

The injured were removed as quickly as  possible, which left rescue workers with the grim task of pulling out the mangled and bloody bodies of the dead, which were trapped in the debris. Train crews used jacks to left the heavy frame of an express car, where dozens of victims had been trapped. In one of the seats, his body pinned, sat a passenger, still conscious but with three dead men crushed against him. The side of the car was chopped away and the man was released, but he died a short time later. The last victims were found late in the day, trapped in the remains of a coach where a boiler had exploded. Their corpses were burned beyond recognition.

Into the early evening, the police kept order at the accident site. The crowd, although curious and restless, was well-behaved. Although suitcases and baggage were strewn about the nearby fields, there were no reports of theft. The streetcars leading out to the wreck remained packed with sightseers and taxicabs did brisk business both coming and going from the wreck. It was estimated by members of the police department that more than fifty thousand people visited the scene. By late that same evening, the wreck had been cleared away and the No. 2 train left Union Station on time for its regular 10:00 p.m. run.

The official records stated that one hundred and one people died in the accident, though some stories listed the death toll as high as one hundred and twenty-one. Spectators lined up at the morgues and the undertaking establishments, gazing at the broken and mutilated bodies. Many searched for family members and friends, while others indulged their curiosity. But even those without missing friends and relatives seemed as deeply affected at the dazed family members who mutely gazed at the mangled remains without word or sound. Reports told of an eerie stillness that settled over the Dorris, Karsch & Co. funeral parlor as survivors filed past the long line of the dead.

Many of the victims were African-American laborers from Arkansas and Memphis who were coming to work at the gunpowder plant in Old Hickory outside of Nashville. Most of them were taken to A.N. Johnson and Taylor's undertaking parlor. Twenty-four unidentified black men were laid out in hopes that someone could identify them. Only three of them were ever recognized.

Nashville newspapers called the aftermath of the collision "the most horrible sight ever witnessed in this city."

In the official report of the tragedy, the Interstate Commerce Commission held the railroad responsible for the accident. A combination of poor operating practices, human error and a lax enforcement of operating rules led to the train wreck, the commission stated. If the signal tower operator had properly signaled the train, if the engineer had seen the signal and checked the train log in the shops as required and if the conductor had monitored the train's progress like he was supposed to, the disaster would have never happened.

But there was more to the story that first appeared. The Nashville, Chattanooga and St. Louis Railroad, like all United States railroads at the time, was being run by the government during World War I. Government officials had changed the railroad's passenger train schedules. In the past, these two trains had always met safely west of Nashville, later in the morning, which might explain both the engineer's and the conductor's seeming indifference. They had always carried out the same routine on each trip, perhaps forgetting about the change. However, because of the changing of the timetables, the trains met somewhere, depending on the timing, closer to Nashville where the possibility for mistakes was more likely.

A gag order was quickly placed on news of the wreck to try and play down public fears about having the government running the country's railroads. The ICC report failed to note the changes in scheduling and did not consider them to be a contributing factor in the wreck. To this day, it remains a mystery as to whether or not the schedule changes had anything to do with the accident – or who was really to blame for what happened that day.

Perhaps unanswered questions like this might be the reason why hauntings connected to the crash are still being experienced today.

According to reports, spectral remnants of the "Great Train Wreck of 1918" are still making themselves known at Nashville's Union Station, which was the destination of many of the passengers of the No. 1 train from Memphis that July morning. Tragically, many of them never arrived.

Union Station officially opened on October 9, 1900. It was constructed from heavy stone in an imposing gothic design with a sixty-five-foot, barrel-vaulted lobby ceiling that featured gold-leaf medallions and stained glass, marble floors, oak-accented doors and walls, a limestone fireplace, twenty gold-accented angels of commerce figures, two-bas-relief panels of a steam locomotive and a horse-drawn chariot, and two alligator ponds.

The station thrived for decades, reaching its peak usage during World War II when it was a shipping-out point for thousands of servicemen and the site of a USO canteen. It began to decline a short time later as passenger service in the United States began to drop off in the 1950s. By the 1960s, it served only a few trains daily. The formation of Amtrak in 1971 reduced service to only two trains daily and when this service was discontinued in October 1979, the station was abandoned.

Despite being listed on the National Register of Historic Places, the station declined further over the next several years. In the early 1980s, Union Station was saved by investors, who turned the building into the luxury hotel that it is today.

**Union Station in Nashville, circa 1900**

During railroading's glory years, the station saw characters such as movie starlet Mae West and gangster Al Capone, who was escorted through Union Station on his way to the federal penitentiary in Atlanta, following his conviction for tax evasion. And while the ghosts of mobsters and movie stars are not reported lingering at the station the phantoms of those who died in the 1918 accident definitely are!

The former railroad station is reported to have at least two ghosts that remain from the disaster, making their presence known in a variety of ways, from opening and closing doors, spectral footsteps, whispering voices and lights that operate mysteriously. On occasion, at least one of the ghosts has been seen. He is an African-American man, wearing soiled clothing, who seems confused as he wanders through the hotel lobby, which was once part of the station. A staff member that was interviewed stated that he believed the man was one of the workers from Memphis who was killed in the wreck.

Another ghost haunts the hallways and one of the hotel rooms on an upper floor. Guests at the hotel claim to have heard knocks on their doors at night – only to find no one there – and have heard strange, weeping sounds in the corridors. One guest claimed that he felt a presence in his room one night and heard a voice asking for help. When he turned on the light to see who was there, he found the room was empty.

Do the souls of those who died in the 1918 train wreck still wander the railroad station and train tracks where their lives came to an end? Some believe they do and as long as that horrific day still lingers in the memory of Nashville, perhaps their spirits will continue to walk.

# 1924: THE MILFORD MINE DISASTER

The state of Minnesota was once scattered with mines that were alleged to be haunted by former workers who were killed there, or who returned to haunt the place after their death, but there are few places that were said to be as haunted as the Milford Mine in Crow Wing County. Even though one of the ghosts was seen only one time -- it was witnessed by several dozen men who were convinced that they had seen the ghost of a dead fellow worker. Other hauntings lingered for years, perhaps until the mine finally closed down for good.

One of the greatest disasters in the state's history happened on February 5, 1924 at the Milford Manganese Mine. The mine was over two hundred feet deep and produced hard and brittle manganese ore, which was once used in steel, aluminum alloys and the original type of dry cell battery. The mine employed several hundred men, including a man named Clinton Harris, who worked at the bottom of the shaft. His job was to operate an electric hoist that dumped ore from the cars into a bucket that was raised to the surface. When it was emptied, it came back down and he repeated the process. Harris was called a "skip-tender" as the bucket was often referred to as a "skip." On February 5, Harris was unfortunately filling in for another skip-tender who had called in sick.

That afternoon, miners blasted a cut near Foley's Pond, which abutted a portion of the mine. Seconds after the explosion, a hurricane of wind rushed through the mine, knocking men down and putting out the electric lights. The lights flickered off, came back on again and then went out for good, plunging the mine into blackness.

Moments later, the deafening roar of water filled the mine. The blasting had caused the earth to collapse next to the pond and the tunnels rapidly began to flood. Miners scrambled for the surface, falling and wading through water that grew deeper by the minute. Some of the miners were slammed into the walls by the force of the water and killed instantly, their bones and bodies crushed against the stone. Others, knocked down by the terrible wind, simply drowned beneath the murky water. Of the 51 men who were working during the shift, only seven of them survived.

Clinton Harris, the skip-tender who was working at the bottom of the shaft, died there. He apparently could have escaped but chose to remain, pulling on the warning whistle that would alert miners on the upper levels of danger. For over four hours, long after mud and water sealed off the shaft, the warning whistle continued to sound. It is unknown whether his body was caught in the rope, or if he had tied himself to it, but eventually someone in the engine room disconnected the whistle and silenced the melancholy sound from the now-flooded mine.

The survivors who escaped from the water made it to the surface and then collapsed, soaked and exhausted, on the frozen ground. Moments later, men from the mine office rushed over with blankets to help them. They quickly began taking a roll of the men who had survived --- and discovering those who were still trapped in the darkness and water below. One of the young men who survived, Frank Hvratin, had a father who perished in the mine.

Word of the disaster spread rapidly through nearby Crosby, where the village siren blew for hours, summoning families to the mine. People watched as the water in Foley's Pond sank lower and lower, flooding into the mine, and clusters of young widows walked arm in arm throughout the village all night. Others silently gathered at the entrance to the mine, now with the horrible realization that the men who had not immediately come out would not be coming out at all.

By midnight, mine clearing operations were underway. In the sub-zero temperatures of northern Minnesota, men took turns operating the water pumps that sucked out over twelve thousand gallons of mud and water each minute. They hoped against all hope that someone could have survived but Crow Wing County mine inspectors began to doubt if any of the bodies would ever be found, let alone any surviving miners.

Finally, it was realized that as long as Foley's Pond held water, the mine could not be drained, so the tasks changed and nearly twelve days were spent emptying the pond. It took another three months to drain the mine. Then, the mud that clogged the passages and shafts had to be shoveled out by hand before the bodies could be found. This grim and filthy task took another nine months to complete. Eventually all 41 of the missing miners were retrieved, making the Milford Disaster the worst on Minnesota's Iron Range.

Despite the horror and the frightening memories, many miners signed on to go underground again when the mine reopened. Manganese was in great demand by the steel industry and jobs were promised to any man who would go back into the Milford Mine. Of course, it should also be remembered that for many of these men, mining was the only work they had ever known.

But the Milford Mine held horrors that few of them had counted on: not only was the shaft filled with the stench of decay and decomposed flesh, but it was also haunted by a ghost. At the base of the shaft, the first workers down caught a glimpse of a figure in the darkness, fluttering away from their approach and sinking back into the shadows. The men pursued it with their lights and their lamps revealed a hideous specter that while semi-transparent, was easily recognized as being the form of Clinton Harris, the heroic and doomed skip-tender. He now looked starved and decayed, as if his flesh had been removed, leaving only molded skin and bones. His deeply sunken eyes were black and vacant sockets and they peered upward along the ladder to which he was clinging. A phantom whistle cord was still knotted about his waist.

The miners bumped and jostled each other in their haste to retreat from this ominous figure, but that haste soon turned to panic --- as the warning whistle, which no longer existed, began to scream through the dark shafts, sounding a warning that no man should enter the mine again. The terrified men scrambled back up to the surface and after that day, not a single one of them ever came back to the Milford Mine.

But others did. Jobs were too hard to come by and the mine paid too well. Men came to work in the darkness and often came away with strange stories to tell. According to a report that was published a few years after the accident, miners told of hearing the warning whistle as it sounded in the lower levels of the mine. Clinton Harris, the doomed skip-tender was never seen again, but it seems he never left.

And he did not haunt the Milford Mine alone. Another story told of a woman's screams in the mine and it was believed that she was the wife of one of the disaster victims who had tried to throw herself into the black water that swirled within the shaft. She died a few months after her husband perished in the accident and some came to believe that she began visiting the distant parts of the mine in search of her husband's spirit.

The stories continued for years but eventually, the mine closed down. Mining continued in the area until 1984 but it soon became cheaper to work surface deposits in other areas and the underground mines faded out of existence. The Milford Mine is abandoned today, but one has to wonder if it's really empty...

# 1931: DYING FOR A LIVING
# THE HAWK'S NEST TUNNEL TRAGEDY

The small community of Gauley Bridge, West Virginia looks like a picture postcard of small-town America. An old rusty railroad bridge stretches out over the water where the New River merges with the Gauley. Houses dot the steep hills and line the banks of the river. A few stores can be found along the town's main street. A renovated old train station serves as the town hall. The speed limit is just 25 miles an hour through town. Children ride bicycles and play in the yards. People smile and say hello to one another as they pass on the sidewalks. A farmer's market in the middle of town sells fresh vegetables in the summer and pumpkins and bales of straw in the fall.

But under the sunny surface of this town lies a dark secret, a horrible memory of death, an almost forgotten horror of one of the worst industrial disasters in American history: the Hawk's Nest Tunnel Tragedy. The disaster occurred during the years of the Great Depression, when times were hard and a man would do just about anything to feed his family. Taking advantage of this fact, powerful and wealthy men started a dangerous project that would claim the lives of an unknown number of men and cause the community of Gauley Bridge to become known as the "Town of the Living Dead."

The Hawk's Nest Disaster resulted from the construction of a tunnel through the mountain near Gauley Bridge. The three-mile-long passage was designed to divert water to an electrical power station by Union Carbide, the sponsor of the plan. However, the subcontractors on the job failed to follow standard safety precautions during the drilling operations, which ended with at least 764 dead workers. None of the companies involved were charged with criminal negligence.

Union Carbide (the company that would later be involved in the chemical explosion in Bhopal, India, in 1984) was formed in West Virginia by the merger of several companies in 1917. By the late 1920s, the company created the New Kanawha Power Co. in order to produce power that would be used in the production of ferro-metals, like aluminum, at a site below Gauley Bridge. The proposal required the damming of the New River just below Hawk's Nest, a spectacular overlook on the river, and the construction of a three-mile tunnel through Gauley Mountain. This tunnel would carry the rushing water to electric generators downstream.

New Kanawha Power contracted with Rinehart & Dennis Co. of Charlottesville, Virginia, to build the tunnel and the dam. Tunneling began on March 31, 1930 and progressed at breakneck speed until it was completed in December 1931. No one knows for sure why the tunnel had to be completed at such a fast pace, but it was believed that uncertainly about the Federal Power Commission's control over the New River was one of the reasons. If the project could be hurried through, the government would have little say over what could, or couldn't, be done during the project. Management drove the workers hard to make sure that the tunnel was completed on time.

Finding workers in Depression-era Appalachia, where numerous coal mines had closed, was an easy task. Word spread through the region, and through the rural south, that jobs were available at Gauley Bridge. Men walked, drove and hopped freight trains to be first in line for the promised work. Rinehart & Dennis hired mostly black workers from outside West Virginia for the project. Reportedly, 75 percent of the 1,494 men who worked inside the tunnel as drillers and mockers – who removed rock debris – and their assistants were African-American. There were another 1,488 workers, also mostly black, who held jobs that involved tasks inside and outside the tunnel. The reasoning behind this is grim in hindsight – in the early

**Workers on the Hawk's Nest Tunnel project were all poor and predominately African-American -- considered expendable by company management.**

**The Hawk's Nest Tunnel under construction -- unknown to the workers, the haze in the air was deadly.**

1930s, black workers were seen as expendable.

Workers labored on the tunnel project for ten hours a day, always under the watchful eyes of bosses who used guns and clubs to force ill or unwilling men to start each day's work. Black workers were paid in company scrip instead of cash, always at lower rates than white workers. When they were dropped from the payroll, they were evicted from company housing, which consisted of overcrowded, segregated boxcars, and run out of town by the Fayette County Sheriff.

Neither Rinehart & Dennis, nor the Union Carbide engineers overseeing the projects, followed even minimal safety precautions during the drilling operations. Workers tunneled from 250 to 300 feet per week through 99 percent silica. Experts knew that miners who inhaled silica dust stood a good chance of contracting silicosis, a deadly lung ailment. But the company ordered that the workers use a dry drilling technique that would create more dust because this method was faster and cheaper. The high-velocity drills that bored cavities in the rock for the insertion of dynamite charges did not spray water on the stone, which was a standard technique to reduce dust. Air ventilation was inadequate. No measurement was taken of dust levels in the tunnel. Ventilators and masks were not issued to tunnel workers, but they were supplied to company executives during inspection tours of the project.

Not surprisingly, few workers stayed on the job for long. Sixty percent of the African-American migrant workers worked less than two months on the project. However, this was long enough to pay a deadly price for signing on at Hawk's Nest.

The men emerged from the hole in the mountain each day with their dark skin covered by clouds of white dust. They looked like phantoms as they came out of the cloud-filled tunnel, blinking and coughing from the dust that filled their eyes and lungs. They began dying two months after they first entered the tunnel. Their deaths were painful. As the silica they inhaled created fibrous nodules in their lungs, their lungs grew stiff and the men found it harder and harder to breath. Eventually, they strangled to death, writhing and choking until they drew their last punishing gasp. It was reported that a man named Cecil Jones struggled so hard for breath that he kicked the wooden slats out of the baseboard of his bed before he died. Silicosis could not be cured, but doctors knew what it was. Rather than diagnose it, a company physician told tunnel workers that they had a new disease called "tunnelitis" and gave them worthless pills.

On May 20, 1931, the local newspaper, the *Fayette Tribune*, tried to break the story of the sick and dying tunnel workers and their unsafe working conditions, but a gag order issued by a local judge stopped publication. But even without the story, local residents knew something was wrong. Gauley Bridge was being dubbed with a nickname – "town of the living dead." A Congressional report from February 4, 1936, described the scene: "The men got down so they had no flesh left on them at all. As they express it down there, the men got so they were all hide, bone and leaders, which means he is just skin and tendons and looks like a living skeleton."

A problem arose as the black workers died. There was no "colored" burial ground in the area. Handley White, local funeral parlor owner in Summersville, located a field on his mother's farm and was given a contract to open a burial ground on the Martha White farm in Summersville. Handley was paid $50 per body with the promise of "plenty of business." Lieber Cutlp, a local resident and friend of White's son, later recalled the days of the burials. White contacted him and asked if he wanted to make some extra money with his flatbed truck. Cutlp, anxious to make any extra money he could, quickly agreed. The dead workers were stacked in rows and strapped on the back of the flatbed truck, he remembered. More of the dead workers were arranged in an upright sitting position as if they were alive for their ride to their final resting place. For years rumors spread about workers buried in mass graves on the Martha White farm, but White family members deny this accusation.

Between July and December 1932, local attorneys filed dozens of lawsuits on behalf of workers who had suffered acute silicosis. The disease had wreaked havoc on the workers, ravaging their lungs and making them susceptible to secondary infections, such as tuberculosis. Silicosis had been recognized as an industrial disease in America since the early 1900s. The United States Bureau of Mines had published warnings in the 1920s about the dangers from it while using high-speed drills. Acute silicosis, from which death could occur within months of exposure, however, was not a recognized disease in 1930. West Virginia did not classify silicosis as an industrial disease at all and the state rejected worker's compensation claims from men who claimed that they had contracted it at Hawk's Nest.

When faced with more than 250 suits that sought more than $4 million in damages by the middle of 1933, Rinehart & Dennis settled out of court, agreeing to pay $130,000, half of which went to attorneys' fees. In accepting these settlements, the plaintiff's attorneys agreed not to file any further suits and to surrender all case records to the defendants. The contractor brokered two additional settlements based on subsequent suits and paid out $200,000 in awards and attorney fees. The average plaintiff received $400, while the defendant took possession of the damning evidence, including x-rays and medical records. Reports circulated that Rinehart & Dennis and Union Carbide bribed witnesses and tampered with juries during the trials prior to the settlements. Few records of the sick workers remains today, most were apparently purposely destroyed.

How many workers actually died in the Hawk's Nest Tunnel? The real number will never be known. This is partly because Union Carbide wiped out the historical record and partly because most of the tunnel workers were dismissed at the end of 1931 and scattered throughout the South. Many of the men did not become sick until later, so their deaths never became a part of the official numbers.

It was also discovered at trial that the field at the Martha White farm was not the only burial ground for black workers. Apparently, Rinehart & Dennis had hired another local undertaker to dispose of the bodies of unclaimed workers and he had buried them in a field near Gauley Bridge. The location of this burial ground remained a mystery until 1972, when the West Virginia highway department stumbled onto 45 of these graves. Martin Cherniack, a medical doctor with a master's degree in public health, attempted to reconstruct the epidemiology of the Hawk's Nest tragedy. After painstaking historical research, his "conservative estimate" was that 746 men who worked in the tunnel had died from acute silicosis, which translated into a mortality rate of 63 percent. African-American workers made up 76 percent of the deaths.

The tragedy forced recognition of acute silicosis as an industrial hazard and a brief and ineffective congressional hearing in 1936, helped focus national attention on the condition. By 1937, all states had adopted laws recognizing the disease in some form – although West Virginia's statute was worthless since it was written solely in the interest of corporations.

The Hawk's Nest tragedy remains a haunting incident in American history today. Dismissed as a product of "mountain gossip" in the 1930s, it has come to be recognized as one of the nation's worst industrial disasters and a chilling reminder of the fact that no man is ever expendable.

## 1830: HELL HOLLOW & THE WINTER OF THE 'DEEP SNOW'

In the early 1800s, America's borders began to spread to the west and the explorers and frontiersmen were followed into the wilderness by settlers and farmers. The rich soil of central Illinois attracted thousands of these settlers and soon homes and fields began to be carved out of the forests. One of the towns that sprang up during the wave of immigrants was the Illinois town of Decatur. The first settlers discovered the land near the Sangamon River around 1820 and began making a life there. By 1829, the small settlement had turned into a full-fledged town.

But the city had barely begun when it was almost wiped out during one of the first winters of its existence. Many settlers died from the extreme cold during the winter of 1830-31, when central Illinois was hit with disaster. This terrible season would be remembered for many years as the "Deep Snow."

During this brutal disaster, a legend was spawned about a place on the south side of the city that would never be the same again. During that horrible winter, the ground there was "soured," some people said, and the area would go on to earn the nickname of "Hell Hollow."

Early in that calamitous winter, snow began to fall and continued to come in intervals, sometimes alternating with sleet and freezing rain. This treacherous mixture formed a layer of snow and ice that blanketed the state with frozen drifts that rose as high as six feet. Storms with high winds continued for sixty days. Many settlers who had depended on going into the nearby forest for firewood found themselves trapped in their homes. Travelers remained wherever they happened to be when the snow first started. Those who tried to continue their journeys often perished. One newspaper report told of "Cold Friday," when a man, his wife, and their six children froze to death, huddled about their half-burned wagon on the prairie.

The snow drifted so high that loaded wagons could be driven over the top of fence rails. Livestock perished and soon game became scarce. At first, the deer and other game became trapped in the snow and were easily caught, but as time wore on, they were eaten by the settlers and by wolves, causing the game population to dwindle almost to nothing. It would be years before the squirrels and prairie chickens could be found to hunt again and it has been said that the winter of the Deep Snow took the last of the buffalo from east of the Mississippi River. It was a horrifying season and one that would be remembered for many decades to come.

Many settlers died in the bitter cold and snow. Some people simply vanished, while others' remains were found when the snows finally melted with warmer weather. A lingering cold damaged the spring corn crop, game was scarce for years and the cotton fields in Southern Illinois perished and never returned. When spring arrived, the snow and ice melted and turned creeks into impassable torrents. Cholera epidemics, caused by the wet conditions, sent many of the survivors of the Deep Snow into their graves.

According to the legend of Hell Hollow, the wooded area on the city's south side, located just west and south of Greenwood Cemetery, was once the location of a small settlement. It was the most secluded of the outposts surrounding the village of Decatur and it was in an area that was mostly avoided by the local settlers. Most went there only for the purpose of burying their dead. The hills above this narrow valley were part of an Indian burial ground that was soon taken over by the settlers. In later years, it would become Greenwood Cemetery but in those days, it was seldom visited and was held in superstitious awe by the pioneers.

In the late 1820s, a group of settlers constructed cabins in the valley west of the burying grounds. They survived there for a few years, until the bitter winter of 1830, which is still remembered as the greatest natural disaster in early central Illinois history. Many settlers died during that season and the storms gave birth to strange legends in Hell Hollow.

It was said that the lack of food struck the small settlement hard. The tiny collection of cabins was cut off from the rest of the settlers in the area. At first, wild game approached the cabins without fear. Food was so scarce that the animals hoped for handouts of grain, but were instead captured and ended up in the stew kettle. As the cold months wore on, the deer, turkey, squirrels and prairie chickens all but disappeared and soon stores of flour and dried meat followed suit. The outlook was growing grim and there was a good chance that the settlers would starve to death long before spring arrived. They made do with what they could forage, boiling the bark from the trees into a bitter soup and then eating shoe leather and rawhide to stay alive. Finally, the legends say, there were no other choices left to them. They had no option but to turn to the only food supply that was still available – each other.

In the early months of the winter, one of the older members of the community had passed away and the body had been stored in an outbuilding so that he could be buried when the ground thawed. This was the first of two corpses that the settlers were forced to eat that winter.

When the weather finally broke, and contact with the outside could be achieved again, the bodies were secretly buried on the hill and the cannibals were sworn to secrecy. No one was ever to know under what unspeakable conditions the community had survived. A few months passed and the settlers from the small community were never heard from again. Apparently, someone had discovered their horrible secret and they vanished from the area without a trace.

Many believe this was the first strange incident to occur in this area and would be the one that truly "cursed" it. The wooded valley near the graveyard had become somehow "blighted," many locals believed, and the tales of starvation and cannibalism would not the last weird stories to emerge from this region.

The seclusion and ruggedness of this secretive area, existing so close to the growing city, attracted the worst of the local criminals. The area became known as an outlaw hideout and few police officers dared to venture there. The stories say that more than one sick or wounded criminal died in the woods, only to be buried secretly under the cover of darkness. For years, the Hollow has been dotted with unmarked graves, which still remain hidden today.

At some point in the late 1800s, the Hollow became the territory of a gang that was called the "Biscuit-Necks" by the local populace. They specialized in extortion and robbery and used the woods south of the cemetery as their base of operations. One night, a lynch mob from town captured the gang there. The crime for which they were pursued remains unknown today, but it is believed to been the robbery of a store, during which the owner was killed. It is said that the authorities failed to find the killers, so a makeshift vigilante group took up the chase. After the gang was captured, they were hanged on the spot. As a message to other criminals operating in the area, the bodies of the Biscuit-Necks were left hanging in the Hollow, swaying in the wind. They remained there until the corpses finally succumbed to the elements and the carrion birds.

The woods of Hell Hollow, and the Sangamon River that flowed through them, claimed many victims over the years and led to mysterious deaths and puzzling disappearances. In August 1896, a young boy named Frankie Ackerman drowned in the river, just beyond the edge of Hell Hollow. Frankie and another boy, Guy Stevens, were wading in the shallows when a strong undercurrent swept them off their feet and carried them out into the deep water. The Stevens boy was rescued by two fisherman just minutes after he was carried out into water. He was not breathing, but the men were able to revive him. Frankie's body disappeared into the current – and was never found.

A few months later, in October 1896, a fifteen-year-old boy who was doing some hunting in the woods of the Hollow found the decomposed body of a man lying a few feet from the river bank. Shaken and scared, the boy went immediately to a grocery store on South Main Street and called the police. Officers had quite a bit of trouble getting a wagon back to the site and eventually, they had to carry out the remains in a canvas tarp. The man had been badly beaten and was likely robbed. He was never identified but the police found a knap-sack nearby that contained a pen knife, five keys, three bottles and an account book that contained the address of several stores on North Main Street. Unfortunately, the bag was so wet from a recent rain that the man's name could not be deciphered.

In August 1905, two brothers, Acy and Luster Woody, decided to try and make a trip downriver on the Sangamon aboard a homemade boat that they had built in their parents' garage. They were never heard from again.

An eleven-year-old boy named Willie Godwin drowned in the river at the edge of Hell Hollow in September 1905. Willie, along with several companions, went down to the Hollow to play in the woods and decided to cool off on that hot afternoon by wading in the river. Willie went out too far into the current and began to run into trouble. Tragically, none of his friends knew how to swim well enough to try and save him and were terrified to

see him go under for the final time. The boys ran to the waterworks at the dam, and called for help. Workers on duty ran down to the river, while another telephoned the police. There was no sign of the boy in the water.

A few minutes later, Dr. T.C. Hunt, along with Officers Gregg and Wheeler, arrived on the scene. The police officers, as well as several of the workmen, offered to go into the river and look for Willie, but it was Coroner Thomas C. Buxton, who arrived in swimming attire, who jumped into the water first. They searched frantically but as time passed, they knew there was no way that the boy could have survived. Rescue efforts soon became a recovery effort for Willie's corpse. After more than an hour had passed and the body could not be found, Coroner Buxton suggested the use of dynamite, which could be used to shake the body loose and bring it to the surface. Several charges were attempted but there was still no sign of Willie. Finally, several boats were launched and the river was dragged with long poles. After more than two hours in the water, Willie's body came to the surface. His corpse had apparently been snagged in the floodgates, although it could not be explained how it had managed to travel upriver, against the current.

In June 1910, an "aged Negro" named Perry Orr committed suicide in the Sangamon River at Hell Hollow, after first taking off all his clothes and singing a religious hymn on the riverbank. The drowning was a mysterious one. Although Orr had been in poor health for some time, he gave no indication that he would commit suicide. He left his West Marietta Street home on the morning of June 15 and went out to the junk wagon that he owned around 10:00 a.m. When he arrived, he handed his pocketbook to Charles Stovall, who worked for him, and asked him to deliver it to his (Orr's) wife. Orr left the wagon in Stovall's charge and walked away. That was the last time that Stovall saw him.

Anna McCoy, who was fishing on the banks of the river, saw Orr a short time later. She looked up when she heard a man loudly singing and saw Orr removing his clothing. Before she could speak, he jumped into the river. She assumed that he was simply going for a swim until she heard a yell and saw his head go under the water. Mrs. McCoy cried out in alarm and two men who were nearby responded. As they looked for any sign of Orr, Mrs. McCoy went to summon the police. The river was searched for hours and Orr's body was eventually found. His identity was learned from the clothing that he left on the riverbank. The clothing, along with his corpse, was taken to Moran's undertaking establishment for an inquest.

In one of Orr's pockets was a card with a telephone number on it, which Charles Bell, Orr's stepson, identified as the number of Dr. Lynn Barnes. Orr had gone to see the physician two days before and had been despondent over the news that he was in poor health ever since. It was thought that he might have committed suicide for this reason. Orr left behind a wife, two stepchildren and many friends. He was known throughout the city as a hard-working, industrious man and he was an active member of the Antioch Baptist Church. Everyone who knew him was shocked by his death and found it impossible to believe that he had killed himself.

The years passed and the edge of the Hollow became known as a "hobo jungle," where transients and small-time criminals camped and lived. The railroad tracks passed close to this area and it was convenient for the hoboes to hop a freight train from one town to the next.

It was during this period, in May 1930, that Greenwood Cemetery caretaker Melbourn Savage was murdered. His death was believed to be linked to the hobo jungle. His murder was never solved.

In 1936, the name "Hell Hollow" was coined for the region by a reporter named Robey Parks from the *Chicago Herald-Examiner*. Parks came to the city to investigate a number of unsolved murders that were all linked to the wooded area. He invented a gang called the "Hounds of Hell Hollow," which he claimed was responsible for not only these murders, but a number of other crimes, as well. Decatur authorities adamantly denied the stories, although there were elements of truth to them. This may have been what frightened and outraged Decatur

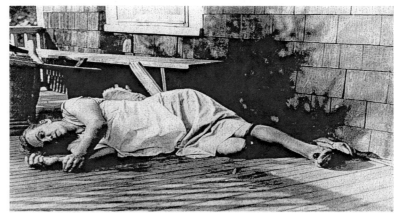

**A number of unsolved murders occurred in the "Hell Hollow" neighborhood, further tarnishing the reputation of the area.**

residents the most – combined with the fact that this area of town had been considered cursed for years.

As the years passed, Hell Hollow maintained its weirdness. The stories of marauding criminal gangs, unsolved murders, weird disappearances, suicides and frequent drownings, blended well with the early stories of death and depravity, further compounding the negative energy of an area that seems to attract crime, violence, mayhem and the unusual.

Hell Hollow grew smaller as the years went on. Acres of woods and brush were cleared away, and finally, only a small valley remained just west of Greenwood Cemetery. This was the original location of the Hollow, the site of cannibalism, murder and lynchings, and the center for the strange activity that has continued to radiate outward from the region. For a long time, the area remained a thick forest of trees and undergrowth through which a narrow gravel road twisted and turned. This became the last reminder of the violence of years gone by, but the legend was not quite dead yet.

The "Hounds" eventually became a forgotten story of the past but the Hollow soon earned a new notoriety among teenagers as a spooky place for a romantic rendezvous. A new collection of stories started to be told about crazed killers with hooks for hands and horrifying murders. Most of the stories were silly, but not all of them could be dismissed as modern folk legends and campfire tales. Every once in a while, something truly unexplainable was encountered in the Hollow. How many of the stories were true and how many were simply products of wild imagination? No one knows but the numerous tales featured everything from glowing apparitions to floating balls of golden light.

One particular story involved a couple who had gone down to the Hollow for a romantic interlude one night and were surprised to hear and feel what seemed to be open hands slamming down on the trunk of their car. Thinking that someone was playing a trick on them, the young man jumped out of the car and looked around. To his surprise, no one was there. He heard a movement to his left and turned to see the tall grass alongside the road being pushed aside, as if some invisible presence were passing through it! He quickly returned to the car, where something caught his eye. There, on the dusty trunk, were the clear impressions of handprints, even though he had seen no one standing behind the car!

The Hollow remained a popular and spooky place for some time. A few years ago, the road that ended in Hell Hollow was closed off and city crews cut and cleared away the thick growth of trees that once filled the valley. A couple more years passed and another road was closed. This time, Lincoln Park Drive, which skirted the edge of Hell Hollow and Greenwood Cemetery, was closed off and turned into a bike trail that is off limits after dark. The official word was that both roads had been closed because trespassers were entering the nearby graveyard at night. Was this true? There are a dozen places to enter Greenwood Cemetery after the sun goes down, so why close just this road? Unofficial sources say that too many odd things have happened there over time, including a few recent deaths and several brutal murders that have shocked the city.

Needless to say, strange things continue to happen in Hell Hollow as if some sort of weird and frightening energy still lingers there, continuing to draw the dark side to the shadows of the abandoned valley.

# 10 MOST DEADLY AMERICAN WINTER STORMS

1. Killed: 400+ - Mar. 11-14, 1888 - The Great Blizzard of 1888 - Northeastern States
2. Killed: 350+ - Nov. 24-30, 1950 - The Great Appalachian Storm of 1950 - Eastern States
3. Killed: 300+ - Mar. 11-15, 1993 - The Storm of the Century - Eastern States
4. Killed: 250 - Nov. 7-10, 1913 - The Great Lakes Storm of 1913
5. Killed: 230 - Jan. 12, 1888 - The Schoolhouse Blizzard - Midwestern States
6. Killed: 154 - Nov. 11-12, 1940 - The Armistice Day Blizzard - Midwestern States
7. Killed: 98, Injured: 33 - Jan. 27-28, 1922 - The Knickerbocker Storm - Mid-Atlantic States
8. Killed: 73 - Jan. 2-4, 1999 - Blizzard of 1999 - Midwestern States
9. Killed: Unknown - Feb. 11-14, 1899 - The Great Blizzard of 1899
10. Killed: 70 - Jan. 9-12, 1975 - The Great Storm of 1975 - Spawned snow and 45 tornadoes

# 1896: THE GREAT ST. LOUIS CYCLONE

The single deadliest incident in St. Louis, Missouri, history occurred on May 27, 1896 when a tornado ripped through the south side of the city, creating a ten-mile path of destruction. Within twenty minutes, 137 people were dead and one hundred and eighteen more were killed across the Mississippi River in Illinois. The tornado destroyed three hundred and eleven buildings and damaged thousands of others. It was unbelievable chaos, like nothing the region had ever seen before, and the effects of the devastation lingered for many years — as did an unusual haunting.

The "Great Cyclone," as it has been called, arrived in Southern Illinois and St. Louis after three weeks of violent storms had pummeled the Midwest. For most of April and May, temperatures and humidity had been well above normal and early on the morning of the storm, newspapers had reported thunderstorms had flattened crops in Missouri's "Boot Heel" and had swamped a riverboat near Cairo, Illinois. The forecast for the day called for "cloudy weather, favorable for local thunderstorms."

The Great Cyclone was actually part of a series of tornadoes that struck Southern Illinois and central Missouri, but it was the deadliest. The eventual death toll, according to the St. Louis Weather Bureau office, was three hundred and six people dead, including six people about one hundred miles west of St. Louis and thirteen in New Baden, Illinois. In St. Louis County, one child died when a tornado struck a farmhouse south of Clayton.

The storm broke around 3:00 p.m. after an oppressively hot day. Rain began to fall and it developed into a fierce thunderstorm with heavy winds from the east. Those winds rose to more than eighty miles an hour, driving the rain before it and tearing loose signs, cornices, chimneys, and just about anything else in its way. A number of buildings were set on fire by lightning and downed power lines. The fire department responded to fourteen alarms.

**Destruction at St. Louis State Hospital (City Hospital) on Arsenal Street.**

**Broadway and Chouteau Avenues**

**The Soulard Market**

As the tornado began to form, the streets were filled with people going home from work and panic ensued as the storm broke. Men were reportedly picked up and hurled against buildings, horses and carriages were overturned and falling wires "added to the horror of the scene," according to a newspaper report.

The tornado touched down in the city near the current site of the St. Louis State Hospital on Arsenal Street, in the southwest part of town. In those days, most of the residents lived downtown and near the river, so this was one of the most populated parts of the city. In 1896, the hospital was the site of the city's poorhouse, a women's hospital, an old people's home and an insane asylum. The storm tore away roofs and porches and knocked down walls on several buildings. The surgical ward was partially demolished, portions of other buildings had cracked walls and several roofs were torn off. Miraculously, only eight people were hurt.

After striking the hospital, the tornado turned and raced southwest, just north of Tower Grove Park, then turned northeast to Grand Avenue and then followed Miller Creek valley to the river. At the levee, it swung at almost a right angle and swept up the river to Madison, where it veered east again. It created more devastation near the warehouses and manufacturing buildings located there. More than twenty men were killed at Seventh and Rutger streets. At Vandeventer Avenue, where the Liggett & Myers Tobacco Co. was erecting a large building complex, 29 men were killed. Many of the workers were still high atop the building when the tornado hit and were buried beneath steel, wood and stone. Twenty-five more workers were killed at the St. Louis Wood Ware factory.

The tornado then headed uphill toward Compton Heights. Nearly every house in the area lost its roof and in some neighborhoods, especially to the east toward Jefferson Avenue, houses were completely destroyed. Whole blocks of homes and buildings lost their upper floors and walls were ripped away and reduced to splinters. The streets were impassable and were covered in places with debris that was ten feet deep.

As it reached Jefferson Avenue, the neighborhood around Lafayette Park was laid waste. The area of homes around the park was quite upscale in those days and prosperous businesses lined Jefferson Avenue, south of Chouteau. Two of the city's cable car systems, which moved cars along underground cables, had their power plants and shops there. The tornado swept in and wreaked havoc. The cable car companies were crippled, churches and homes were destroyed and all but a few of the trees in the park were snapped off at the trunk. City Hospital, just east of the park, also suffered great damage. Another miracle occurred there, where out of the 458 patients housed here, only one was killed outright. Two others died a few hours later, including one woman who was said to have died of fright.

**The Union Club at Jefferson & Lafayette Avenues**

Further east, the Soulard neighborhood was the scene of even greater horror. Buildings were wiped away by the tornado and one area, now a dark parking area beneath the Interstate 55 viaduct at the corner of Seventh and Rutger streets, was called the "vortex" by newspapers of the time. This was the deadliest spot in the tornado. At this location, fourteen people died as the three-story Mauchenheimer tenement collapsed into a pile of wood, stone and rubble. Among the victims were the building's owners, Fred and Kate Mauchenheimer, who ran a tavern on the ground floor and a seven-year-old girl named Ida Howell. She died in the arms of her mother, next to the body of her father, John Howell.

The storm continued on. It curved just south of downtown, where it was still strong enough to tear the roofs from downtown buildings and to break windows. It crossed the river along a line from the St. Louis approach to the current MacArthur Bridge to the East St. Louis approach of the Eads Bridge. The wagon way on the bridge, and one of the towers, were reduced to a crumbled pile of masonry and stone. There were sixteen boats in the harbor that day and all of them were wrecked. There is no way of estimating the number of lives that were lost on river craft that happened to be near when the cyclone came. Hundreds of barges were moored along the riverbank, in some instances with as many as ten or twelve persons on board. The men were blown into the river and the barges were capsized. After the storm, a rumor spread that the excursion steamer *Grand Republic* had gone to the bottom with five hundred people on board. The rumor was denied by the company the following day; it reported that the steamer had left for Alton, Illinois, at noon, hours before the storm struck the city.

The tornado tore through the rail yards and warehouses on the Illinois side. It devastated three locomotive roundhouses, the riverfront grain elevator and four freight stations, killing 35 depot workers. The railroad hotels were also destroyed, although beneath the remains of the Martell House, a maid named Mary

**The heavily damaged Eads Bridge across the Mississippi River**

**Wrecked homes in Lafayette Square**

Mock survived for two days and was found alive by rescue workers.

The catastrophe of that day has never been equaled in St. Louis history and its lingering memory can still be felt in the city today. There are stories that the effects of the Great Cyclone of 1896 reverberated in other ways, as well.

The tornado that struck St. Louis has a more tragic impact in Lafayette Square than in any other part of the city. As the storm reached Jefferson Avenue, it destroyed Lafayette Park and then turned its terrifying attention to the neighborhood around it. The park and square were located on the summit of a hill and that seemed to offer a particularly attractive target to the tornado.

By the time the center of the storm was directly over Lafayette Avenue, its tail had begun to swing to the north. It swept past Grand Avenue and then descended onto Jefferson. It pushed up against the side of the hill, with the tail of the storm now swinging around toward Chouteau, ripping a path along Jefferson Avenue from Chouteau to Russell. The tail of the storm continued to move from north to south, while the dense body of the tornado remained in the area, revolving in the direction of Geyer Avenue. All the while, the winds that accompanied it ripped apart the homes and the neighborhoods in their path.

The tornado moved above the Scullin power plant and as it did, the tail of the cyclone whipped down and ravaged the streetcars, men, machinery and buildings located there. Then, it swung toward the old South Side racetrack, on the current site of McKinley High School, and literally obliterated all trace of it. The storm then rolled on, flashing lightning in its belly, destroying more homes and stripping Lafayette Park.

By the time that the storm reached Lafayette Square, its path had widened to nearly three-quarters of a mile. A statue of U.S. Senator Thomas Hart Benton was the tallest thing remaining in the park as the trees around it were torn to pieces. Those not torn out by the roots were broken and splintered and stripped of their leaves and branches. The massive iron fence was pounded flat on the ground and the horticultural splendor of the park had been turned into a wasteland. Obviously, the houses that surrounded the park and those along the nearby avenues fared no better. The mansions and churches were unroofed and their walls demolished. Broken bits of wood, brick and stone were scattered in the streets and across lawns. Survivors wandered about the area in the aftermath of the storm, bemoaning the destruction of the once-gracious neighborhood.

Almost every home was damaged and many others were wrecked beyond repair. The Soderer House, located on the corner of Missouri and Park, was badly damaged. The stable was a ruin and the family's horse and driver were buried under the rubble. Dr. Soderer's brother, Julius, who lived farther down Park Avenue, was left with a "house not fit to live in." Two of the houses next to his, owned by his mother-in-law, were totally wrecked.

The Alexander Selkirk house was also destroyed and the family lost everything it owned.

The home belonging to cotton magnate Jerome Hill was nearly dismantled. Great gaps had been ripped throughout the structure, the roof was gone and the glass had been blown out of the windows.

John Endres, who lived next door to Hill, ended up with his home devastated but according to a contemporary account, he "good-naturedly said that he was only glad that nobody in the house was hurt." As he directed the removal of belongings from the house, he took the time to spread a luncheon on the parlor mantle, along with some bottles of wine that had been salvaged from the cellar. He insisted that everyone in the house sit down and eat before his daughters were sent off to stay with their grandmother. Endres spent the night on the floor of the Carr residence next door, getting up every half-hour to make sure that the remains of the house were undisturbed. The accounts went on to say that "Mr. Endres' courage and philosophy over his loss did much to inspire his neighbors with the same sort of feelings."

Next door to Endres was the home of Mrs. James Carr, the widow of Judge Carr. She and her children resided in what turned out to be the least damaged home on that side of the street. The structure had been relatively untouched, although not a single pane of glass remained in it. Her sons spent most of the night after the storm replacing windows and helping Endres restore some amount of order to the immediate neighborhood. In addition to Endres, Mrs. Carr also housed other homeless people from around the Square and nursed those who were injured or cut and bleeding from flying debris. Fortunately, the entire family escaped from the disaster unscathed, although Mrs. Carr's daughters were in the midst of the danger. The young women had just returned from a wedding at a nearby church. The guests had barely left the church when the roof blew off, sending everyone running for their lives. The Carrs sought refuge from the storm in a cellar "between two large brick piers," which swayed and rocked but didn't give away.

One of the most horrifying stories of the neighborhood came from the John Bene home, located just off Park Avenue, where the house was first wrecked and then burned. Mrs. Bene and her two children, ages five and two, were buried under the debris and the youngest child burned to death in the fire that followed. The older child was also badly burned but rescuers managed to dig him out from beneath the rubble before the fire could claim him. Mrs. Bene had been pinned beneath several heavy timbers but she refused to be removed until those who came to her assistance had dug out her children first. When she was finally taken out, she was found to have been badly burned about the legs, hips and feet. She had been struck in the head by falling bricks and wood and when she learned of the fate of her youngest child, she fainted – not from her serious injuries, but from grief.

In the end, the murderous storm lasted less than a half-hour and yet it created such destruction that its repercussions would last for years. After the tragedy was over, many of the homeowners from Lafayette Square fled to the central West End. It took until the early 1900s for the square to recover from both the cyclone and the abandonment by so many of the residents, but the recovery would be a brief one. By the 1920s, the area had lost its fashionable image and the once-stately private homes became apartments and boarding houses for the working class. The decline continued through the Great Depression and World War II and the neighborhood declined even further. Lafayette Square became a crime-riddled ghetto and the once-elegant neighborhood simply began to be called "Slum D."

All of that slowly began to change in 1945 when architect and historian John Albury Bryan purchased a house at 21 Benton Place. He renovated it and then began a fierce, and at first quite lonely, battle to take back and restore Lafayette Square. Through the 1960s and 1970s, things started to happen, first at a tedious snail's pace and then much faster. Little by little, brave people began moving into the neighborhood and they organized the Lafayette Restoration Committee. A campaign was launched to restore the area and to bring Lafayette Square back to its former glory.

And undoubtedly, their efforts have been successful. To visit Lafayette Square today is to take a trip back in time and to recapture a bit of an era that has long been forgotten. If you get a chance, take a short trip there some day and take a stroll around Lafayette Park, past the mansions and homes that have been so gloriously restored.

You may also hear a story or two about ghosts, one of which is directly connected to the Great Cyclone of 1896.

The haunting at that location was first reported in the 1970s. Today, it is a former apartment house that is located directly on the site of the stables that once belonged to Alois Soderer. In the earlier account of the Great Cyclone of 1896, readers will remember that the destruction of the stables took the life of the carriage driver who was employed by the Soderers. His name was William Taylor and he had been with the family for many years. As the storm approached, Taylor had hidden in the basement of the Soderer home with the family but over the sound of the wind and the house ripping itself apart, he heard the cries of the family's horse, Bess. She had been left out in the stable and it was said that Taylor was passionately devoted to the animal.

Even though the Soderers urged him to stay, Taylor ran outside to the stable. He arrived just as the storm was reaching its peak, but he was unable to free the mare in time. The roof of the building collapsed, killing both the coachman and the horse.

*And Hell Followed With It – Page 97*

Years later, the foundation of the stable was used to construct an apartment building on the site, which later became a rooming house. And while there were rumors of a murder that took place in the building at one point in its history, it seems to have been the storm of 1896 that left the greatest ghostly impression on the place. Shortly after the building was restored in the early 1970s, residents began to complain about hearing unnerving sounds. Many of them were frightened about living here, especially during thunderstorms, when they would claim to hear the sound of a panicked horse's neighing and hooves beating on the pavement outside. Eerie memories of the events that occurred in 1896?

Many believed so and while the apartment building is the site of three condominiums today, the days when this was a stable have not quite been forgotten. It is said that on certain nights, the sounds of a horse's screams and the animal's frantic hoofbeats can still be heard in the darkness.

# 1900: "A NIGHT OF HORRORS" THE GREAT GALVESTON HURRICANE

The city of Galveston, officially founded in 1839, was a booming deep water sea port in 1900. The city was built on a barrier island just two miles off the coast of Texas. With the natural harbor of Galveston Bay on one side and the Gulf of Mexico on the other, Galveston was a center for shipping and commerce. It ranked consistently among the top five American ports for exporting goods. With a population of nearly 40,000, it was the largest city in Texas. It was a wealthy city as well, one of the wealthiest cities in the United States.

But all of the money in the world could not save the residents from the legendary storm that arrived in September of 1900 – leaving death and hauntings in its wake.

The barrier island upon which this lovely city was built was not much more than a glorified sand bar, roughly three miles across at its widest point and 28 miles long. The island's highest elevation was less than nine feet above sea level. Galveston had weathered many storms and on occasion, had gotten its feet wet when the waters from the gulf rolled in a bit too far. Regardless as to how high the sea rose or how hard the wind blew, Galveston was still standing proud when it all died down.

The same could not be said for her neighboring port city of Indianola on Matagorda Bay, second only to Galveston in its size and importance to shipping. Indianola had been hit with two severe hurricanes, the latest only 25 years earlier and it had nearly been destroyed. After the second hurricane, Indianola had never really recovered and Galveston grew even faster as a result.

There were some concerned residents of Galveston who worried that the time would come when their own city would experience a head-on collision with a severe hurricane and suffer the same consequences as Indianola. They pushed for a seawall to be built to protect them from just such a possibility. However, there were even more people who believed just the opposite - that Galveston had weathered the worst storm that could happen and had withstood the test without too much fuss. A seawall, they believed, would spoil the beaches and waste a lot of money. To further support this position, Isaac Cline, the section director for the U.S. Weather Bureau in Galveston wrote an article in 1891 for the *Galveston Daily News*. In the article, he strongly stated that a seawall was not needed to protect the city. He further offered his belief, as a weather expert, that there was no way a hurricane of significant strength could ever strike the island city. With such a strong statement from the man the U.S. Weather Bureau had put in charge of its Galveston office, it was difficult to argue the point, so the seawall was never built.

As the island continued to be developed, it became even more vulnerable to the sea when large sand dunes on the gulf side were cut down. The sand was used to fill in sunken areas and make them more appropriate for construction. This resulted in the removal of the last protective barrier between the city and the Gulf of Mexico.

In 1900, weather-watching and reporting was making great improvements. The United States had set up a network of stations that would allow the weather bureau to follow storms as they moved about, and provide warnings whenever and wherever possible. This worked out very well, except when the storm was out to sea. Then they had to rely on reports from ships that just happened to be in the right place at the right time.

Unfortunately, wireless communication was still a new technology and wasn't terribly reliable, or in some cases, not yet installed on the ship observing the storm. Once a storm passed away from land, the bureau had to make its best educated guesses as to where it would surface next or where it was headed.

In early September of 1900, a tropical storm was brewing off the coast of Cuba. It crossed over Cuba and continued on its westerly journey while passing over Key West, Florida. From there, a few ships were able to report on its position. It moved over the exceedingly warm waters of the Gulf of Mexico, gaining strength as it went. The tropical storm, feeding off the gulf's "bathtub warm" waters, quickly rose to hurricane strength. The area around Galveston received warnings that they were in danger of a direct hit. The red and black hurricane warning flags were raised and the alarm went out across the island. A large number of people took heed and left the island for safer surroundings on the mainland. However, most of the residents were determined to ride out the storm, just as they always had, just as they always would.

### *Official Record - Galveston branch, U.S. Weather Bureau:*

**Tuesday, September 4, 1900**
**U.S. Weather Bureau Report**
**Galveston, Texas**
Nimbus, cumulus, strato-cumulus and alto-stratus clouds. Fresh to brisk easterly winds. Light rain. Heavy rain. Thunderstorm. Advisory message stating "Tropical disturbance moving northward over Cuba" was received and distributed at 5:00 p.m.

**Wednesday, September 5, 1900**
**U.S. Weather Bureau Report**
**Galveston, Texas**
Scattered nimbus, strato-cumulus and cumulus clouds. Fresh easterly winds. Light rain. The following advisory message was received and distributed at 11:20 a.m. "Disturbance central near Key West moving northwest. Vessels bound for Florida and Cuban ports should exercise caution as storm likely to become dangerous."

**Thursday, September 6, 1900**
**U.S. Weather Bureau Report**
**Galveston, Texas**
Scattered cumulus, strato-cumulus and alto-stratus clouds. Fresh northerly winds. Advisory message in regard to tropical storm central over southern Florida received and distributed at 2:59 p.m.

**Friday, September 7, 1900**
**U.S. Weather Bureau Report**
**Galveston, Texas**
Broken cumulus and strato-cumulus clouds. Fresh to brisk northerly winds. Special observations taken at noon and 3 p.m. Order to hoist storm flag northwest 10:35 a.m. received at 11:30 a.m. and hoisted at 11:35 a.m. Rough sea with heavy southeast swells during afternoon and evening.

**Saturday, September 8, 1900**
**U.S. Weather Bureau Report**
**Galveston, Texas**
Strato-cumulus and nimbus clouds. Fresh to high northerly winds. Gale of 84 miles an hour from the northeast at 6:15 p.m. when anemometer blew away. Higher wind after this time probably reaching 110 or 120 miles per hour. Special observations taken at noon and 3 p.m. Order to change northwest storm warning to northeast at 10:30 a.m. received at 11:10 a.m. and warning northeast hoisted at 11:15 a.m. Warning only

remained up a few hours until it was blown down. Instrument shelter with instruments blown down. All instruments not yet found.

Light rain began at 6:45 p.m. and continued into the night; rain gage blown down and record lost, amount up to 3:30 p.m., 1.37 inches. Exceptionally heavy rain after this time continuing into the night. Impossible to obtain records of instruments on roof for p.m. observation as they had blown down. Conditions were also dangerous to approach of roof as entrance was a partial wreck and gave way soon after observation time.

The following special barometer readings were taken during the rapid fall during the late afternoon. The lowest barometer apparently occurred between the two last observations when the barometer stood at about 28.44. The barometer began rising at about 8:30 p.m. and rose about as rapidly as it had fallen.

The tide commenced coming in over low portions of city in early morning and the following telegram was sent at about 7 a.m.: "Unusually heavy swells from southeast, intervals one to five minutes overflowing low places south portion city three to four blocks from beach. Such high water with opposing winds never observed previously." The tide continued to rise all day. A sudden rise of four feet occurred at 7:30 p.m.

The entire city was under water from eight to fifteen feet deep at 8 p.m. The entire south, east and west portions of the city from one to five blocks inland are swept clean, not a house remaining. Many other houses blown down over the city and all other buildings damaged more or less.

Many men, women and children drowned, some entire families, and the number of persons killed or drowned will probably reach more than five thousand when all reports are received. The streets are one mass of debris and it will be many days before all the dead bodies can be found. Many lives were saved after floating on the drifting debris for several houses. Thousands of people were injured by flying timbers while endeavoring to save themselves.

The tide began to fall slowly at about 11 p.m. and comparatively no damage resulted after this time. I.M. Cline Local Forecast Official and Joseph L. Cline, Observer, badly injured in wreck and drift among drifting houses from 7:30 to 10:30 p.m.

**Sunday, September 9, 1900**
**U.S. Weather Bureau Report**
**Galveston, Texas**

Broken stratus, nimbus, strato-cumulus, alto-stratus and cirrus clouds during the day. High subsiding to brisk southerly winds; record lost until 8:00 a.m., highest velocity estimated at fifty miles or more from the south in early morning.

The rain of yesterday ended sometime in early morning and time unknown; record lost. Light scattered showers during the day but beginning and ending unknown; no rain gage and amount of rain, also, unknown.

The tide had receded so that the high places of the city were dry this morning. Low places still covered with water tonight but tide almost normal. All office force reported at office today except Mr. T.C. Bornkessell, printer. Time of beginning and endings of rain could not be obtained today on account of being where no time could be ascertained. Observations were made and completed as was possible considering the loss of instruments. Thermograph found and put in working order but mechanism of same injured.

**Monday, September 10, 1900**
**U.S. Weather Bureau Report**
**Galveston, Texas**

Broken cumulus, nimbus and cirrus clouds, Fresh southerly winds prevailed. Light rain from 12:40 p.m. to 12:50 p.m., amount trace.

I.M. Cline, Local Forecast Official, absent today on account of injuries received in storm. Joseph L. Cline, observer, left in charge but unable to do much. Mr. Ernest E. Kuhnel, map distrubutor, absent today on account of looking for bodies of his relatives. Mr. T.C. Bornkessell, printer, still missing.

Rain gage No. 750 temporarily erected today. A temporary instrument shelter was erected from pieces of old shelters and other pieces of lumber and the following instruments were put up today: Maximum thermometer No.

5148, minimum No. 5635, dry No. 3082 and wet No. 3647.  Sunshine recorder cannot be found.

**Tuesday, September 11, 1900**
**U.S. Weather Bureau Report**
**Galveston, Texas**
Scattered cumulus and strato-cumulus clouds. Fresh easterly winds. I.M. Cline, local forecast official, still unable for duty.  Mr. T.C. Bornkessell, printer, still absent.  Presumed lost.

## *End - U.S. Weather Bureau Reports*

The Weather Bureau reports are particularly devoid of emotion or excitement, however they do offer a simple reflection of what was happening in the city of Galveston before and after the hurricane hit. The storm approached and things were done that should be done but otherwise, everything went on as usual. Then the storm hit and things started to go wrong. Damage was occurring faster and more severely than they would ever have expected.  Suddenly, there was nothing more that could be done except ride the storm out, hoping that they would still be there in the morning. Then, when the storm had passed, they took stock of what had happened around them. They did their best to repair what was possible to repair, doing what they could with what they had to work with. Some   people returned in fairly good condition, some were injured, and others were never seen again. What happened inside the tiny weather bureau office was a mini tableau of the entire island.
Galveston was experiencing a Category 4 storm on the Saffir-Simpson Hurricane Scale and no one had any idea what to expect.

The best possible descriptions of that terrible night and the following days come from the stories of survivors in their own words.
John D. Blagden, from Memphis, Tennessee, was on temporary assignment at the Galveston branch of the U.S. Weather Bureau. He was in the bureau office when the storm hit and stayed at his post throughout the night. The bureau office survived the storm in good shape but the instrumentation did not.
Blagden was boarding with a family on the south part of the island, the part that received the most damage. The morning after the storm, he left the office to return to his lodgings.  It took him hours to walk the single mile to the house in which he was staying but was unable to find it: it was gone. The entire block was gone. Every block around where the house once stood was gone. Nothing was left but a pile of wreckage that was otherwise unrecognizable as having been a number of houses.   Everything was swept clean and part of it was still under water.

Also in the southern part of town was the family home of Isaac Cline, the local forecast official, the man who had argued against the construction of a seawall. Cline had lived in what he felt was the strongest, most solidly built house in his neighborhood. The Clines had invited forty friends and neighbors into their home to weather the storm. Cline's house, just as every house around it, had collapsed under the pressure of the wind and the water. Of the forty people inside, fewer than twenty survived the night, including

**Massive debris field with only a few scattered buildings still standing in the background.**

**Wagon load of bodies, headed for the barges and then out to sea.**

**Recovery team searching debris for bodies.**

Cline's pregnant wife, Cora. He and his brother, Joseph, who also worked for the weather bureau, had been able to save all three of his daughters but the youngest was severely injured.

Blagden wrote in a letter to his family, "I could not help seeing many bodies though I was not desirous of seeing them...I soon got sick of the sights out there and returned to the office to put things in order as best I could...There is not a building in town that is uninjured. Hundreds are busy day and night clearing away the debris and recovering the dead. It is awful. Every few minutes a wagon load of corpses passes by on the street. The more fortunate are doing all they can to aid the sufferers but it is impossible to care for all. There is not room in the buildings standing to shelter them all and hundreds pass the night on the street. One meets people in all degrees of destitution. People but partially clothed are the rule and one fully clothed is an exception."

"We had warning of the storm and many saved themselves by seeking safety before the storm reached here," Blagden's letter continued. "We were busy all day Thursday answering telephone calls about it and advising people to prepare for danger. But the storm was more severe than we expected."

Mrs. Ida Smith Austin lived farther north on the island, at 1502 Avenue D. She fared better than the Clines but still spent a terrible night. She was aware that a powerful storm was nearing but she, like so many others, didn't pay much attention. She was so unconcerned that on Friday, the night before the storm, she gave "a most beautiful and well attended moonlight fete" in her home. The following day she busied herself with cleaning up after the party.

In the afternoon, a man ran past her home yelling that the waters of the bay and the gulf had come together from opposite sides of the island and met on Fifteenth Street. She went out onto her gallery (front porch) to see that it was so. She assured her niece that all was still well and it would soon pass, but a few minutes later, water was creeping up into her yard. "In an incredibly short time the water surged over the gallery driven by a furiously blowing wind. Trees began to fall, slate shingles, planks and debris of every imaginable kind were being hurled through the air. We brought our cow on the gallery to save her life but soon had to take her in the dining room where she spent the night. Ten very large trees were soon uprooted and fell crashing, banging, and scraping against our house. We opened all downstairs and let the water flow through. Soon it stood three feet in all rooms."

Mrs. Smith continued: "The wind seemed to grow more furious reaching the incredible velocity of one hundred and twenty miles an hour. Blinds were torn off windows, frames, sash and all blown in, and the rain water stood an inch and a half on upstairs floors. Then slowly dripped through, taking paper and plastering from

**(Left) Horse waiting amid debris with a body cart.**
**(Right) A recovery team finds removes a body from the debris.**

ceilings in rooms below."

Mrs. Smith spent a fearful night but she and her niece survived the storm, as did her house and her cow. Hundreds of other families didn't have the same luck.

Milton Elford, a young man living with his parents and nephew Dwight, was the only member of his family to survive the night. He and his family were in their own home but as the storm intensified, they decided at about 4:00 p.m. to cross the street to seek shelter in a larger, sturdier house with a brick foundation until the storm blew over. But within another hour, they became worried about the safety of that house as the wreckage of other destroyed buildings began slamming against it. By this time, fifteen other refugees had found their way into the house. The little family were about to leave and take their chances, using floating debris as rafts, when the rest of the group talked them out of going, insisting that the house the were in was sturdy and would withstand the storm.

The group was gathered in a close pack when the house was suddenly raised up and knocked off its foundation. Within seconds, the room was waist-deep in water and they all ran for the door. The door was jammed shut but just a quickly, the large living room window burst open and young Milton was the first one there, keeping his nephew in tow. "I had only got part way out when the house fell on us. I was hit on the head with something and it knocked me out and into the water head first. I do not know how long I was down, as I must have been stunned. I came up and got hold of some wreckage on the other side of the house. I could see one man on some wreckage to my left and another on my right. I went back to the door that we could not open. It was broke in, and I could go part way in as one side of the ceiling was not within four or five feet, I think, of water. There was not a thing in sight. I went back and got on the other side but no one ever came up that I could see. We must all have gone down the same time, but I cannot tell why they did not come up."

Milton spent the remainder of the night moving from makeshift raft to makeshift raft. Much of the time, he used a wooden tool chest he had found floating as a protective helmet, which he believed had saved his life several times throughout that perilous night. By 3:00 a.m., the water started to recede and Milton found himself a mere five blocks from where he had started out. At first light, he returned to the collapsed house, searching for his family or anyone who might have survived. Finding no one, he feared the worst and headed toward city hall to talk to the police chief and get help with removing the bodies. With everything he had been through, he somehow believed that the loss of his family had been an isolated incident, but he was soon to discover this was not the case.

When he got to City Hall, he saw that firemen were bringing in piles of corpses by the wagonload and laying them out in a line in the street for identification. But by the next day, the bodies were decomposing so rapidly,

**A family searches the wreckage near their home, looking for anything from their life before the storm.**

they had to be disposed of immediately. They were loaded by the hundreds onto barges and taken out into the gulf and buried at sea. However, the bodies had not been properly prepared and began washing back ashore. Some of the bodies floated along the gulf coast and Galveston Bay for many days, washing onto distant shores for hundreds of miles, but most of them returned to Galveston.

The next plan for body disposal was to bury the bodies were they were found. This worked for a short while until the recovery teams realized that this was taking too long and the corpses were decaying too fast in the near one hundred degree heat. After that, the bodies were burned. As soon as any bodies were discovered, a bonfire would be started and the corpses would be placed in the fire. Once a good fire was going, the men would toss more bodies on as they were found. There was no possibility for identification. There were just too many bodies. It was too hot, too wet, and the odor too foul to contemplate trying to give names to the corpses before disposing of them. Officials kept the body crews well supplied with free whiskey, as they had to "throw the bodies of their wives and children on the burn piles,"

according to the *Houston Chronicle.* The pyres were kept burning for several weeks after the storm had passed.

Most of the victims had either drowned or were crushed by the waves pounding against their houses. Many people survived the storm but were trapped in their demolished houses or within the debris in the streets. Rescuers could hear their screams and cries for help as they walked through the wreckage trying to save anyone they could. Hundreds died waiting for help that never came.

Charles Law, a traveling salesman, was staying at The Tremont Hotel on the night of the hurricane. The Tremont, built in 1872, was an imposing five-story brick building. On September 8, there were two hundred paying guests, but as the weather worsened, the number of people inside the hotel increased by between eight hundred and one thousand. The newcomers were people searching for shelter anywhere that looked like it could withstand the wind and water. The hotel guests and those who had come in for shelter were all huddled in the stairways, hallways and lobby. It was impossible to enter any of the guest rooms as all the windows were blown in. Law had tried to retrieve some of his belongings from his room around 6 p.m. but when he opened his door, the windows and ceiling fell in on him. Amazingly, he was not seriously injured but he was badly bruised about his head and shoulders. He spent the rest of the night with the others, lying on the sopping wet carpeting in the hallway.

Law later wrote to his wife, "On Sunday morning after the storm was all over I went out into the streets and [saw] the most horrible sights that you can ever imagine. I gazed upon dead bodies lying here and there. The houses all blown into pieces; women, men and children all walking the streets in a weak condition with bleeding heads and bodies and feet all torn to pieces with glass where they had been treading through the debris of fallen buildings. And when I got to the gulf and bay coast I saw hundreds of houses all destroyed with dead bodies all lying in the ruins, little babies in their mothers' arms."

"I went from the shores to the interior of the City and every step you would take, dead bodies of all kinds: horses, mules, cats, dogs, chickens and even snakes. Monday they took the bodies up and carried them out to sea and buried them there and Tuesday they could not take them up fast enough so they cremated them wherever they run up on them and when I left there today I saw them still working with hundreds of hands cremating the bodies. None of the bodies the last two days were identified. They could not allow them to do so as the air was so foul. Most horrible! Most horrible!"

George Hodson, a stenographer for a Galveston insurance agency wrote a letter to his wife, who had been visiting family with their young daughter. In it he described a little of what he saw the following morning, "The entire roof of the Ball School is off, the City Hall is one mass of ruins, the opera house is entirely gone, the First Baptist Church and St. John's Church are each a mass of ruins and so the story goes from one end of the town to another, but sadder and more serious still is the great loss of life which is beyond computing. This is something utterly beyond my ability to describe."

Realizing that his family was much safer where they were, Hodson ended his letter by begging his wife to stay away, "Now my good girl I have to make an appeal to your good sense. I have told you that I am well and sound, but I must ask you if you have any love whatever for me that you stay where you are and make no effort whatever to come home."

An unidentified survivor gave this account to a newspaper reporter, "But the whole town was a perfect wreck, you can't picture the awfulness of it all, and as for dead bodies, we couldn't sit on the galleries at all without seeing wagon loads of them going by. At first, people didn't realize there would be so many, and they were carried by one at a time on litters, but later they had to be carted away like so much debris. There were two wagons full taken from the wreck right here in front of us on the esplanade and the poor things had stiffened in the positions in which they died, most of them with their hands clasped high in the air, in the attitude of prayer. The ones I saw will stay with me to my dying day!"

Sarah Hawley and her husband were caring for her wealthy parents' house while they were away vacationing. She, her husband, baby son and two servants stayed in the house all night and fared quite well. Sarah wrote of some of what she witnessed the next day, "The hospital is badly injured and over 100 patients are dead, the schools and churches are all down but the jail is standing firm. The forts are nothing but mounds of dirt, at the camp out at the Denver thirty-five soldiers were lost."

The Galveston railroad yard was severely damaged during the storm.

Most of the boats and ships in the harbor and Galveston Bay were destroyed.

She also wrote of her neighbors, Mr. and Mrs. Irving. They had spent the entire night in the water before drifting to safety in a nearby convent. Their house was gone, as was everything they owned. Mrs. Irving arrived with all her clothes washed from her body. She had lost everything but her husband and her life. Many other victims were left with only what they wore upon their backs.

Sarah wrote very unkindly about the plight of her servant girl, Nancy, displaying her attitude toward her privileged position in life before the hurricane. She had allowed Nancy to "go and see what she had left" which meant that she had to care for her baby all day by herself, which had greatly displeased her. She was rather perturbed when Nancy didn't return home until they were ready for bed that night.

"She hasn't a sign of a relative and little else than the things at our house which were scarcely hurt at all yet she behaved awfully - wouldn't do a thing towards helping and when I left her with the baby she left him as soon as my back was turned. She wanted to see all the horrors and to talk about them in fact as simply daft and behaved as if out of her head."

Sarah's heart did soften later, however, when she saw two young parents, climbing over the wreckage in the street in front of her house. The clothes they wore were in shreds and they were carrying with them a seven-week old-baby. She took them in, got them fed and the baby into dry swaddling. Sarah learned that they had stood on chairs all night, in water up to their necks while holding their baby above their heads on a small mattress. It had been a horrible night for them but they had made it through until the sun came out and they were all three alive.

Perhaps the saddest story of the hurricane tragedy happened at the St. Mary's Orphan Asylum, operated by the Sisters of Charity. In 1866, Catholic Bishop Claude M. Dubuis assigned the Sisters of Charity to Galveston to care for the sick and infirm. An outbreak of yellow fever had taken the lives of many people in Galveston leaving numerous children orphaned. The sisters were assigned to care for them, as well.

After opening the hospital, St. Mary's Infirmary, the nuns were able to open an orphanage, housed in the hospital building. It soon became apparent that the children needed to be distanced from the ailing patients in the infirmary, so they were moved three miles west to the beachfront property of a deceased sea captain. They were far from town and far from the yellow fever patients. As time passed, the Sisters were given the care of children from all over the state of Texas.

St. Mary's Orphan Asylum was made up of two separate two-story dormitory buildings, the older one for the boys and the newer one for the girls. These buildings were just off the beach behind some rather large sand dunes, which were held in place by salt cedar trees. With galleries looking onto the gulf, the nuns, along with the children, could keep a close watch as the storm continued to build.

The nuns and children were gathered in the girls' dormitory, the newer and stronger of the two. They watched and waited as the monster outside gained strength. The wind hammered the sides of the buildings and the waves pounded the beach. One of the young boys from the orphanage described how the tide ate away at the dunes "as though they were made of flour." Too soon, the rising gulf waters had reached the orphanage buildings. The nuns and their charges had taken refuge in the chapel on the first floor. Trying to calm the children, they had them sing the hymn "Queen of the Waves."

As the water continued to rise, it entered the building. The nuns moved the children up to the second floor. Again, they had the children sing "Queen of the Waves" and sent Henry Esquior, the custodian, in search of clothesline rope. A young survivor later said that the Sisters were very brave and the children were very frightened.

**St. Mary's Orphan Asylum. The boys' dorm is on the left, the girls' dorm farther back.**

The main tidal surge struck the south shore at about 7:30 p.m. Houses all along the beachfront were lifted from their foundations and slammed into other houses, ramming them off their foundations. Houses fell upon other houses, crushing each other to splinters.

In town, St. Mary's Infirmary wasn't fairing much better than the orphanage, except that there were sturdy masonry buildings around them that at times, seemed to provide some shelter from the winds. The building itself was in poor condition. The first floor was completely flooded and every window in the building had been blown out. The Sisters and what helpers they had, moved all the patients to the second floor. Once there, they worked frantically, pulling victims into the overcrowded hospital as they floated past the windows, clinging to whatever debris they could catch hold of.

The orphanage buildings were isolated so there was no chance for shelter, and they were in the area of the island that was catching the greatest winds and the worst of the storm surge. They had chosen their location well. As they huddled in the girls' dorm, the heard a monstrous crash as the boys' dorm collapsed and was carried away by the floodwaters.

Sensing a great urgency, the Sisters cut the clothesline rope into shorter pieces and tied them around each child, linking them together so they would not be separated should they have to evacuate the building. Each nun tied herself to between six and eight children. Two of the youngest children were terrified and one of the nuns scooped them up in her arms, promising that she would never let them go. Some of the older children chose to take care of themselves and climbed out onto the roof, clinging fast for their very lives.

Finally, the building could hold out no longer. It, too, was lifted from its foundation and slammed back down, collapsing the walls. The roof came crashing down on those still inside, trapping them underneath. Only three boys survived the storm. William Murney, Frank Madera and Albert Campbell had climbed onto the roof with a few others and were somehow thrown clear when the building crumbled. The three of them were able to make their way to a tree floating past. They floated randomly in their tree for most of the next day until they were able to make their way into town and to the infirmary, where they delivered to sad news of the destruction of the orphanage to the other Sisters.

At the time the nuns' bodies were discovered, recovery workers were still trying to bury victims where they were found. The nuns were thus buried rather than burned. The workers chose to bury the nuns with the children they had tried so disparately to save still attached to them. Two of the Sisters and their charges were found to have floated across Galveston Bay before washing ashore on the mainland. One of the nuns was still holding tightly to two small children; even in death she had kept her promise to them.

St. Mary's Infirmary building was still standing but few others around it had been spared. It became a place of shelter for the sick and injured along with many who had nowhere else to go. They repaired and reopened the infirmary and within a year, had opened a new orphanage. Its first occupants had been orphaned by the storm.

Because the bridges and telegraph lines were taken out very early by the storm, there was no way to inform the outside world about the destruction of Galveston until 11:00 a.m. the morning of September 9. The *Pherabe*, one of the only ships to survive the storm, limped into Texas City carrying six passengers from the island. It was then that a short, shocking message was telegraphed to Governor Joseph Sayers and President William McKinley: "I have been deputized by the mayor and Citizen's Committee of Galveston to inform you that the city of Galveston is in ruins." At the time, the estimated death toll was five hundred, and that was considered an exaggeration.

Temporary shelters in the form of surplus army tents were set up along the shoreline where most of the debris had been washed away. The area became known as the "White City on the Beach." Others made their own shelters that they called "storm lumber homes," using salvaged materials from the wreckage.

An aid organization that is today very familiar at scenes of great or small tragedies, the American Red Cross, had only been in operation for nineteen years in 1900. It started raising money almost immediately by selling postcards and photographs around the country of the storm destruction. After they arrived in Galveston, the volunteers quickly established an orphanage for storm victims and helped acquire lumber to rebuild houses.

The Red Cross was sharing office space with the *New York World* on The Strand, the most historic neighborhood on Galveston Island with the largest and strongest buildings. The head of the newspaper office believed that if Clara Barton herself would come to Galveston, the charitable response from the rest of the country would greatly increase. The *World* offered to give every dollar it raised to the Red Cross efforts if only Clara Barton would come and they would publicize her visit.

Clara Barton, now 78 years old, agreed to come from Washington, D.C., to help administer the donations and to help the penniless and homeless people who were suffering so terribly. Barton later wrote of her experience there saying her workers "grew pale and ill," and that she herself "who had resisted the effect of so many climates, needed the help of a steadying hand as I walked to the waiting Pullman on the track, courteously tendered free of charge to take us away."

When the sun rose on Sunday morning, September 9, the death and destruction must have been unimaginable, but within hours, the dying city began to plan for its rebirth. By 10 a.m., Mayor Walter Jones had called together what was left of the city council, and later that day they appointed a Central Relief Committee. The *Galveston Daily News* never missed an issue. They printed a single sheet for September 9 and 10 together. The back of the sheet held names of the known dead thus far.

By the end of the first week, the telegraph lines were back up and most of the water service was restored. New telephone lines were being laid during the second week. At the end of the third week, many relief groups went home, saloons reopened, the trolley resumed a few routes and the harbor opened again for processing freight.

Some of those who had survived the storm decided to move off the island. Most, however, chose to stay and rebuild. But they knew that things would have to change and that their city would never be the same. One immediate change was on the beautiful shores that Galveston was known for. No visitors would walk those sandy beaches for many months to come. Instead of shells, it was bodies that were washing ashore; those who had been carried out into the gulf by the hurricane and those who had been improperly buried at sea during the cleanup.

The city hired three engineers, Alfred Noble, Henry Robert and H.C. Ripley, to study the problem and make recommendations. The plan to protect the city of Galveston from future hurricanes would involve two massive civil engineering projects. They would build a seawall and raise the overall elevation of the entire city.

Construction of the seawall began in 1902 and the first three miles were completed in 1904. The wall was curved toward the gulf and was nearly sixteen feet tall. The wall of concrete was sixteen feet wide at the base and five feet wide at the top and weighed 40,000 pounds per linear foot. It was designed to protect the city from up to Category 5 hurricanes. Over the next sixty years, the seawall was extended in both directions and today is ten miles long.

The other project, to be constructed concurrently with the seawall, was to raise the elevation of the island by seventeen feet. This was a major engineering feat for the time. There was also to be a slight slope designed into the plans to help drain away any water that might top the seawall. This work continued from 1902 until its completion in 1911.

The engineers reasoned that if they dredged the shipping channels of Galveston Bay and pumped the slurry of sand and mud onto the island, the water would drain off, leaving the solid material behind. To do this, they partitioned off quarter-mile sections of the city with dikes. They then lifted every building in the section with hand-turned jackscrews, along with the accompanying infrastructure such as streetcar tracks, fireplugs, water and sewer pipes. Elevated sidewalks were built of wood framing and planks. Then the slurry was pumped into the section until the solid material filled the cavity created by the dikes. Before moving on to the next section, new foundations were constructed for each building they had raised. Cemeteries also had to be raised but the coffins were left in place. The new depth allowed for as many as three coffins to be buried one on top of the other. When the project was completed, over two thousand buildings had been raised anywhere from a few inches to seventeen feet.

The first real test of the new seawall and elevated island came in 1915, when another hurricane struck the island with approximately the same force at the deadly one in 1900. There was again flooding, but minor in comparison. Most of the structures outside of the protection of the new seawall were severely damaged or destroyed, while those inside the seawall were largely undamaged. There was loss of life, but the 53 people killed by that storm was a very different number from the thousands who were killed fifteen years earlier.

The Strand, a neighborhood in Galveston where a greater concentration of buildings survived, contains numerous stately mansions, built mainly of masonry. The heavy construction was most likely the reason so many of these structures survived. The Strand itself is now a historical landmark, as are all the existing buildings in the city predating the storm.

Its status as a historical landmark is not the only thing for which The Strand is noted. It is also considered to be the most haunted area in all of Galveston. There is hardly a building that doesn't have at least one resident ghost and several of them are believed to be that of people who died during the great storm. One of the strangest apparitions on The Strand occasionally appears in Bistro LeCroy, located at 2021 The Strand. While dining in this charming Louisiana seafood grill, customers have noticed what appear to be transparent bodies, or sometimes a single body, floating in thin air near the ceiling. Many believe that these are residuals from the storm. When the floodwaters suddenly washed into buildings, people often became trapped and were floated to the ceiling by the rising waters and drowned, their bodies remaining there until the waters receded. Many diners who have seen the

**The Strand after the hurricane**

transparent figures believe that they are witnessing a replay of that horrible drowning.

In 1994, the state of Texas put up a historical marker at the site of the original St. Mary's Orphan Asylum, to commemorate the loss of life there and the brave actions of the nuns in their attempt to save the children. Descendants of the three orphan boys who survived attended the ceremony. To this day, The Sisters of Charity of the Incarnate Word remember and pay their respects to the Sisters who died during the Galveston hurricane. Each year, on September 8, wherever they are or whatever they are doing, they stop and sing the old French hymn "Queen of the Waves."

A visit to this marker would find a visitor in the parking lot of the Galveston Wal-Mart Supercenter. Other than the striking contrast of an orphanage site turned discount department store, there is reason to consider this location a bit closer. The Galveston Wal-Mart has been plagued with strange and unexplained occurrences almost since it opened. People working the night shift have reported the most frequent activity, and the toy aisle seems to be the most popular location. Employees will leave the area clean and tidy and when they come back, several toys will be spread out on the floor as if a child had been playing with them. On one occasion, a stockman reported witnessing a small riding toy float gently from a shelf to the floor and roll the length of the aisle, then stop right in front of him. During the night or day, workers have reported leaving an aisle after tidying it up and turning around to see it "wrecked." Late night shoppers have commented on hearing what they thought were children playing in the toy section. Thinking it strange that children should be awake and in a store so late at night, they checked it out and found no one there. Could it be that the orphans who died over a century ago on that same spot have lingered where they died and are now enjoying the playthings they never had in life?

The seawall seems to be another place where hurricane victims return time and time again. A weeping woman with a lost-looking little girl, both dressed in tatters, have been known to attach themselves to visitors and follow them around as they walk up and down the seawall, before fading away to nothing. Farther up the seawall to Stewart Beach, a man in old-time clothing has been seen running along the top of the seawall. He stops and stares intently out at the gulf, then runs on until he disappears.

There is no shortage of ghosts and hauntings on Galveston Island. There are Civil War soldiers, Victorian ladies, grouchy politicians and even the famous pirate Jean Lafitte. But most of all, there are ordinary people, poor lost souls washed out of their lives by a hurricane's tidal surge or crushed by their own homes. But their lives may not have been lost in vain because the lessons learned in 1900 have saved countless lives over the past century.

Statistics bear this out. More people were killed during the unnamed hurricane that struck an unprepared Galveston Island in 1900 than all the other hurricanes to strike the United States since - combined!

## 1918: "BEHOLD, A PALE RIDER.."
## THE SPANISH INFLUENZA EPIDEMIC OF 1918

Even in an era of rumored pandemics and flu outbreaks, no modern Americans can imagine the death and devastation caused by the epidemic that swept across the country in 1918. It was the most lethal epidemic to ever strike the United States and has largely been forgotten by history, despite the fact that it killed between fifty million to one hundred million people worldwide. The flu epidemic caused almost 675,000 American deaths and ranks with the bubonic plague in Europe in the fourteenth century and the decimation of the American Indians from European diseases a few centuries later as one of history's most catastrophic outbreaks.

The first outbreak of what became known as the Spanish Flu occurred in Haskell County, Kansas, in January 1918, just nine months after the United States had declared war on Germany and entered World War I. Within weeks, the flu spread to Camp Funston, which was located at Fort Riley, near Manhattan, Kansas. The camp was one of the country's largest military facilities, quickly put together to train soldiers for the war. The wartime conditions provided a perfect breeding ground for influenza, because America's entrance into the conflict brought together large groups of soldiers and sailors to encampments and naval installations across the country. From these locations, troops were transported across the Atlantic to the front lines in France. Some of the ships literally became death traps and thousands of flu victims were buried at sea. Freighters and troop ships from other countries then served as carriers of the disease, connecting the battlefields to other cities and countries around the world.

Although the first cases of the disease were discovered in the United States and the rest of Europe long before getting to Spain, the epidemic received its nickname of "Spanish Flu" because Spain, a neutral country in World War I, had no special wartime censorship for news about the disease and the accompanying death toll. Since it received reliable press coverage in Spain, people got the false impression that Spain was the most – if not the only – affected country.

The first European outbreak of the flu occurred in April in Brest, France, the principal port of disembarkation for American troops in Europe. From there, the disease spread across the continent, then on toward Asia and Africa. By the fall of 1918, the disease had reached a lethal stage. Army leaders were unprepared for such a

monumental health crisis and largely ignored the warnings about troop movements since they were more concerned about building up strength in Europe for a final thrust against Germany. Despite General John J. Pershing's request for more troops, the draft was canceled in October. On the other side of the lines, the flu contributed to Germany's failure to stop the final Allied assault in late 1918. Germany agreed to an armistice on November 11.

The second wave of the 1918 pandemic was much deadlier than the first. The first wave had resembled typical flu epidemics; those most at risk were the sick and elderly, while younger, healthier people recovered easily. But in August, when the second wave swept across the United States, the virus had mutated to a much deadlier form.

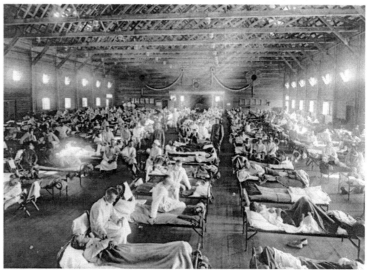

**Temporary hospitals that were used to quarantine those with the Spanish flu began springing up all over the country. The number of those sick overwhelmed the standard hospitals of the time.**

Thousands died. The new wave of the disease spread by soldiers returning from Europe, and for Americans, the flu turned out to be more devastating than the war that accompanied it. By the fall of 1918, the Surgeon General of the Army reported that the disease had "exploded" in port cities where soldiers were entering the United States from overseas. In the early stages of the illness, the epidemic had been largely ignored by the public health departments and was regarded as merely a minor outbreak. Most doctors cited pneumonia on the death certificates of those killed, since flu came first and weakened the resistance of those who were sick. Pneumonia usually followed and was the eventual cause of death for most.

Late in the year, though, as port cities and naval bases began to report large numbers of illnesses and death, the public began to realize that something was very wrong. However, little was done to curb the spread of the virus. Doctors warned local health departments to quarantine the sick and to restrict attendance at large public gatherings. However, most towns, in the grip of patriotic fervor, resisted the advice and held rallies and parades for returning soldiers. In Philadelphia, a massive Liberty Loan parade was held in October, despite the pleas of some medical officials to cancel it. The city paid a horrible price for continuing with the event, as fatalities soon approached one thousand per week.

In the days and weeks that followed, the disease began to spread to the interior parts of the country. The Navy carried the flu from coast to coast on their troop ships and the Army did the same via the railways. Soldiers packed into tight quarters on the trains guaranteed the rapid spread of respiratory illnesses, and when they arrived in the various stations, they passed the flu on to all who came into contact with them.

Large public gatherings in support of the war, such as parades, bond rallies and loan drives, brought masses of people together and they quickly spread the flu even further. The people simply did not appreciate the amount of danger they were in and they ignored orders calling for the closure of schools, churches, theaters and other public meeting places. Most cities refused to halt their public transportation services until hundreds of transit authority workers fell ill and forced them to do so. Soon, those who collected the dead and interred them found themselves overwhelmed in some cities. The accumulation of corpses then served to create secondary epidemics, making the larger cities the hardest hit by the flu.

**PREVENT DISEASE**

CARELESS
SPITTING, COUGHING, SNEEZING,
SPREAD INFLUENZA
and TUBERCULOSIS

As the death toll mounted around the country, the social fabric of many communities began to unravel. In San Francisco, schools were closed for six weeks; in Philadelphia, bodies were "stacked like cordwood" and went uncollected. The police were forced to remove bodies from homes and families had to dig graves for their loved ones, as gravediggers refused to work. Factories closed due to high absence rates. Normal social intercourse, even kissing, stopped. The epidemic so affected everyday life that schoolgirls in Massachusetts jumped rope to a new song:

*I had a little bird*
*And its name was Enza.*
*I opened up the window*
*And in-flew Enza.*

The people's indifference to the flu led directly to the rapid and deadly spread of the disease. Most considered the flu as merely a side note to the terrible war and in those days, epidemics of one sort or another were a common part of life. Most people had already lived through an epidemic of some sort, although usually on a much smaller scale. Influenza moved quickly. It arrived in a town, flourished for a time and then left before most people had the opportunity to realize how great the danger was. Also, the flu did not always kill and when it did, it killed quickly, especially young adults. Normally the healthiest of age groups, individuals in their twenties had the highest rate of mortality from the Spanish flu. Many of their deaths were agonizing. Historian John Barry described a flu death: "Blood poured from their noses, ears and eye sockets; some victims lay in agony; delirium took others away while living." Coughing was sometimes so violent that the muscles of the rib cage were torn apart. When the extremities such as lips and cheeks turned black, death followed soon after. In some cases, victims who were fine in the morning were dead by evening.

Nearly one-fourth of all Americans caught the flu between the fall of 1918 and the late winter of 1919. Even if sufficient numbers of doctors had been available, they could have done little to intercede. No flu vaccines existed at the time and caregivers could do little but encourage patients to drink plenty of fluids, hand out aspirin and keep the dying comfortable. Emergency Red Cross hospitals were set up from coast to coast but doctors and nurses were scarce as the war effort had taken many of them into the military and to France. Despite frantic appeals, calls for more nurses went unanswered.

In many cases, entire families were incapacitated with illness, unaided by doctors and avoided by their neighbors, who refused to enter homes that had "Influenza" signs nailed to the front door. Some cities required people to wear surgical masks, which were actually ineffective to the microscopic virus. Because death rates were highest among people in their twenties, many of whom were parents, the flu produced thousands of young orphans around the country.

The federal government offered little assistance to flu victims. The U.S. Public Health Service, aside from issuing a handful of warnings, played a very small role in the epidemic. This was in part because President Woodrow Wilson did not publicly acknowledge it. His priorities in 1918 were the defeat of Germany and the supervision of the peace settlement when the war was over. Following the president's lead, American newspapers downplayed the epidemic, urging citizens to not become fearful and pumping up the patriotic fervor that came with the end of the war. The deliberate suppression of bad news during the war helps to explain why the Spanish Flu epidemic received so little attention when compared with other catastrophes that struck the United States during the twentieth century.

After Germany surrendered, President Wilson went to France as the head of the American delegation for the peace negotiations held at Versailles. In April 1919, the president contracted the flu, which came on very suddenly. He later recalled that night was "one of the worst through which I have ever passed." Prior to getting sick, Wilson had resisted the Allied demands to punish Germany, but even before he was fully recovered, he changed his mind and went along with the Allied position, including the imposition of expensive financial reparations on Germany. It's unknown just how much effect the flu had on Wilson's reversal but some believe that it may have contributed to his debilitating stroke the following September, an event that clouded his judgment when the Senate considered the ratification of the Versailles Treaty.

The flu may, or may not, have had an effect on world politics but it's certain that it had an impact on the social history of the United States, as well as the role of medical research in years to come. The epidemic was slowly brought under control and almost seemed to vanish as a few more months passed. By then, however, the damage was done. Millions were dead around the world, entire families were wiped out, towns had been laid waste and never recovered, and American history had been altered in a way that had never happened before.

And all because of the flu...

There are a number of locations around the country where the Spanish Flu left a lasting impression as a haunting. Stories tell of former emergency hospitals where the weeping sounds of the dying can still be heard and places where lost children have been known to walk, still searching for their deceased parents after more than nine decades.

One haunted location is Fort Riley, Kansas, one of the first places where the flu was reported in early 1918. Fort Riley had a long history on the frontier. It was used as a Confederate prison camp during the Civil War and later, troops from the fort were needed to protect workers from Indian attacks as they built the Kansas Pacific Railroad. In 1866 and 1867, Lieutenant George Armstrong Custer was stationed there and in 1867, Wild Bill Hickok served there as an Army scout. In 1893, Fort Riley became the site of the Cavalry and Light Artillery School, which continued until 1943, when the Cavalry was disbanded. Through both world wars and up until today, the post has remained active. The military reservation covers more than 100,000 acres and has a population of nearly 25,000, including the 1st Infantry Division, nicknamed the "Big Red One".

But one soldier at the fort is not supposed to be there – at least, not anymore.

Fort Riley was the location of Camp Funston when the United States entered World War I. The camp was the largest of sixteen temporary training camps that were set up at the start of America's involvement in the war. Located at Fort Riley because of its central location, the camp was opened in December 1917. With a capacity for fifty thousand soldiers, it drew trainees from all over the Midwest and the Great Plains. However, not long after it was completed and filled with soldiers, the Spanish Flu hit the encampment and swept through Camp Funston, claiming scores of lives. In 1922, the camp officially ceased to exist and its many buildings are used as temporary housing today.

The soldiers from World War I are long gone now, but at least one of them has chosen to stay behind at the former camp. First reported in the late 1960s, a ghostly soldier in uniform from the World War I era has been seen on guard

## 10 MOST DEADLY AMERICAN EPIDEMICS

1. Killed: 500,000 - March to November, 1918 - Spanish Influenza - Entire United States
2. Killed: 13,000+ - 1878 - Yellow Fever - Southern States: Lower Mississippi Valley
3. Killed: 7,790 - 1853 - Yellow Fever - New Orleans, LA
4. Killed: 7,340 - 1832 - Cholera - July-Aug. 3,000+ in New York City - Oct. 4,340 in New Orleans, LA
5. Killed: 7,000, Cases: 27,363 - 1916 - Polio (Infantile Paralysis) - Entire United States
6. Killed: 5,000+ - 1848 - Cholera - New York City, NY
7. Killed: 4,000+ - 1793 - Yellow Fever - Philadelphia, PA
8. Killed: 3,300, Cases: 57,628 - 1952 - Polio - Entire United States
9. Killed: 3,093 - 1867 - Yellow Fever - New Orleans, LA
10. Killed: 2,720, Cases: 42,173 - 1949 - Polio - Entire United States

duty. He was first spotted by a public works employee while repairing downed electrical lines during a snowstorm. He noticed a soldier, in a heavy wool overcoat and a rifle over his shoulder, pacing back and forth near the site of the old World War I gymnasium. After repairing the lines, he decided to share his thermos of hot coffee with the young man. However, when he approached the area where he had seen him, the soldier was gone. Strangely, he realized that there were no sign of any footprints on the snow-covered ground where the soldier had been standing.

Since that time, the specter has been seen dozens of times, always near the same place – a gymnasium that had been temporarily turned into a hospital during the flu epidemic. Many believe that this long-forgotten soldier is one of those who died during from the terrible disease that ravaged the camp back in 1918.

# 1935: HEMINGWAY'S HURRICANE

The most devastating hurricane to ever impact America's tropical paradise, the Florida Keys, struck on Labor Day weekend of 1935. Florida residents had lived through violent hurricanes before, but they had been nothing like this one. On Labor Day, September 2, 1935, a Category 4 storm, packing winds of 140 to 150 miles per hour with gusts up to two hundred, struck the Keys, a series of islands that bend westward from the foot of Florida to the island of Key West, the southernmost point of the United States.

Originating in the southeastern Bahamas, the storm gained velocity as it moved toward the Keys. One of the most intense storms to ever make landfall in the United States, it destroyed everything in its path, including buildings, vegetation, and much of Henry Flagler's famed Florida East Coast Railroad, which connected most of the Keys to the Florida mainland. The storm surge measured as high as fifteen to twenty feet, swamping the islands with elevations of a foot or less.

Despite the Great Depression, the sparsely settled Keys had experienced a real estate boom during the early 1930s. Popularized by the residency of celebrated author Ernest Hemingway, who lived on Key West, the population of the islands was well over twelve thousand by 1935.

According to the American Red Cross, at least 423 of them lost their lives in the storm. Officials believed that many more people disappeared, likely blown into the sea and drowned. Two hundred and fifty-nine of the known casualties were veterans of World War I and other campaigns. Most of them were employed by the New Deal's

Federal Emergency Relief Administration as workers on U.S. Highway 1, which would later link the Florida mainland with Key West. The workers were newly arrived in the Keys and lived in bunkhouses and army tents. The veterans, along with vacationers and the locals, were unaware of the strength of the storm as it approached the islands. The torrential rains and driving winds prevented the local residents from being rescued. Writing about the hurricane later, a survivor recalled, "Objects careened through the air with deadly speed. Sheet metal roofs became flying guillotines, decapitating several victims, amputating the limbs of others. Like exploding atoms, pounding sheets of sand sheared clothes and even skin off victims, leaving them clad only in belts and shoes, often with the faces literally sandblasted beyond identification."

Called by some historians "the storm of the century," the 1935 Florida hurricane left a permanent mark on the Florida Keys and changed the fabric of the region forever. It not only destroyed Flagler's railroad, which was the only way to get to Key West except by boat, it also created an eerie legend of a phantom train that still steams its way toward paradise.

On September 1, 1935, a tropical storm was brewing in the Caribbean. As it approached Andros Island in the Bahamas, less than one hundred miles from the American mainland, it was packing winds of about 75 miles per hour. This would be considered a minimal, Category 1 storm today. Bulletins that were issued by the weather service suggested that by the following morning, the storm was likely to hit Havana, one hundred miles south of Key West, and pass westward into the Gulf of Mexico. But, of course, nature is always unpredictable and no one had any idea that the relatively benign storm would, less than forty hours later, veer northward toward the Keys and become a Category 5 monster, devouring everything in its path.

Even if anyone had known where the hurricane was going next, little could be done about it. Even with the small population of the Keys, it would have taken at least 24 hours to evacuate the islands in those days. In 1935, weather experts had access to charts that detailed the workings of previous hurricanes, and where they were likely to appear, but they couldn't say when the next one might appear – or where it might go when it did.

Much of what was known about hurricanes in those days came from the research of Father Benito Vines, a nineteenth century Jesuit priest who was one of the first meteorologists to specialize in hurricane forecasting. Father Vines had established a weather observatory in Havana and while he had little access to instruments, his predictions became so accurate that the locals came to believe that he had supernatural powers. As to what to do about a hurricane that was bearing down on you, though, Father Vines was as perplexed as everyone else. He suggested an appeal to a higher authority – in other words, pray.

And when the people of Key West learned that a huge hurricane was coming in their direction, that's exactly what they did. Believe it or not, it seemed to work. The island's most famous resident, Ernest Hemingway, wrote, "... a little after two o'clock [the storm] backs into the west and by the law of circular storms you know the storm has passed over the Keys above us. Now the boat is sheltered by the sea wall and the breakwater and at five o'clock, the glass having been steady for an hour, you get back to the house. As you make your way in without a light you find a tree is down across the walk and a strange empty look in the front yard shows the big, old sapodilla tree is down too. You turn in. That's what happens when one misses you."

Whether by divine intervention or plain luck,

**Driving to Key West on the Overseas Highway in the early 1930s. The construction during the New Deal -- and the hurricane -- would forever change the highway.**

Key West escaped the worst of it. But for the thousand or so residents and workers caught in the Middle Keys, their prayers apparently never made it through. The storm, this time swelled into a massive hurricane, slammed into the Middle and Upper Keys. Islamorada, Craig Key, Long Key, and Upper Matecumbe and Lower Matecumbe Keys suffered the worst. The locals who lived on these islands were hammered by the high winds and rain and lost everything as the seas washed over the low elevations and destroyed their homes. There was simply no escape from the storm.

The outlook was just as dire for the men working on the Overseas Highway. The "vets" as the highways workers had come to be called by the locals, were mostly World War I veterans who had marched on Washington a few years before, demanding payment of bonus money that had been promised by Congress but never delivered. Although President Hoover had dispersed the veterans with armed troops and tear gas, Franklin Roosevelt arranged employment for the men building the new highway across the Keys. He had done this with the best of intentions, never dreaming that he had sent most of them to their doom.

The biggest problem was that the workers were not being supervised by project engineers who knew anything about the Keys, but rather by officials from the Federal Emergency Relief Administration, bureaucrats who had little knowledge of that they were getting themselves into. The three work camps that were established for the men at various points along the route were not the kind of sturdy, reinforced barracks that had been built by the Florida East Coast Railroad when the line was constructed years before. The highway workers had tents and flimsy temporary buildings that could be easily taken down and moved as the roadway progressed toward Key West. Certainly anyone with experience in the Keys would have been aware of the danger a hurricane posed, but there was no one with the necessary knowledge in charge and no contingency plan in place.

As the storm descended on the Keys, the tropic paradise became like a little piece of Hell. "You could see nothing. The winds are howling. And the rains are pounding. It was chaos," a survivor named Bernard Russell later remembered. "It felt like eternity. It could have been thirty minutes. It could have been two hours. Time was nothing then."

With evacuation by sea from the Keys impossible because of the storm, a last-ditch effort was made to try and save as many as the highways workers and residents as possible. A rescue train was sent from Homestead by the Florida East Coast Railway, the main transportation route linking the Keys to mainland Florida. With J.J. Haycraft in the engine of Old 447, he set off in the evening of September 1 to save as many people as he could.

**Henry Morrison Flagler at a station on the East Coast Railway**

When he steamed away from the station and into the heart of the hurricane that night, he earned his rightful place in the colorful history of the Florida Keys.

The Florida East Coast Railway was developed by Henry Morrison Flagler, an American tycoon, real estate developer and John D. Rockefeller's partner in Standard Oil. Formed in Cleveland, Ohio, in 1867, Standard Oil moved its headquarters to New York City in 1877 and Flagler and his family moved along, too. He was joined by Henry H. Rogers, another Standard Oil executive who was also involved in America's railroad development, including those on Staten Island, the Union Pacific and elsewhere. Flagler was at what he believed was the peak of his career in 1878 when, on the advice of a doctor, he took his ailing wife,

Mary, to Jacksonville, Florida, for the winter. But the warm climate didn't save her and she soon died. Two years later, Flagler was married a second time to Ida Alice Shourds, Mary's former nurse. For their honeymoon, the couple returned to Florida, this time vacationing in St. Augustine. Flagler fell in love with the city but found the hotel facilities and transportation to be inadequate. He recognized Florida's potential for tourism and commerce and decided to relocate there. He remained on the board of directors for Standard Oil, but gave up his day-to-day involvement in the company to move to Florida.

In 1885, he began building the grand Ponce de Leon Hotel in St. Augustine. He then turned his attentions to the transportation in Florida. He purchased the Jacksonville, St. Augustine & Halifax River Railway on December 31, 1885 and then realized a major problem – all of the Florida railway systems operated on different gauges, making it impossible to connect them. He soon set about changing the entire rail system in the state, starting with his purchase of three additional railroads: the St. John's Railway, the St. Augustine and Palatka Railway, and the St. Johns and Halifax River Railway. He switched the railroads to a standard gauge system and also used them to transport materials for the construction of other hotels Florida's east coast, which was almost completely undeveloped at the time. He was soon offering rail service between Jacksonville and Daytona. He continued to develop hotel facilities to entice northern tourists to visit Florida and in 1889, Flagler bought and expanded the Ormond Hotel, located along the railroad's route north of Daytona in Ormond Beach.

Beginning in 1892, when landowners south of Daytona petitioned him to extend the railroad eighty miles south, Flagler began laying new railroad tracks. He decided to no longer purchase existing railroads and merge them into his system. He built entirely new ones. Flagler obtained a charter from the state of Florida authorizing him to build a railroad along the Indian River to Miami, and as the railroad progressed southward, cities such as New Smyrna and Titusville began to develop along the line.

In 1894, Flagler's railroad system reached what is today known as West Palm Beach. Flagler constructed the Royal Poinciana Hotel and The Breakers Hotel in Palm Beach, and Whitehall, his private, sixty-thousand-square-foot winter home. The development of these structures, along with the railroad line that reached them, established Palm Beach as a winter resort for the wealthy members of America's Gilded Age.

Palm Beach was meant to be the final point on the Flagler railroad, but during the winter of 1894-1895, central Florida was plagued with several hard freezes, during which the Miami area was unaffected. This caused Flagler to re-think his original plan to not continue the railroad south of Palm Beach. There is a legend that says that Julia Tuttle, one of the two largest landowners in Miami, sent orange blossoms to Flagler to prove to him that Miami was unaffected by the frost. This part of the story is untrue, however, Mrs. Tuttle, who was eager for development in the area by Flagler, did wire him to say that, "the region around the shores of Biscayne Bay is untouched by the freezes." Flagler sent his two lieutenants, James E. Ingraham and Joseph R. Parrott to investigate and they brought boxes of produce and citrus back to Flagler. He immediately contacted Julia Tuttle to ask what she proposed.

To convince Flagler to continue to Miami, both Mrs. Tuttle and the other major landowner, William Brickell, offered half of their holdings north and south of the Miami River to Flagler. Mrs. Tuttle added fifty acres for shops and yards if Flagler would extend his railroad to the shores of Biscayne Bay and build one of his hotels. An agreement was made and the rest was history. On September 7, 1895, the name of Flagler's company was officially changed to the Florida East Coast Railway Company.

On April 15, 1896, the track reached Biscayne Bay, the site of present-day downtown Miami. At that time, it was a small town of fewer than fifty residents. When the town incorporated in July 1896, its citizens wanted to name it in honor of Flagler, but he declined, persuading them to keep the old Indian name of Miami. To further develop the area around the new railroad station, Flagler dredged a channel, built streets, instituted the first water and electrical systems, financed the town's first newspaper and constructed the Royal Palm Hotel. There is no question that Flagler was a visionary and can be credited for the development of the entire east coast of Florida. He was wrong about one thing, though: he never believed that Miami would ever be anything more than a quiet fishing village.

Flagler was widely praised for all of his projects, except for one. In 1905, he began what everyone considered his folly, a project doomed to fail: the extension of his railway to Key West. The Overseas Railway would become

Florida East Coast Railway, Key West Extension.
Finishing Concrete Piers for Steel Bridge over Sea.
Knights Key, Florida.

**Postcard showing the construction of the Florida East Coast Railway and the work that had to be done to extend the line over the long reaches of water between the Keys.**

Flagler's greatest challenge but he did not approach it lightly. Extending the railroad to Key West, 128 miles from the end of the Florida peninsula, was a solid business decision. He made his announcement about the railroad soon after the United States announced the construction of the Panama Canal. Key West, as America's closest deep-water port to the canal, could not only take advantage of Cuban and Latin American trade, but the opening of the canal would allow significant trade possibilities with the West.

The construction of the railroad required many engineering innovations, as well as vast amounts of money and labor. At one time during the construction, four thousand men were employed to lay the rails, pour the concrete and create the overpasses that took the railroad over vast expanses of water. During the seven years of construction, three hurricanes threatened to halt the project.

Despite the many hardships, the final section of the Florida East Coast Railway was completed in 1912. On January 22, a proud Henry Flagler rode the first train into Key West, marking the completion of the railroad's connection to Key West and the linkage by railway of the entire east coast of Florida.

Tragically, Flagler only lived for one year after the completion of his greatest project. In 1913, he fell down a flight of stairs at Whitehall. He never recovered from the fall and died in West Palm Beach of his injuries on May 20, 1913. He was 83 years old. He was buried in St. Augustine alongside his daughter, Jenny Louise, and his first wife, Mary. Nearly a century later, the effects of Henry Flagler's incredible accomplishments can still clearly be seen throughout Florida.

The Stock Market Crash of 1929 and subsequent Great Depression were particularly hard on the Florida East Coast Railway, but it would be the Labor Day Hurricane of 1935 that destroyed the Key West Extension. Unable to afford to rebuild the ruined sections, the roadbed and surviving bridges were sold to the state of Florida, which built the Overseas Highway to Key West, using much of the remaining railway infrastructure. Today, U.S. Highway 1, following Flagler's dream, continues to provide the link between mainland Florida and Key West, America's southernmost point.

During Labor Day weekend of 1935, the Florida East Coast Railway was the only connection between the Keys and the mainland and there was little choice but to send a rescue train to bring back as many people as possible from the Upper Keys. It was nearing 8:00 p.m. when Old 447 approached the Islamorada station on Upper Matecumbe Key. There had been no power to the station lights or the approach signals for hours and with wind-whipped sheets of rain pelting the engine and waves sweeping over the seven-foot right-of-way, engineer J.J. Haycraft was traveling blind.

He was slow to stop when he approached the station. A group of refugees had gathered under the overhang of a cluster of buildings along the track but Haycraft feared that the station house, post office and warehouse were liable to come crashing down in the high wind. Despite the cries of those who feared he was leaving them behind, he ran the engine nearly a quarter mile past the station, finally coming to a stop at a point where the landmass of the island was the widest. He later told reporters that he believed if he had stopped at any other point, the train would have ended up at the bottom of the ocean.

Rain-soaked figures chased after him, dimly lit in the engine's headlamp, fighting against the ferocious winds to get onto the train. Haycraft, with the train in reverse, watched as men, women and children struggled past his cab to the passenger cars, where his crew frantically pulled them aboard. For a few moments, Haycraft must have felt a glimmer of hope, that all of his efforts had been worthwhile, but then he felt a terrible rumbling under his feet and spotted a gigantic "wall of water" bearing down on the train.

As the hellish winds howled and the tidal surge rushed toward the train, Haycraft threw open the throttle in a desperate attempt to save those who were already on board. But the engine lurched forward only a few feet before it came to a sudden halt. The train's conductor, J.F. Gamble, flung himself into the cab and blurted out the horrifying news --- one of the hundred-ton boxcars at the rear of the train had been knocked over by the wind and the waves, automatically locking the brakes on the entire train. There was no way to move as the huge wave advanced on them. Haycraft believed they were as good as dead.

As the water wall slammed down on the train, Haycraft felt a great lurch as the remainder of the eleven cars attached behind the engine toppled over. The linked cars went over sideways. The windows of the passenger cars shattered inward and the interiors were instantly filled with water. The scores of men, women and children inside, who thought they were safe, now found themselves trapped in what must have seemed like watery coffins. In the surging darkness, desperate parents groped for the children that had been torn from their arms. Panicked people flailed blindly against the water and a few did manage to escape from the cars through the broken windows. Ironically, most of them were swept out into the storm-tossed sea to die.

Engine 447, an old workhorse that had been built for duty and not for grace, was simply too heavy for the tidal surge to overturn. Haycraft and the crew in the cab, including conductor Gamble and fireman Will Walker, emerged alive from the battering of the giant waves. But for forty miles flanking that single, sixty-foot stretch of tracks where Engine 447 sat, the bed of the railroad had been completely obliterated. It was gone – as was everything else that had been in the path of the storm, including the station, the solidly built homes of the locals, and the nearby Long Key Fishing Camp. The islands had simply been wiped clean. Engine 447 was eventually returned to Homestead by way of a sea barge.

One stunned reporter, who made his way to the location by boat, wrote, "The Florida East Coast Railway is a total wreck... tracks have been picked up and tossed aside, sometimes fifty yards from the roadbed. The trestles through the cuts are ruined. The hospital building at Camp No. 1 was swept so completely that not a splinter except the concrete base remains. Not a building stands there... the foliage has literally vanished... everywhere one sees bedding, clothing and other bits of household necessities clinging to the brush, almost as if laid out to dry. Always it is high in the bushes, almost above a man's

**The rescue train was swept off the tracks during the storm.**

head... The entire mass of lumber used in the construction of all the homes and cottages along the east coast of the islands lies high in the underbrush fully 300 yards inland. You'll go a long way before you'll see such wreckage again."

The Keys were a scene of total devastation. Survivors on the fringes of the storm told chilling tales of men disemboweled by sheets of metal roofing that had been torn loose in the wind, of skulls crushed by fifteen-pound rocks that were hurled through the air like pebbles. The darkness was often illuminated by flashes of "ground lightning," a phenomenon generated by the wind lifting millions of bits of sand into the air, where they clashed and created eerie static charges.

A highway worker named Melton Jarrell, whose leg was pinned under a huge section of rail, was ready to cut off his own foot to free himself before he drowned. However, he passed out from pain and shock before he could carry out his gruesome plan. When he regained consciousness, he found that the tidal surge that had dropped the heavy rail on his leg had somehow lifted it away – but he was being swept out to sea! Jarrell blacked out after colliding with something hard but somehow managed to survive his ordeal.

Another vet, Lloyd Fitchett, had run to the railroad embankment, hoping to escape the rising waters. When he found a telephone pole, he climbed as high as he could. "I took my belt off and strapped myself to it," he later recalled. "I heard a swishing noise, then a shriek, and realized I had been hit by flying debris. I learned later it was the roof of the barracks that had fallen on my chest. A barrage of stones kept hitting me all over the body and then I partly lost consciousness. I hung on through the night in a semi-dazed condition and when daybreak came I could see the bodies of my dead comrades all around me. I counted fifteen."

Witnesses reported seeing an entire roof lift off a house on Windley Key. Moments later, the walls of the house collapsed, disappearing when hit by a tidal surge. Sofas, chairs, tables and household goods of all kinds churned away in the raging water, followed by a piano. This was strange enough but then the onlookers realized there was a desperate woman clinging to the piano. She was draped over it, clinging tightly to it as she rushed past at incredible speed. She was hurled two hundred yards inland before the wave crashed down against the railroad embankment. The massive piano fell onto the woman and crushed her underneath it.

The first doctor to arrive in the Matecumbes after the storm was G.C. Franklin of Coconut Grove. He discovered the bodies of 39 men in the first pile of debris that he encountered. Corpses were scattered everywhere, many of them swelling and decomposing in the heat.

A mind-boggling account of the hurricane's aftermath described a victim who was found on the day after the storm. He was impaled by a two-by-four that had passed completely through him, just beneath his ribs and somehow missing his kidneys and surrounding organs. The man was still alive and appeared calm as a doctor prepared to remove the piece of wood. The doctor offered the man a shot of morphine to dull the pain but the man refused. He was sure the operation was going to kill him and he said that he would rather have two beers instead. He was given the beers and he ordered the doctor to pull out the board. The doctor yanked the timber out of the man's body – and he died.

Ernest Hemingway, trapped in Key West by residual winds until the second morning after the storm, joined one of the first rescue parties to reach the Middle Keys. He later wrote a stunning article on what he found in *New Masses* magazine. Hemingway wrote, "When we reached Lower Matecumbe, there were bodies floating in the ferry slip. The brush was all brown as if autumn had come, but that was because all of the leaves had blown away. There was two feet of sand over the island where the sea had carried it and all the heavy bridge-building machines were on their sides. The island looked like the abandoned bed of a river where the sea had swept it."

Soon, the rescue party found greater horrors: "The railroad embankment was gone and the men who cowered behind it were all gone with it. You could find them face down and face up in the mangroves... Then further on you found them high in the trees where the water had swept them."

"On the other hand," Hemingway also wrote, "there are no buzzards. Absolutely no buzzards. How's that? Would you believe it? The wind killed all the buzzards and all the big winged birds like pelicans too. You could find them in the grass that's washed along the fill."

In a letter to his friend and editor, Maxwell Perkins, Hemingway presented the most disturbing things the rescue party found, in terms that would have made it impossible for any publication of the time to print: "Max,

# 10 MOST DEADLY AMERICAN HURRICANES

1. Killed: 6,000 - 12,000 - Sept. 8, 1900 - Great Galveston Hurricane - Galveston, TX
2. Killed: 1836 - Sept. 16-17, 1928 - San Felipi - Okeechobee Hurricane – FL
3. Killed: up to 1,800 (1464 in LA, 340 in MS) - Aug. 25-29, 2005 - Hurricane "Katrina" - LA and MS.
4. Killed: 1,000 - Aug 28, 1893 - Unnamed - Savannah, GA; Charleston, SC; Sea Islands, SC
5. Killed: 787 (287 on land, 500 at sea) - Sept. 10-14, 1919 - Unnamed - FL and TX
6. Killed: 600 - Sept. 20-22, 1938 - Long Island Express - NC and NY
7. Killed 423 - Sept. 2, 1935 - The Great Labor Day Storm - Florida Keys
8. Killed: 400 - Aug. 11, 1856 - Unnamed - Last Island, LA
9. Killed: 390+ - June, 26, 1957 - Hurricane "Audrey" - TX and LA
10. Killed: 390 (46 on land, 344 at sea) - Sept. 12-16, 1944 - NC to New England

you can't imagine it, two women, naked, tossed up into the trees by the water, swollen and stinking, their breasts as big as balloons, flies between their legs. Then, by figuring, you located where it is and recognize them as two very nice girls who ran a sandwich place and filling-station three miles from the ferry. We located sixty-nine bodies where no one had been able to get in. Indian Key swept absolutely clean, not a blade of grass, and high over the center of it were scattered live conchs that came in with the sea, crawfish, and dead morays. The whole bottom of the sea blew over it... we made five trips with provisions for survivors to different places and nothing but dead men to eat the grub..."

The official Red Cross death toll from the hurricane was four hundred and eight but most agreed that the official count was too low. The Islamorada coroner put the figure at 423 but the final tally will never be known. With an uncertain Keys census and scores of people being washed out to sea and vanishing without a trace, we'll never know just how many residents and workers lost their lives in the storm. Some twenty years later, an Islamorada developer was digging out a rock pit when he unearthed three automobiles with out-of-state license plates dated 1935 – with the skeletons of their owners still inside. And to this day, those poking about on one of the hundreds of small, uninhabited islands in the region will still uncover remains suspected to be victims of "Hemingway's Hurricane."

Strange, haunting stories later began to be told about Islamorada and spectral memories of the 1935 Hurricane. One of the most frightening accounts involved sightings of a group of people that have been spotted wandering through the swamps and woods at night. Many locals believed these people were actually the spirits of those who perished in the storm.

For three weeks after the hurricane, the decomposing bodies of hundreds of victims were pulled from the swamps and creeks. Although the search was thorough, many bodies were never found, perhaps trapped under the roots of cypress trees or simply washed out to sea. To this day, government land workers and environmentalists will still find an occasional skeleton lodged in the swamp beds, a grim reminder of the storm. Eerily, though, there have been a number of reports of large groups of people trudging through the swamp at night. They are hunched over and slow, as if beaten down or injured. They always seem to disappear into a thicket – or simply vanish. The figures are always seen staggering to the north, as if trying to escape from the storm-wrecked Keys, and are perhaps re-living their final hours on earth.

And they are not only the ghosts of those who died in the Labor Day Hurricane. They also seem to seem to serve as a foretelling of future horror. Legend has it that they were seen several times just before Hurricane Andrew hit Homestead, Florida in 1992.

And these shambling spirits are not the only phantoms that remain from the hurricane. According to numerous accounts, witnesses have also spotted a ghost train lumbering along railroad tracks that no longer exist.

Most believe this is a ghostly re-enactment of the Engine 447 rescue train as it tried in vain to save the residents of Islamorada on the night of the hurricane.

The Key West Extension of the Florida East Coast Railway was never rebuilt after the storm but in the early 1940s, weird events began to be experienced along the old line. The sound of a steam engine and a train whistle could sometimes be heard later at night and occasionally, a headlight could be seen silently rolling by in the early hours of the morning. An old man once told of fishing near a railroad bridge and hearing a train whistle that was so loud that he had to hold his ears. He heard the rumble of the engine and actually felt the vibration of a train as it passed over the bridge – but there was nothing there. No train had passed over the bridge in years.

# 1937: "OH, THE HUMANITY!" HISTORY & HAUNTINGS OF THE *HINDENBURG* DISASTER

On May 6, 1937, one of the most photographed and familiar disasters of the twentieth century occurred as the German zeppelin airship *LZ 129 Hindenburg* burst into a massive ball of flames as it descended over Lakehurst, New Jersey. Seven million cubic feet of ignited hydrogen incinerated the dirigible in just 34 seconds, long before it could hit the ground. The disaster shocked the world, dealt a blow to Nazi propaganda, effectively ended the era of lighter-than-air travel and claimed the lives of 35 crew members and passengers and one person on the ground.

To this day, the anguished cries of radio reporter Herbert Morrison, as he broadcast from the scene, can still send chills down the spine of the most jaded listener. But Morrison's famous radio report is not all that lingers of this fiery calamity. Some believe the spirits of the *Hindenburg* dead still linger, as well.

Dirigibles, or airships, first came to the attention of the public as a method of air travel in the late 1700s. They were really considered more of a novelty than for practical use until the latter part of the 1800s, when a few inventors began to attach propulsion motors to their balloons in order to get from one place to another.

However, the "Golden Age of Airships" really began in July 1900 with the launch of the Luftschiff Zeppelin LZ1. This grand experiment led to the most successful airships of all time: the Zeppelins. They were named after Count Ferdinand von Zeppelin, who began working with rigid airship designs in the 1890s. The airships had a framework composed of triangular lattice girders, covered with fabric and containing separate gas cells. Tail fins were added for control and stability and two engine and crew cars hung beneath the hull driving propellers, which were attached to the sides of the frame by means of long drive shafts. Additionally, there was a passenger compartment located halfway between the two cars.

Airships turned deadly during World War I. Oddly enough, the idea of using airships as bombers had been thought of long before they were actually up to the task. In H.G. Wells' *The War in the Air* (1908), he described the obliteration of entire cities by airship attack. On March 5, 1912, Italian forces became the first to use airships for a military purpose, scouting west of Tripoli, behind Turkish lines.

Soon, however, they began to be used as a weapon. The Germans, French and Italians began operating airships for reconnaissance and bombing missions. Count von Zeppelin and others in the German military believed that that airships could be used to not only counteract Britain's naval superiority but could be used to strike at Britain itself. Zeppelins proved to be a terrifying but inaccurate weapon. Navigation and target selection proved to be difficult under the best of conditions. The darkness, high altitudes and clouds that were frequently encountered by Zeppelin missions reduced accuracy even further. Their flammable hydrogen lifting gas made them vulnerable at lower altitudes. Several were shot down in flames by British defenders, and others crashed en route. They began to fly higher, above the range of other aircraft, but this made their accuracy even worse.

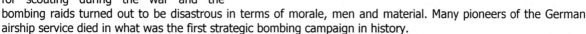

In the end, airships were best suited for scouting during the war and the bombing raids turned out to be disastrous in terms of morale, men and material. Many pioneers of the German airship service died in what was the first strategic bombing campaign in history.

After the war, a number of nations operated airships, including Britain, the United States, Italy, France, Russia and Japan. Most discontinued their use by the early 1930s and, within a few years, only Germany was still in pursuit of the superior airship. The Zeppelin company was operating a passenger service between Frankfort and Recife in Brazil, which took 68 hours. In the middle 1930s, the company started building an airship that was specifically designed to offer passenger service across the Atlantic to the United States.

After Adolph Hitler's rise to power, around this same time, the Zeppelin lent itself to exploitation by the Nazis. The German public perceived the development of the airships as a national achievement, rather than as a business one. Nazi propaganda minister Joseph Goebbels employed airships in mass events, as a daunting symbol of Nazi power. With no other country in the world employing the massive airships on a regular basis, Germany flaunted its superiority in this area, starting a regular transatlantic service in March 1936.

On May 3, 1937, the *Luftschiff Zeppelin 129 Hindenburg* departed from the Rhein-Main Airport in Frankfort, Germany, lifting into the air toward the United States. The airship's namesake was the recently deceased Paul von Hindenburg, a World War I field marshal, president of the Weimar Republic and a national figure. The *Hindenburg* was over eight hundred feet long, 135 feet in diameter, and weighed approximately two hundred and fifty tons. To provide the lift that was required to get the monstrous ship off the ground, its sixteen gas cells had to be filled with combustible hydrogen.

Since its maiden flight in 1936, the *Hindenburg* had completed twenty flights across the Atlantic Ocean and had broken the speed record of previous Zeppelins. Under normal conditions, its engines accelerated the airship to 84 miles per hour, but favorable winds had allowed for top speeds of up to 188 miles per hour. A westward trip from Germany to the United States took an average of 36 hours and 42 minutes. Although the *Hindenburg* had been built to accommodate between fifty and seventy passengers, it carried only 36 travelers in addition to 61 crew members when it embarked on its fatal final flight. The passengers could rest in twenty heated cabins at the center of the hull's lower decks. Amenities on board included a dining room, a reading, writing and smoking room, and centrally located restrooms with showers. Panoramic windows embedded in the concave hull provided spectacular views for those on the promenade deck.

From the start of the trip, Captains Max Pruss and Ernest Lehmann had to confront a number of problems, all of them due to bad weather conditions. Storms first kept the airship from crossing the English Channel and then delayed its journey across the Atlantic. Blown off course to Newfoundland, it passed over Manhattan behind

Passengers disembarking from the *Hindenburg* during a previous, uneventful flight.

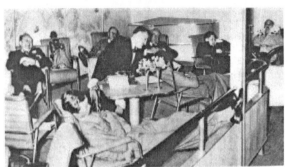

The passenger lounge (with grand piano for entertainment) where passengers could rest, eat, sleep and socialize during the flight.

A two-berth cabin on the *Hindenburg*. A wash basin was included in each small cabin, with the toilets and shower on another deck.

schedule at 3:00 p.m. on May 6. It finally reached the Naval Air station in Lakehurst, New Jersey, at 6:00 p.m. but heavy rain kept the airship from initiating landing procedures. After an hour, the storm passed and the *Hindenburg* approached the mooring mast. It was to be a high landing, known as a flying moor, after which the airship would be winched down to ground level. This type of landing maneuver reduced the number of necessary ground crew, but required more time. The landing was initiated at 7:00 p.m. At 7:09 p.m., however, the airship made a sharp full speed left turn to the west around the landing field because the ground crew was not ready. Two minutes later, it turned back toward the landing field and began to slow. Three minutes later, Captain Pruss ordered all engines full astern so that the airship could be stopped. At 7:17 p.m., the wind shifted direction to the southwest and Pruss was forced to make a second, sweeping sharp turn, this time to the starboard. Two minutes later, the airship made another sharp turn and dropped its water ballast because the *Hindenburg* was stern-heavy. Six men were also sent to the bow to trim the airship, which allowed it to be on an even keel as it stopped. At 7:21 p.m., the mooring lines were dropped from the bow. The starboard line was dropped first, followed by the port line. The port line was connected to the post of the ground winch. The starboard line was left dangling.

At 7:25 p.m., a few witnesses saw the fabric ahead of the upper fin flutter as though gas was leaking. Other witnesses also reported seeing blue discharges, possibly static electricity, moments before fire erupted on top of the ship. Several other eyewitness testimonies suggest that the first flame appeared on the port side just ahead of the port fin, and was followed by flames that burned on top. On board, people heard a muffled explosion and those in the front of the ship felt a shock as the port mooring rope jerked on its winch. The officers in the control car initially thought the shock was caused by a broken rope.

Moments later, the *Hindenburg* caught fire and became engulfed in flames.

The fire quickly spread. Almost instantly, a water tank and a fuel tank burst out of the hull

The *Hindenburg* bursts into flames. The series of photos on the next page show it as it falls to the earth.

due to the shock of the blast. This shock also caused a crack behind the passenger decks and the rear of the structure imploded. The stern of the ship lost its buoyancy and the bow lurched upwards. As the *Hindenburg's* tail crashed into the ground, a burst of flame came out of the nose, killing nine of the twelve crew members in the bow. As the airship continued to fall with its bow pointing upwards, part of the port side directly behind the passenger deck collapsed inward and the gas cell there exploded. The airship's gondola wheel touched the ground, causing the burning ship to bounce upwards. At this point, most of the fabric had burned away. Finally, the airship went crashing onto the ground, bow first. The *Hindenburg* had been completely destroyed.

Various theories have been suggested as to the cause of the fire on board the airship. Contemporaries suspected sabotage or a lightning strike, while more recent experts believe that maneuvering in the storm may have caused a build-up of static electricity in the ship's envelope. An electric discharge could have ignited the hydrogen. To this day, no one knows for sure.

Unbelievably, despite the violent fire, most of the crew and passengers survived. Of the 36 passengers and 61 crew members, thirteen of the passengers and 22 members of the crew perished. As the burning airship had crashed down on the landing field, the American landing crew had fled in a panic, but one linesman, Allen Hagaman, had been killed by falling debris.

The majority of the airship crew who died were up inside the ship's hull, where they either had no easy escape route or were too close to the bow of the ship, which hung burning in the air, for them to find a way out.

Most of the passengers who were killed were trapped in the starboard side of the passenger deck. Not only had the wind blown the fire toward the starboard side, but the ship had also rolled slightly to that side when it hit the ground, sealing off the observation windows and cutting off the escape of any passengers on that side of the ship. To make matters worse, the sliding door leading from the starboard passenger area to the central foyer and gangway stairs (through which rescuers led many passengers to safety) jammed shut in the crash, which also trapped the starboard side passengers. A few of them did escape, but most did not. By contrast, all but a few of the passengers on the port side of the dirigible survived the fire, most escaping virtually unscathed.

Some of the survivors were only saved by pure luck. Werner Franz, a fourteen-year-old cabin boy, was initially frozen in a state of shock when he realized the ship was on fire. As he stood in the officer's mess, where he was putting away dishes, he was unable to move. It was only when a water tank above him burst open and he was soaked to the skin that he came to his senses. The exploding tank also managed to put out the fire that was swirling around him. He made his way to a hatch that he knew about because he had seen it used to stock the kitchen before the flight. He dropped through it just as the forward section of the ship was rebounding into the air. He started to run toward the starboard side, but then turned in the other direction when he noticed how the flames were being pushed that way by the wind. He managed to make it out of the wreck with nothing more than singed eyebrows and wet clothes.

When the control car crashed to the ground, most of the officers jumped out of the windows and became separated. First Officer Albert Sammt found Captain Max Pruss going back into the wreckage to look for survivors. Pruss was badly burned on his face and he required months of hospitalization and surgery, but he survived. Captain Ernst Lehmann escaped the crash with burns to his head and arms and severe burns across most of his back. Although his injuries did not seem as severe as those of Captain Pruss, he died at a nearby hospital the next day.

Out of the twelve crewmen in the bow of the ship, only three of them survived. Four of these men were standing on the mooring shelf, a platform at the very tip of the bow from which the front landing ropes and mooring cables were released to the ground crew, and which was directly in front of gas cell #16. The rest were standing either along the lower keel walkway ahead of the control car, or were on platforms beside the stairway that led up the curve of the bow to the mooring shelf. During the fire, as the bow hung in the air at a steep angle, flames shot forward and burst through the bow, roasting the unfortunate men alive. The three men from the forward section that survived, elevator operator Kurt Bauer, cook Alfred Grözinger and electrician Josef Leibrecht, were those furthest aft of the bow, and Bauer and Grözinger happened to be standing near two large triangular air vents, through which cool air was being drawn by the fire. They managed to escape with only superficial burns.

The other men either fell into the fire or tried to leap from the *Hindenburg* when it was still too high in the air. Three of the four men standing on the mooring shelf inside the very tip of the bow were actually taken from the wreck alive, though one of them, a rigger named Erich Spehl, died shortly afterward in the Air Station's infirmary. The other two,

The *Hindenburg* burning on the airfield.

helmsman Alfred Bernhard and apprentice elevator operator Ludwig Felber, initially survived the fire but died at area hospitals later that night.

The four crew members who had been in the tail fin survived the disaster. Although they were closest to the origin of the fire, they were sheltered by the structure of the lower fin. They escaped by climbing out of the fin's access hatch when the tail hit the ground.

The *Hindenburg* disaster remains one of the most widely known calamities in American history, thanks largely to the wide press coverage that the airship fire attracted. There was a large amount of newsreel coverage and photographs taken of the crash, as well as Herbert Morrison's recorded, on-the-scene, eyewitness radio report for station WLS in Chicago, which was broadcast the next day. This was the first transatlantic flight by a Zeppelin to the United States that year and it was heavily publicized, bringing many journalists to the scene.

The photographs and film footage of the scene were tragic but Morrison's radio broadcast remains one of the most famous in history:

*It's practically standing still now. They've dropped ropes out of the nose of the ship; and (uh) they've been taken ahold of down on the field by a number of men. It's starting to rain again; it's... the rain had (uh) slacked up a little bit. The back motors of the ship are just holding it (uh) just enough to keep it from...It's burst into flames! It burst into flames, and it's falling, it's crashing! Watch it! Watch it! Get out of the way! Get out of the way! Get this, Charlie; get this, Charlie! It's fire... and it's crashing! It's crashing terrible! Oh, my! Get out of the way, please! It's burning and bursting into flames and the... and it's falling on the mooring mast. And all the folks agree that this is terrible; this is the one of the worst catastrophes in the world. [indecipherable] its flames... Crashing, oh! Four- or five-hundred feet into the sky and it... it's a terrific crash, ladies and gentlemen. It's smoke, and it's in flames now; and the frame is crashing to the ground, not quite to the mooring mast. Oh, the humanity! and all the passengers screaming around here. I told you; it—I can't even talk to people Their friends are out there! Ah! It's... it... it's a... ah! I... I can't talk, ladies and gentlemen. Honest: it's just laying there, mass of smoking wreckage. Ah! And everybody can hardly breathe and talk and the screaming. Lady, I... I... I'm sorry. Honest: I... I can hardly breathe. I... I'm going to step inside, where I cannot see it. Charlie, that's terrible. Ah, ah... I can't. Listen, folks; I... I'm gonna have to stop for a minute because [indecipherable] I've lost my voice. This is the worst thing I've ever witnessed.*

The film footage at the scene, as well as Morrison's passionate recording, shattered public faith in airships and marked the end of the giant passenger-carrying airships. The *Hindenburg* crash certainly marked the end of an era – closing the story with a scene of horror that still resonates today as an eerie haunting at the Naval Air Station hospital.

The hospital, know officially at that time as Naval Dispensary Lakehurst, was in the middle of the disaster on the night the *Hindenburg* fell burning from the sky. The doctors, nurses and corpsman that were stationed there in 1937 offered their assistance during the tragic event, although little detail is known about how the medical personnel on the site triaged the wounded or cared for the dead. It is known that the dispensary was utilized after the crash, though, and that many of the injured were brought there. The role the hospital played has been commemorated by the state of New Jersey and has been listed on the registry of historical sites.

And many New Jersey ghost buffs have listed the hospital as one of the state's haunted sites, as well.

The Naval Air Station in Lakehurst played an important role in transatlantic airship flights. The base commanding officer at the time was Lieutenant Commander C.E. Rosendahl, who eventually rose to the grade of vice admiral, and was a longtime proponent of airship aviation. The base hospital, which is now known as the Branch Medical Clinic of the National Naval Medical Center, became a key player in the events that followed the *Hindenburg* crash.

Lieutenant Carl Victor Green, Jr., the Naval Air Station base physician, along with his son, Robert, was among those watching the airship as it approached the mooring tower. The *Hindenburg* was running late and Robert had anxiously looked forward to seeing it arrive at the base. "It was evening, but quite light," Lt. Green recalled in an interview many years later. "The nose of the silver ship was pointed toward the town of Lakehurst. She was poised for her pulling down and landing tower docking."

Suddenly, there were three rapid explosions. Green remembered, "The rear half of the vessel was totally enveloped in bright orange flame. A blast of heat blew over us, standing a half-mile away." He and his son watched in shock and terror as the mighty Zeppelin fell to the ground in a blazing ball of fire.

"I hurried to the base hospital. I watched people walking in, carried into the hospital or ambulance garage, which had become a temporary morgue," Green said. Fortunately, only one man from the ground crew died at the hospital. The hull of the ship fell on him after he tripped and fell on the railroad tracks used to stabilize the airship after mooring. Many of the injured were treated at the hospital and several of them died.

On the morning after the disaster, smoke was still rising from the black and twisted skeleton that had once been the world's largest flying vessel. Eyewitnesses on the scene claimed they would never forget the horrible smell of burning flesh that was in the air. A number of bodies were unidentified and they were moved into the crew's quarters in the hangar. It had been hastily transformed into a temporary morgue. A small group of men and women filed past the charred remains of 26 of the victims in an attempt to identify them. Detachments of sailors were posted as guards around the ruins of the airship and no information was given out to the curiosity-seekers who flocked to the area. Men who served on the base at that time stated that they would never forget those darks days in 1937.

The Branch Medical Clinic of today, once a full-service naval hospital, was built in 1921 when the base first opened as an airship station. Officers and corpsmen stationed at the clinic will say without reservation that it is a great duty station for enjoying the Jersey Shore and nearby cities like Philadelphia, Atlantic City and New York but they will often add that strange things happen at the old hospital that cannot easily be explained.

It is not uncommon, they have said, to hear mysterious footsteps, rattling doors, loud crashes, voices, and to see lights flashing off and on. Many who have been stationed here have come to believe that some of those who have died in the building do not rest in peace. The majority of them believe that the spirits of those who died in the *Hindenburg* disaster have remained behind to haunt the clinic and the surrounding buildings.

Recently, a staff member reported hearing footsteps and the rattling of his office doorknob, when working late one evening. He said, "I was sitting in my office writing a report when I heard footsteps in the hallway and someone or 'something' attempting to open my office door. When I got up and opened the door, just a few seconds later, I saw nothing and the hallway leading to my office was dark and empty."

Such things happen on a regular basis. A former staff member said he was standing watch when he heard a loud crash in the clinic area. When he went to look, he said he saw a large pamphlet rack had been tipped over and pamphlets were scattered all over the floor. "I was irritated by that," he said, "so I yelled, 'I didn't make the mess. I'm not cleaning it up, you are.' The next morning the pamphlets were all back in their place."

There are also reports of a naval officer who walks the grounds of the historic hangar deck where the *Hindenburg* was housed during its initial visit. There is also a ghost woman in a white gown who has been seen in the clinic area at night and an airman in vintage flying gear who has been said to greet workers with a cheery, German-accented "good morning!" when he has been encountered.

Other reports claim that, on certain rainy evenings, if you listen closely, you might hear the muffled voices of men shouting "Away the lines! Away the lines!" and "She's afire!" coming from the tarmac near the hangar.

Is the naval station haunted? Many who have worked here believe that it is. But whether you believe in ghosts or not, the crash of the *Hindenburg* remains a tangible part of the history of the Lakehurst Naval Station that will never be forgotten.

# 1947: OKLAHOMA'S DEADLIEST TORNADO

In Oklahoma, a state that has often been called "the middle of Tornado Alley," the Woodward tornado of April 9, 1947, still ranks as the deadliest storm to ever wreak havoc there. In the wake of the calamity were the bodies of 185 dead, more than one thousand injured, and the lingering haunting of the old Woodward Memorial Hospital.

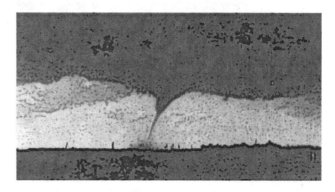

No one saw it coming. The Woodward tornado struck without warning, destroying everything in its path. A few days before, a warm Pacific low-pressure system had come ashore and collided with a large cold front near Amarillo, Texas. Winds just north of Amarillo were clocked at more than one hundred miles per hour. Six major tornadoes dropped out of the storm. One of them, the twister that would eventually ravage Woodward, first touched down near Canadian, Texas. Its base was an incredible two miles across and it stayed that way for the next six hours as it traveled more than one hundred miles across the Texas and Oklahoma plains.

At 7:00 p.m. on April 9, it struck Glazier, Texas, about fourteen miles from Canadian, killing sixteen people and destroying 25 buildings. In nearby Higgins, the tornado destroyed all but three buildings in town. A woman, who had crawled under her bed, believing that she would be safe, was sucked up into the wire bedsprings when the tornado passed over her house. She was one of 45 people killed in Higgins.

Even though Glazier and Higgins were literally wiped off the map, no warning of the approaching storm reached the Oklahoma just across the border from the Texas Panhandle. It was the third day of a national telephone strike and only emergency operators were running the switchboards across the country. Grace Nix and Bertha Wiggins were the operators on duty in Woodward when the first warning call came in. An operator in Shattuck, Oklahoma, less than twenty miles from Higgins, called the women to ask if they were all right. The operator in Shattuck was watching a massive black storm cloud moving toward Woodward. A few minutes later, at 8:00 p.m., another call about the dark cloud came in from Cestos, south of Woodward. Until that moment, no one in Woodward had any idea that they were in danger.

At 8:15 p.m., the tornado leveled the small farming community of Gage, 21 miles southwest of Woodward.

The monster storm tore across western Oklahoma, devouring sixty farmhouses, destroying the small town of Fargo and killing eight more people as it charged northeast toward Woodward.

Meanwhile, in Woodward, it was an ordinary Wednesday evening. Many in town commented on how humid the air was that night, but nothing else seemed strange about the weather. Church services were being held, people were having dinner and downtown, the two movie theaters were filled with high school students. The Woodward Theater was showing an Ingrid Bergman film and the Terry Theater was showing *The Devil on Wheels,* a juvenile delinquent genre film about the dangers of speeding. Down the street, the usual patrons were hanging out at the pool hall and at the high school, the band had just finished practicing for its trip to Alva, Oklahoma, the next day.

Dr. Joe Duer, head physician at the Woodward Hospital, walked into Gill's Café for his ritual cup of coffee as Erwin Walker drove past on his way to work at the power plant on the north side of town. There is no record to say that the two men acknowledged each other on that night, but both of them would go on to play fateful roles in the disaster that followed.

By 8:42 p.m., the wind was starting to blow hard. Large raindrops hit the sidewalks, followed by hail. As the tornado passed over Experimental Lake on the west side of town, it sucked up so much water that the level of the lake dropped by an entire foot.

At the power plant, Erwin Walker was one of the first to actually see the massive tornado bearing down on the town. Live electric lines began to snap all across Woodward. Walker threw the plant's master switch, cutting off the town's power, just as the tornado hit the building head-on. Walker was instantly killed but his quick thinking was later credited for saving countless lives.

At his café, Gill Gillard's attention was drawn to the front windows of the place when he heard the tapping of hail as it hit the sidewalk outside. As several customers peered out, Gillard glanced over at the barometer hanging on the wall – it had bottomed out. Moments later, the lights went out and all of Woodward was plunged into darkness. The only illumination was provided by the violent arcs of lightning that blazed across the sky.

George MacLaren, a regular at the pool hall in town, stayed there most nights until about 11:00 p.m. On this night, he was just walking inside when he saw full-grown trees in the nearby park being pushed over by the wind until they were bent all of the way to the ground. Changing his mind about playing pool, MacLaren hailed a passing taxi and headed for home. The cab was hammered by strong winds as it zigzagged down streets, trying to avoid fallen trees and downed power lines. But when MacLaren reached his home and got out of the taxi, everything was calm – no wind, no rain, no hail. Then he noticed the leaves of the trees were standing straight up, pointing into the night sky. He knew that something was seriously wrong. He ran across his porch and into the house just as the porch enclosure was suddenly torn away.

MacLaren screamed for his children as he ran into the living room. There was a thunderous, roaring sound described by survivors as sounding like a freight train – and he fell to the floor. MacLaren's son, Gayner, saw the

top of the room's walls separate from the ceiling, fall down, and then lift up as the windows imploded. He blacked out and when he came to his senses, he was lying in the front yard with rain pelting his face. His father was standing in the ruins that had been their house, searching for Gayner's younger brother, Merritt, in the rubble.

Just then, a chill swept over them and sleet and snow began to fall from the sky. The shirt that Gayner was wearing was covered in his own blood. He walked over to his father to try and help as the elder MacLaren pulled loose boards from the pile of debris in a panic. He couldn't find his other boy. He looked down at his bloodied son and asked Gayner if he was all right. When the boy nodded, his father immediately sent him off to find help. Gayner began to run toward the large fires that were burning downtown. It was just after 9:00 p.m.

Movie patrons at the Woodward and Terry theaters also heard what sounded like a roaring train, followed by explosions, screams and cries for help. People tried to run out the front doors but were stopped by the theater staff. One man who managed to push his way out of the Terry Theater was picked up by the wind and hurled down the street to his death. As the tornado roared overhead, the roof of the theater collapsed. Moviegoers ducked under the theater seats and the stiff metal backs kept them from being crushed by the falling ceiling. A large air conditioning unit broke through a rear wall and some escaped the ceiling collapse by fleeing out into the storm.

Downtown Woodward was soon burning as factories, warehouses and the grocery store were engulfed in flames. At the high school, several students who stayed late after band practice were killed. Their bodies were later found in the rubble. Trees were ripped out of the ground. Deadly flying debris filled the air, whipping through hail, rain and snow. The streets were filled with bricks, power lines, downed trees and broken bodies. Telephone poles and timber beams were driven into the walls of the Woodward County Courthouse. Above, the black sky pulsed with an unearthly display of eerie lightning.

The tornado leveled one hundred city blocks with winds that ranged from 225 to four hundred and forty miles an hour. After leaving Woodward, it traveled northeast almost 45 miles toward the Kansas border. There were no fatalities along this route, although 36 more homes were destroyed and thirty people were injured. At some point, west of Alva, the Woodward tornado lifted back into the sky and vanished.

Its deadly work was completed.

In Woodward, Dr. Duer tried desperately to organize a hospital that was filling with people, mostly children, who had compound fractures and severe injuries. He had to figure out a way to decide which patients were most in need of urgent care. "It just broke your heart," he said later.

The most serious patients remained at the hospital, while the Baker Hotel was converted into a temporary triage unity for those with minor injuries. The hotel's windows had been blown out by the storm, but the building was structurally sound and there were soon two patients for every bed. There was no running water, however, to clean wounds, wash patients or even to flush the toilets. Everyone was covered with mud from Experimental Lake, which had blown all over the town by the storm. One girl's eyes were so heavily caked with mud that her optic nerve was pinched, leaving her blind for several weeks.

Duer saw some horrific cases that day. An infant who died early in the night was covered with splinters of wood that had embedded themselves in her body. He was called to a house across the street from the hospital during the night to see a badly injured young woman. She had been impaled with a two-by-four and did not survive the night. The hospital's front lawn was transformed into a temporary morgue after trucks began driving up and down the streets, collecting the dead.

A young mother of two, named Thelma Irwin, had a close call with the temporary morgue. When the tornado hit, her husband, Raymond, was asleep on the living room couch. He grabbed their young son, Joe, and held him to the floor. Thelma had just run into the bedroom, where their baby girl, Jennifer, was sleeping when the tornado hurled a milk truck through the wall of the house. The next thing she remembered, someone was washing her face off with milk as she lay on her front lawn. She closed her eyes for what she thought was only a moment and felt the sensation of being lifted. When she opened her eyes again, she discovered that she was surrounded by dead bodies. She tried to scream but she couldn't and then she lost consciousness again. When Thelma Irwin woke again, she was lying among the rows of the dead on the front lawn of the hospital. She was still unable to speak but she managed to get the attention of a passing nurse. Thelma later remembered the nurse saying, "I don't think this woman's dead."

Later that night, rescuers found a bloody, confused and frightened Gayner MacLaren roaming the streets. As he was taken to the hospital, he kept crying, "My brother's trapped! My brother's trapped!" Eventually, a nurse had to sedate him. He woke up on a cot around 3:00 a.m. with a bandage around his head and a pool of blood drying beneath him. A person he knew who was lying on a nearby cot told him that his brother Merritt had died.

And poor Merritt was far from alone. Scores of people had died. The pool hall where George MacLaren had planned to spend the evening had been leveled. The five men inside were so badly mangled that they could only be identified by their wristwatches. An elderly woman, a Mrs. Chance, had been sucked out of her home and was found in a nearby field, rolled in barbed wire. Her husband, Daniel, was killed. Mrs. Chance's granddaughter, who had come to Woodward to visit her, was still in the house but was covered in wooden planks that were held to her body by nails.

A Mrs. Boattmann was on her way to the hospital to volunteer when she saw a baby's arm sticking up from the mud on the side of the road. When she saw the hand move, she quickly dug up the baby and ran home. She was able to get her into the sink, where she washed the mud from the child's eyes, ears and mouth.

Another little girl, also covered in mud, was brought to Wilma Nelson's home. She wrapped the child in a blanket and tried to rock her to sleep, only to have the child scream in terror every time a boom of thunder was heard. When dawn finally came, Wilma decided to wash the mud off the girl with dishwater that was still in the sink. When she did, she discovered that the child's skin with filled with wooden splinters. She rushed her to the hospital only to be told by a nurse that she had to wait: there were more critical injuries to deal with. Wilma held the girl for hours until a doctor was finally able to see her.

The wire chief for the telephone service in town, L.L. Orel, along with Carl Brown, traced down the lines south of Woodward for three miles before being able to send word to Oklahoma City about the devastation. Eight of the striking telephone workers reported to work to help with the crisis; a week later, the union dismissed all eight of them.

As with all tornadoes, the storm that came through Woodward left oddities in its wake. Hundreds of chickens roamed the town without feathers. A milk bottle was found sitting upright on the back steps to a house that was no longer there. The grown children of Sam and Jessie Smith made their way through what had been downtown Woodward, expecting the worst. The Smith home was at the center of the destruction – but they found it untouched. Sam and Jessie were just waking up. Both of them were hard of hearing and were unaware that the tornado had even taken place.

Assistance began to arrive in Woodward as three inches of snow blanketed the town. With telephone lines down, local Boy Scouts delivered messages around town on their bikes. Bulldozers were brought in to remove the remains of what had been homes and businesses just 48 hours earlier. The Woodward Army Air base, which had been closed down after the war, was re-opened for housing and was soon dubbed "Tornado Town." Barracks were divided into apartments. Families stood watch over the rubble of their homes to prevent looting. One man

## 10 MOST DEADLY AMERICAN TORNADOES

1. Killed: 695, Injured: 2,027 - Mar. 18, 1925 - The Tri-State Tornado - MO, IL, IN
2. Killed: 317, Injured: 109 - May 7, 1840 - The Great Natchez Tornado - Natchez, MS (Note: slave deaths were not counted)
3. Killed: 271, Injured: 3,000 - Apr. 11, 1965 - Palm Sunday Tornados - 37 funnels in IA, WI, MI, IN, OH
4. Killed: 269, Injured: 1,874 - Mar. 21, 1932 - AL Tornados
5. Killed: 240-250, Injured: 1,000 - May 27, 1896 - St. Louis, MO, East St. Louis, IL
6. Killed: 233, Injured: 700 - Apr. 5, 1936 - The Tupelo Tornado - Tupelo, MS (Note: African American deaths were not counted)
7. Killed: 203, Injured: 1,600 - Apr. 6, 1936 - Gainesville, GA
8. Killed: 181, Injured: 980 - Apr. 9, 1947 - Southern Plains Tri-State Tornados - TX, OK, KS
9. Killed: 192, Injured: 770 - Apr. 24, 1908 - Swarm in AL, LA and S
10. Killed: 116, Injured: 200 - May 12, 1899 - New Richmond, WI

who was caught stealing from the ruins of a house was jailed for eighteen hours and then driven fifteen miles from town and told to start walking. Badly injured people were flown to Oklahoma City, while less serious cases were loaded onto trains and transported in freight cars to the hospital in Alva.

Two of the tornado victims were never identified: a blonde girl of about twelve who bit her fingernails and a six-week-old baby girl. Some speculated that they had been carried from Texas by the power of the storm.

The biggest mystery surrounding the Woodward tornado turned out to be the disappearance of a little girl named Joan Gay Croft. On the day of the tornado, Joan was taken to the hospital with a pencil-size splinter of wood embedded in her thigh. Her family had been scattered by the storm. Her mother, Cleta, a telephone operator, had been killed when the tornado struck the Croft home. Her stepfather, Olen, was so badly injured that he was taken to Oklahoma City. Her half-sister, Jerri, was also at the hospital and after a frantic search, the girls' aunt found the two girls there. Leaving them in the care of the hospital staff, the aunt then went to volunteer at the hospital in Moreland, ten miles to the east, where many Woodward victims had been taken.

On the night after the storm, two men dressed in khaki Army uniforms came to the hospital and asked for Joan. As they carried her out, a staff member later remembered hearing Joan crying that she didn't want to leave her sister behind. One of the men told her not to worry and promised they would come back for the other girl. Joan's protests got the attention of several staff members who challenged the men. One of them said that they were friends of the family and that they were simply taking Joan to another hospital, where family members were waiting. The men were allowed to leave with the little girl – and little Joan Croft was never seen again.

Even though he had not yet fully recovered from his injuries, Olen Croft hurried back to Woodward when he learned that Joan was missing. He and Joan's grandfather, Raymond Goble, went from town to town posting fliers and placing missing person ads in local newspapers and on radio stations. Goble died a short time later of a massive heart attack, but Olen spent the next forty years searching one small town after another, following tips and rumors about where Joan might be. He died in 1986, broken-hearted and still obsessed with finding the lost girl.

In 1994, the television series *Unsolved Mysteries* featured a story about Joan Croft. Within 48 hours, Joan's aunt received more than two hundred telephone calls with potential leads about the long-lost girl's whereabouts. One of them seemed promising: a woman living in Phoenix, Arizona, who had the same blood type as Joan and even had a scar on her leg where Joan had been injured during the tornado. A Croft family member stayed with the woman for two weeks and became convinced that she was Joan. Sadly, a DNA test later showed that she was not related to the Crofts.

The Croft family never speculated publicly about the identities of the two men who took Joan from the hospital, or why they might have taken her. Some believed that perhaps she was kidnapped for ransom, although a ransom demand never came. Olen Croft was not a wealthy man, but he was doing better than a lot of other people in town at the time. He likely would have paid a ransom if one had ever been demanded. Others believed that perhaps Joan's mother's family might have taken her after learning that Cleta had been killed in the storm. This theory would explain how the men knew Joan by name and why they took her and not her half-sister. The Woodward authorities, and Olen Croft, questioned Cleta's family, but there was nothing to suggest that they had any idea about what had become of the girl. What happened to Joan Gay Croft remains a mystery to this day.

The Woodward Hospital, which saw so much pain and suffering during the tornado, was only used for about three years after the storm. The massive number of injured people who descended on the place after the devastation in town proved that the old, 28-bed hospital was outdated and sadly obsolete. In 1950, a new, modern hospital was erected and the original building passed into the hands of private owners. It still stands in Woodward today, although it had been abandoned for many years.

It's abandoned, but some say it's not empty.

Over the years, there have been many reports of a haunting at the old hospital. Voices have been heard in the deserted rooms and corridors, faces have been seen peering out the windows and the apparitions of small children have been spotted both inside and outside the structure. They reportedly vanish whenever they are approached. Many of the owners of the building have had their own experiences, including many who purchased the property where the former hospital stands and who did not believe in anything as frivolous as ghosts. They quickly became believers that something very strange was going on in the old building that stood in their backyard.

Numerous ghost hunters have investigated and spent the night in the hospital and many of them leave the next morning with eerie tales to tell, from mysterious shapes on video to disembodied voices imprinted on their recordings. And while many hospitals allegedly become haunted because of the trauma experienced and the lives lost within their walls, the old Woodward hospital seems to fit into a category all its own -- a haunting reminder of the deadliest day in Oklahoma's history.

# 1948: THE DONORA DEATH FOG

"Smoke means money." That mantra was repeated up and down the Monongahela River Valley throughout the first half of the twentieth century. Sadly, for Donora, Pennsylvania, in 1948, smoke also meant death.

For nearly one hundred years, two words had defined southwest Pennsylvania: coal and steel. For a select few, these two words meant vast wealth, the level of which had rarely been seen before in America. But for everyone else, the stout, hard-working residents of this region, these words meant long hours of hard work under very hazardous working conditions and a shortened life expectancy. However, coal and steel also meant the possibility of achieving the American Dream, of having their own homes and providing food and clothing for their families. As long as smoke billowed across the sky, they would be all right --- or so they thought.

In the 1940s, southwest Pennsylvania was sprinkled with hundreds of small towns, nestled in the foothills of the Allegheny Mountains. Many of these were "patch towns," clusters of houses constructed around coal mines by coal companies to house the miners and their families. This region sat on some of the richest veins of bituminous coal in the world. Today, very few of these patch towns are inhabited by miners and many exist solely in the memories of the "old timers." Coal mining no longer requires the huge numbers of workers it once did and the demand for coal has diminished drastically over the years.

But in the 1940s, the hills were still lined with coal patch towns, looking down on rivers that were lined with mill towns. These towns were filled, not with miners, but with mill workers who kept the steel mills and their support industries in production around the clock, seven days a week. The massive amounts of coal and thousands of gallons of water needed to produce coke and steel made this region, along the rivers banks, a logical place to build, with most of the main ingredients right at hand - and all that water.

Winding its way through these coal-laden hills is the Monongahela River, lovingly known to locals as the

"Mon." This unusual, north-flowing river runs from West Virginia until it reaches Pittsburgh, where it joins with the Allegheny River to form the Ohio River before heading west. The Mon is an old river, with twists and turns and deep horseshoe bends, making it ideal for the infrastructure of making and processing steel.

In 1900, R. B. Mellon's American Steel & Wire Co. (a U.S. Steel subsidiary) broke ground in a bowl-shaped site inside one of the Mon's horseshoe bends to build an iron mill just thirty miles south of Pittsburgh. Soon, people seeking work, including a large number of Eastern European immigrants, flocked to the new mill to fulfill the labor needs. Within a year, enough workers and their families had arrived to incorporate the town of Donora. The mills continued to expand and immigrants continued to arrive to work the mills. Soon, Donora was home to one of the largest mill complexes in the country, employing over 6,500 people. For nearly fifty years, the town's sole purpose for existing was to supply workers for those mills. The rest of the town's population existed to support the mill workers and developing community.

There were now several rod mills, rolling mills, wire mills, a billet

**The Donora Steel Mill**

An aerial view of the Donora zinc smelting plant

mill, a coking plant, steam engines, open- hearth furnaces and the largest train depot south of Pittsburgh. The furnaces alone had the capability of producing one hundred and ten tons of steel per heat, or batch, of steel. On an average day, the mills consumed 45 train carloads of iron ore, forty cars of coke (coal baked at incredible temperatures to remove the oils), six cars of limestone and six cars of various other materials. The Donora mills burned more coal daily than all the homes in Pittsburgh combined. Every mill operation produced thick, unfiltered smoke. The raw materials consumed by the mills were transported to Donora with coal-fired barges on the river or coal-fired locomotives, all producing even more smoke. No one ever questioned whether all that smoke could make people sick as long as they had jobs and could put food on the table.

The waters of the Mon were as abused as the skies. Water was sucked from the river to flush impurities, clean dirty raw materials, and quench the coke. It was then returned to the river, unfiltered and laden with tons of pollutants. As a result, nothing lived in the Mon.

In 1920, a few farmers from the town of Webster, across the river from Donora, tried to sue the mills for crop losses and the deaths of hundreds of head of livestock; they were unsuccessful. The effects of air pollution were still unknown to most and impossible to prove by others – but at least some were starting to take notice.

Oxygen is the enemy of steel. Protecting steel from rust caused by oxygen became extremely important.

The zinc plant's smokestacks issued fluoride gas, sulphur dioxide and a variety of particulates in the smoke.

Hills surrounded the Donora works

Houses were built right next to the mills and were frequently engulfed with smoke.

Dipping the steel elements such as nails and wire in molten zinc, known as galvanizing, did the trick. In 1915, Donora received a great gift. The world's largest zinc smelting plant was to be built on 45 acres along the Monongahela River. Smoke from the zinc plant was added to the smoke from the steel mills and coking plant.

The nearly 14,000 residents of Donora were accustomed to the smoke. It had been their daily companion since the first mill was fired up. Living in a river valley meant that they were also very used to fog, but that was not much of a problem as it usually burned off a few hours after the sun rose - usually.

Life in Donora was hard, and work in the mills was harder. People were mostly young but seemed to age uncommonly fast. Strong, healthy people were sickly invalids by the time they reached their fifties. Lung and heart disease were commonplace for anyone lucky enough to get past that age. Oxygen tanks were typical accessories in many households.

The hills surrounding Donora are steep, so steep that many of the streets have stairs instead of sidewalks. The hills are also very high, most between four hundred and six hundred feet. The smokestacks at the mills were only about sixty feet tall, far too low to clear the hilltops. The hillsides surrounding the zinc plant were completely barren. Nothing would grow there. Houses under the zinc plant's smoke plume could only grow gardens on the sides facing away from the plant, if at all.

There was always a layer of soot on everything. A freshly washed car in the evening would be covered with grime by morning. On window washing day, the first window that had been washed sparkling clean was dirty again by the time the last window was finished. Curtains were washed every week and plastic covered every piece of upholstered furniture. Venetian blinds became popular because they could be wiped down. When snow fell, it was gray by the time it reached the ground and shortly after it stopped falling, there would be a layer of dark gray soot on top. People who drove in the late afternoon needed to turn on their headlights, hours before sunset. Some people continued to live in their basements even after their ground floor had been built - just to keep it clean.

The men typically had two jobs. After they left work at the mills, they went home to work on their houses. Since the steel mill companies didn't provide housing for their workers, the men bought small lots and built their own. They first built a basement with concrete block-lined walls. The family lived there until they could save up enough money to build a floor above ground. People with skilled positions and higher wages might even have houses with a second story. Bigger houses were needed to provide for parents, brothers, sisters and cousins who were coming from the old country to fill more positions in the mills. Similar stories could be told of the mill towns up and down the Mon Valley. Donora was unique in only one respect - the zinc smelting plant.

Despite their hardships, the people of Donora were immensely proud of their community. There were 22 churches and a synagogue, six schools and one hundred and 135 cultural and civic clubs. They met, fell in love, married and raised their children. They cheered on their local sports teams every weekend and at least one of their baseball teams was playing somewhere nearly every summer evening. They visited their neighbors and cared for their sick. After dark, during fair weather, they sat on their porches admiring the spectacular display as impurities in the molten iron popped and spat in the open-hearth furnaces, sending sparks shooting into the sky. For the most part, their lives echoed those of millions of hard working families all over the country.

Sports were especially important. An unusually large number of athletes for such a small town went on to achieve national fame. Stan Musial, who played for the St. Louis Cardinals, grew up in Donora. Also calling Donora home were Arnold "Pope" Galiffa, All American quarterback for West Point in 1949 and "Deacon Dan" Towler, of the Los Angeles Rams. Ken Griffey, Sr. was another hometown athlete. He went on to play for the Cincinnati Reds and was considered to be the second-fastest runner in baseball.

The years ticked by and life went on as usual. Fogs rolled in and burned off. The sky ran gray. The river ran brown.

Wednesday, October 27, 1948, started out like any other day. Unsuspecting residents went about their business while a rare weather phenomenon was developing over the Mon River Valley. A thermal inversion was causing a mass of warm, stagnant air to become trapped by a dense mass of cold air. As a result, a thick fog formed all along the valley. Fogs were common along the river so no one paid much attention. It would burn off soon - it always did.

This time was different, though. The inversion had stalled, and rather than dissipating, the fog stayed put. People went to bed that night without worry, expecting everything would be back to normal the next day. It wasn't. The following morning the fog was still there, and it seemed to be getting worse.

Pollutants from the mills' smokestacks were mixing with the fog, causing a thick, choking smog. The fog kept the pollutants close to the ground and people complained that the air tasted bad. By noon, the thickening smog had so darkened the sky that it was as if night had fallen. That evening, a few workers actually got lost trying to get home from work. Again, people went to bed without too much concern. After all, it was just fog and smoke and that could not be harmful.

The mills continued working at full capacity.

Friday, October 29, dawned much the same. It remained dark with smog all day. Still, people tried to go on with their lives as best they could. The annual children's Halloween parade was planned for that afternoon and it went on as scheduled. Halloween only comes once a year and no one wanted to disappoint the children. Spectators described how eerie it was as the costumed children slowly appeared, then vanished into the mist as they made their way along the two-block parade route.

Attorney Arnold Hirsh described what he saw, "The air looked yellow, never like that before. Nothing moved. ...looking down towards the river, you could just barely see the railroad tracks. Right there on the tracks was a coal burning engine puffing away. It issued a big blast of black smoke that went up about six feet in the air and stopped cold. It just hung there, with no place to go, in air that did not move."

People were starting to get sick. Dr. William Rongans, a member of the Donora Board of Health, and the other town doctors started making house calls. They went from door to door, treating anyone they could. Dr. Rongans recommended that everyone with any type of heart or lung disorder should leave town immediately. He later recalled leading the ambulance on foot through the smog to the hospital or to the temporary morgue that had been set up in the basement of the community center.

By Friday night, people had started leaving town. It was slow going as the roads out of town were congested with traffic and smog. Some said that the only way they could drive was to hang their head out of the window and to let the car wheels scrape along the curb. Area hospitals began to fill with Donora residents. They arrived

**Photo taken in the early afternoon on October 28, 1948. It is full daylight but the streetlights are on and it looks like nighttime.**

with crushing headaches, stomach cramps and vomiting. Some were so seriously ill that they were gasping for breath and coughing up blood.

Although the townspeople were worried when they went to bed that night, most had no idea how bad things really were. They thought surely the fog will have lifted and the smog will be gone by morning....

And the mills continued operating at full capacity.

On Saturday, October 30, Donora was still engulfed in the same stinking soup. The smog was thickening with sulfur dioxide, soluble sulphants and fluoride gas. Routines were apparently hard to break so the high school football game between the Donora Dragons and their rivals from Monogalela High scheduled for that afternoon went on as planned. It was difficult for spectators to keep track of what was happening on the field since they were only able to follow the action by listening for the referees' whistles. It was equally difficult for the players. Footballs were thrown or kicked and the players were unable to see where they went or find them when they landed. John "Chummy" Lignelli, who attended the game remembered, "You couldn't' identify the ballplayers. You could see movement on the field but you didn't know who had the ball and what was going on. But we stayed and watched."

During the game, the announcer called for the family of Bernardo DiSanzi to return home immediately. Unbeknown to them, their father had just died. A short time later, another announcement came over the loudspeaker ordering Donora's star tight end, Stanley Sawa, to "Go home. Go home now." The player left the field and ran home in full pads and uniform. His father had become desperately ill. The doctor was with him when Stanley arrived, but he was too late. His father was dead. After the game, spectators learned that nine people had died by 10:00 a.m. that morning.

Fire bells rang throughout that afternoon. Firemen were being called to take tanks of oxygen to people who were having difficulty breathing. Area hospitals had sent oxygen tanks to Donora but they were still very limited, and there weren't nearly enough for all who were in need. They lugged the heavy tanks through the town, feeling their way from house to house, delivering relief to those who needed it. Unfortunately, as the number of tanks were so limited, they were only able to give each suffering individual three or four breaths from the tank before having to move on to the next house.

Bill Schempp, then a Donora volunteer fireman, described what it was like by Saturday afternoon, "If you chewed hard enough, you could swallow it. It almost got to the point where it was claustrophobic, it was so thick. You couldn't see a thing. You had to get right up to the door and guess where you were. It sounds dramatic but without exaggeration, that's the way it was."

After a time, it became far too dangerous for the firemen to be out and they were sent home to be with their families and wait out the fog.

Dr. Rongans was still working around the clock, answering as many calls for help as he could. He began telling everyone who would listen that they needed to leave town as soon as they could, whether they were sick or not. Unfortunately, by mid-afternoon on Saturday the roads were so clogged with abandoned cars and smog that they were closed. Those still in town were now trapped with no means of escape.

John Gnora's wife, Suzanne, was extremely ill and he was unable to move her, much less get her out of town. "She was weak. That smoke was awful bad," he recalled. Gnora sat by her bed and watched helplessly as his wife coughed and gasped for hours before she died.

Palmer Park sat high on a hilltop, overlooking the smog-choked town. This park was one of the only green spaces in the area. Because the smoke from the mills rarely blew over the park, grass was able to grow there. Several families decided to try to get to the park, which sat high above the smog. Those who were able to get there seemed to feel better

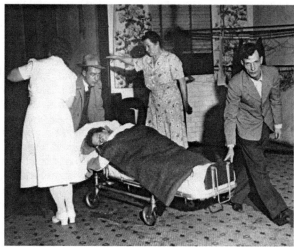

**Smog victim being taken into a local hospital**

shortly after arriving. Decades later, Dr. Rongaus remembered how he and his brother "hauled women and children in horse-drawn wagons up to the park. Soon as we got them above the smog, they would get much better."

Church volunteers from nearby towns began bringing food and blankets to the park for the families who were camping there. The remainder of the residents, unable to leave town or get to the park, shut themselves in their houses, sealing up their doors and windows as best they could. It was Saturday night and the streets of Donora were completely deserted.

On Saturday evening, Walter Winchell, the famous radio personality, started his broadcast with his customary "Good evening America," then proceeded to describe the killer fog – calling it a weather phenomenon and an act of God -- bringing national attention to the plight of the people of Donora. All of America was now focused on the tiny Pennsylvania town.

And the mills continued operating at full capacity.

The massive thermal inversion that had caused all this trouble had descended on the Mon River Valley, stretching for miles, yet no one had died outside of Donora and Webster, which was just across the river. Even though there were several steel mills and coking plants all along the river, no one else was dying. The difference that made the fog so deadly in that area was the zinc smelting plant.

Finally, at about 3:00 a.m. on Sunday, October 31st, Roger Blough, then the chief counsel for the American Steel and Wire Company, called Michael Neale, the superintendent of the zinc works. He ordered Neale to dead fire the furnace without any zinc ore. If the fire heating a zinc smelter were ever to be extinguished completely, the smelter would cool and break itself apart, effectively destroying the furnace. A "dead fire" was a fire maintained just to keep the furnace hot, without any molten zinc. Neale, upset with the inconvenience the dead fire would cause, and believing that the zinc plant was not the cause of the deaths, ignored the order for three more hours, until a team of company chemists arrived at the plant and he was forced to comply.

After the zinc furnace was dead fired, the levels of toxins in the fog remained just as they were – neither declining nor increasing. All day Sunday the smoke-filled fog continued to smother the town and the streets remained deserted. Everyone had either left town, escaped to Palmer Park, or had sealed themselves in their houses. No one dared to venture out.

However, by late afternoon on Sunday, everything was about to change. It started to rain. By the time it stopped raining, the air was cleaned of toxins and the fog was finally gone. The crisis had ended -- but not without a huge loss. Eighteen people from Donora and two from Webster were dead. Fifty more people were dead within the next month. Six thousand people had been seriously sickened. Over eight hundred family pets and livestock animals were dead. Houseplants and gardens were dead. Donora had spent five days in hell and had paid a heavy toll.

On Monday, the very next day, the zinc plant was fired up and was back to full capacity by the next week.

Officially, the American Steel & Wire Company and U.S. Steel formally denied any responsibility for the Donora smog, claiming the event an "act of God." Oddly, this statement of cause had already been pronounced by the great Walter Winchell to the American people so it was easy to sway the convictions of the local workers. Behind closed doors, however, they settled several lawsuits out of court for the deaths that had occurred.

The first twenty people to die were buried on Tuesday. The day dawned clear and bright. Funeral-goers commented to each other that it was the clearest day they had seen in years, maybe even decades. The sky was blue and the clouds were white. Prevailing winds blew the smoke away from the cemetery that day.

It was time to start forgetting, although many would instead use the word "denying." Many people, such as Dr. Rongaus, used angry words like, "It was murder from the mills" and started talking about moving the zinc works, but most were not so quick to call for action. Michael Duda, a zinc worker and city council member announced during a meeting that, "I got a darn good job and I'm going to keep it, I don't care what it kills." This sentiment was echoed across Donora. LIFE Magazine published a photo-article on November 15 and it was noted that, "Although four groups were investigating the deadly source, Donorans were cautious about getting tough with the industry that provided their living." The smog became a deep, dark secret that no one wanted to talk about for decades to come.

President Harry Truman ordered a study to be conducted by the Public Health Service (PHS) into the deadly events that occurred in Donora. The steelworkers union also paid for a $10,000 study of the event. Extensive studies were conducted, including X-rays of the dead, tissue analysis and air samples. To this day, the records from both studies, neither of which were released, have ever been found. Records of the study conducted by U.S. Steel were sealed and were never been released to the public.

The PHS report was released in 1949, stating that no one substance caused the Donora deaths and the blame was determined to be the stalled temperature inversion. Industrial consultant Philip Sadtler, then considered to be a leading expert on fluorine pollution, including investigations stemming from the Manhattan Project's development of the atom bomb, was very vocal about the PHS report, calling it a "whitewash." During an interview in 1996, not long before his death, he was asked about Donora. "It was murder. The directors of U.S. Steel should have gone to jail for killing people." He further explained that he believed that the PHS report aided U.S. Steel in avoiding costly liability for the deaths and also allowed a variety of other fluoride polluting industries to continue unabated.

There were other questions. The zinc works had been in operation for over thirty years and nothing like this had ever happened. True, plants and livestock had been killed, but up until that point, no people had died. Was there something different about the zinc that had been smelted that week? Was it possible that this had been some sort of experiment with intended or unintended results? The answers to these questions will never be known because as soon as the fog cleared, orders came down Pittsburgh to get the heat out of town immediately. By "heat", they meant all the zinc that was in the smelter at the time of the disaster. What happened to that heat, no one knew, or at least no one was saying.

---

## DEATH IN DONORA

Dan Hoffman, folklorist, received this ballad from Donora resident John P. Clark:

### Death in Donora

I have felt the fog in my throat --
The misty hand of Death caress my face;
I have wrestled with a frightful foe
Who strangled me with wisps of gray fog-lace.
Now in my eyes since I have died.
The bleak, bare hills rise in stupid might
With scars of its slavery imbedded deep;
And the people still live -- still live --
in the poisonous night.

The University of Cincinnati conducted its own study of the tragedy in 1948. The resulting report predicted that if the fog had lasted 24 to 48 hours longer, thousands would have died.

Though everyone who lost his or her life lived within one-half mile of the zinc plant, the only definitive evidence of the cause came decades later. The body of a victim who had died in the first few days of the fog was exhumed. Tissue tests revealed lethal levels of toxic fluoride gas - as much as twenty times higher than normal.

In the 1950s the demand for American steel began a steep decline. The zinc furnaces were shut down for good in 1957, leaving three hundred men out of work. By the time the coal-fired plant closed, it had been outdated for decades. Modern zinc smelters all had gas or electric furnaces, making them much cleaner and more economical. Even so, some people in Donora were bitter, blaming the closing of the plant on negative publicity from the killer smog.

View of the Donora mills from the cemetery. This cemetery was located under the mill's smoke bloom, making it impossible to grow grass over the graves of the people who had given their lives to the mills.

By the time the last remnants of the old steel mill were shut down in 1967, the last 825 workers of the original 6,500 were laid off. Donora found itself with fifty percent unemployment across the entire population. That would not last, however. With the majority of people out of work, there was no money to spend and no place to go. The downtown area became a near ghost town, with row upon row of empty storefronts. Soon, almost no one was employed and those who were had to drive a great distance every day to get to new jobs. There were few reasons to stay in Donora and the rapid influx of people that had occurred at the beginning of the century began to reverse itself. Just sixty years later, Donora had become a place to leave. By 2000, nearly 63 percent of Donora's population had gone.

There is a silver lining to this story. Ironically, Donora's blinding smog opened the eyes of the general public to how dangerous air pollution could be. Soon after the fog cleared, a string of state air quality laws were passed culminating in the passage of the nation's first Clean Air Act of 1970. Many experts attribute the start of the environmental movement with the pollution disaster that occurred there.

The skies over Donora and the entire Monongahela River Valley are now clear and bright, unobstructed by smoke. The hillsides are covered with thick, lush vegetation. The Mon runs blue again and life abounds within its waters.

An environmental legacy was not the only remembrance left behind by the killer fog. Bits and pieces of those who lived and worked in Donora remain. Fog continues to roll in and roll out, as it does all along the Mon Valley, but the fog in Donora is a bit different. It no longer carries toxins and pollutants, but it does have its secrets.

A leisurely stroll along the streets on a foggy night may find you with some unexpected company. For over thirty years, countless numbers of people have described seeing shadowy figures appear in the mist and then disappear again, without the slightest sound. These figures typically appear to be adults and reportedly have never interacted with or acknowledged the presence of the living witnesses. These shadowy women and men seem to be lumbering along as if in distress, walking with difficulty and somewhat hunched over. Some believe these are the spirits of Donorans, trying to find their way home in the fog, just as they did in October of 1948.

Palmer Park is the location of other reported hauntings. Visitors to the park frequently report feeling uneasy or having a chill run up their backs. Strange sounds can be heard coming just behind a tree or bush -- often described as a coughing or wheezing sound. Cold spots are a common occurrence, even on the hottest days.

An interesting incident happened in Palmer Park in the late 1960s. "Joe," a veteran police officer, had worked in and around Donora for quite some time. He was on patrol one early evening in late October, just about dusk when he decided to swing up through Palmer Park to check for kids up to mischief. When he got to the park, he noticed a small cluster of people sitting on the ground about one hundred yards from the road. This seemed odd and he decided to check it out. When he got to where the people were, he found what appeared to be a family, sitting or lying about on blankets on the ground. There were two little girls, both of whom seemed to be ill; coughing and curled up into balls. "Joe" described what he saw: "They were just a cute as could be but their color was just awful. Come to think of it, the whole family looked a little the worse for wear." Seeing no car in the area, he tried to talk them into riding back into town with him in the police car but the father flatly refused, insisting they were safer where they were.

Worried about the children and the chilly night air, "Joe" decided that he would walk back to his patrol car and radio in to the station to see if he could get some help for the family. About halfway back to the car, he decided to try one more time to talk them into coming with him. Upon turning back, he was astonished to see that the grassy area where the family had been was completely deserted. There was no one anywhere in sight and there hadn't been enough time for them to have hidden.

Quite shaken up by the incident, "Joe" sat in the patrol car until he felt calm again and decided that this was one police call that he was going to keep to himself. Could this family have possibly taken refuge in Palmer Park, just as they had in 1948? We will never know for sure but so far as anyone knows, they have never returned to that grassy knoll, high on a hill in Palmer Park, just out of reach of the fog.

# 1972: GHOSTS OF FLIGHT 401

On the cold winter's night of December 29, 1972, Eastern Airlines aircraft number 310 waited in a dimly lit jet runway outside of New York's John F. Kennedy International Airport's Terminal One. It was set to take off that night at 9:00 p.m., bound for Miami. But unknown to the crew and passengers on board, the plane would never arrive.

When it departed that night, it was designated Flight 401 – a name that has since become one of the most famous aircraft flights in the annals of the supernatural.

The plane that became Flight 401 was a new Lockheed L-1011 Tristar, the pride of Eastern's fleet. It stood as tall as a five-story building and Eastern's version of the aircraft was designed to carry 229 passengers. As far as the company was concerned, the new Tristar planes were the most comfortable aircraft ever built. They boasted eight-foot ceilings, indirect lighting, individual temperature control, music headsets and the kind of comfort that could be found in most living rooms. A chandelier decorated the front of the airplane and there was a standup, padded bar in the back. Perhaps the most interesting feature of the L-1011 was the kitchen, which was equipped to server dinner for more than three hundred people. It was tucked away below decks, accessible by two elevators from the main cabin.

Aircraft 310 was one of a dozen L-1011s that Lockheed had delivered to Eastern Airlines that year. They were excellent aircraft but their design, manufacture and maintenance were not without problems. While the fleet was being built by Lockheed, Rolls Royce, the manufacturer of the engines, faltered under the pressure of the development costs and

**A photograph taken of Aircraft 301 in St. Louis, a few weeks before the crash.**

went bankrupt. This forced the project behind schedule and it went into financial disarray. When the new airplanes were finally delivered to Eastern in the spring of 1972, they were plagued with problems, particularly in the new advanced engines. The L-1011s were constantly taken out of service for maintenance that winter but Aircraft 301 seemed to have fewer bugs than the other planes. Lockheed delivered it on August 18 and it was put into service on August 21. By December 29, it had been flying for only a little over four months. It had been regularly maintained and the current flight log showed only minor issues. There had been no entries for more than sixty days complaining of trouble with the landing gear. Altogether, the aircraft had made five hundred and two landings, including the one that had brought it into JFK earlier that evening when it had flown in from Tampa. Routine service was carried out on the plane at 7:43 p.m. and the flight dispatcher cleared the plane for a 9:00 p.m. departure to Miami as Flight 401.

The engineer and second officer for Flight 401 was Donald Luis Repo, a 51-year-old pilot who had worked for Eastern Airlines for 25 years. He was a native of Massachusetts, now living in Miami. He had gone to sleep early the night before because he was trying to shake off a cold. When he awoke, he flew to Tampa, where he boarded Aircraft 310 for the flight to New York. He was flying back to Florida with the same crew.

One of the duties of the flight engineer is to board the plane early, before the captain and first officer, and go through a checklist that made sure the plane was equipped with various items like spare light bulbs, a first aid kit, rain repellant, smoke goggles, a hand ax, and other things. Repo would also fill out the takeoff data card, which had to match the weight limits on the manifest. The manifest listed nine passengers in the forward cabin and 144 in the rear, with a total of 153 in all. As it turned out, there would be one hundred and sixty actually on board. For balancing purposes, it was estimated that each passenger weighed an average of one hundred and seventy pounds, which figured out to be a total payload, with luggage and freight of almost 35,000 pounds. The manifest, despite the fact that there was a miscount on the passenger number, was meticulously detailed. Four hundred pounds were also added for the additional men who would occupy the flight deck jump seats during the trip. Warren

**(Left to Right) Capt. Bob Loft, Albert Stockstill, Donald Repo**

Terry, a co-pilot, and Angelo Donadeo, a maintenance specialist, were off-duty airline employees who were "dead-heading" – airline slang for employees hitching a ride as they returned from a duty assignment.

Flight 401 was in the very capable hands of Captain Robert Loft, a tall, trim 55 year old who had been working for Eastern Airlines for 32 years. He was comfortable and relaxed before takeoff, having flown the route many times before. He was in great health and had spent the morning working in his yard in Plantation, Florida.

First Officer Albert Stockstill occupied the co-pilot seat on the right side of the cockpit during takeoff. He was a former Air Force pilot and a native of Louisiana who now lived in Miami. Stockstill had even more flying time in the L-1011 than Loft. He had slept late that morning and after getting up, had spent a couple of hours in his home workshop building a light airplane.

The crew started the engines and at 9:20 p.m., words came from the tower that it was their turn to take off. Once on the runway, Stockstill released the brakes, applied thrust and Aircraft 310 rolled forward and gathered speed for nearly a mile down the runway. Loft rested his hands on the thrust levers with the assurance of a man who had done this many, many times before. As captain, he was the final authority on whether the takeoff was aborted, or the plane left the runway. Everything was fine with the flight, he decided, and the jet soared upward into the night sky.

Flight 410 flew south over Norfolk, Virginia, over Wilmington, North Carolina, and then out over the Atlantic. When the airplane passed east of Jacksonville, Florida, it would be 155 miles out to sea. A computer-stored flight plan would bring Flight 401 inland over West Palm Beach, and then south to Miami.

The flight attendant crew on board Aircraft 310 was a close-knit, fun-loving group of young women. Their uniforms in the winter of 1972 were dark brown, beige and powder blue. Flight attendants had the option of wearing skirts, slacks or shorts with boots that zipped to the knee. The senior flight attendant on Flight 401 wore blue shorts with her brown boots. Her name was Adrienne Hamilton, age 27. The pretty, slender Texan had been flying with Eastern for five years.

The day's trip was a quick turnaround for the flight attendants: Miami to New York and then back to Miami. The crew had checked into Eastern's in-flight office at Miami International at 3:35 p.m., and by 11:50 p.m., they were schedule to be off-duty. From Miami to New York, the ten women flight attendants few on Flight 26, a dinner flight. At JFK, they changed planes to work Flight 410. Flight 26 had arrived late into JFK and Adrienne and her crew had only 23 minutes to get from one plane to another. They almost missed Flight 401.

Immediately after takeoff, Warren Terry, the dead-heading pilot who occupied one of the jump seats in the cockpit, moved to an empty seat in first class. This left four crew members on the flight deck for the remainder of the trip. The first officer and copilot, Bert Stockstill, flew the plane. Bob Loft, the captain, operated the radio. This was normal operating procedure for Eastern Airlines with the pilot and co-pilot alternating turns flying the plane. The other man was then in charge of radio traffic. Behind Stockstill sat Don

**The flight service crew on Aircraft 301, taken in Miami earlier that day.**

Repo, the flight engineer. The fourth man in the cockpit was Angelo Donadeo, who was not there in a working capacity. He was also no stranger to the L-1011. He had been Eastern's maintenance manager in Miami and since September, had been working as a technical supervisor specializing in troubleshooting the new L-1011 fleet. On Friday morning, he had been in New York examining an L-1011 that was having engine trouble. With this job completed, he was anxious to return to Miami in order to close on a new house.

For the most part, the flight was mundane and uneventful. Once the plane was out of the New York area, the weather was good and Stockstill put the aircraft on autopilot and dimmed the cockpit lights to allow for better visibility outside. The cockpit speakers were turned on, so even without headphones, it was possible to listen to the conversations between Loft and the air traffic controllers, as well as conversations between various planes also in the sky.

For most of the trip, a DC-10, National Airlines Flight 607, was flying ahead of the L-1011. But as it approached the Miami International Airport, Flight 607 began experiencing difficulties with its landing gear. At 11:19 p.m., the north arrival radio operator gave Flight 607 its final approach course. The National pilot, however, asked for an extended pattern because they were going to have to crank down their landing gear. One minute later, National 607, with a light indicating a hydraulic leak radioed the controller and asked for fire trucks to be out on the runway when they arrived.

The men on Flight 401's flight deck listened to the pilot on the National plane as he dealt with the troubled gear. With the emergency equipment rolling onto the field near runway Nine Right, in anticipation of National 607, Eastern 401 was assigned the other parallel runway, Nine Left.

At 11:32 p.m., the north approach controller instructed Flight 401 to change radio frequencies and initiate contact with the local controller. Loft contacted the Miami tower and advised them that Flight 401 was on its final approach. He instructed Stockstill to lower the landing gear when a message came back from the tower to continue their approach to runway Nine left. Loft acknowledged the controller and then began a series of practiced, terse, checklist exchanges with the rest of the flight crew in preparation for landing.

From his jump seat behind the captain, Angelo Donadeo looked out a side window and noticed that they were making a west to east approach. The plane was crossing the Palmetto Expressway, a major highway just west of the airport. It was at that moment that Donadeo realized they had a problem.

Stockstill was landing the plane and he announced that they had no nose gear. The flap position warning horn began to sound and from that point on the cockpit was periodically filled with the clang of various warning signals, as well as voices coming from the radio speakers. Captain Loft spoke, "I gotta... I gotta raise it back up," he said. "Goddamn it. Now I'm gonna try it down one more time."

For a moment, the two horns sounded in the cockpit and then the flap position warning horn became silent. Stockstill spoke in a calm voice. "Want to tell 'em we'll take it around and circle around and fart around?"

At 11:34 p.m., Loft spoke to the Miami control tower. "Well, ah, tower, this is Eastern 401, it looks like we're gonna have to circle; we don't have a light on our nose gear yet." The light, located on the lower right side of the center instrument panel, indicated when the nose gear was down and locked in position for a landing. However, it was still dark at this point, the local controller advised then to climb back to two thousand feet. They had lowered to less than one thousand feet in preparation to land. Stockstill reached for the landing gear handle as he prepared to take them out of their descent. However, Loft stopped him. He suggested, "Put the power on first, Bert. Thataboy. Leave the goddamn gear down until we find out what we got." Donadeo saw that while Stockstill was still flying the plane, Loft applied power to the throttles and the plane began to pull out of its descent.

From behind Loft and Stockstill, Repo offered to check the lights but his test still failed to illuminate the small, square light for the nose gear. Stockstill suggested that perhaps the light assembly was not properly seated in the fixture and asked Loft to jiggle it. Loft was unable to reach the light since it was on the co-pilot's side of the panel. He was using the radio and Stockstill was still flying the plane. Repo came forward and attempted to make the light work, but nothing happened.

At 11:35 p.m., Loft radioed the approach tower and reported their position. They were instructed to remain at two thousand feet and maintain a route that would taken them in a wide U-turn, swinging first to the north and slowly around away from the airport and out toward the Everglades. Loft told Stockstill to put the plane on autopilot and see if he could get the light to work. Stockstill managed to extract the light fixture from the instrument panel. Inside of the plastic square were two small light bulbs. Donadeo glanced around the flight deck and saw Repo examining the fixture. He did not see the flight engineer remove the old bulbs and put in two new ones, even though there were spare bulbs on board. Then the fixture was replaced in the socket – sideways. Loft noticed and pointed out the error to Repo. Unfortunately, inserted sideways, the fixture had jammed and the light was still off.

There were other ways to confirm that the gear was down and Loft chose one of them. He turned to Repo and told him to climb down into the forward avionics bay, a space beneath the flight deck that was often referred to as the "hell hole." The bay was accessible through a trap door in the floor of the cockpit and inside was an optical sighting device that could be used to actually see the landing gear.

Meanwhile, Stockstill was still trying to remove the jammed light assembly. He was considering using pliers, cushioned with a tissue, to try and pull it out. Loft told him that it would break if he tried to do that. Stockstill continued his efforts, with which Loft quickly lost patience. Again, he ordered Repo down into the avionics bay. "To hell with this," he said, "to hell with this! Go down and see if it's lined up...that's all we care. Fuck around with that goddamned twenty-cent piece of light equipment we got on this bastard!"

The cockpit voice recorder picked up the sound of laughter. It was clear that the crew viewed the malfunction as more of an annoyance than any sort of emergency. At 11:38 p.m., Loft calmly spoke into the microphone to the Miami tower and told them that Flight 401 would go out a little further west and see if they could get the light to come on. The controller responded that they had them now traveling westbound.

While Flight 401 was flying over the Everglades, the skies above Miami were busy with other flights. At the airport, National 607, the plane that had experienced landing gear problems, was finally given clearance to land on runway Nine Right. Fire trucks were standing by. Unlike the problem with Flight 401's faulty light, National 607's issue was seen as a real emergency. At the same time, Avianca 781 took off from runway Nine Left, followed by Eastern 470. Eastern Flight 111 landed on runway Nine Left. West Indian Flight 790 entered a final approach and immediately behind it was Lan-Chile 451. Backed up and waiting to land was National Flight 437. In the midst of all of this holiday traffic, National Flight 607 landed without incident.

On Flight 401, Stockstill was still fighting with the light. "I don't know what the hell is holding that son of a bitch in," he said. "Always something - we could have made schedule."

They turned their attention back to the problem with the landing gear and decided that it was probably down. A test on the light showed that it was not working anyway and were convinced that Repo would discover the gear was in place when he returned from the avionics bay. Unfortunately, when he came back up, he was unable to confirm it. It was too dark, he said, even with a little light shining in the right direction, he was unable to tell if the landing gear was down. Loft threw a switch on the overhead panel and told him to look again.

Repo went back down the ladder and this time, Donadeo followed him down. When Donadeo left the flight deck, he noticed that Stockstill had his right hand on the yoke and was pushing or pulling on the jammed light assembly with his left. Loft had loosened or unfastened his seat belt and was reaching across the center control pedestal, trying to help with the irritating light. The captain's left arm was braced against the top of the glare shield (a fixture that shades the control panel from outside light through the windshield) and he was reaching for the light with his right hand, crossing just forward of the throttles.

At the airport, the approach controller looked at the altitude reading for the blip on his radar screen that represented Eastern 401. The plane was supposed to be at two thousand feet, but the green numerals read nine hundred. The controller radioed the plane. "Eastern 401, how are things coming along out there?"

Loft replied. "Okay, we'd like to turn around and come back in."

The controller radioed back. "Eastern 401, turn left heading one-eight-zero."

Loft acknowledged and the L-1011 began a gradual left turn. On the radio speakers, the approach controller could be heard telling Lan-Chile 451 to descend to fifteen hundred feet. The Lan-Chile pilot acknowledged the instructions.

The next voices on the flight recorder were the last ever heard from Loft and Stockstill.

"We did something to the altitude," Stockstill said.

Loft: "What?"

Stockstill: "We're still at two thousand, right?"

Loft: "Hey, what's happening here?"

At the airport, the approach controller handled another plane and then looked again at the radar screen. In the data block next to Flight 401, the words read "CST" – for "coast," which is shown when a beacon target is lost or becomes too weak for three sweeps of the radar antenna.

He quickly radioed the plane. "Ah, Eastern 401, are you requesting equipment?"

There was only the whisper of static over the line.

He tried once more. "Eastern, ah, 401, I've lost you, ah, on the radar there, your transponder. What's your altitude now? Eastern 401, Miami."

There was no reply from Flight 401.


The airplane crashed northwest of Miami, almost nineteen miles from the end of runway Nine Left, in the heart of the Everglades, a vast swamp region of water, saw-grass, marshland and alligators. The L-1011 was traveling 227 miles an hour when it hit the ground. The left wingtip hit first, then the left engine and the left landing gear. Together, they slashed three long trails through the heavy saw-grass. Each trail was five feet wide and more than one hundred feet long.

When the main part of the fuselage hit the ground, it continued to move through the grass and water, coming apart as it went. It hit once, lifted into the air and then slammed back down again with a hard, grinding sound. About halfway along its path, the nose of the plane spun clockwise and careened around until it was sliding backwards. As the plane was skidding through the swamp, a fireball rushed through the cabin, from front to rear. Passengers felt a blast of cold air and then a wet wave of fuel as the plane broke apart. The huge white fuselage crumpled and tore into five large sections and countless smaller pieces. From the first impact to the point that it came to a shuddering halt, the plane traveled more than one-third of a mile.

Passengers drowned in the murky water. Others were thrown from the plane, suffering broken bones, paralyzing injuries and death. As the plane broke apart, an apparently random pattern of death and survival was repeated throughout the aircraft. Some died, while people seated next to them survived. One woman was thrown out of the plane, her seat intact, and died from multiple injuries, while the poodle she brought with her in a pet carrier under her seat survived. Two passengers in first class were thrown out of the plane and ended up fifty yards away from one another. Both lived. A two-year-old boy was hurled three hundred feet from the plane. He was unmarked except for two small cuts on his face. He died. A young mother was killed on impact but her six-month-old daughter survived.

At 11:42 p.m., a private plane that had just taken off from Miami International Airport radioed the tower. The pilot reported seeing a "tremendous flame" in the Everglades. One minute later, at 11:43 p.m. National Airlines Flight 661 reported a "big explosion out west."

Earlier that same evening, a local man named Robert Marquis and a friend, Rayburn Dickinson, were out in the Everglades in an airboat, hunting bullfrogs. By 11:40 p.m., Marquis and Dickinson had caught about thirty pounds of frogs and were working their way east, toward the glow of lights from Miami. Suddenly, Marquis noticed the lights of a large jet. The plane was flying west and seemed very low. Although he couldn't hear it over the sound of the airboat's motor, he knew it was very close and could see the strobe lights flashing on the ends of its wings. Moments later, he saw "a ball of fire, an orange, orange glow that just lit up and spread out for about eight thousand feet across the Glades; looked like maybe it went up a hundred foot high, just for a short duration of eight or ten seconds."

He yelled to Dickinson, "That was a plane crash, wasn't it?"

Marquis pushed forward on the throttle and started the airboat darting across the swamp toward where he had seen the flash.

Two minutes after Flight 401 disappeared from the radar screen at Miami International, the telephone rang at the U.S. Coast Guard station at Opa-locka operations center and an alarm was sounded. By 11:45 p.m., the ready crew was airborne in Sikorsky Sea Guard helicopter. Allan Pell, a lieutenant commander, was the senior office on board. At this point, it was only known that the plane has disappeared from radar. Pell had doubts about a crash. The L-1011 was a brand new plane and it was a clear night; it seemed unlikely that the plane had actually gone down.

Meanwhile, Robert Marquis was racing to the scene in his airboat. He cut through the dark swamp for almost fifteen minutes and then cut the engine to listen. He heard screams in the distance that sent chills down his spine. He continued in the direction of the screams and stopped again. Now, the cries were coming from behind him. He ran the airboat around a thick stand of saw-grass and suddenly saw a huge piece of wreckage directly in front of him. He literally ran right into it and had to stop the boat, get out and turn it around. He soon discovered the path where the plane had hit the ground. It was about fifty to a hundred yards wide and filled with trash and debris.

Marquis later recalled, "When I first started working into the wreckage, I began seeing people - some of them laying in the water, some of them wandering around, walking, but very slowly. I got as close as I could without running over anybody, and then I got out. There were dead people everywhere. And everywhere I looked were half-naked people, some completely naked. I felt so helpless. The first one I came to was a man who looked like he was about to drown. Looked like both his legs were broken. Couldn't move. The only thing he could move was his head, and it kept falling into the water. He said, 'Help me; I can't hold my head up much longer.' So I pulled him up and rested his back and propped his head up out of the water. There were lots of people in turned-over seats, their heads in the water. I tried to help the ones that possibly were drowning."

After a few minutes of struggling to assist the survivors that he could find, Marquis noticed a helicopter in the sky. It was obviously searching for the crash, but it was looking in the wrong area. Marquis waded back to his airboat, grabbed a helmet light that he had made and began wildly waving it in the direction of the helicopter.

The Coast Guard chopper crew saw the faint light flashing in the distance and the pilot swooped toward it. As the wreckage came into sight, Lieutenant Commander Pell saw bodies, a few people stumbling through the water and the tall grass and the looming tail of the plane, one of the few distinguishable pieces of wreckage. The helicopter made one full sweep of the area and then climbed back up to three hundred feet to establish radio contact. Pell called the air station. "We've got one hell of a mess out here," he reported.

Pell landed the helicopter and took on survivors, three men and a woman, and then lifted off into the night sky. They would be the first four of 167 victims – dead and alive – who would be transported from the horrific scene. The chopper lifted off at 12:46 a.m., one hour and four minutes after the crash.

When the helicopter took off, it left Coast Guard Petty Officer Don Schneck behind. Carrying only small flashlight, he climbed aboard Marquis' airboat for a ride to the main sections of the wreckage. He was dropped off about fifty feet from a large section that still had the right wing of the airplane attached to it. After wandering in the darkness for about 25 yards, he came upon a man standing in the water, calling for help. The man told Schenck that his wife was hurt. In the blackness of the swamp, the Coast Guard officer had not seen a woman sitting next to the man. She was bleeding from the thigh. Schneck used the man's belt to apply a tourniquet and then continued on.

He soon came upon the cockpit section, jutting from the water at a 45-degree angle. The roof was smashed and it was cluttered with wreckage. He was stunned when he heard voices coming from the debris. He later wrote, "I could not imagine anyone surviving inside the twisted remains of the cockpit. I heard two voices yelling that they could see my light. I peered into a few small holes [in the side of the wreckage] and could see someone, who was moaning slightly."

Schenck went around to the other side of the wreckage and found senior flight attendant Adrienne Hamilton and another crew member, Sue Tebbs. After checking their injuries and providing what little help he could, Schneck began to move some pieces of debris away from Hamilton. As he did, he discovered the co-pilot, Stockstill, suspended off the ground, wrapped in a tangle of wires that were the remains of the cockpit's wall. He could only see the man's head and shoulders but Schenck checked his eyes and knew that he was dead. He then worked his way into the ruins of the flight deck and found Captain Loft sprawled across the control panel under the windshield. He was alive and moving around and Schenck told him to remain still. Loft, however, told him that he was going to die and tried to get out of the cockpit. After Schenck calmed him down, he went below to try and help the two men trapped in the avionics bay. Loft died before he could be rescued.

By now, ambulances were speeding west from Miami on US Highway 41. The nearest road was eight miles from the crash site but it was eventually determined that rescue vehicles could proceed single file along the top of a flood control levee to within one hundred yards of the scene. The levee was also used as a helicopter landing pad.

Rescue workers soon began to arrive on the scene, finally coming to assist Schenck, Marquis and Dickinson, who, up until that time, were the only people helping the survivors. The rescuers found a scene of carnage and horror. One man was still alive under the center fuselage section with just his head and feet sticking out of the mud. His hips and pelvis were obviously broken since both his

The crash site, photographed on December 30. The cockpit section is on the upper left. On the right is a life raft that inflated on impact.

legs were perpendicular to his torso with each foot next to his head. It took six men more than thirty minutes to dig around him and pull him out. They were only able to do so by rocking the huge section back and forth and causing the man even more agony. Victims were scattered throughout the swamp in various states of injury. Far too many were dead.

Survivors were taken to several hospitals around Miami, all of them the closest to the crash site. Palmetto was the most convenient and had a helipad. Hialeah Hospital was also close and when the helicopter pilots complained that it was difficult place to land because of the numerous power lines around it, police cars marked an alternate site in the parking lot of the Hialeah Race Track. Both hospitals received six chopper loads of survivors – 32 people in all.

Mercy Hospital also received four flights. The first survivor handed from a helicopter at Mercy Hospital was the white poodle that had managed to live through the crash under her owner's seat. The first human victims were received by a veteran nurse named Ferne Pletchan, who came out to the helipad to help with the unloading. She was struck by their silence. None screamed. A few moaned. Others wept softly. A little boy cried for his mother. Most of the victims seemed to be in a daze and yet were touchingly grateful for blankets and caring hands that wiped away the mud from the faces. Over and over again, they said only two words: "Thank you."

The first light of dawn brought a swarm of chartered helicopters to the crash site, each of them filled with television cameramen and reporters. They hovered over the remains of Flight 401 for a few minutes and then flew back to Miami. The images of the crash would soon shock the American public.

In the swamp, Jimmy Duckworth, a police sergeant, would supervise the recovery of bodies from the wreck. Duckworth and his team waited while Dr. Joe Davis, the medical examiner, attended a meeting in Miami with the National Transportation Safety Board investigators who had arrived during the night from Washington, D.C. When Davis and the NTSB team made it to the crash site, the recovery teams were finally allowed to leave the levee where they had been gathered and wad out into the murky water. Behind them waited airboats piloted by wildlife officers from the Game Commission. They would be in charge of ferrying the dead out of the Everglades.

The search began at a spot they designated as point zero: a spot that was distant enough from the wreckage

**(Left) Rescue workers in airboats at the scene. The cockpit section rests on its side, the numbers "310" visible on the nose.     (Right) The nose of the plane resting in the swamp the morning after the crash.**

that all agreed no bodies would have been thrown beyond. From that point, the searchers spread out in a long line and slowly advanced toward the remains of the plane. When a body was found, the team was to mark it with an indelible number, photograph it, tag the body, plant a small yellow flag near the head with the same number on it, and place the corpse in a body bag. The airboats would then come and pick up the body.

After dredging through the muck for thirty minutes, Duckworth's team found the first body at 12:30 p.m. It was the naked body of a young woman. A second corpse, a naked man, was found fifteen minutes later. The body of a young boy was discovered about four hundred yards away. He was laying in two inches of water, fully dressed, and had no apparent signs of injury. Another young woman was found next. She was lying on her back, eyes open, her right hand extended as though reaching out for something or someone.

And the search continued. The grueling, heart-breaking work went on for several days until the sun was shining down on a forest of bright yellow flags, each with a number scrawled on it.

On New Year's Day, a passenger named Braulio Corretjer, died in the hospital from his injuries. Searchers also found the body of a flight attendant named Stephanie Stanich in the Everglades. She was still strapped in her seat. On Tuesday, the medical examiner and the airline agreed for the first time about the number of survivors and casualties; 77 people had lived through the crash and 99 bodies had been found in the swamp. But by then, two of the original survivors – Don Repo and Corretjer – had died in the hospital. Two more would die later. In the end, Flight 401 had carried 176 passengers and within a month of the crash, the death toll stood at one hundred and three victims.

In the days that followed, the NTSB conducted an investigation of the crash. Its investigators searched through the wreckage, interviewed survivors and witnesses and studied the flight data. When investigators climbed into the crushed cockpit, they found the control panel virtually intact. The clock had stopped at the moment of the crash. The airspeed needle on Loft's side of the flight deck read 198 knots. The altitude select panel was set at two thousand feet. The nose gear light assembly was found jammed on its side and protruding one-quarter inch from its normal position. It contained two burned-out light bulbs. All three throttles were in the full forward position, an indication that the pilots discovered the problem at the last moment and tried to pull out of it.

Angelo Donadeo, whose spot in the cockpit jump seat made him a crucial observer of what occurred on the flight deck, was interviewed on January 8. He was under heavy sedation at the time in a Miami hospital and he reluctantly signed the transcript of his interview, believing that his medical condition may have altered his version of the events.

But Donadeo's testimony wasn't needed to discover a peculiarity in the forward avionics bay – two autopilot computers, which controlled the plane's nose up and down attitude, were mismatched. One of the computers was a model 1-7 and the other a model 1-8. The difference between the two was that while one required fifteen pounds of pressure on the column to disengage the system, the other needed twenty pounds of pressure. Although the two computers were slightly different, both worked properly when tested, along with the five other computers that survived the crash. Regardless, it was a troubling anomaly.

Eventually, all of the evidence that was gathered – investigations, Flight Data Recorder printouts, and voice recordings of the pilots – and presented in a public hearing on March 5, 1973. Investigators now had a clear picture of what had occurred.

The flight had been normal until the final approach into Miami. When Stockstill had looked at the landing gear indicator, the green light that stated that the gear was properly locked into the "down" position did not illuminate. This failure had two possible explanations: either the gear had not come down, or the light was not working. The pilots recycled the gear. When the light still failed to come on, they aborted the landing to examine the situation. The tower instructed the L-1011 to pull out of its descent, climb to two thousand feet, and circle out over the Everglades. The cockpit crew removed the malfunctioning light assembly and Repo, the flight engineer, was sent down into the avionics bay to visually check the landing gear. Fifty seconds after they had reached their assigned altitude, and when the plane was halfway through its U-turn, the captain instructed the co-pilot to put the L-1011 on autopilot. For the next eighty seconds, the plane maintained level flight. Then it dropped one hundred feet, flew level for the next two minutes, and then began a descent that was so gradual that it was not perceived by the crew. In the next seventy seconds, the plane lost only two hundred and fifty more feet but this was enough to cause the altitude warning alarm to go off, which was clearly heard on the cockpit recordings. During the NTSB investigation, one Eastern captain stated that modern aircraft like the L-1011 have so many "clickers and clackers and bells" that the cockpit becomes overwhelmingly filled with alarm tones. Perhaps so much so, he theorized, that pilots begin to stop hearing them, to simply tune them out. For whatever reason, there was no indication on Flight 401's voice recordings that pilots heard the alarm.

Meanwhile, the crew continued to attempt to reinstall the light assembly, which had been taken out to see if it was working or not and then had been incorrectly pushed back into the panel, causing it to become jammed. During the NTSB investigation, an Eastern L-1011 captain noted that after the accident he and a mechanic tried to remove and replace the gear lamp only to find that, although it is square in shape, it has a small track and groove which only line up when the lamp is positioned correctly. He testified that the track started halfway in, so if you started to push it in incorrectly, you wouldn't realize the mistake until it was wedged in the housing.

Within fifty seconds, the plane was at half of its assigned altitude and was slowly continuing to drop. At the moment when Stockstill's radio altimeter beeped, the plane was dropping at fifty feet per second. This time, the crew heard the warning, but it was too late.

The question remained – why did the airplane that was locked on autopilot dive into the Everglades?

The answer came in small pieces. One of the first clues came from the testimony of Eastern pilot Captain Daniel Gellert, who stated that he had noticed that the altitude hold function could be disengaged by bumping the control column. Many pilots doubted Gellert's testimony, but the incident was strikingly similar to a situation encountered by Thomas Oakes, another Eastern pilot. Oakes had been one of the first captains qualified to fly the L-1011. He had the altitude hold function disengage on a flight on January 8, ten days after the crash of Flight 401. Oakes testified that he and the co-pilot noticed the malfunction and then proceeded to re-set the autopilot and then trip it off by bumping the control column several times. They noted the problem in their logbook. Although these may have been freak occurrences, Eastern took them seriously and sent a printed notice about the malfunction to their L-1011 pilots on January 15.

Given this information, the NTSB hypothesized that Loft had probably bumped the control column when he turned to tell flight engineer Repo to go down into the avionics bay and check on the landing gear. The NTSB report noted: "If the captain had applied a force to the control wheel while turning to talk to the second officer, the altitude hold function might have been accidentally disengaged." The autopilot had apparently not turned off completely, but rather had switched into the "Control Wheel Steering" mode. The plane was no longer locked at two thousand feet, but would fly steadily at whatever level the pilots selected, purposefully or accidentally, by pressure on their control wheels. From this point on, even a slight nudge would be enough to edge the plane up or down.

A part of the mystery that was never solved was whether the altitude hold light extinguished when the function disengaged. In both Gellert's and Oakes' cases, they noted the autopilot light went out when they bumped the columns. But Stockstill might have been deceived by the mismatched autopilot computers on the plane. Because the computers were mismatched, Loft's side required fifteen pounds of pressure to disengage, and Stockstill's side required twenty pounds of pressure. If Loft bumped the column with more than fifteen, but less than twenty pounds of pressure, Loft's altitude hold light would have gone out, and Stockstill's light would remain on, giving him the erroneous impression that the autopilot was still engaged and holding the plane at two thousand feet. No one could know for sure what happened, but either way, the NTSB did not believe this was a crucial factor in the accident.

The final report cited the cause of the crash as pilot error, specifically, "the failure of the flight crew to monitor the flight instruments during the final four minutes of flight, and to detect an unexpected descent soon enough to prevent impact with the ground. Preoccupation with a malfunction of the nose landing gear position indicating system distracted the crew's attention from the instruments and allowed the descent to go unnoticed."

In the tragic ending, one hundred and three people died – all because of two burned out light bulbs that would have cost twelve dollars to replace. And ironically, the landing gear on the plane was found to be in the down and locked position, which meant that the disaster should have never happened at all.

As it happened, the crash of Flight 401 was not the end of the story.

Captain Bob Loft and flight engineer Dan Repo were among the one hundred and three people who lost their lives when Flight 401 crashed into the Everglades on that December night in 1972. Initially, both men were among the survivors but Loft succumbed to his wounds about an hour after the crash before rescuers got him to the hospital. Repo, critically injured, was reportedly angry when he was pulled from the wreckage. He survived about thirty hours before he, also, died.

Both of the men would be found to be at fault by the NTSB investigation, although most of the blame fell on Loft's shoulders. They were accused of being preoccupied with finding a source for the indicator light problem and ignoring the fact that the plane was steadily losing altitude. When they discovered what was wrong it was too late – a fact that apparently haunted both men after their deaths, for their ghosts soon began to be encountered aboard other Eastern L-1011 jets.

Apparently, to save costs, Eastern ordered the salvageable parts of the aircraft Number 310 to be removed and incorporated into other Eastern planes. Soon after, reports of the ghosts of Repo, Lofts and even some unidentified flight attendants were encountered on various Eastern flights. For the next year or so, they were most often seen on Eastern's aircraft Number 318, or on other L-1011s, all of which contained salvaged parts from Flight 401. Eastern crew members and passengers saw the ghosts or heard them speak on the plane's intercom systems or received verbal messages and warnings from them. Witnesses also experienced cold sensations and sensed invisible presences, aircraft power turning on by its own volition and a tool inexplicably appearing in a mechanics hand when no one was in the area.

Substantiation of the sightings was difficult, however. Eyewitness reports made to Eastern's management were met with skepticism and a fear of further damaging the airline's reputation and causing a further loss of business. The crash had done enough damage and for the public to hear that the ghosts of some of the lost plane's crew were visiting other flights could make for a public relations disaster. For the most part, eyewitness crew members were told that perhaps seeing a psychiatrist would be in order, which most took as a precursor to being fired. After that, most were reluctant to talk to anyone investigating the hauntings and the sightings that did occur were often covered up. Log sheets that contained the sighting reports, as well as the names of witnesses, mysteriously disappeared from the planes where they occurred. Normally, a logbook would contain entries for several months, but these pages vanished. To this day, many hotly deny the stories of the ghosts from Flight 401, despite the scores of credible witnesses that eventually came forward.

Of course, denying the existence of the ghosts did not stop them from being seen. The eyewitness reports continued and were so widely circulated throughout the aviation community that Eastern finally removed the parts associated with Flight 401. Many believe the reports were so numerous because the ghosts allegedly visited different planes at various times of the day and night, thereby exposing themselves to a wide range of people. In addition, Repo and Loft were often recognized by people who had once worked with them. Both men, especially Loft, had been with Eastern for many years and had literally worked with hundreds of different crew members.

Repo was seen more often that Loft and was often seen in aircraft Number 318's galley, where flight attendants claimed to see his face reflected in the door of an oven. The attendants also reported that the galley felt unusually cold and clammy, or that there was the strong presence of someone in the room with them. During one incident, Repo's ghost allegedly

**Eastern ship N318EA, the main aircraft allegedly haunted by the "Ghosts of Flight 401." The tall building behind the plane is Building 16 at MIA, the former headquarters of Eastern Air Lines.**

repaired an oven that had an overloaded circuit. It wasn't until another engineer came to fix the oven, and told a flight attendant that he was the only engineer on the plane, that she realized something was strange. She looked up Repo's photograph and realized that he was the man who had first come to make the repairs.

But Repo's ghost seemed to be especially concerned about the safety and operation of the plane. When his ghost appeared, he often made suggestions or gave warnings to crew members who only realized that he was an apparition after he had vanished. Repo's ghost was seen on the flight deck, either sitting at the engineer's instrument panel or with just his face reflected in it. During one visit, a flight engineer was making a pre-flight inspection when he recognized Repo's ghost. Before vanishing, the spirit told the engineer that he had already made the inspection.

Repo's ghost once warned a flight engineer that there would be an electrical failure on the plane and a check revealed that there was a faulty circuit. Another time, his ghost warned an attendant about a fire on the plane and on still another occasion, the phantom pointed out a problem in the plane's hydraulic system. Repo's ghost even told a captain that there would be another crash on an L-1011, but that "we will not let it happen."

On several occasions, Captain Loft's ghost was seen sitting in the plane's first class section. During one incident, a flight attendant approached Loft and asked him why his name was not on the passenger list. When he didn't respond, she called her supervisor over, along with a flight captain. It was the captain who recognized Loft sitting in the seat and cried out in shock, "My God! It's Bob Loft!" Moments later, the ghost disappeared. Loft's ghost also appeared in the crew compartment and it was suspected that his voice was heard during one flight, warning passengers about seat belts and smoking rules. No one else claimed to have made the announcements.

Eventually, once the parts from Flight 401 were removed from the various planes, the hauntings came to an end. Eastern Airlines ceased operations in January 1991, leaving behind a mystery of what actually happened in the planes that were said to have been visited by ghosts.

# 1979: THE LINGERING SPIRITS OF FLIGHT 191

Before the horrific events of September 11, 2001, the worst airline-related disaster in American history occurred on Memorial Day weekend of 1979 in Chicago. On Friday, May 25, American Airlines Flight 191 took off from O'Hare International Airport en route to Los Angeles and at just after 3:00 p.m., literally fell from the sky.

# 10 MOST DEADLY AMERICAN AVIATION DISASTERS

1. Killed: 2,976 - Sept. 11, 2001 - American Airlines FL 11 & United Airlines FL 175 - NY, NY. American Airlines FL 77 - Arlington, VA. United Airlines FL 93 - Shanksville, PA
2. Killed: 273 - May 25, 1979 - American Airlines Flight 191 - Chicago, IL
3. Killed: 265 - Nov. 12, 2001 - American Airlines Flight 587 - Belle Harbor, Queens, NY
4. Killed: 230 - July 17, 1996 - Trans World Airlines Flight 800 - off East Moriches, NY
5. Killed: 217 - Oct. 31, 1999 - Egypt Air Flight 990 - Cape Cod, MA
6. Killed: 156 - Aug. 16, 1987 - Northwest Airlines Flight 255 - Romulus, MI
7. Killed: 153 - July 9, 1982 - Pan American World Airways Flight 759 - Kenner, LA
8. Killed: 144 - Sept. 25, 1978 - Pacific Southwest Airlines Flight 182 collision - San Diego, CA
9. Killed: 135 - Aug. 2, 1985 - Delta Air Lines Flight 191 - Ft. Worth/Dallas TX
10. Killed: 134 - Dec. 16, 1960 - United Airlines Flight 826 collided with Trans World Air Lines Flight 266 - Staten Island and Brooklyn, NY

Just after takeoff, the left engine of the McDonnell-Douglas DC-10 tore loose and plummeted to the ground. With the aircraft's hydraulic system fatally compromised, the plane stalled, banked into an uncontrollable dive and plunged wing-first into a nearby trailer park, instantly killing all of the 271 passengers and crew members on board.

The flight was meant to be a non-stop journey from Chicago to Los Angeles but as fate would have it, the plane never left the Windy City.

It was a beautiful holiday weekend in Chicago with a clear blue sky and warm weather. Throngs of people filled O'Hare International, the world's busiest airport. The passengers of Flight 191, including a number of Chicago literary figures bound for Los Angeles and the annual American Booksellers Association conference, boarded the McDonnell-Douglas DC-10 shortly before 3:00 p.m. There seemed to be nothing out of the ordinary about the flight. The DC-10 was a top-of-the-line aircraft and this particular model had logged more than twenty thousand trouble-free hours since it left the assembly line. The crew was top-notch, as well, including Captain Walter Lux, a pilot with many years experience who had been flying DC-10s since their introduction into service eight years before, First Officer James Dillard and Flight Engineer Alfred Udovich, who had nearly 25,000 flight hours between them.

At 2:59 p.m., the plane was cleared to begin its taxi to the runway 32-R's holding point. Then, at 3:02 p.m., Flight 191 started down the runway. All went smoothly until a point about six thousand feet down the runway, just prior to rotation. The tower controller saw parts of the port engine pylon falling away from the aircraft and a "white vapor" coming from the area. A moment later, the plane pitched into rotation and lifted off. As it did so, the entire engine and pylon tore loose from their mounting, flipped up and over the wing, and crashed down onto the runway. The engine separation disabled the aircraft's hydraulic system, making it impossible to control both the retractable flaps necessary for takeoff and landing and the captain's electrical controls, which were not duplicated in the co-pilot's instrumentation. Since the engines were not visible from the cockpit windows of the plane, the pilots knew that something was wrong, but had no idea what it was.

Immediately, the tower controller tried to raise the plane on the radio: "American 191, do you want to come back? If so, what runway do you want?"

It would not have mattered if they wanted to return or not. There was no reply from the aircraft. It proceeded to climb normally only dipping the left wing for a moment. It quickly stabilized and continued its descent, but after 31 seconds in the air, at a height of about three hundred feet, the DC-10 banked left into a dizzying dive and crashed to the earth.

The left wingtip hit the ground first and the sound of tearing metal was followed by a massive explosion. The fireball went down about a half-mile northwest of O'Hare and slammed into an abandoned hangar on the site of the old Ravenswood Airport on Touhy Avenue, just east of a mobile home park. It was mostly vacant ground, although the plane narrowly missed some fuel storage tanks on Elmhurst Road and the busy I-90 Expressway. However, two people were killed on the ground and several homes were damaged in the trailer park. As for the crew and passengers aboard the aircraft --- all of them had been killed instantly.

The NTSB started an investigation immediately after the crash and released their findings seven months later. Early on, investigators eliminated possible causes such as terrorism, bad weather, other aircraft and pilot error. Since there had been three other fatal crashes of DC-10s, they focused on the plane itself. They soon found a broken bolt from the mount connecting the wing to the engine had fallen off. Then two mechanics discovered metal dust on the engine mount of a United Airlines DC-10 and cracks behind access panels with broken rivets and other defects. The Federal Aviation Administration ordered all 138 American DC-10s to be grounded, which caused chaos in the airline industry.

The real problem with Flight 19, however, turned out to be a maintenance procedure that had been performed in Tulsa, Oklahoma, on the doomed plane. Instead of separating, removing and reinstalling the engine and its mount, mechanics had performed their work in a single step to save time and money. A forklift used to hold the engine up was left unattended for a while and a hydraulic problem caused the tilting of the engine, creating enough pressure on the mount to develop a small fracture. This problem worsened over several flights, cracking further with each takeoff and

American Airlines Flight 191 as it goes into a dive and (below) a plume of smoke and fire erupts in the distance as the plane slams into the ground.

landing. Eventually, as Flight 191, the DC-10's mount simply fell apart. At the point of rotation, the engine detached and was flipped over the top of the wing. A tiny crack had caused the flight to end in disaster.

Weird legends sprang up about Flight 191 almost at once. One of them claimed that television actress Lindsay Wagner had a premonition before boarding the flight and decided not to fly. Another story involved Ohio

**An aerial view of the Flight 191 crash site**

resident David Booth, who had recurring nightmares about a plane in a steep bank prior to a fatal crash. On May 22, 1979, three days before the flight, he telephoned the FAA, American Airlines and a psychiatrist in Cincinnati to tell them about what he had seen in his nightmares. Whether he was presumed insane or taken seriously, nothing was done before May 25. Strangest and most frightening were the stories of the ghosts. They soon began to spring up around the crash site of Flight 191. According to Des Plaines police officers, motorists began reporting odd sights within a few months of the crash. They called in about seeing odd, bobbing white lights in the field where the aircraft had gone down. First assuming them to be flashlights carried by ghoulish souvenir hunters, officers responded to the reports to find the field was silent and deserted. No one was ever found, despite patrols arriving on the scene almost moments after receiving a report.

More unnerving, though, were the accounts that came from the residents of the nearby mobile home park, which was adjacent to the crash site. Many of these reports came within hours of the crash, when residents claimed to hear knocking and rapping sounds at their doors and windows. Those who responded, including a number of retirees and off-duty police and firefighters, opened their doors to find no one was there. Dogs in the trailer park would bark endlessly at the empty field where the plane had gone down. Their owners could find no reason for their erratic behavior. This continued for months and even escalated to the point that doorknobs were being turned and rattled, footsteps were heard approaching the trailers, clanging was heard on the metal stairs, and on some occasions, actual figures were confronted. According to some reports, a few residents opened their doors to find a worried person who anxiously stated that he "had to get his luggage" or "had to make a connection" standing on their porch. The figure then turned and vanished into the darkness.

The tragedy, and the strange events that followed, caused many of the residents to move out of the park but when new arrivals took their place, they, too, began to report the weird happenings. One sighting was described by a man out walking his dog one night near the area where Flight 191 went down. He was approached by a young man who explained that he needed to make an emergency telephone call. The man with the dog looked at this person curiously for he reeked of gasoline and appeared to be smoldering. At first, he just assumed the man had been running on this chilly night and steam was coming from his clothing, but when he turned away to point out a nearby phone and then turned back again --- the man had vanished! The man with the dog had heard stories from other local residents about moans and weird cries emanating from the 1979 crash site, but he never believed them until now. He was now convinced that he had encountered one of the restless passengers from Flight 191 for himself.

In 2008, I spoke with a man named Andrew Cook, who had his own strange connections to Flight 191 – although it was one that would eventually become even stranger. On May 25, 1979, Cook was a small boy living in Bloomingdale, a Chicago suburb. On that day, he was playing with his school class in a park that was located across the street from his family home. He and his friends had just climbed to the top of the tallest slide in the park when a bright light caught his attention. He said later that, "it was like someone shined a mirror on my face, but from a long distance away." Just then, he looked up to see Flight 191 as it banked to the left over the airport and then crashed to the earth.

"Seeing that haunted me for my entire life," he said.

Years later, in 2000, he met a man named Gary Schwartz. Cook's wife had just started working at the same company as Schwartz and Cook met him one day at a breakfast gathering. During a conversation that he was having with one of his wife's co-workers, he happened to mention his fear of flying. It was a fear that was caused by what he had witnessed as a small boy in 1979. The co-worker called Gary Schwartz over to the table. Schwartz's parents had been killed on Flight 191 but Schwartz said that he had never been told much about the crash and had never been to the site. For whatever reason, Cook decided that he wanted to track it down.

**The Flight 191 crash site today.**

He knew the site was near I-90 and near a trailer park and he eventually asked a local policeman for directions. They chatted for a few minutes but the policeman sent him to the wrong part of the field. Cook went to look around, convinced that he was at the crash site. He parked his car for a few minutes along a dirt road, then started to leave. As he was driving away, he saw a strange-looking woman standing in the middle of the road. He stopped his car and rolled down the window to ask her to move. Instead, he ended up telling her about his own experience with Flight 191 and why he had come to the crash site. The woman listened intently but never spoke. Instead, she simply smiled and started to walk in the direction from which Cook had come. He passed her and when he looked in his rearview mirror, the woman was gone! She had just vanished in a matter of seconds.

Cook immediately stopped the car and got out to make sure that he was not mistaken about the woman's disappearance, but she was definitely gone. He stood there for a moment, scratching his head, and then started back to his car. He was very unnerved by what had happened and he quickly locked the doors. Hands shaking, Cook put the car into gear and started to drive off. He glanced into the rearview mirror again and this time, the woman had returned! She was standing at the back of the car and she lay a bouquet of what looked to be wildflowers on the trunk. Cook slammed on his brakes and jumped out of the car. By the time he got to the rear of the vehicle, the woman had again vanished. The flowers remained, though, although he refused to touch them. He got back into his car and drove away, bothered by what had happened.

The following weekend, Cook brought Gary Schwartz out to see the field. As they were standing there, looking around, a police car approached and asked them if they needed help. When Cook explained what they were doing, the officer told them that they were at the wrong spot. The actual crash site was a short distance away. Cook was actually relieved to hear it. He had spent the last week believing that the strange woman with the flowers was a ghost. Now he knew that she was just a bizarre woman who liked to play practical jokes. In time, he forgot about the weird incident.

A few years later, Schwartz invited him to attend a gathering that was being held to commemorate the twenty-fifth anniversary of the Flight 191 crash. Cook met a number of people with close ties to the disaster and one of the people he spoke with that day was a woman who had lost her older sister in the crash. She told him stories about her sister, including the fact that she was a former hippie and volunteer worker who always helped out other people whenever she could. When Cook asked to see a photo of the sister, he was shocked to discover that it was the same woman that he had met in the field a few years before. Startled and upset, he took the woman aside and told her what had happened that day. He mentioned the incident with the flowers and the woman suddenly burst into tears. She said that her sister was always giving flowers to people and that was one thing that everyone always loved about her.

# FIRE

## 1871: CITY IN FLAMES
## THE GREAT CHICAGO FIRE

According to the legend, the Great Chicago Fire was started by a cow belonging to an Irishwoman named Catherine O'Leary. She ran a neighborhood milk business from the barn behind her home. She carelessly left a kerosene lantern in the barn after her evening milking and a cow kicked it over and ignited the hay on the floor. The story started as a rumor and was soon accepted as truth, although history tells a slightly different story.

In 1871, Chicago was truly a boomtown. It had become one of the fastest-growing cities in America and because of this, construction standards had been loose, to say the least. Beyond the downtown area, the city was miles and miles of rickety wooden structures. Most of the working-class neighborhoods consisted of wooden cottages and tenements, all of which made for dangerous fuel in the event of a fire.

And fire was always a possibility. "The absence of rain for three weeks," reported the *Chicago Tribune* in the fall of 1871, "has left everything in so flammable a condition that a spark might set a fire that would sweep from end to end of the city."

For several years after the end of the Civil War, a respectable but poor laborer named Patrick O'Leary lived with his family in the three rear rooms of a cottage at No. 137 De Koven Street on the city's West Side. He lived there with his wife, Catherine, and their five children. The two front rooms of the cottage were rented to the family of Patrick McLaughlin and on the night of October 8, 1871, the house was a very lively

**The O'Leary Cottage on De Koven Street in 1871**

*And Hell Followed With It – Page 158*

place. The O'Leary family had retired for the evening and was already in bed, but McLaughlin, a fiddler, along with his family and friends, was entertaining his wife's cousin, who had recently arrived from Ireland. The rooms were filled with music and drinking and at some point, a few of the young men who were present went out to get another half-gallon of beer – or some milk, depending on the story that was told.

It is believed that at some point in the evening, some of the McLaughlin clan decided to prepare an oyster stew for their party and a couple of the young men were sent to get some milk from the cow that the O'Learys stabled in a barn at the rear of the house. A broken lamp found among the ashes of the stable a few days later gave rise to the legend that the cow, or a careless milker, had started the fire that destroyed Chicago.

Late on the evening of October 8, a man named Dennis Sullivan called on the O'Learys and roused Patrick from his bed. The two men chatted for a few minutes and as Sullivan walked slowly along De Koven Street toward Jefferson, he stopped on the curb to light his pipe. As he raised his head to light the tobacco, shielding his pipe from a strong wind that was blowing, he saw a flickering light in the O'Leary milking barn. Crying an alarm, he rushed into the building and managed to drag out a calf, whose hair had caught on fire. But when he went back inside to try and save the horse and the cow, his wooden leg caught in a crack between two boards and he barely escaped with his own life.

This was the beginning of the Great Chicago Fire. Within two hours, it was raging over a hundred acres, devouring the wood frame homes, barns and buildings and burning wildly out of control. Chicago was soon a city in flames.

By 10:00 that evening, the fire had spread from the O'Learys' across the West Side in two swaths so wide that all of the fire engines in town were clanging on the streets and the courthouse bell, in the downtown section, pealed incessantly. Many things conspired to give the flames such headway in

## MRS. O'LEARY'S COMET?

Could a comet from space have started the Great Chicago Fire? Aside from the O'Learys' unfortunate cow, there have been other causes suggested for the fire, including one that was first brought up in 1882. The Chicago Fire was not the worst conflagration to sweep through the Midwest; it was not even the worst one to start on October 8, 1871!

On that hot and windy autumn night, three other major fires occurred along the shores of Lake Michigan. About 400 miles to the north, a forest fire consumed the town of Peshtigo, Wis., along with a dozen other villages, killing 1,200 to 2,500 people and charring approximately 1.5 million acres. The Peshtigo Fire remains the deadliest in American history, but the remoteness of the region meant it was little noticed at the time. Across the lake to the east, the town of Holland, Mich., and other nearby areas burned to the ground. Some 100 miles to the north of Holland, the lumbering community of Manistee, Mich., also went up in flames. Farther east, along the shore of Lake Huron, another tremendous fire swept through Port Huron, Mich., and much of Michigan's "thumb." That four large fires occurred all on the same day, all on the shores of Lake Michigan, suggests a common root cause and some believe that cause was Biela's Comet, which broke up and rained down over the Midwest at that time. It has been theorized that the eyewitness accounts of spontaneous ignitions, a lack of smoke from all of the fires, and flames falling from the sky could have been the result of pieces of the comet falling to earth.

Could one of these sparks have landed on the O'Leary barn, thereby letting the cow off the hook for Chicago's greatest fire?

**Contemporary illustrations, like these from Harper's Weekly, show the madness and panic that was described in first-hand accounts of the Great Fire.**

such a short amount of time. The watchman on the City Hall tower had misjudged the blaze's location and called for a fire company that was located a mile and a half out of the way, causing a terrible delay. In addition, a strong, dry wind from the southwest was blowing. Furthermore, most of Chicago's fire companies had been exhausted by a fire on the West Side the day before and had celebrated the defeat of the blaze by getting drunk. The firemen had been working almost day and night all summer, battling one conflagration after another, and had needed to relax. The residents of "the city of shams and shingles," had believed that it would never burn. Fires might damage small neighborhoods, but not the great city.

Within half an hour, all of Chicago was on the streets, running for the river. Most could not believe what they were seeing as a wall of flames, miles wide and hundreds of feet high, devoured the West Side and was carried on the wind toward the very heart of the city. By 10:30 p.m., it was officially out of control and soon the mills and factories along the river were on fire. Buildings, even across the river, were hit by fiery missiles from the main blaze, and began to burn. Owners of downtown buildings began throwing water on roofs and walls as the air filled with sparks and cinders that contemporary accounts described as resembling red rain.

Even then, the crowds were sure that the flames would die out when they struck the blackened, four-block area that had been burned during the previous night's fire. But with the force of hundreds of burning homes and buildings behind it, the blaze passed over the burned-out path, attacked the grain elevators along the river, and fell upon the Union Station.

From the West Side, a mob poured into the downtown section, jamming the bridges and flooding the streets. It was believed that the river would stop the fire in its path, but a blazing board that was carried on the wind settled on the roof of a tenement building at Adams and Franklin, one-third of a mile from any burning building. The fire hungrily jumped the river and began pushing toward the center of the city. Fire engines, frantic to save the more valuable property of the business district, pushed back over the bridges from the West Side.

Great masses of frightened and now-homeless people surged ahead of the flames. They were blistered and scorched by the horrific heat. They carried bundles, babies and invalids, dragging trunks and carts, stumbling, falling, trampling fallen children, crying and screaming so loudly that sometimes the shouting could be heard above the roar of the flames.

Among the first downtown buildings to be engulfed was the new Parmalee Omnibus & Stage Company at the southeast corner of Jackson and Franklin streets. A flying brand also struck the South Side Gas Works and soon this structure burst into flames, creating a new and larger center for the fire. At this point, even the grease- and oil-covered river caught fire and the surface of the water shimmered with heat and flames.

In moments, the fire also spread to the banks and office buildings along LaSalle Street. Soon, the inferno became impossible to battle with more than a dozen different locations burning at once. The fire swept through Wells, Market and Franklin streets, igniting more than five hundred different buildings. One by one, these great structures fell. The *Tribune* building, long vaunted as "fireproof," was turned into a smoking ruin, as was Marshall Field's grand department store, along with hundreds of other businesses.

Many of the great hotels, like the Palmer House and the Sherman, were reduced to blazing ash. The Grand Pacific Hotel, which had just been completed and was not yet open, crashed down in flames. Another new hotel, the Bigelow, with its art gallery, Turkish carpets and carved wood furniture, was also consumed. The Tremont House burned for the fourth time in its history and the manager, John Drake, left the place in a hurry, carrying the contents of the hotel safe in a pillowcase. Unshaken, Drake passed by the Avenue Hotel on Congress Street and noting that it was untouched by fire, he entered and approached the distracted owner with a startling offer to buy the place, right then and there with $1,000 from the Tremont's safe as a down payment. The deal was made and a hasty bill of sale was written, witnessed by fleeing guests. Drake then departed and went home with his pillowcase full of silver. He knew that he had an even chance of being a hotel owner the next morning. As it turned out, the Avenue Hotel survived, but Drake had to insist on his ownership rights with a pistol.

In the early morning hours of Monday, the fire reached the courthouse, which stood in a block surrounded by LaSalle, Clark, Randolph and Washington streets. A burning timber landed on the building's wooden cupola and it soon turned into a fire that blazed out of control. The building was ordered evacuated. The prisoners, who had begun to scream and shake the bars of their cells as smoke filled the air, were released. Most of them were allowed to simply go free, but the most dangerous of them were shackled and taken away under guard. The prisoners that were released immediately went across the street to a nearby jewelry store and looted it.

Just after 2:00 a.m., the courthouse bell tolled for the last time before crashing through the remains of the building to the ground beneath it. The roaring sound made by the building's collapse was reportedly heard more than a mile away.

Around this same time, the State Street Bridge, leading to the city's North Side, also caught fire and the inferno began to devour the area on the north side of the river. Soon, stables, warehouse and breweries were also burning. The lumber mills and wood storage yards on the riverbanks were eaten by the fire and many people who were dunking themselves in the water had to flee again to keep from being strangled by the black smoke. Some people threw chairs and sofas into the river and sat with just their heads and shoulders visible. Many of them stayed in the river for up to fourteen hours.

Then, the fire swept into the luxurious residential district surrounding Cass, Huron, Ontario, Rush and Dearborn streets. Here stood the mansions of some of Chicago's oldest and most prominent families. By daylight, these beautiful homes were nothing but ruins. Servants desperately buried their employers' valuables in hidden places on the grounds. Oddly enough, at least a dozen pianos were later unearthed in gardens. Also discovered were family silver collections that, despite being buried, had melted into twisted masses from the heat.

Members of the Chicago Club, the expensive enclave of the rich, never dreamed that the fire would dare to affect them. Many of them had breakfast while the city burned and they toasted their defiance of the fire. The building burned, though, almost as the men lifted their glasses, and they ran for their lives, after having stuffed their coats with wine bottles from the best years' vintages and fine Havana cigars. The club's celebrated red satin lobby sofas were carried in grand fashion down to the lake.

The flames were not the only threat that the city's residents of had to worry about. In the early hours of the fire, looting and violence had broken out. Saloonkeepers, hoping that it might prevent their taverns from being destroyed, had foolishly rolled barrels of whiskey out into the streets. Soon, men and women of all classes were staggering in the streets, thoroughly intoxicated. The drunks and the looters did not comprehend the danger they were in and many were trampled in the streets. Plundered goods were tossed aside and were lost in the fire, abandoned by the looters as the fire drew near.

From the burning lairs of the underworld came throngs of gunmen, thieves and prostitutes, hurrying to snatch up the loot that had been left behind or was being carried by the panicked citizens. They roamed singly and in packs, taking what they wanted from wagons and carriages, breaking into saloons, stores and homes. They drank liquor, stuffed their pockets with cash and jewelry and covered themselves with fine clothing, rings, necklaces and bracelets. The *Chicago Post* later published, "They smashed windows with their naked hands, regardless of the wounds inflicted, and with bloody fingers rifled till and shelf and cellar, fighting viciously for the spoils of their forage. Women, hollow-eyed and brazen-faced, with filthy drapery tied over them, their clothes in tatters and their feet in trodden-over slippers, moved here and there – scolding, stealing, fighting; laughing at the beautiful and splendid crash of walls and falling roofs."

Alexander Frear, a New York alderman, who was caught in the fire, remembered seeing Wabash Avenue choked with crowds and discarded bundles.

"Valuable oil paintings, books, pets, musical instruments, toys, mirrors and bedding were trampled under foot. Goods from stores had been hauled out and had taken fire, and the crowd, breaking into a liquor establishment, was yelling with the fury of demons. A fellow standing on a piano declared that the fire was the friend of the poor man. In this chaos were hundreds of children, wailing and crying for their parents. One little girl in particular I saw, whose golden hair was loose down her back and had caught fire. She ran screaming past me and somebody threw a glass of liquor upon her, which flared up and covered her with a blue flame," Frear later wrote.

On Lake Street, Frear saw a man loading a wagon with loot that he had stolen from Shay's, a dry-goods store. Someone with a revolver shouted at him not to drive away and the thief replied, "Fire and be damned!" The man put the pistol back into his pocket. Frear recalled that everyone seemed to be shouting at the top of his lungs. He saw people pushed off bridges and into the river to drown, while boat crews fought to keep crowds from clambering onto their decks.

Frear also wrote that rough-looking men carried women and children to safety and then went back into danger to find more. Police officers saved countless lives as fireman dashed into the flames and carried out unconscious victims. Horses broke out of stables, or fought loose from their handlers, and ran frenziedly through the streets. Rats, smoked out from under houses and wooden sidewalks, died squealing under the feet of the fleeing masses.

During the early morning hours, the flames jumped the river to the north and the panicked residents ran ahead of the fire, edging eastward, toward the lakefront and Lincoln Park. Women's dresses caught on fire. Sick

**Chicagoans took refuge in any safe place they could find, both during and after the fire, including in the open graves of the City Cemetery, which is now Lincoln Park.**

and injured people, carried on mattresses, stretchers, and chairs, were knocked to the ground and trampled. Some of the fugitives, insane with fear, plunged into blazing alleyways and were burned alive. Many of the elderly were crushed under the feet of the frantic crowds and a number of housewives, rushing into their homes for cherished possessions, perished in the inferno. The Chicago Historical Society was destroyed, losing city records of incalculable value and the original draft of the Emancipation Proclamation, which Abraham Lincoln had written during the Civil War.

Lincoln Park -- only recently a cemetery -- became a macabre location during the fire as it served as a gathering place for uprooted families and fleeing fire victims. Graves in what had once been the old City Cemetery had been opened so that their occupants could be moved and now the yawning pits and the haphazardly stacked tombstones were being used to shelter huddled masses of adults and children.

On the lakefront, thousands took refuge away from any buildings that might burn but they were still tortured by the heat and the storm of falling embers. Men buried their wives and children in the sand, with a hole for air, and splashed water over them. Many fled to stand chin-deep in the waters of Lake Michigan, breathing through handkerchiefs.

Throughout the day on Monday, the fire kept to its wind-driven task, finishing the business section and the North Side. The wind blew so hard that firefighters could get water no more than ten feet past the nozzles of their hoses. Streams of water could not carry above two stories. Fire engines were destroyed in the flames and companies were separated from their officers. The fire department, like the city of Chicago, was destroyed.

Thankfully, the fire began to die on the morning of October 10, when steady and soaking rains began to fall.

The Great Fire, as it was called from then on, was to be the most disastrous event in America until the San Francisco earthquake and fire of 1906. The people of the city were devastated, as was the city itself. Over three hundred people were officially reported dead. The fate of many more was never discovered, or their bodies were never found. Another one hundred thousand were without homes or shelter. The fire had cut a swath through the city that was four miles long and about two-thirds of a mile wide. Over $200 million in property had been destroyed. Records, deeds, archives, libraries and priceless artwork were lost although a little of it survived in public and private vaults. In the destruction of the Federal Building, which, among other

Devastation of Chicago after the Great Fire

**Left to Right -- Ruins of the Courthouse; Monroe & Dearborn Streets; Remains of Trinity Church**

things, housed the post office, more than $100,000 in currency was burned.

Chicago had become a blasted and charred wasteland.

On Tuesday, sightseers poured into town; among them were hundreds of criminals from neighboring regions, eager for pillage. Local business owners hired Allan Pinkerton to assign his detectives positions around the remains of stores and banks and soon, six companies of Federal troops were deployed under the command of General Phillip Sheridan to assist in maintaining order. Two days later, Chicago's Mayor Roswell Mason placed the city under martial law, entrusting Sheridan and his troops to watch over it.

Sheridan recruited a volunteer home guard of about one thousand men to patrol unburned areas of the city. He also enforced a curfew, much to the chagrin of Illinois governor John M. Palmer, who felt that martial law was uncalled for and unnecessary. Mayor Mason was heavily influenced by local business leaders, however, and ignored Palmer's order to withdraw the troops.

The state of martial law didn't last long. A few days after it went into effect, a local businessman - one of those responsible for pushing Mason into enacting martial law - was accidentally killed by a member of the volunteer home guard. In spite of this, Sheridan received orders from President Grant that left four companies of men on active duty in the city through the end of the year.

Bizarre cases of arson, which seemed to follow every large conflagration, were discovered. Seven men who were caught setting fires were shot and an eighth was beaten to death by a group of angry Chicagoans at Fourteenth Street and Fourth Avenue. His body was left lying in the street for 24 hours as a warning to others who might be inclined to start their own blaze.

On the morning of October 10, 1871, W.D. Kerfoot, a well-known real estate agent, went to the ruins of his office on Washington Street, between Clark and Dearborn. With the assistance of his clerk and the clerk's father, he cleared away the still smoldering ashes and hastily constructed a wooden shanty where his office once stood. In front of it, he placed a sign that read "Kerfoot's Block – W.D. Kerfoot – Everything Gone but Wife, Children and Energy."

This was the first building erected in Chicago after the fire. But by October 18, just ten days after the start of the disaster, business was being carried on in more than five thousand temporary structures, and within a year, more than ten thousand permanent structures had been erected.

By the end of the decade, Chicago was a bigger and grander city that it had ever dreamed of being. The vigor of the city's rebirth amazed the rest of the nation and within three years, it once again dominated the western United States. It soared from the ashes like the fabled phoenix and became the home of the nation's first skyscraper in 1885. The city then passed the one million mark in population five years later. The Great Chicago Fire marked the beginning of a new metropolis, much greater than it could have ever become if the horrific fire had never happened.

Despite the widespread devastation of Chicago, only a handful of ghostly tales concerning the Great Fire survived into modern times. Perhaps the most famous story is connected to the Chicago Water Tower, which stands on North Michigan Avenue. The limestone tower and the pumping station across the street were built in 1869 by acclaimed architect William W. Boyington. The interior of the water tower was a 138-foot-high standpipe to hold water. It was to be used as a storage tank for firefighters and in addition, the pressure in the pipe could be regulated to control water surges in the area.

The tower gained prominence after the Great Fire. With the city in ashes, only a handful of buildings in the downtown district remained. One of them was the tower and in the years that followed, it has become a symbol of old Chicago and of the city's recovery after the fire.

It's also become known as a haunted place.

Eyewitness accounts say that passersby and shoppers on Michigan Avenue have often gotten a glimpse of what appears to be a hanging man in one of the tower's upper windows. When they take a closer look, the man always disappears, leaving them shaken and unsure about what they have seen. Those with the responsibility of maintaining the upkeep on the tower say that they have had many of these eerie reports over the years and don't know what to make of them.

There is a legend, though, from the days of the Great Fire, that just might explain what people have been seeing in the tower window. According to the story, the structure is haunted by the ghost of a man who stayed on the job during the fire, continuing to pump the water as the fire got closer. This heroic man waited until the last possible minute and then took his own life rather than be engulfed in the flames. He had no way of knowing, as the wall of flame drew closer, that the tower would escape destruction. Perhaps this terrible regret is what keeps his spirit attached to this place.

Since the fire, his ghost has reportedly been seen through an upper window of the tower, dangling from the end of a rope, and his footsteps are said to have been heard inside as he scrambles away from the approaching flames.

There is one other unsettling story in regard to the Great Fire, which may (admittedly) be more speculation than fact. It involves the LaSalle Street Bridge, which crosses over the Chicago River. There have been many strange reports over the years of people being frightened, unnerved and just plain terrified while on this bridge. Others say that they have been overwhelmed with feelings of sadness. There are even reports of screams, cries and the occasional sounds of running feet, as though a large group of people is trying desperately to get away from something. What could cause such weird stories to be told and how can they be connected to the Great Fire when the bridge that currently exists at LaSalle Street had not even been built at the time of the fire?

Directly beneath the LaSalle Street Bridge is something that even many long-time Chicagoans don't know about: a tunnel that travels beneath the river.

From the early days of Chicago, the low bridges crossing the Chicago River frequently had to be opened for

**La Salle Street Tunnel**

masted vessels to pass through, cutting off street traffic to the North and West Sides. City officials began discussing tunnels as early as 1844. The LaSalle Street Tunnel was the city's second tunnel under the river. It was started in November 1869 and finished on July 4, 1871 – just a few months before the fire.

When the Great Fire broke out, the wooden bridges over the river were almost immediately consumed, which turned the tunnels into a valuable escape route. According to some reports, when the buildings on LaSalle Street began to burn, flames were sucked into the tunnel, turning it into a death trap. Unfortunately, because of the lack of accurate records for the fire, we have no idea how many – if any – people actually perished in the tunnel. However, it is believed that a number of victims never made it to the south side of the river.

Although the tunnel originally only served private vehicles and pedestrians, a cable car company took it over in the 1880s because the cable car line, which operated on a constant source of electricity, could not cross the LaSalle Street drawbridge. In 1906, the tunnel was closed with the end of cable car operations but a wider, deeper replacement was built beneath it that opened to streetcar service in 1911-1912.

The tunnel was finally closed for good in 1939, although the entrance to the Reid-Murdoch building's parking garage is actually the entrance to the tunnel and it's still used today. The tunnel itself still exists, although the entrance was sealed off and filled with sand in the 1950s, and it still runs beneath the present-day LaSalle Street Bridge.

Could the existence of this tunnel – which served as an escape route and possible death scene for fleeing residents during the Great Fire – explain the supernatural events that still occur today on the bridge? Many believe so, especially those who have had a strange and chilling encounter at this spot.

# 1871: THE GREAT PESHTIGO FIRE
## "THE WOODS & HEAVEN WERE ALL ON FIRE"

On October 8, 1871, the single most destructive fire in American history devastated a portion of the Midwest. It was not the Great Chicago Fire, which occurred on this same date, but a much less widely known conflagration a few hours to the north in Wisconsin. To those who experience the terrifying events of the Peshtigo Fire, it must have seemed that the world was coming to an end. The smoke blocked out the sun, the rising moon turned red and one witness later wrote that, "the woods and heaven were all on fire."

The blaze, pushed by hurricane force winds, consumed more than one million acres of farms, forests, sawmills and small towns in Wisconsin and upper Michigan. In the path of destruction, an estimated 1,500 people lost their lives, making this the greatest natural tragedy of its kind in North America. With the fire occurring on the same day as the Great Chicago Fire, it has been relegated to a lesser place in the annals of American disaster and yet it left perhaps even a greater mark on the landscape of the country than this much more famous blaze.

The summer of 1871 had been a dry season for the upper Midwest. Almost no rain had fallen between July and October and the Peshtigo and Menominee rivers were at their lowest levels in years. The forests of Wisconsin were ready to burn.

Despite the ever-present threat of fire, those who lived in the region went about their everyday lives. Farmers worked their fields and kept their livestock healthy and fed. The dry weather even gave them the opportunity to clear more land and smoldering stumps of trees littered the newly cleared and parched landscape for much of the summer and into the early fall. Even with the drought-like conditions, the slash and burn method was still the best way to clear hundreds of acres of ground. This left scattered piles of flammable debris, just steps away from homes, barns and fields that had been baked dry by the weather.

Loggers in the region worked hard all summer, too. The vast tracts of immense white pines and the numerous fast-moving rivers had lured lumber and railroad magnates like Chicago millionaire William Butler Ogden to Wisconsin and provided a way of life for the increasing number of immigrants arriving in the area. Communities like Peshtigo and Marinette were supported by the lumber industry and logging camps dotted the landscape for miles around.

William Ogden was the man responsible for much of the growth that had come to the region. He was greatly respected and admired, both in Peshtigo and Chicago, where he had served as the city's first mayor. His venture in the north woods made him a millionaire many times over. He built and owned the prosperous Peshtigo Company and built a community for his employees that included a company store, schools for the workers' children and a rooming house for two hundred of the unmarried men.

Lumber was a booming business in the region but this summer it had been problematic. The unusual low river levels had prevented the lumberjacks from floating logs downriver to the mills. They were usually ordered to leave the cut timber in piles alongside the Peshtigo and Menominee rivers, providing potential fuel for any fire that might break out. The logging practices of the era also produced a large amount of waste, called slash, made up of unusable tree branches. Tons of this material littered the logged-over land north and west of Peshtigo and Marinette. In their wake, lumberjacks had unknowingly left behind a deadly fuel to help the coming inferno.

Where there was logging, there were sawmills. Thanks to the massive amount of trees cut down in the surrounding forests, there were eight sawmills in the towns of Peshtigo and Marinette alone. They turned out millions of boards and thousands of finished goods every year. These mills so dominated the landscape that a fine layer of sawdust blanketed the towns. The dust was carelessly disposed of – shoveled into the streets, placed under wooden sidewalks and pine board houses or simply piled into enormous mounds near the mills. The sawdust was merely a by-product of progress, the locals knew, and they learned to embrace the inconvenience of it with a sense of grim resignation. And while the sawdust represented prosperity, it added more fuel for the fire to come.

The new work being done by rail gangs added to the volatile nature of the forests. Prior to the Civil War, the region had been slow to grow and during the war itself, nearly all of the men left the woods and marched into battle. After 1865, though, Wisconsin's population nearly tripled and the lumber industry contributed greatly to those numbers. Peshtigo soon became one of the three largest cities in the state, north of Green Bay. William Ogden, always with an eye for expansion, encouraged the railroads to move north. The railroads could move both men and machinery and link farm and industry together. It was faster, less expensive, and safer than shipping lumber by barge via Lake Michigan to Milwaukee and Chicago. The lake was notoriously dangerous during the winter months, and gale-force winds could easily sink a cumbersome lumber barge, taking product down with it. Railroads seemed to be the answer to the problem and by September 1871, the Chicago & Northwestern Railroad was piercing the north woods, bringing rail and telegraph lines along with it.

The rail gangs worked feverishly and by October, the line had advanced from Green Bay to a point just south of Peshtigo. In their haste, they left smoldering logs and vegetation piled along the railroad right-of-way.

The nineteenth century methods of land clearing, logging and rail construction, combined with the drought-like conditions, created the perfect setting for a massive forest fire. The only thing missing was the right combination of metrological conditions that would create such a destructive scenario. On October 8, 1871, the elusive weather conditions arrived – and the region would never be the same again.

By late September, the area was experiencing small fires in the woods. The eyes of Peshtigo residents were red from the ever-present smoke that choked the air. At night, they watched the flames from the fires stretch beyond the canopy of the forest and into the black sky. Some of the railroad crews were nervous enough about the situation – both the small fires and the lack of drinking water-- that they went on strike. They could find plenty of whiskey and beer in the saloons of Peshtigo, but good clean water was getting harder and harder to come by.

The residents of Peshtigo and surrounding communities like Oconto and Little Suamico began to prepare for the worst. Logging crews dug fire ditches along the forest edge, and in the towns, workmen set aside barrels of what water could be spared in order to wet down the sawmills.

On September 23, a slight change in the wind sent sparks across the Peshtigo River and set fire to some sawdust and boards adjacent to the woodenware factory. Loggers, lumbermen and shopkeepers alike turned out to fight the fire, passing buckets along a human chain that stretched from the river to the blaze. Several other fires broke out on the same day in a number of surrounding communities, destroying barns, homes and mills.

Fires burned in every direction from Peshtigo and it seemed that as soon as one was extinguished, another started in a neighboring town. There were later reports of a fire so intense that it burned up from under the ground. Months of drought and very low humidity levels had caused organic materials under the earth's surface to dry out. Not only were the trees on fire, even the ground beneath them crackled with flame.

Peshtigo's makeshift fire company successfully fought several fires over a three-day period, starting on Saturday, September 23. On Monday, the wind cleared the smoke away and miraculously, the town had been saved. By Wednesday, the tired and worried residents tried to resume their usual activities, hoping that the worst danger had passed. Many believed that the burned trees bordering the town would provide a natural fire barrier and would protect them if a large blaze broke out. Instead, the trees would act like giant sticks of charcoal in the days to come.

Outside of Peshtigo, farmers began to bury their possessions in an attempt to save them from certain destruction, while others wrestled with the decision to evacuate the area for safety in the city of Green Bay. No one was sure what to do for it seemed hard to believe that a danger could be created that they could not face. One local resident later wrote, "The surrounding woods were interspersed with innumerable open glades of crisp brown herbage and dried furze, which had for weeks glowed with the autumn fires that infest these regions. Little heed was paid them, for the first rain would inevitably quench the flames. But the rain never came…"

During the first days of October, thick smoke blanketed Peshtigo, forcing the inhabitants to cover their mouths with handkerchiefs in order to breathe. The sun, which was barely visible, threw an eerie, yellowish pall over the land.

Then, on October 8, a low-pressure system over southwestern Minnesota, coupled with a slow-moving high-pressure system over the Mid-Atlantic states, created moderate southwesterly winds in northeastern Michigan. It was this terrible weather scenario that would create a nightmare for the entire region. This cyclonic storm, with counterclockwise winds that would eventually reach more than sixty miles an hour, fanned the flames of the small fires into a hellish inferno that could devour the forests, homes and residents of the north woods.

*And Hell Followed With It – Page 168*

As the wind began to blow in Peshtigo, one resident later remembered, "the forest rocked and tossed tumultuously." The air became saturated with heat – enough to almost burn the skin. The noise of the wind became louder and impossible to ignore. Father Pernin, a priest in Peshtigo, later wrote that the deafening sound was like "the confused noise of a number of cars and locomotives approaching a railroad station, or the rumbling of thunder, with the difference that it never ceased, but deepened in intensity each moment."

Terror mounted as the people listened and looked at the town around them, hazy and yellowish from the smoke. Some came from church, others poured from the saloons, but all came to stand on the sidewalks and in the streets, looking at the towering, swaying trees past the edge of town. Suddenly, at 9:00 p.m., the first fire alarm was raised in Peshtigo. Swirling blasts of fire came from every direction at once. One witness wrote, "A great flame shot up in the western heavens, and in countless fiery tongues struck downward into the village." In less than ten minutes, the entire town was engulfed in flames.

The fires that came on October 8 were unlike any of the fires that had previously threatened Peshtigo and the surrounding areas. Many of the survivors claimed that the winds from the fire whirled about like a tornado, attaining speeds like the famers, loggers and rail gangs – all experienced with past fires – had never seen before. It seemed to feed on itself, sucking up everything in its path, including trees that had already been burned.

What the witnesses experienced was a phenomenon known as a "fire vortex" and these vortices contributed to the speed and destructive nature of the Peshtigo fire. Fire whirlwinds of this nature consisted of violent updrafts forming over the fire center. When survivors told of "fire tornadoes," they were referring to the rotating movements of the fire whirlwinds, which developed within, and immediately downwind, of the wildfire. They made it virtually impossible to escape the flames. The rapidly moving vortices scattered burning debris in a wide area, torching buildings and people located miles from the edge of the main fire.

The whirlwinds seemed almost alive. A series of events provided the necessary fuel to keep the deadly vortices spinning. The burning ground cover provided heat for the whirlwind air column, destabilizing the air and creating strong updrafts and drawing surface winds inward toward the center of the tornado. Horizontal surface winds fed the insatiable fire by transporting fuel into the whirlwind, heating the air, enhancing its buoyancy, and increasing the whirlwind circulation. The fire was not only feeding itself, it was

**The remote location of the Peshtigo Fire, combined with its overshadowing by the fire in Chicago at the same time, caused it to receive little attention from the press of the day. Almost no photographs of the damage exist -- only a handful of contemporary illustrations.**

creating its own weather pattern.

Survivors from Peshtigo said that the "tornado swept in currents and eddies of fire, in which many were caught and smothered on the spot, while others with great difficulty worked their way, some to the river and some to an open field on one side of town." Others believed that the large boarding house in town simply would not, on the basis of its size, succumb to the flames. Hundreds crowded into the structure only to be burned alive as the fire swept over it. After the disaster, the building was described as "a mass of ashes." No one escaped from the boarding house alive and all that remained was "a pile of human ashes, from which can be picked out pieces of human bones, the largest not two inches long, and these split and broken."

Those who could make it sought refuge in the river. Unfortunately, the speed of the fire prevented many from reaching the water. Panicking onlookers groping their way to the river watched as waves of fire ignited everything in their path. Men, women, and children burst into flames in an instant. Many believed that the river bridge led to safety, but flames engulfed both sides of the river. People attempting to escape from either side collided in the middle of the bridge. Then, the bridge caught fire, dumping everyone into the water below and many drowned. Others poured into the water from the riverbanks and immersed themselves in the protective water. For the next five hours, they watched in horror as their city burned to the ground. In the glare of the flames, they saw "the sloping bank covered with the bodies of those who fell by the way. Few living on the back streets succeeded in reaching the river, the hot breath of the fire cutting them down as they ran."

Those who plunged into the river thought they would be safe in the water, but even the river could not provide complete protection from the superheated air, burning logs that floated downstream and flaming embers from the sky. Only by constantly throwing water upon their heads did the waterlogged survivors manage to avoid injury from the flames. Many of them had every hair burned off their head during the fire and many lost their lives protecting others. But fire was not the only danger. The cool waters of the Peshtigo River began to chill the refugees and despite the superheated air around them, many were in danger of succumbing to hypothermia. People finally emerged from the river at daylight but others, caught in the chaos of fleeing people, panicked livestock and burning logs, did not survive. A report taken from an observation of the scene the next day spoke of mothers and children, unable to escape the clutches of the fire, lying in "rigid groups, the clothes burned off and the poor flesh scarred to a crisp."

Peshtigo had been literally wiped off the map. The fire had destroyed everything. The heat and tornado-like winds of the firestorm had melted the wheels of railroad cars, leveled buildings, and uprooted the charred remains of trees. Less than seven hundred people remained from the once happy and prosperous town of two thousand souls Survivors began the heart-breaking search for friends and loved ones. Nearly everyone had lost someone to the blaze. The dead were not always recognizable and lay in the streets where they had fallen. One account stated, "Where houses stood the ground was whipped clean as a carpet and the hope of identifying human ashes was idle." One horror-stricken man found the remains of his nephew only recognizable by the boy's treasured pen knife – which was embedded in a mound of ashes.

On Monday evening, about twenty-four hours after the fire arrived at Peshtigo, the long-awaited rain finally arrived. It came, one survivor wrote "gratefully to the living, and kindly to the fleeting ashes of the dead."

Stories of heroism and horror followed in the wake of the fire. The inferno had struck with such suddenness that there was hardly time for people to save themselves and yet many risked their lives to save others. One farmer west of Peshtigo found himself in a clearing with his wife and fourteen children when the fire swept over the forest. The children were not all his own – eight of them belonged to a neighbor who had sent them to the clearing for safety. The farmer kept his wits about him as the fire came closer. Using only his hands, he dug a hole and then covered all of the children and his wife with dirt and then threw handfuls on himself. All survived.

A little girl who had managed to survive the fire in Peshtigo, and yet had lost her entire family, was taken in by generous strangers in Oconto who eventually adopted her.

A poor cobbler who was fleeing to the river stopped and picked up a frightened little girl and carried her to safety. The child turned out to be a relative of the governor of Michigan, who handsomely rewarded the cobbler's bravery.

Some preferred to die by their own hand rather than face a painful death by fire. One young man reportedly returned to his family home, found his parent's dead and slashed his own throat in despair. Another, apparently uncertain whether he was safe from the flames by hiding in his well, wrapped the bucket chain around his neck and hanged himself. One man, search parties believed, murdered his children and then himself after watching his wife die in the flames.

About two hundred and sixty people died in the Upper, Middle and Lower Sugar Bush settlements west of Peshtigo. The farms were isolated and the residents had nowhere to flee once they found themselves surrounded by the flames. The desolation caused by the fire was so complete that many who survived the fire starved to death before rescue parties could find them.

It is estimated that at least 1,500 people perished in the October 8 fire. At Peshtigo, it was written, "The names of half the dead will never be known. They are buried all over Peshtigo, and the boards that mark their graves are marked '2 unknown', '3 unknown,' etc."

The injured packed into a nearby, understaffed and overwhelmed hospital and spoke of the tragedy. "Most of them suffer

more from hurts of the mind than hurts of the body," it was reported. One woman cried of hearing the screams of her daughter and her crippled son as they perished in the flames.

To make matters worse, communications between the burned-out areas and the outside world were hampered by the destruction of the telegraph lines. A telegram from Green Bay did not reach the state capital of Madison until October 10. By that time, news of the Great Chicago Fire was known throughout the country. At the same time that Chicago was burning, an even greater fire was engulfing the land a few hundred miles to the north. It was America's greatest natural disaster but was overshadowed by the fire in Chicago. William Ogden turned out to be a victim of both fires, losing well over $3 million to the flames.

By the time that news of the Peshtigo Fire reached Madison, Governor Lucius Fairchild was already on his way to Chicago with a trainload of supplies for fire victims in the city. It was the governor's young wife, Frances, who received the telegram with news of the north country devastation. She immediately took charge of the situation and began to organize a relief effort to provide material goods to meet the needs of Wisconsin's fire victims. She even commandeered a supply train headed for Chicago. In a matter of hours, Mrs. Fairchild had gathered enough blankets to fill a train car, and it was soon on its way to Green Bay. Over the following days, Mrs. Fairchild continued her efforts to acquire more supplies, and with the return of her husband from Chicago, the state began a massive relief effort for the survivors. A number of private agencies and communities throughout the state offered their assistance, and support eventually came from every state in the Union as well as from foreign countries. Frances Fairchild is still considered a hero to the people of northern Wisconsin.

The Peshtigo Fire remains today a unique disaster in American history. It was a "perfect storm" of various

## 10 MOST DEADLY AMERICAN WILDFIRES

1. Killed: 1,500 - Oct. 8-14, 1871 - 3.8 million acres burned - Peshtigo, WI
2. Killed: 800 to 1,000, Injured/Displaced: 52,000 - Oct. 13-15, 1918 - 250,000 acres burned - Cloquet, MN
3. Killed: 600-800 - Sept. 1, 1894 - 200,000 acres burned - Completely destroyed Hinkley, Mission Creek and Brook Park, MN
4. Killed: 282 - Sept. 1, 1894 - 1 million acres burned - The Thumb Fire - Port Huron, MI
5. Killed: 200 - Oct. 8-21, 1871 - 1.2 million acres burned - The Port Huron Fire of 1871 (same time as Peshtigo, WI and the Great Chicago Fires) - Port Huron, MI
6. Killed: 160 - Oct. 1825 - 3 million acres burned - Maine and New Brunswick, Canada
7. Killed: 85 - Aug. 20-21, 1910 - 3 million acres burned - The Big Blow Up or the Big Burn - ID and MT
8. Killed: 38 - Sept. 1902 -1 million acres burned - Yacoult Fire - WA and OR
9. Killed: 25 - Oct. 20, 1991 - 1,520 acres burned - Oakland, CA
10. Killed: 24 - Oct. 2003 - 800,000 acres burned - Southern California

events that came together to create a conflagration unlike any other. Specific weather conditions and an abundance of fuel combined to create a series of tornado-like fires that dramatically – and permanently -- altered the landscape of northwestern Wisconsin.

Entire towns were destroyed, homes were wiped out and entire families perished in the flames and yet, the people of the region wasted little time in rebuilding their lives. William Ogden vowed to resume operations as soon as possible, to rebuild Peshtigo and "do a larger winter's logging than ever before." His positive, and much-publicized outlook infected others and the area became a hive of activity in the aftermath of the fire. Homes were rebuilt, stores reopened and farmers returned to their land.

In the face of tragedy, strong wills prevailed.

# 1876: FINAL ACT AT THE BROOKLYN THEATRE

The audience sat in hushed silence, awaiting the rise of the curtain for the fifth and final act of "The Two Orphans." They had come to the elegant Brooklyn Theatre to see Miss Kate Claxton, the popular and talented American actress. She had created the role of Louise, the impoverished blind girl who had been abducted and separated from her twin sister. The French play had been very successful in Manhattan and now in Brooklyn, but it was about to close. No doubt, the crowd was excited to have the opportunity to see it before it moved on. When the curtain rose for the final act, no one had any idea that it really *was* the final act, or that in less than thirty minutes, nearly 300 of them would be dead.

Built on the site of the old St. John's Episcopal Church, the Brooklyn Theatre opened its doors on October 2, 1871. The theater was intended to be one of the premier production houses in the sister cities: Brooklyn and New York. Within a short time, it became highly respected within the legitimate theater. It was originally managed by Frederick and Sara Conway and was designed under Sara's close supervision. Sadly, they both died a few years after opening and management passed on to their children, with poor results. In August of 1875, a new lease on the theater was taken on by Albert Palmer and Sheridan Shook, who were already very successful as managers of the Union Square Theatre Company in New York. They had charge of the Brooklyn Theatre until it was destroyed by fire in 1876.

The structure, which seated 1,600 patrons, was an L-shaped building on the corner of Washington and Johnson streets, just one block from the former Brooklyn City Hall. The Dieter Hotel was tucked into the "crook" between the two wings of the theater. The larger of the wings housed the proscenium theater with the rear stage wall fronting onto Johnson Street. Included in the proscenium theatre wing was the auditorium seating area, the stage, dressing rooms and storage for scene decorations, flats, furniture and props. To accommodate bringing in and removing large scenery flats and props, there were twenty-foot-wide scene doors opening onto Johnson Street. The stage doors, located on the same side as the scene doors, were smaller but still wide enough to allow people carrying large loads to enter with ease. Though these doors were readily accessible to the stage, they were used solely for production purposes and never available to the general public.

As "The Two Orphans" was nearing the end of its run, materials for the next two productions were already being stored at the theater. The backstage area, usually fairly open and spacious, was now packed with stored items. These extra materials made it difficult for actors and support personnel to navigate backstage and in the wings. The managers ordered that the fire buckets filled with water be removed, so people would not knock them over and spill them while trying to maneuver around all the extra set pieces. The additional flats were piled up against the back wall, blocking the fire hose apparatus.

Washington Street wing of the Brooklyn Theatre. The theater is the tallest building with the ornate Mansard roof. The shorter, white building to the right is the First Precinct Police Station.

The smaller wing, fronting on Washington Street, was the public face of the Brooklyn Theatre. Here were the public street entrances, the main and secondary box offices for ticket sales, the lobby and the staircases leading to the two balconies. The production offices were located on the upper floors of this wing.

Each of the theater's three seating levels had its own special designation and commanded different ticket prices accordingly. There were six hundred floor-level seats in two sections known as "parquet" and "parquet circle." Parquet circle seats were the best of the floor seats and tickets sold for a dollar fifty. Parquet seating was very close to the stage and considered to be less desirable so the cost was lower at seventy-five cents. The lower balcony, known as "dress circle." contained 550 seats and tickets sold for one dollar. The "family circle," made up the upper balcony and seated 450 patrons. These seats were farthest from the stage and nearest the ceiling so tickets were just fifty cents. The most choice and elegant seating was in eight private boxes, four on each side of the stage. Each box held up to six seats at a premium ticket cost of ten dollars.

The theater's architect, Thomas R. Jackson, was very conscience of safety. He designed the structure so that it could be completely emptied within five minutes in case of emergency, even though there were no external fire escapes. In addition to the public entrances and the large scene and stage doors, he built three special exits into the long wall that made up the far side of the seating auditorium at ground level. These were large six-foot-wide double doors opening onto Flood's Alley, which in turn led to Washington Street. One set was near the rear corner, the second in the center of the wall and the third just in front of the stage. Although these doors were kept locked to thwart intended gate crashers, the ushers had keys so they could be opened easily and quickly.

The staircases were also designed for ease and safety. The main flight from the dress circle on the first balcony was ten feet wide and opened into the box office lobby. There was also a narrow emergency staircase on the opposite side of the balcony that lead to the Flood's Alley exit nearest the stage.

The family circle had a different design than the parquet and dress circles on the two lower levels. It had only one exit staircase leading from the upper balcony. Though it was a generous width at nearly seven feet, guests still needed to traverse two full flights separated by a long corridor. As was the custom of the day, the theater's family circle was viewed much as the steerage on a ship. Third class ticket holders were basically third class citizens. They had a separate entrance, separate box office and a separate set of stairs, so they could not mingle or interact with those patrons in dress circle or parquet.

On that fateful night in December 1976, there were nearly 1,200 people inside the Brooklyn Theatre including over a hundred theater employees and members of the acting company. The house manager reported that they had sold approximately 250 tickets for parquet and parquet circle, 360 tickets for dress circle and 400 for family circle. Not quite a packed house, but still, a very sizable crowd for a frigid Tuesday night.

Backstage, the area above the presentation platform was the fly space, or flies. Suspended in the flies were several scenic elements known as drops. In 1876, drops were large pieces of painted canvas mounted on wooden frames. Using the rigging loft in the fly space, drops and borders were raised or lowered as needed when scenes or acts called for a different setting. On the night of

**Kate Claxton as Louise in *The Two Orphans* at the Brooklyn Theatre.**

the fire, several additional drops were stored in the fly space and against the rear wall in preparation for the next play to open, but all was in working order.

The lighting for the body of the theater was provided by gaslights. The stage itself was lighted with gas-lit border lights equipped with reflectors. These lights were ignited by an electric spark and the level of light from each was controlled by regulating the gas flow. To ensure that these "open-flame" lights didn't ignite drops, props, furniture or curtains, they were covered with a protective wire frame, intended to keep objects at least a foot away from the flame.

The fifth and final act of "The Two Orphans" involved a major setting change. This act was to take place inside an old, derelict boathouse, poor Louise's family home. First, the drop and borders from the previous scene were raised into the fly space and the new set moved onto center stage. The set was a simple wooden frame draped with dark brown painted canvas. There was little in the way of set pieces, just a pallet of straw in the center of the "boat house."

It was just past 11:00 p.m. on December 5. The border drop from the previous scene had been raised and the stage crew was preparing the stage for the boathouse scene. Shortly before the curtain was to rise, stage manager J. W. Thorpe noticed that a border that had just been raised into the fly space had a broken frame corner and seemed to be hanging down at an angle, as if it had snagged on something. More importantly, he saw a small fire, not much larger than a fist, burning in the torn corner. Apparently the drop had gotten caught on the protective wire cage over one of the boarder gaslights and had ignited.

Kate Claxton had taken her place on stage and was lying on her back upon the straw pallet. Also on stage were two other actors, Henry Murdock and J. B. Studley. Waiting in the wings for their entrance cues were Mary Ann Farren and Claude Burroughs. Everyone had taken their places. Everything was ready to go. The audience was waiting.

Thorpe was unable to get to the fire hose that was behind the stored flats on the back wall and the fire buckets had been removed. He thought that the fire could be easily extinguished, and not wanting to disrupt the play, he directed two nearby carpenters to put the fire out and for the curtain to be raised for the final act.

Waiting to start the scene, Kate heard a rumbling sound "as if the roof were coming down" as the two carpenters, armed with long poles, were attempting to beat the fire out over their heads. Kate, looking up as she lay on her bed of straw, could see sparks floating down from the flies. But the curtain went up and she began the scene, delivering her first few lines without hesitation. As she lay there, Lillian Cleaves knelt just behind her on the other side of the canvas, out of sight of the audience, and whispered, "Save yourself, for God's sake! I am running now!"

More sparks and tongues of flame drifted down and were now in full view of the audience. Mary Ann Farren came on stage and knelt next to Kate, as if she were playing her roll, but instead whispered that the fire was steadily gaining. The audience, seeing the smoke and flames jumped up and began to lunge about as panic overtook them. A few, who were seated closest, tried to crawl up onto the stage. J.B. Studley, one of the actors on stage, tried to take command of the situation by addressing the audience directly. He stepped to the edge of the stage and shouted out at them that, "The play will go on and the fire will be put out. Be quiet. Get back in your seats." The crowd began to quiet and some returned to their seats.

Kate, in a further attempt to quiet the crowd, stepped forward and tried to tell the audience that the fire was part of the play and to remain calm. Within seconds, it became apparent that this could not be true as sparks continued to rain down. Studley continued, "If I have the presence of mind to stand here between you and the fire, which is right behind me, you ought to have the presence of mind to go out quietly." Kate Claxton then said, "The passage is clear. Get down. We are between you and the fire." As she spoke those last few words, a burning piece of wood fell to the stage at her feet and all attempts to calm the crowd were abandoned and panic took over, on the stage and in the audience.

Most of those in the stage area made their way to the large stage doors and out to safety, a route blocked from audience members by the growing fire. However, Henry Murdock muttered something about it being December and wanting a coat so he and Claude Burroughs left the stage heading upstairs to their dressing rooms. Sadly, these dressing rooms were directly over the growing fire and they were never seen alive again.

In an interview for the *Philadelphia Times*, just days before the ninth anniversary of the fire, Kate Claxton described her next actions as only a longtime actress of that era could. "For an instant I stood petrified with horror. For an instant there seemed no way of escape... Access to the stage door and all other exits in the rear had long ago been cut off by the flames. Suddenly, like an inspiration, there flashed upon me the recollection of a subterranean passage that led from the star dressing room to the box office... Maude Harrison's dressing room was next to mine. She was hastily gathering together some portions of her wardrobe. I knocked on her door and screamed that she must come with me quickly or we should both be lost. In a few seconds we were in the dark, narrow passage, and then an awful thought came into my mind. The door at the other end, which led into the box office, closed with a spring latch, and one of the ushers carried the key. What if it should be closed? The agony of suspense caused by this question made the few seconds that intervened before I learned its answer seem like years. We reached the door at last to find it open, thank God, and were soon in the box office. With the strength of madwomen we burst the box office door open against the seething, struggling crowd without, and were soon among them in the vestibule, within a few feet of the open street and life."

She continued, "We thought we were acting for the best in continuing the play as we did, with the hope that the fire would be put out without difficulty, or that the audience would leave gradually and quietly. But the result proved that it was not the right course. The fire broke out, as I have already said, just before the commencement of the last act. The curtain should have been kept down until the flames had been extinguished, or if it had been found impossible to cope with them, the audience should have been calmly informed that indisposition on the part of some member of the company or some unfortunate occurrence behind the scenery compelled a suspension of the performance, and they should have been requested to disperse as quietly as they could. Raising the curtain created a draft which fanned the flames into fury."

Whether their intentions were well meant or misguided, we can only speculate as to the effects of delaying the crowd for those few minutes in an attempt to quell their panic.

As the crowd attempted to flee en masse, head usher Thomas Rochford was able to unlock the emergency exit onto Flood's Alley at the rear of the floor seating area. Audience members in the parquet and parquet circle easily found their way out through that exit or to the Washington Street foyer. However, when Rochford opened the rear exit door, a rush of fresh air reinvigorated the fire and it rushed towards the back of the auditorium and up toward the balconies.

The story was quite different on the dress circle level. Almost no one knew of the emergency stairs on the opposite wall from the main staircase. In a panic, people will nearly always try to exit the same way they entered. And so, those in the dress circle all headed toward the main staircase that would take them directly into the Washington Street lobby and then out into the street. This should have been a simple process, but for the panic. As the frenzied crowd rushed toward the stairs, it quickly became jammed. Some stumbled and fell, and others piled on top of them. Feet were tangled up in the balusters. Still others pulled and clawed at those in front, trying to climb over the mass to get to safety. Escape became next to impossible.

Fortunately for these poor trapped individuals, the First Precinct Police Station was just next door so assistance was quickly at hand. Several police officers and theater employees, working at the bottom of the stairs, were able to untangle the crowd as the crush pushed them down toward the exit. Nearly everyone from the dress circle eventually made it out of the building. Almost all of their injuries stemmed from falls or the massive crush, rather than from the fire.

An anonymous witness described the scene in the dress circle balcony for the *Brooklyn Daily Eagle*. "With few exceptions, the audience in the orchestra [floor seats] rushed headlong toward the doors. Those in the dress circle followed suit, and the most fatal and appalling evils resulted. Bereft of calmness and self possession...the panic stricken throng dived headlong forward, using brute force to escape the disaster which was still comparatively distant, and which was only converted from an ordinary accident into an awful calamity by that very ruthless and reckless haste. The weaker went down before the charge of the stronger, and women and children were the sufferers, as usual. In the body of the theater and in the corridor scores were crushed and jammed almost to death, and many were thrown to the floor and trampled on."

In the family circle, conditions were far worse. The seating area with the most people had the poorest evacuation possibilities. Within seconds, all four hundred of the family circle patrons moved toward their only exit. As in the dress circle, the stairs became immediately jammed with bodies packed in so tightly that almost no movement was possible. Down below, the fire was raging, sending heat and smoke toward the ceiling where it collected in the upper balcony. In a short time, those who were trapped up next to the ceiling began to collapse, unable to breath in the thickening smoke and hot gasses.

Charles Straub and his friend Joseph Keramer, seated in the family circle, were lucky enough to be sitting very near the stairs. They both ran for the exit almost as soon as they saw the flames, but still found themselves very quickly packed in. Because they were near the front of the pack, they were able to make some headway. Part way down the first flight, Straub stumbled and fell, with dozens of people falling on top of him. He was able to partially get up and was carried along the rest of the way down to the exit doors by the pressing mass. He estimated that a few dozen people got out ahead of him and that many more were forcing their way out after him. He was wrong. After Charles burst into the street, only about ten or twelve people followed him out. His friend Joseph was not one of them. Joseph Keramer never made it out alive.

Also seated in the family circle was Charles Vine, but on the opposite side - far from the stairs. He had been enticed into remaining in his seat for those extra few minutes by Kate Claxton's charming entreaties. By the time he awoke to the serious danger in which he now found himself, the stairs were already packed with people and offered no possibility for escape. His first thought was to open a window and jump onto Flood's Alley, but the sixty-foot drop was just too much. Instead, he made his way to the rail and jumped onto the dress circle balcony. He struck a chair and was badly cut, but was still able to run to that stairs. It was still tightly packed but the crowd had started to move down again as the mass was being untangled from the bottom. Vine was believed to be the last person to make it out of the family circle alive. He later estimated that it took no more than four minutes from the first glimpse of flames on the stage till the smoke reached the upper balcony

In the Washington Street lobby, District Engineer Farley and fireman Cain along with several policemen and theater janitor Mike Sweeny, had finally succeeded in clearing the dress circle stairs. They made their way up to

**(Left) View of the Brooklyn Theatre showing the Johnson Street wall, which was the rear wall of the backstage area. This wall was the first to collapse. (Right) Period illustration of the body recovery efforts from the ruins of the Brooklyn Theatre.**

the dress circle balcony but found no signs of activity. They then opened a connecting door to the family circle stairs. Met with thick black smoke, they were unable to continue any further. They shouted up but got no response. They heard no human sound or movement upon the stairs. Believing that everyone who had been sitting in the family circle had already escaped, Farley ordered everyone out of the building. Within minutes of their evacuation, large cracks appeared in the theater wall along Johnson Street. Just under half an hour after the tiny fire was first spotted, bystanders heard a giant crash as the entire wall collapsed into the burning theater, just feet from where the fire had started.

It took only a matter of minutes for anyone arriving at the site to acknowledge that the building was lost. When Brooklyn Fire Department Chief Engineer Thomas Nevins took command just before 11:30 p.m., he understood that his job was not to save the theater, but to keep the fire from spreading to other buildings. The Dieter Hotel, nestled in the crook of the theater, was at the greatest risk. With its lower profile, the chance that floating embers and burning debris landing on the roof and setting it alight was very likely. Several other buildings in the general vicinity were also in jeopardy. Nevins ordered that fire-fighting apparatus be positioned throughout the area, on and around buildings most likely to catch and spread the fire. As for the Brooklyn Theatre, she would burn herself out without any possibility of being saved.

Several of those who had made their escape, found refuge in the police precinct next door. At some point in the night, Kate Claxton was found standing alone in the frigid street, still wearing only the thin, ragged costume of Louise, her character in the play. She seemed to be in a daze, not really aware of the chaos around her. After being led into the police station she sat quietly, only occasionally asking of the whereabouts of some of her fellow actors.

The fire raged into the night, the crowd of onlookers grew; some merely curious, others frantic with worry as they searched for friends and loved ones among the survivors. Despite the growing number of people inquiring about the missing, authorities believed that few, if any had been lost to the fire. A physical search had been done of the dress circle balcony and it was found to be empty. No one had been able to get into the family circle balcony but rescuers had found no evidence of anyone still up there. They believed they had every reason to be optimistic.

Uncontrolled until well after 1:00 a.m. when the Flood's Alley wall collapsed, the fire began to burn down. At about 3:00 a.m., Chief Nevins made his first attempt to enter the building through the Johnson Street lobby into the vestibule but was forced back by heat and smoke. Eventually, he was able to enter the building to just inside the lobby doors where he found the body of a woman, sitting on the floor propped up against a wall. She was horribly disfigured and her legs had been largely burned away. Nevins exited the building with a new understanding that where there was one body, there would likely be many more. He kept his discovery to himself, fearing the crowd might storm the crumbling building.

No one entered the building again until well after 6:00 a.m. The fire was nearly out and nothing remained of the auditorium except for a very small portion of the vestibule (seating area) nearest the lobby doors. The entire structure had collapsed into the cellar. Chief Nevins decided it was time to take in a recovery party.

The first sight that greeted them was a mass of charred and tangled debris in the cellar toward the rear of the auditorium. As they descended into the rubble, they made a grim discovery. The tangle of debris was in reality a tangle of human corpses. They had fallen into the cellar when the family circle balcony and staircases collapsed. Though their bodies were horribly burned, they had fallen victim to the smoke and heat long before the flames had reached them.

News rose from the smoldering crater that as many as twenty people had perished. The search, and body removal continued but by 9:00 a.m. the number had risen to nearly seventy. Within two more hours, twenty more were added to the growing total. By early afternoon the true depth of the tragedy became apparent as the estimation surpassed two hundred.

It would take nearly three days to remove all the bodies from the building's wreckage. Some had been scattered when the balcony collapsed and became tangled in the debris. The task was made particularly difficult by the extremely poor conditions of the remains. Recovery became problematic as many body parts disintegrated at the slightest touch. Some bodies simply fell apart when rescuers tried to lift them from the floor of the cellar.

The crowd around the ruins grew throughout the day. Worried, distraught, and sometimes frantic people wandered from person to person, officer to officer, imploring of anyone who would listed for information about some missing person. In several cases, the only reason someone might have been thought to have been at the

**The inside of the theater being inspected by authorities. Note the highest arch at the far end of the wall on the right. This is the doorway through which the first staircase from the family circle balcony entered the Washington Street wing.**

theater was that they didn't come home that night, didn't appear for work the next morning, or simply hadn't been seen since the previous evening.

The stories of grief were all too similar. A man searched for Hugh Doner, his thirty-one-year-old brother: a neighborhood milkman who hadn't returned home the night before. Doner eventually did make it home, but not until after his body was identified by his watch chain. He was taken home by his brother to prepare for his funeral.

Reverend Father Kiely searched for and found his brother. Nicholas Kiely was found, not with the survivors at the precinct station, but in the morgue. He was the first victim to be identified.

Three prim ladies arrived from Syracuse, N.Y., inquiring about their nephew, Harry Anderson, who was in Brooklyn visiting his sister. He was known to have been at the theater that evening but had not returned to his sister's home. His body was never identified.

W.H. Fletcher's brother spent the day searching the area for him. He had no idea whether his brother attended the theater the previous night but he frequently did so, and he hadn't come home. His body was not identified and there was no evidence that he had even been present, but he was never seen or heard from again.

Mrs. John Turner, the butcher's wife, searched in vain for her husband, who had attended the theater the night before and hadn't come home. His was later found to be among the dead.

German cigar maker Morris Solomon, 46, had treated his four children to a night at the theater. They were a close family and Mary, Deborah, Lena and Philip, ages eighteen through 24 all still lived at home. Mrs. Morris had chosen not to accompany them that evening. She alone was left to bury her entire family.

Discovered amid the fire debris was the body of Officer Patrick McKeon. Assigned to the Sanitary Police out of the First Precinct, it was not known if he was in the theater as a patron but most believed that he was one of the first responders and fell victim to the flames. His body was found just inside the lobby doors.

 Police officer William Collins, also of the First Precinct, was in the first recovery teams to enter the building with Chief Nevins. To Collins' utter horror, one of the bodies was that of his fourteen-year-old brother, Daniel. Collins was relieved from duty so he could take the body of his little brother home. The experience must have been too much for him. Three days later, he died at the age of 28. His official cause of death was recorded as "congestion of the brain."  One week after the fire, the funerals of brothers Daniel and William Collins were held together and they were laid to rest side by side.

The city morgue filled quickly. An unused market was found nearby on Adams Street for the overflow. In the end, the market floor provided the best location for the victim's remains and shreds of clothing, jewelry and personal items that survived the inferno. Identification was going to be difficult as most faces were burned beyond recognition. In many cases, the damage from the fire was so great that even gender was not evident. The victims who were identified were largely done so by personal items found on or near the bodies.

With the large open market space of the temporary morgue, human remains, extracted from the theater, could be prepared and arranged for viewing in the hopes of possible identification. A steady flow of mourners passed through the office of Kings County Coroner Henry C. Simms, requesting passes to enter the morgue. As they moved up and down the rows of the dead, they were guided by an official because so many had collapsed or passed into fits as they saw something they recognized on a particular body. As each individual was identified, their body was removed to their home or that of a family member. This procedure ensured a fairly rapid and simple reduction in the mass of human bodies laid out upon the floor. Regrettably, it also ensured that mistakes in identification would surely be made as well.

Brooklyn fell into a period of mourning. Funerals were held all over the city. Several neighborhoods and organizations held memorial services for the victims of the fire. Prayer vigils and special church services and masses were performed for those who died and their friends and families.

Nearly one hundred of those who lost their lives in the Brooklyn Theatre fire could not be identified. The City of Brooklyn secured a large plot in the Green-Wood Cemetery to use as a mass grave. A large arch-shaped common grave was dug for those who remained unidentified and for families who couldn't afford to pay for private burials.   One hundred and three people, in donated coffins

**Artist's rendering of the inside of the temporary morgue set up in the empty Adams Street market. Note the candles placed on each body to illuminate what was left of their faces for possible identification.**

**The granite memorial marking the Brooklyn Theatre's mass grave in Brooklyn's Green-Wood Cemetery. (Marianne McCarthy)**

trimmed in silver, were laid to rest in the common grave, arranged with their heads towards the center of the arch. Over two thousand mourners braved the bitter cold to attend the graveside service and mourn the victims. After two hours of speeches, ceremonies and music performed by a sixty- voice German choir, fresh soil was shoveled over the long lines of coffins creating a large burial mound topped with a floral crown and cross. Later, the mass grave was marked with a thirty-foot-tall granite memorial, engraved with a brief history of the disaster. The memorial, also purchased by the City of Brooklyn, was placed atop the mound.

The final number killed would fluctuate for several days. It was hard to determine how many complete bodies could be made up from the piles of arms, legs, heads and torsos, and impossible to account for the body parts that had burned completely away. Henry Simms, the Kings County Coroner announced the death toll as 293 on Friday, but later scaled that back to 283. The number engraved on the memorial marker erected in Brooklyn's Green-Wood Cemetery was 278. That number is by no means definitive however as researchers have estimated the true number is likely nearer to 300. Regardless of the final count, the horrific tragedy could not be denied, nor its impact on a stunned city.

Coroner Simms convened an inquest almost immediately, lasting through December and into January. The coroner's jury found that Sheridan Shook and A. M. Palmer, the theater's lessees and managers, were responsible for failing to take appropriate precautions against fire. The previous owner, Mrs. Sara Conway, had been nearly obsessive about her insistence on fire safety. Shook and Palmer were also faulted for not properly training stage personnel for fire, allowing the backstage area to become cluttered with additional props and drops, and not maintaining the fire suppression equipment and emergency exits.

Minor faults were found with the design of the five-year-old building. They found that the family circle staircases lacked a firewall between the audience and stage. They believed that these who died in the highest balcony had likely been suffocated by smoke within the first few minutes after it arrived at their level.

Police Fire Marshall Patrick Keady also conducted an investigation in which he interviewed 62 witnesses directly. His report was completed and delivered on December 18. In it, he included a strong reprimand for the lax management demonstrated by Shook and Palmer. He noted the lack of the use of water in any way, even though there was a large pipe leading to the hydrant in the rear of the stage.

Keady also reported on the design of the building. His official findings were that the theater had better means of exits than most of the other public buildings in Brooklyn at that time. It was further noted that Thomas Jackson, designer of the theater, had estimated that a full house could be emptied within five minutes. However, his calculations were based on a quiet, orderly evacuation, without consideration for the extreme panic of the patrons when faced with an actual fire.

The immediate response to the fire was to place most of the responsibility on managers Shook and Palmer, but as time went by, common theater production practices started to be reconsidered. Activities that were considered to be acceptable risks in the past were being recognized as hazardous and avoidable. By the end of

# THE CLAXTON CURSE?

**Later photograph of Kate Claxton. Was she a cursed actress?**

Hours after the fire, Kate Claxton had been discovered wandering about in a Manhattan park, burned and in shock. After she had recovered her senses and her wounds had healed, she returned to acting. She was now being billed as "Kate Claxton of the Big Brooklyn Fire" and began touring the country performing in a variety of plays, but most often reprising her role as poor, blind Louise in "The Two Orphans."

On April 11, 1877, just four months after the Brooklyn Theatre tragedy, Kate Claxton found herself once again fleeing a burning building, barely escaping with her life. She was touring with "The Two Orphans" and was appearing at the Olympic Theatre in St. Louis, Missouri. She and other members of the theater company were staying at the Southern Hotel in downtown St. Louis.

The fire alarm at the Southern Hotel sounded at 2:00 a.m. Claxton, well known for her cool composure and steady nerves at the onset of the Brooklyn Theatre fire, was able to stay calm and think clearly. She wrapped herself in wet towels and rolled down the stairs to safety. It was later reported that the staircase was on fire as she fled and it collapsed within seconds of her foot leaving the last step. She was physically unharmed. The same could not be said for many of the other guests at the hotel. At least 45 people lost their lives and dozens of others were severely injured. The hotel was a total loss.

A special dispatch to the *New York Times* described the scene after the fire had been extinguished: "This morning Miss Kate Claxton visited the ruins, and had the good fortune to recover the manuscript of her play 'Conscience' and several contracts with different theatrical managers. The papers were badly scorched, but were still legible. Miss Claxton is very much prostrated by the excitement attending her escape from the fire, though she appeared last night and tonight at the Olympic Theatre in the role of Louise. She lost $2,000 by the fire and her entire wardrobe, including a splendid costume she had received a few hours before the fire. A performance for her benefit and that of Rose Osborn and Marion Chifton, two other actresses who are impoverished by the fire is announced for Friday night."

After experiencing - and surviving - her second major fire in less than five months, many superstitious people began to avoid the theaters where Claxton was performing, believing her to be bad luck. In reality, structure fires were common in the nineteenth century and actors were frequently in large wood-framed public buildings, such as theaters and hotels, which are particularly susceptible to fire. Just the same, several members of the press capitalized on her misfortunes and proclaim her a fire pariah. Her career was not particularly hurt by the negative publicity. Instead the public seemed to become more interested in her and displayed great sympathy, which she used to her advantage as she toured the country as a fire survivor.

Bad luck, pariah, or just a victim of circumstance? It is impossible to determine for certain. However, the following short news item appeared in the local newspaper in tiny Oil City, Pennsylvania, on December 12, 1884: "An alarm of fire was sounded in the Oil City Opera House here tonight as Kate Claxton's company began playing 'Sea of Ice.' Great excitement prevailed but no one was hurt and the fire was easily extinguished"....

**The approximate site of the Brooklyn Theatre today.**
**(Marianne McCarthy)**

1880, the New York City fire code incorporated several changes designed specifically for theaters. Some of the changes included barring the construction of props and set pieces or any painting to be done on the stage area, or to use the stage for storage of anything other than what was needed for the current production, and required a widening of all exit doors and doorways.

By the early twentieth century, the New York City building codes were also amended for theaters. Now, proscenium walls and arches (the wall separating the audience from the stage area, hiding the wings and fly spaces) had to be built of brick or masonry and must extend from the cellar to the roof. Stage curtains were required to be made of non-flammable materials to keep any fire starting backstage from advancing out into the seating areas. The fly spaces had to have heat activated sprinkler systems installed.

The biggest change was the use of fire department members as regular attendees of all theater productions. The duties of the Theatre Detail Officer were to attend every performance, arriving half an hour early to test fire alarms, test fire retardant materials in the production and to inspect fire suppression equipment. During performances, they were required to keep all aisles and exits clear and accessible.

Three years after the Brooklyn Theatre had been reduced to ashes, Haverly's Theatre was built on the same site, but was torn down just eleven years later. The next structure was a simple office building, used by the *Brooklyn Daily Eagle* until it went defunct. The approximate site is now a lovely wooded park-like seating area just north of the New York Supreme Court Building. Sadly, there is no marker of any sort, recalling or commemorating the terrible tragedy that had taken place there.

For the first two days, while the recovery efforts were continuing, much of the work going on inside the ruin and guard duty around the crumbling structure was done by the Brooklyn Police Department. Many of these men had been working around the clock with very little rest. They were near exhaustion and there were few officers on their regular patrol of the city. It was noted in the *Brooklyn Union* that: "The city is comparatively uncovered, and if New York thieves should make raid it would, no doubt, be highly successful."

One hundred members of the Thirteenth Regiment of the New York National Guard presented themselves to the Brooklyn Police Commissioner, offering their services to take over for the police officers, that they might get some rest and return to their regular duties protecting the city. The Fourteenth Regiment did likewise and it was determined that they would rotate duties every twelve hours until the work was completed. The Fourteenth Regiment would have the night shift, starting at 6:30 p.m.

Those long nights in the frigid December weather must have worn heavily on the men of the Fourteenth. At first, they kept busy, as there were still crowds of mourners, curiosity seekers and scavengers. Soon enough, the crowds began to thin down to almost nothing after the bodies had been removed and the novelty of the tragedy had worn off. The long, dark vigil had gradually become a quiet one. The men walked or stood their posts and chatted quietly when they had occasion to pass each other.

But the nights were not completely quiet. As the guardsmen spoke in hushed tones, their attention was on occasion called to the cellar floor, where they reported hearing the soft sound of a woman's sobs. This would continue until someone would call down for the woman to come out; that it was dangerous, especially at night, and that no one was allowed inside. Two of the men went so far as to venture into the building to find and escort her safely out. They later described what they saw as the dark, shrouded shape of what they thought was a woman.  She was walking through the debris, bent over and weeping, as if she were looking for something. She stopped here and there as if to peer into some cavity, then moved on. One of the men climbed toward her to entice her away from the danger, but she simply vanished as he got closer. They knew that there was no other way out and that she hadn't gone past them. They left the cellar area frightened and confused, but wondering if a poor lost soul was left searching for someone she had gotten separated from on that terrible night. The mysterious apparition appeared two more times over the next week, then was seen no more.

# 1903: THE SHOW THAT DIDN'T GO ON
# THE IROQUOIS THEATER DISASTER

*This is the most flammable goddamn mess of scenery I ever saw...*
**Will J. Davis, co-owner of the Iroquois Theater**

In addition to the Great Fire of 1871, the city of Chicago has had a number of other tragic blazes in its colorful and often bloody history. Perhaps the most heartbreakingly tragic Chicago fire occurred at the famed Iroquois Theater on December 30, 1903 as a blaze broke out in the crowded venue during a performance of a vaudeville show. The fire claimed the lives of hundreds of people, including children, who were packed in for an afternoon show during the holidays. It remains one of the deadliest theater fires in American history.

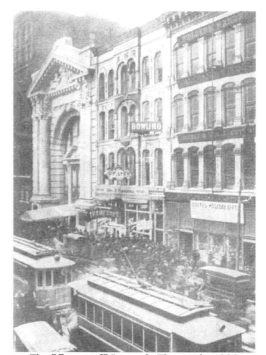

The Iroquois Theater, the newest and most beautiful showplace in Chicago in 1903, was believed to be "absolutely fireproof," according to newspaper reports. The *Chicago Tribune* called it a "virtual temple of beauty," but just five weeks after it opened, it became a blazing death trap.

The new theater was much acclaimed, even before it was unveiled to the public. It was patterned after the Opera-Cominque in Paris and was located downtown on the north side of Randolph Street, between State and Dearborn streets. The interior of the four-story building was magnificent, with stained glass and polished wood throughout. The lobby had an ornate sixty-foot ceiling and featured white marble walls fitted with large mirrors that were framed in gold leaf and stone. Two grand staircases led away from either side of the lobby to the balcony areas. Outside, the building's façade resembled a Greek temple with a towering stone archway that was supported by massive columns.

Thanks to the dozens of fires that had occurred over the years in theaters, architect Benjamin H. Marshall wanted to assure the public that the Iroquois was safe. He studied a number of fires that had occurred in the past and made every effort to make sure that no tragedy would

**The "fireproof" Iroquois Theater in 1903**

Another view of the Iroquois, just to the right side of the brick corner building.

occur in the new theater. The Iroquois had 25 exits that, it was claimed, could empty the building in less than five minutes. The stage had also been fitted with an asbestos curtain that could be quickly lowered to protect the audience.

While all of this was impressive, it was not enough to battle the real problems that existed with the Iroquois. Seats in the theater were wooden with cushions stuffed with hemp and much of the precautionary fire equipment that was to have been installed never actually made it into the building. The theater had no fire alarms and in a rush to open on time, other safety factors had been forgotten or simply ignored.

The horrific fire occurred on the bitterly cold afternoon of December 30, 1903. A holiday crowd had packed into the theater on that Wednesday afternoon to see a matinee performance of the hit comedy *Mr. Bluebeard*. Officially, the Iroquois seated 1,602 people, with approximately 700 in the expensive "parquet," the seats down in front that overlooked the orchestra pit; more than 400 in the first balcony and probably just under 500 in the steep, upper balcony. There were four lower boxes, each seating six people, and two upper boxes designed to hold four people in each, but the owners had managed to crowd eight chairs into those boxes.

Added to those who had purchased tickets to the show in advance were the usual late arrivals. Some came to buy tickets for available standing room; others had guest passes from connections they had with the management, contractors, actors, and theater employees. Others had been given tickets by city inspectors who had done favors for the owners of the theater. Estimates varied, but because the managers wanted to make up for earlier, smaller shows, that there may have been considerably more than two hundred standees that afternoon. By curtain time, an estimated 1,840 people, most of them women and children, were packed into the house. This was far beyond capacity. The overflow had people filling the seats and standing four-deep in the aisles. Another crowd filled the backstage area with four hundred actors, dancers and stagehands.

As the show was about to begin, actor Eddie Foy was delighted at the size of the crowd. "That Wednesday afternoon, the house was packed and many were standing," he later said. "I was struck by the fact that I had never seen so many women and children. Even the gallery was full."

Eddie Foy was a popular vaudeville actor and comedian of the day and was perhaps one of the most beloved performers in America at the time. He was the star of *Mr. Bluebeard* and many have attributed the packed crowds to Foy's popularity. What Foy did not see beyond the bright stage lights that afternoon was that the Iroquois auditorium was not merely full, it was dangerously overcrowded. Not only was the standing room only crowd packed into the designated area behind the last row of seats, they were also sitting in the aisles and standing along both side walls. One usher would later claim there were at least five hundred people standing in the auditorium.

Anticipation mounted as the lights dimmed for act one of the show. In accordance with the owner's standard operating procedures, most of the doors leading from the balcony and gallery had been locked or bolted by the ushers to keep out gate crashers and prevent those sitting or standing in the upper tiers from sneaking down in the darkness to the more expensive seats. This was done regardless of the fact that it was obvious that there were no empty seats anywhere.

The audience was thrilled with the show's first act. During the intermission, those in the expensive sections and boxes retired to the smoking room, or went to freshen up, relax on the plush couches and mingle on the promenade. Those in the balcony and gallery, behind the locked and bolted gates, flowed through the upper promenade and used the restrooms.

By 3:20 p.m., the second act of *Mr. Bluebeard* was well under way. During one of the early scenes, possibly while Foy was riding a baby elephant, Nellie Reed of the aerial ballet was hooked to a thin trolley wire that would send her high above the audience during a musical number. The sequence was made spectacular through the use of hundreds of colored lights. Some of the bulbs were concealed inside two narrow concave metal reflectors that were located on each side of the stage. Called "front lighting," each reflector was mounted on vertical hinges and, when not needed, was supposed to be pivoted by stagehands so that they disappeared into niches in the wall. The lights were not needed for the number that was about to start, but a member of the stage crew, for some reason, had not retracted the right stage reflector. It was left slightly extended, an edge of it in the path of the curtains. In the usual business of moving scenery, adjusting lights, moving backdrops, and the hundreds of other things that needed to be done, no one noticed the error.

In the scene that followed, all of the house lights were extinguished, bathing the stage in a soft blue glow from one of the backstage carbon arc lamps, a powerful spotlight that was created by an electric current arcing between two carbon rods. The spotlight was positioned on a narrow metal bridge that was about fifteen feet above the stage and within a foot or so of the theater's drop curtains and the fixed curtain that prevented the audience from seeing into the wings. The spotlight was a bulky piece of machinery, with a large metal hood and reflector, and could generate temperatures as high as four thousand degrees Fahrenheit.

As the action continued on the stage, bringing beautiful chorus girls and young men in uniform into the softly lit gardens, the carbon arc lamp suddenly began to sputter and spark. A cracking sound was heard and then a few inches of orange flame appeared and began to spread out, dancing along the edge of the fixed curtain. On the stage below, the cast went into an up-tempo song as stage hands tried to slap at the small flame with their bare hands. Within seconds, though, the tiny blaze had grown, consuming the material above their heads and beyond their reach. It was soon spreading into the heavier curtains and they shouted to a man on a catwalk above to try and put the fire out. He also began slapping at the fire with his hands.

The audience was engrossed in the romantic musical number onstage as on either side of the garden set, stagehands, grips, and those on the catwalks frantically tried to get to the fire and put it out. But the flames had grown larger and were now out of reach. Black smoke was starting to rise.

William Sallers, the house fireman, was on his usual rounds to make sure that no one was smoking and as he made his way up the stairs from the dressing rooms in the basement, he spotted the flames. He immediately grabbed some tubes of Kilfyre (a powdery flame retardant) and ran up the vertical stairs of the light bridge and began frantically tossing powder onto the still-growing fire. The platform was only eighteen inches wide, so he had to hold onto a metal rail with one hand as he threw the powder with the other. But it was too late. The flames had spread to the point that the small amount of powder was almost comically ineffectual.

At first, the actors on stage had no idea what was happening, but after a few sparks began to rain down, they knew something was seriously wrong. They continued to sing and dance, waiting for something to happen. Later, some of the actors would recall hearing shouts and bells that signaled for the curtain to come down, but they were muffled by the music.

In the orchestra pit, the musicians spotted the fire and an order was given for them to play as fast as they could. The tempo picked up, but soon faltered as more of the musicians spotted the flames and began to get rattled. Several of them calmly put down their instruments and exited through the orchestra pit door beneath the stage.

Depending on where they were sitting or standing, some members of the audience saw the fire by simply following the gaze of the actors, who were now looking up. At first, many of them were merely puzzled, but others were becoming alarmed. Most of the children in the front main floor rows remained in their seats, believing that the glow that was spreading across the upper reaches of the theater was another of the show's magical effects.

Those in the upper gallery who saw the eerie flickering of the flames had no idea at first about what was happening, until bits of burning fabric began falling down around members of the cast who were still trying to go on with their number. But it was becoming obvious that some of them had fallen out of step with the music and others seemed to have lost their voices. Most were terribly frightened but survivors of the fire would later say that seeing those girls remaining there, still dancing in an effort to quiet the audience, was one of the bravest acts they had ever witnessed.

Backstage, things became more frightening and chaotic. The stage manager, William Carelton, could not be found (he had gone to the hardware store) and one of the stagehands, Joe Dougherty, was trying to handle the curtains from near the switchboard. But Dougherty was filling in for the regular curtain man, who was in the hospital, and could not remember which drop should be lowered. The asbestos curtain ran on an endless loop of wire-enforced rope but he was not sure which rope controlled which curtain.

High above him, Charles Sweeney, who had been assigned to the first fly gallery, seized a canvas tarpaulin and, with some of the other men, was slapping at the flames. The fire was out of their reach, however, and it continued to spread. Sweeney dashed down six flights of stairs to a room filled with chorus girls and led them down to a small stage exit. In the rush to escape, most of the girls dropped everything and left the building wearing only flimsy costumes or tights. Other men raced downstairs to rescue girls who were in the dressing rooms under the stage.

High up in the theater's gridiron, The Grigolatis, a group of 16 young German aerialists (12 women and four men), had a horrifying view of the scene. Clouds of thick, black smoke was rising toward them and blazing pieces of canvas the size of bed sheets were falling down on the stage and the footlights. William Sallers, still above the stage, saw the same thing and knew the theater was doomed.

The Grigolatis had only seconds to act. One of them, Floraline, who was perched some distance away from the others, was suddenly engulfed in flames from a burning piece of scenery. Before the others could reach her, she panicked, lost her grip on the trapeze, and plunged to the stage, 60 feet below. By the time her companions were able to unhook themselves from their harnesses and scramble down some metal scaffolding to the stage, Floraline had vanished. They could only hope that she had been carried to safety.

**Beautiful Nellie Reed of the Flying Ballet**

In all of the confusion, no one remembered Nellie Reed, who was still attached to her wire.

In one of the dressing rooms, five young female dancers were sitting and talking when they heard the cries of "fire!" In the rush to get out, one of them, Violet Sidney, twisted her ankle and fell. The other girls ran, but Lola Quinlan stopped to help her. She managed to drag Violet down five flights of stairs and across the back of the burning stage to safety. She was badly burned in the process, but she refused to leave her friend behind.

Voices screamed for the asbestos curtain to come down, but nothing happened. Joe Dougherty and others were still confused about which curtains should be lowered and more time was lost. A stagehand who had been ordered to sound the fire alarm found that no alarm box had ever been installed. He burst out of the theater and ran as fast as he could through the streets to notify Engine Company 13 of the blaze.

Inside his dressing room, Eddie Foy, in tights, misshapen shoes, short smock, and red pigtailed wig, was preparing for his novelty act as the Old Woman Who Lived in a Shoe. Foy heard the commotion outside and rushed out onto the stage to see what was going on. As soon as he opened the door, he knew something was deadly wrong. He immediately searched for his young son, who had accompanied him to the theater that day, and quickly found him in the darkness. As he stumbled with the boy in his arms, he heard terrified voices raising a cry of "fire!" At that moment, the nearly 2,000 people packed into the "absolutely fireproof" Iroquois Theater began to panic.

Some of the audience had risen to their feet; others were running and climbing over the seats to get to the back of the house and to the side exits. Many of the standees were blocking the aisles and, since the new theater was unfamiliar to them, were unsure about which way to turn. The initial runners soon turned into a mob that was trying to get out the same way they had come in. Their screams and cries were muffled by the music and by the show's cast, which was still singing as the burning scenery fell around them. Terrified families were quickly torn apart from one another.

Eddie Foy grabbed his son and rushed to the stage exit, but felt compelled to go back and try and help. He pressed the boy into the arms of a fleeing stagehand and went back to try and help calm down the audience and finally bring the curtain down. By the time he arrived, the cast had abandoned the stage and he stood there alone, the blazing backdrop behind him and burning bits of scenery raining down around him. Smoke billowed around him as he stepped to the edge of the footlights, still partially clothed in his ridiculous costume. He urged everyone who could hear him to remain calm and remarkably, some of the people in the front rows took their seats again. Even some of the people in the gallery sat back down. From the edge of the stage, Foy urged musical director Herbert Gillea to get some of the remaining musicians to play an overture, which had a temporary soothing effect on the crowd.

A few moments later, a flaming set crashed down onto the stage and Foy asked everyone to get up and calmly leave the theater. He told them to take their time, to not be frightened, and to walk slowly as they exited. The, he dropped his voice to stagehand who was on the brink of fleeing from the theater himself. He ordered him, "Lower that iron curtain! Drop the fire curtain! For God's sake, does anyone know how this iron curtain is worked?"

Foy heard timbers cracking above his head and he made one last entreaty that everyone proceed slowly from the theater, but by now, no one was listening. As he looked out into the auditorium, he later recalled seeing many of the people on the main floor leaving in an orderly fashion, but what he saw in the balcony and the gallery terrified him. In the upper tiers, he said, people were in a "mad, animal-like stampede."

Lester Linvonston, a young survivor who vividly recalled seeing Foy standing at the edge of the stage, pleading for calm, was only distracted from the comedian by a macabre sight that appeared above Foy's head. "Almost alone and in the center of the house," he later said, he watched "a ballet dancer in a gauzy dress suspended by a steel belt from a wire. Her dress had caught fire and it burned like paper." The gruesome vision was Nellie Reed, the British star of the aerial ballet.

Finally, the asbestos curtain began to come down. Most of the stage crew had fled the theater but someone had figured out a way to lower what was thought would be a fireproof shield between the stage and the audience. It began inching its way down a steel cable between two wooden guide tracks. As if in slow motion, it descended and then, less than 20 feet above the stage, it suddenly stopped. One end was jammed on the light reflector that had not been properly closed and the other end sagged down to about five feet above the stage. The wooden guide tracks tore apart and the curtain, which was supposed to have been reinforced and made stiff by steel rods and wires, began to billow out over the orchestra pit and the front rows of seats, pushed by the draft coming from an open stage exit that had been mobbed by the cast and crew.

Some stagehands tried to yank down the curtain, but it was no use. The rest of the crew ran for their lives. The theater's engineer, Robert Murray, ran down to the basement and told his crew to shut off the steam in the boilers heating the building, bank all of the fires to prevent an explosion, then get out as fast as they could. Then he helped a group of chorus girls escape from a basement dressing room by pushing them one at a time through a coal chute than led to an alley. One or two of them were wearing street clothes, but the others were clad in their thin costumes or worse, in nothing but undergarments.

Murray rushed back up to the stage level and found a young woman whose costume and tights were shredded and burned and whose skin was charred and blistered. Nellie Reed had somehow unhooked herself from her wire, but was seriously injured and in great pain. He managed to get her out into the street, where he handed her to some rescuers.

The entire stage had been turned into a blazing inferno and if one of the stagehands had not opened one of the big double scenery doors, the entire cast might have perished. Opening the doors undoubtedly saved the lives of the cast and crew, but it sealed the fate of the audience in the upper tiers. The contractors who had built the theater not only failed to connect the controls for the roof's ventilating systems, but had nailed shut the vents over the stage and left open vents above the auditorium, creating a chimney effect. The blast of cold air that rushed in the scenery doors, which caused the curtain to billow out from the stage, instantly mixed with the heated air fueled by the flames and the result was a huge deadly blowtorch that one fire official later described as a "back draft."

A churning column of smoke and flames burst out of the opening under the curtain, whirled above the orchestra pit and floor seats, and swept into the balcony and gallery under the open roof vents like a fiery cyclone. The fireball sucked the oxygen from the air, burning and asphyxiating anyone in the upper tiers who remained in their seats or were trapped in the aisles.

Moments later, the last of the ropes holding up the scenery flats on stage gave away and with a roar that literally shook the building, tons of wood, ropes, sandbags, pipes, pulleys, lights, rigging, and more than 280 pieces of scenery crashed to the stage. The force of the fall instantly knocked out the electrical switchboard and the auditorium was plunged into complete and utter darkness.

The aisles had become impassable and as the lights went out, the crowd milled about in blind terror. The auditorium began to fill with heat and smoke and screams echoed off the walls and ceilings. Many of those who died not only burned but suffocated from the smoke and the crush of bodies. Later, as the police removed the charred remains from the theater, they discovered that a number of victims had been trampled in the panic. One dead woman's face even bore the mark of a shoe heel. Mothers and children were wrenched away from one another and trampled by those behind them. Dresses, jackets, trousers and other articles of clothing were ripped to shreds as people tried to get through to the exits and escape the flames and smoke. When the crowd reached the doors, they could not open them as they had been designed to swing inward rather than outward. The crush of people prevented those in the front from opening the doors. To make matters worse, some of the side doors to the auditorium were reportedly locked.

In desperation, some of those whose clothing had caught fire jumped from the first balcony to the floor below. Many of them died instantly. Others suffered agonizing deaths from broken backs that were caused by landing on armrests and seat backs.

A brief burst of light illuminated the hellish scene as the safety curtain burst into flames. The curtain, it turned out, was not made completely from asbestos, but from some cheaper material that had been chosen by the theater's co-owner, Will Davis.

At that moment, Eddie Foy made a fateful decision. He needed to get out of the theater as quickly as possible and first considered following the crowd through the Randolph Street doors. But, wanting to find his son, he changed his mind and made his way through the burning backstage and out of the scenery doors. He would only realize how lucky his decision had been after he learned of the hundreds of victims found crushed inside those doors.

Inside the theater, the badly burned house fireman William Sallers was shoving members of the cast and crew out of the scenery doors and into the alley. By now, he believed that Engine 13 should have arrived and he stepped outside and began shouting for the commander, Captain Jennings. Sallers believed that if he could get the fire crew through the scenery doors and onto the stage, they could prevent the blaze from reaching the audience. But when he looked behind him, he saw flames roaring out of the doors. He later recalled, "I knew that anybody who was in there was gone. I knew there was no chance to get out."

In the time that had been lost because the Iroquois had no alarm system, before Engine 13 and other units began arriving, the theater had turned into an oven. When collecting valuables after the fire, the police found at least a dozen watches that had been stopped at about the same time, 3:50 p.m. This meant that nearly 20 minutes had elapsed from the time that the first alarm had been raised. This certainly accounted for the jamming at the exits and the relatively few people that eyewitnesses saw leaving the theater. Some of the witnesses later stated that nearly seven minutes passed from the time they saw fire coming from the roof of the theater and the front doors on Randolph Street being opened.

Strangely, when Engine 13 arrived at the Randolph Street doors, the scene outside of the theater was completely normal. If not for the smoke billowing from the roof, the firefighters would have assumed that it was a false alarm. This changed when they tried to open the auditorium doors and found they could not --- there were too many bodies stacked up against them. They were only able to gain access by actually pulling

**Crowds gathered when it was realized that the Iroquois Theater was on fire. Hundreds were trapped inside.**

the bodies out of the way with pike poles, peeling them off one another and then climbing over the stacks of corpses. It took only 10 minutes to put out the remaining blaze, as the intense heat inside had already eaten up anything that would still burn.

The gallery and upper balcony sustained the greatest loss of life because the patrons who had been seated there were trapped by locked doors and gates at the top of the stairways. The firefighters found 200 bodies stacked there, as many as 10 deep.

A few who made it to the fire escape door behind the top balcony found that the iron staircase was missing. In its place was a platform that plunged about 50 feet into Couch Place, a cobblestone alley below. Across the alley, behind the theater, painters were working on a building occupied by Northwestern University's dental school. When they realized what was happening at the theater, they quickly erected a makeshift bridge using a ladder, which they extended across the alley to the fire escape platform. Several people made it to safety, but then as another man was edging his way across, the ladder slipped off the icy ledge of the university building and the man plummeted to his death.

After the ladder was lost, three wide boards were pushed across to the theater and the painters anchored them with their knees. The plank bridge worked for a time, but it could not handle the crush of people spilling out of the theater exit. The painters helped as many people as they could but when what sounded like a bomb went off in the theater (the sound of the rigging and scenery falling to the stage), they watched helplessly as the people trapped inside tried in vain to escape.

Those who swarmed from the fire escape exit were pushed to the edge of the railings with nowhere to go. It was impossible for them to turn back because of the crowd behind them and they were pushed over the side. Some of people tried to crawl across the planks but in the confusion and smoke, slipped and fell to the alley. Others, whose clothing was on fire, simply gave up and jumped from the railings.

The boards began falling away and as the fire grew, flames shot out the doors and out of the windows along the theater's wall, many of those hoping for rescue were burned alive in full view of the painters and the students at the dental school. From some of Northwestern University's windows, onlookers could see directly into the theater, which was a solid mass of flames. In the middle of the inferno, they could see men, women, and children

**Couch Place -- or Death Alley as it came to be known -- after the fire. The makeshift bridge that was created to get people out of the upper balcony can still be seen in the smoke and haze.**

running about and students later said that they did not even look human.

In the aftermath of the fire, Couch Place was dubbed "Death Alley" by reporters who arrived on the scene and counted nearly one hundred and fifty victims lying on the slush-covered cobblestones. The bodies had been stacked there by firemen, or had fallen to their death from above.

For nearly five hours, police officers, firemen and even newspaper reporters, carried out the dead. Anxious relatives sifted through the ruins, searching for loved ones. As the news spread, public response was immediate and overwhelming. A nearby medical school sent one hundred students to help the doctors who had been dispatched to the Iroquois. A hardware company down the street emptied its stock of two hundred lanterns. Marshall Field's, Mandel Brothers, Carson, Pirie, Scott and other department stores sent piles of blankets, sheets, rolls of linen, packages of cotton and large delivery wagons, and converted their ground floor restrooms and lounges into emergency medical stations. Montgomery Ward sent one of its new, large, motorized delivery wagons, but even with its bell ringing, it could not get through the crowds that were jammed into the streets and had to turn back. Other bodies were taken away by police wagons and ambulances and transported to a temporary morgue at Marshall Field's on State Street. Medical examiners and investigators worked through the night.

Within a short time, small restaurants, saloons, and stores in the vicinity of the Iroquois had been turned into improvised aid stations as medical workers and volunteers began arriving in large numbers. Chicago's central telephone exchange was overwhelmed by emergency calls.

Because the hardware store lanterns were not powerful enough to illuminate the blackened auditorium, the Edison Company rushed over forty arc lamps and, when they were turned on, fire and rescue workers were stunned by what they saw. Some of the audience had died sitting up in their seats, facing the stage, staring straight ahead. Others had no burn marks or bruises on them because they had suffocated quickly from the smoke. Many women were found with their heads resting on the back of the seat in front of them. A young boy's head was missing. One woman was bent back over the seat she had been sitting in, her spine severed. Hundreds had been trampled. Clothing, shoes, pocketbooks, and other personal belongings were strewn about. Some of the bodies were burned beyond recognition.

Scores of victims had been wedged into doorways. A husband and wife were locked so tightly in one another's arms that they had to be removed from the theater together. A mother had thrown her arms around her daughter in a hopeless effort to save her and both had been burned beyond recognition. The number of dead children was heartbreaking. Many were found burned, others trampled. Two dead children were found with the kneeling body of their mother, who had tried to shield them from the flames.

At the edge of the auditorium, a fireman emerged from the ashes with the body of a little girl in his arms. He groped his way forward, stumbling toward Fire Marshall William Henry Musham, who ordered him to give the child to someone else and get back into the auditorium. Another senior officer also ordered him to hand the child off to someone else. As the fireman came closer, the marshal and the other officers could see the streaks of tears on the man's soot-covered face. "I'm sorry, chief," the man said, "but I've got a little one like this at home. I want to carry this one out."

# AFTER THE IROQUOIS THEATER FIRE...

The gutted auditorium of the Theater

Firemen survey the ghastly damage and death

Fire-blasted seats in the balcony

Interior hallways of the Theater

A lounge area that was scorched by the fire. The new paint literally melted off the walls.

The lobby of the Theater was almost untouched by the fire, but many died there as they tried to force their way out of the Randolph Street exit.

A line of victims was laid out after the fire.

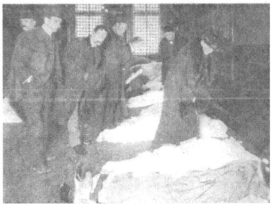

A woman searches for her children among the dead

Musham told him to go ahead and the other officers stepped aside. The weeping fireman carried the little body down the steps of what only an hour before had been the glittering promenade of the grandest theater in Chicago.

With the aid of the Edison arc lights, Deputy Fire Chief John Campion searched the theater's interior while his men continuing to douse hot spots that occasionally still burst into flames. Campion called out for survivors, looking around at the burned seats, the blackened walls, and the twisted piles of debris that littered the stage.

The devastated Iroquois Theater was silent.

In possibly less than a quarter of an hour, 572 lives had ended in the Iroquois Theater. More died later, bringing the eventual death toll up to 602, including 212 children. Hundreds more had been injured in what was supposed to be the safest theater in the city. The number of dead was greater than those who had perished in the Great Fire of 1871. A few hours before, the Iroquois had been a luxurious palace but, as newspapers reported that evening, "From the galleries, it looked like a burned-out volcano crater."

The next day, the newspapers devoted full pages to lists of the known dead and injured. News wires carried reports of the tragedy around the country and it soon became a national disaster. Chicago mayor Carter Harrison, Jr. issued an order that banned public celebration on New Year's Eve, closing the night clubs and making forbidden any fireworks or sounding of horns. Every church and factory bell in the city was silenced and on January 2, 1904, the city observed an official day of mourning.

Someone, the public cried, had to answer for the fire and an investigation of the blaze brought to light a number of troubling facts, including the faulty vents and that one of them was nailed shut. Another finding showed that the supposedly "fireproof" asbestos curtain was really made from cotton and other combustible materials. It would have never saved anyone at all. In addition to not having any fire alarms in the building, the owners had decided that sprinklers were too unsightly and too costly and had never had them installed.

To make matters worse, the management also established a policy to keep non-paying customers from slipping into the theater during a performance -

-- they quietly bolted nine pair of iron panels over the rear doors and installed padlocked, accordion-style gates at the top of the interior second and third floor stairway landings. And just as tragic was the idea they came up with to keep the audience from being distracted during a show -- they ordered all of the exit lights to be turned off! One exit sign that was left on led only to ladies restroom and another to a locked door for a private stairway. And as mentioned already, the doors of the outside exits, which were supposed to make it possible for the theater to empty in five minutes, opened to the inside, not to the outside.

The investigation led to a cover-up by officials from the city and the fire department, which denied all knowledge of fire code violations. They blamed the inspectors, who had overlooked the problems in exchange for free theater passes. A grand jury indicted a number of individuals, including the theater owners, fire officials and even the mayor. No one was ever charged with a criminal act, though. Families of the dead filed nearly 275 civil lawsuits against the theater but no money was ever collected. The Iroquois Theater Company filed for bankruptcy soon after the disaster.

Nevertheless, the building was repaired and re-opened briefly in 1904 as Hyde and Behmann's Music Hall and then in 1905 as the Colonial Theater. In 1924, the building was razed to make room for a new theater, the Oriental, but the façade of the Iroquois was used in its construction. The Oriental operated at what is now 24 West Randolph Street until the middle part of 1981, when it fell into disrepair and was closed down. It opened again as the home to a wholesale electronics dealer for a time and then went dark again. The restored theater is now part of the Civic Tower Building and is next door to the restored Delaware Building. It reopened as the Ford Center for the Performing Arts in 1998.

There are a number of oddities and mysteries about the 1903 Iroquois Theater fire that still linger today. It seems that official Chicago police and fire department records on the fire do not exist, nor does the Chicago Historical Society possess such records. According to the Cook County Courts, the records of the legal proceedings that followed the disaster were thrown out decades ago to make room for new documents.

The building next to the Iroquois still stands at Randolph and State streets, looking just as it did back in 1903, except there is a McDonald's where a cigar store was once located. The Delaware Building, as it is known, has a small lobby with a collection of framed photos of the some of the prominent hotels and theaters in the vicinity. However, there is no photograph of the Iroquois and no mention of the horrible events that occurred next door. Instead, there is a later photograph of the theater building after it was refurbished, renamed, and turned into a vaudeville house.

Worst of all, there is not a single marker or plaque that is dedicated to the hundreds of victims who perished in the blaze. There was a plaque unveiled by politicians and city leaders in 2003, the one hundreth anniversary of the fire, but it has never been installed at the theater, in Couch Place, or anywhere else.

The controversy over the fire may have faded away many years ago, but the lessons learned from it should never be forgotten. The Iroquois Theater Fire ranks as the nation's fourth deadliest blaze and the deadliest single building fire in American history. It remains as one of Chicago's worst tragedies and a chilling reminder of how the past continues to reverberate into the present.

The Iroquois Theatre is long gone. In its place stands the even more majestic Oriental Theatre, which was erected on the spot in the 1920s. But there has never been anything but a theatre on the site, and ghosts began to be reported early on.  In fact, they've stuck around to this day.

According to employees, the curtain has a tendency to get stuck at about five feet down - just as the fire curtain did. Others claim that one spotlight - right near the location of the light that started the fire - tends to break off from the now-computerized circuits and behave as through it had a mind of its own.

Many employees claim to have seen people in the balcony, particularly during rehearsals, and found no one there - and the doors locked - when they go to ask them to leave.

Still others have reported backstage encounters with the ghost of a woman wearing a tutu. Traditionally, this has been attributed to Nellie Reed, the aerialist who was killed in the fire. However, details of Reed's death are sketchy - the *Chicago Tribune* alone has reported several different stories, some claiming that she was stuck on a high platform and unable to get down during the fire, and others saying she was in a high dressing room and,

**Couch Place -- Death Alley -- today. Although revitalized and well-lit after renovations a few years ago, it remains a haunted spot.**

afraid of elevators, took the burning staircase instead. Still other reports claim that she didn't die in the theatre, but in the hospital shortly afterward.

If the ghost isn't Nellie, it may be the ghost of Floraline, the other performer who was killed.

But the woman in the tutu is not the only specter seen around the theatre. Recently, several employees have reported the apparition of a man in a red shoulder cape. Several others have reported a ghost in the balcony ventilation system. The identity of the man in the cape would be is anyone's guess - there were, however, over a thousand costumes in use in *Mr. Bluebeard*, and the idea that one might have been wearing a red shoulder cape is certainly possible. The phantoms could also be ghosts of the other employees killed - one other actor, a bit-part player named Burr Scott, was killed, along with an usher and two female attendants.

It's also possible that some of these ghosts may not be the ghosts of the victims of the Iroquois fire. The theaters that have occupied the spot since 1904 have their share of horror stories, too. They have included stories of violence, death and suicide. In 1943, a patron attending a movie at the Oriental put a note to his wife, mentioning the song "You'll Never Know How Much I Miss You," a song from the movie, in his pocket. As the song played in the movie, he shot himself to death. There have also been at least two suicides in the alley behind the theatre - Death Alley - in which people have jumped from high buildings to their doom in the alley.

Death Alley, in fact, is often said to be more haunted than the theatre itself. Cold spots - localized areas that are about ten degrees cooler than they ought to be - are common in haunted sites, and some say that the whole of Death Alley is a cold spot.

Poltergeist activity has been reported around the Dearborn Street entrance to the alley, particularly by mothers of small children.

Farther back, around the area where the bodies fell, more strange things are reported. Pictures have been taken in which the very bricks in the wall seem to show a woman's screaming face. The woman in a tutu appears here, too, in the form of a silhouette that is seen from time to time. Digital camera batteries frequently drain mysteriously in the alley, only to be charged up again a short time later.

Many who pass through Couch Place often find themselves very uncomfortable and unsettled there. They say that faint cries are sometimes heard in the shadows and that some have reported being touched by unseen hands and by eerie cold spots that seem to come from nowhere and vanish just as quickly. A number of women claim that they have been touched as they walked though the alleyway, often experiencing something like a small hand holding onto their own as they walk along. Others claim to have heard the sounds of singing, shouting, and, perhaps most eerie of all, a group of children laughing and playing.

Is this alleyway actually haunted? And do the spirits of those who met their tragic end inside the burning theater still linger here? Perhaps, or perhaps the strange sensations experienced here are "ghosts of the past" of another kind --- a chilling remembrance of a terrifying event that will never be completely forgotten.

# 1908: COLLINWOOD SCHOOL FIRE

March 4, 1908 dawned bright and crisp. It was Ash Wednesday. Spring was rapidly approaching but there was a definite chill in the air. Fritz Hirter, a father of eight and the custodian for the Lake View School, left his home early to walk the short block between his home and the school. He wanted to stoke the basement furnace with coal in plenty of time to get the building well warmed for the children when they arrived. By 6:30 a.m., he had set to work cleaning the classrooms and sweeping the hallways. Promptly at 8:00 a.m., Hirter opened the doors, admitting the children - among them were four of his own.

The day had begun in much the same way as any other day but this peaceful routine was not to last long.

**Collinwood's Lake View School before the fire.**

Collinwood was a small community of eight thousand citizens located just outside of Cleveland, Ohio. The Lake View School, built in 1901, was an imposing, three-story brick building with an interior made of wood. It was a neighborhood school. Most of the families it served lived within walking distance.

On March 4, there were between 310 and 325 children between the ages of five and fifteen in attendance. In the basement, beneath three floors of happy, unsuspecting children and teachers, a malfunctioning furnace was hard at work. The steam pipes running under the first floor became dangerously overheated, so much so that the wooden floor joists ignited from the excessive heat. Thirty short minutes later all that remained of the Lake View School would be a smoking pile of rubble inside a burned-out brick shell.

After the children were settled into their classrooms and the halls and stairways were quiet, Fritz Hirter returned to the school basement. He described what happened next: "I was sweeping in the basement when I looked up and saw a wisp of smoke curling out from beneath the front stairway. I ran to the fire alarm and pulled the gong that sounded the alarm throughout the building. Then I ran to the front and then to the rear doors." Hirter explained that he had first opened the doors to help the children escape. Unfortunately, air rushing through the school with the doors open only served to increase the intensity of the flames and they were soon closed. He ran to a first-floor classroom and yelled for his five-year-old daughter, Ida, to run home and for the other children to leave immediately.

Hirter said the next moments were confusing. "I cannot remember what happened next, except that I saw the flames shooting all about and the little children running down through them screaming. Some fell at the rear entrance and others stumbled over them. I saw my own little Helena among them. I tried to pull her out, but the flames drove me back. I had to leave my little child to die."

The signal for fire was three loud raps on a gong. When the teachers and children on the second and third floors heard the gong, they didn't get excited immediately, assuming it was just another fire drill. Falling into line with their teachers, they quietly headed for the stairways leading to the main doors on the first floor. At first, they marched in an orderly fashion until the children at the head of the lines saw the flames. Order quickly turned to chaos and most of the children either ran screaming headlong into the flames in an attempt to get past them, or they turned to flee back up the stairs and down the narrow halls.

Katherine Weiler, a teacher at Lake View School, was a strong young woman in her mid-twenties. At nearly six feet tall, she was a commanding presence and was known for being a strict but caring teacher, having been raised in Pittsburgh by her father, a German Methodist minister. She had been teaching since she was eighteen.

When her students realized that the fire drill wasn't a drill at all, Miss Weiler did her best to calm her 39 second grade students as they made their way from their second-floor classroom toward the front stairs. When they saw their way was blocked by flames, they quickly ran to the stairs leading to the rear exit. By the time they got there, they found the narrow staircase and hallway beyond packed with children. As more children arrived, they tried to climb over the pile but only succeeded in wedging themselves in even tighter. She could have left to save herself, but instead she stayed. Katherine Weiler spent her last few minutes trying desperately to pull children free of the tangled pile and relieve the pressure as they tried to force their way toward the rear doors. At some point, she lost her footing and was trampled to death under the building mass of children. She was later heralded as a hero.

Laura Brodey, a teacher on the third floor, worked to calm her panicked fifth graders. She called to them: "Courage children! Everyone in line. You will be safe." Trying to lead her students to safety, she, too, found the front staircase was blocked by flames and the rear staircase was wedged tight with children. She turned back and returned with the children to the third floor and to the fire escape mounted to the side of the building. Most of them followed her into the room but others, fearing they would become trapped, tried to run past her back into the hallway. She grabbed hold of the fleeing children and forced them back into the classroom. She broke a window with a chair and lifted each student onto the fire escape platform. A short time later she found herself on the school lawn, along with nearly all of her students, watching as the school continued to burn. It was later found that nearly all students from the third floor were able to escape the fire unharmed. Only four or five who had managed to get away from Miss Brodey were killed.

The fire started in the basement, just under the staircase leading to the front doors. During fire drills, the children had been trained to go directly to those doors but were never trained to seek another way out if those doors were blocked. When the children reached the foot of the stairs they found the flames already raging up through the floor, blocking the way to the front doors and safety. The rush for the doors was so swift that the children were very quickly packed into a tight mass in the vestibule against the closed doors, which opened inward. The children approaching the foot of the stairs, seeing what was ahead of them, turned and attempted to fight their way back up while those who were coming down forced them back into the flames. From that moment on, there was no hope for the children at the front door and first floor stairs.

A Cleveland newspaper reporter tried to describe the scene in this way: "What happened at the foot of the first flight of stairs will never be known, for all of those who were caught in the full fury of the panic were killed. After the flames had died away, however, huge heaps of little bodies, burned by the fire, and trampled into things of horror told the tale as well as anybody need to know it."

After the general fire alarm was sounded, Collinwood Chief of Police Charles McIlrath was among the first to arrive. Even knowing that three of his own children were likely still inside the burning school, Chief McIlrath set to work directing rescuers and firefighters and later containing the thousands who came to help or simply watch, out of morbid curiosity.

Within minutes, hundreds of frantic parents and family members who had heard of the fire arrived at the scene. Their numbers were too vast for the police to hold back. Also arriving to help were a number of men from the nearby train yard and railroad shops at the Lake Shore Rail Yard.

George Getzien, a passerby, ran to the rear doors and, with the aid of police officer Charles Wall, managed to get the doors open but was forced back by the flames and heat. They both said that at that time, there were no children in

**The Lake View School engulfed in flames and smoke.**

that area so they ran to the front doors in an attempt to get them open - but to no avail.

Mrs. Walter Kelley, mother of two Lake View students, and an unknown man were among the first parents to reach the building. Mrs. Kelley was trying to open the rear doors and the man came to help her. Pulling and tugging as hard as they could, believing that the doors opened outwards, they could not to get the doors to budge. Unable to find anything with which to break down the door, they abandoned their effort and began smashing windows and pulling children out until the fire became too intense. They were able to save a few children this way.

Rescuers believed that had there been more men trying to force the doors, many more children could have been saved. What they didn't realize was that by that time, on the other side of those doors, there was a solid mass of children packed in so tightly that there would have been no way possible for the doors to be forced open. Despite previous attempts to open the doors, men from the rail yard "kicked and pounded on the solid wood doors until their fists were bloody."

Eventually, the rear doors collapsed from the weight of the children, exposing a horrifying sight: a solid wall of children, all white faces and struggling bodies. Fritz Hirter, the custodian, was still in the building. He was able to save several children by tossing them through windows as he made his way out, in an attempt to pull them away from the doorway from the inside. Though his face and hands were scorched black, he continued pulling children from the pile until he could save no more. He fled the building at the last second, as more children were shoved onto the pile that was now over six feet high.

**Right side view of the building showing the only fire escape.**

**The Collinwood Fire Department didn't have enough water pressure to even reach the second floor.**

As the flames grew closer and closer to the children, rescuers tried everything to untangle them and pull them free of the pile, but none could be saved. Eventually, the heat drove the rescuers back, and they were forced to watch helplessly as their children were engulfed in flames.

Two of Police Chief McIlrath's children, seven-year-old Benson and nine-year-old Viola May, who had been burned about her head and had lost her hair to fire, were among the children who found their way out of the building. However, his oldest son, ten-year-old Hugh, was lost in the fire but he died a hero's death. Several witnesses, including his father, described Hugh's actions that day. He was seen leading a number of younger children down the fire escape, but when they got to the bottom they saw it was a long jump to the grass. Frightened of the distance, a few ran back into the building. Hugh followed them in an attempt to bring them back out but a wall of flames appeared before he could do so and he was never seen alive again.

When Johanna Sprung first noticed the fire, she rushed across the street in search of her seven-year-old son, Alvin. When she got to the school, the first floor was engulfed in flames but she saw her son with his face pressed against a window. Unable to reach him, she ran home to get a stepladder, which she leaned against the building and climbed up. She reached in through the window and caught her son by the hair but it burned off in her hand and he fell back into the flames.

When the front doors finally gave way, people saw an awful scene, similar to the one at the rear doors: a wall of children. This time however, most of the children were already dead. Wallace Upton, a father who had been helping the police and firefighters, realized that his own ten-year-old daughter was caught near the bottom of the pile. She was badly burned and had been trampled, but she was still alive. He tried with all his strength to tear her from the pressing weight as the flames moved ever closer, but he was unable to free her. He continued until most of his clothes were reduced to ashes and he was severely burned himself. Despite his serious injuries, he could not be persuaded to get medical attention for several more hours.

Three little girls, unable to escape, took refuge in the building's attic. Rather than wait for the flames to reach them, Anna Roth, Gertrude Davis and Mary Ridgeway, all ten years old, leapt to their deaths from an attic window to the ground below.

The school's principal, Anna Morgan, along with teachers Katherine Gollmar and Lulu Rowley, stayed with the children until they felt they could do no more for them. They made their escape through a rear window. Miss Gollmar later described her experience, "It was awful. I can see the wee things in my room holding out their tiny arms and crying to me to help them. Their voices are ringing in my ears yet, and I shall never forget them." She went on to explain that her students had marched to the front stairs but were met with flames. They panicked and ran to the rear stairs where they soon became jammed in the narrow stairway. She made her way to the bottom by climbing out a window then back in again. Unfortunately, she was unable to pull even a single child free from the mass. "Those behind pushed forward and as I stood there, the little ones piled up on one another. Those who could, stretched out their arms to me and cried for me to help them. I tried with all my might to pull them out and stayed there until the flames drove me away."

Ethel Rose, who taught some of the youngest students, was able to get all but three out and to safety. She was seen carrying the last two under her arms as she herself ran from the structure.

Teacher Pearl Lynn was carried away in the rush of panicking children as they ran toward the rear stairs. She stumbled and fell at the bottom. Several children stumbled and fell on top of her. None of them were able to get back up because of the weight of other children upon them. She was later pulled from under a pile of burned children just as the flames reached her. Though severely injured, her body had been insulated by those of the very children she was trying to save.

Mrs. John Phillis was alerted to the fire when her four-year-old son, while looking out their front window, asked to go watch the children play on the fire escape. She found her fifteen-year-old daughter, Jeannie, penned in around the front entrance. Mrs. Phillis pulled on her arms in vain, trying to free her. When she realized that she could not save her daughter, she reached in and patted her hair, trying to keep the fire away from her. The

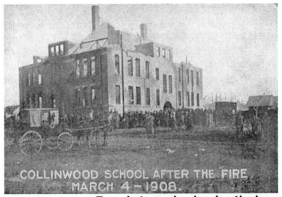

**Two photographs showing the burned-out shell of the Lake View School**

distraught mother stayed with her child until a heavy piece of glass fell, nearly severing her hand. She was forced to move back and Jeannie died before her eyes.

The Collinwood Fire Department was made up entirely of volunteers, many of them quite inexperienced. They had difficulty getting everything in order and were slow in getting to the building. When they finally arrived, they found their fire fighting apparatus to be sorely inadequate. Lacking in water pressure, the water stream was not even strong enough to reach the second story windows. In addition, they didn't possess a ladder long enough to reach the third floor. The firefighters did all they could, but in the end, they had very little effect on the outcome.

In very short order, there was little need for fighting the fire. Most of it had burned out within the first thirty minutes. All that was left to water down were smoldering embers, making it safer for volunteers to remove the children's remains. This was a fairly dangerous task. The only thing left standing was the outer brick shell of the building. The walls had lost most of their internal supports and were in imminent danger of collapsing. Fortunately, the walls remained standing until after the victims were taken from the ruins.

Removal of the bodies was done by the firefighters and the railroad workers from the Lake Shore shop. It was a gruesome task as they pulled blackened torsos and bits of human remains from the site. The rescuers formed a line and as each body was untangled from the debris, it was passed down the line to a stretcher. After each body was covered with a blanket, they were carried to one of the dozen waiting ambulance wagons. A nearby railroad shop was used as a makeshift morgue. As each ambulance was filled with victims, the remains were carried to the morgue and unloaded so that the ambulance might make a return trip for another load as quickly as possible.

As the bodies arrived at the morgue, they were laid out in rows of ten. There were sixteen rows. Many of the little bodies had fallen to pieces as they were removed from the debris making identification even harder. The scene at the morgue was sorrowful as parents and family members walked the rows of the dead searching for their lost children. Families were allowed into the morgue ten at a time, giving them ample time and space to find their loved ones in peace.

Deputy Coroner Harry McNell was put in charge at the morgue. He was nearly beside himself with worry about how identification of the victims could be possible since the faces of nearly all were badly burned. "I have many portions of bodies and dozens of hands and feet which have been torn off and burned away, but which cannot possibly be identified," he said.

Little Nels Thompson was the first to be identified; his mother recognized him by his suspender buckle. Nine- year-old Henry Schultz was identified by a fragment of sweater. Irene Davis, fifteen, was known only by a fragment of skirt. Dale Clark, eight years old, by a small pink-edged handkerchief wrapped around his favorite green marble. Russell Newberry, nine, was known by a fragment of watch chain. A daughter was recognized by a favorite pencil still clutched in her hand. A young girl identified her sister by the plaid pattern of her skirt. A boy was identified by a repaired tear in his pants; his mother having mended them only the day before. Heart-wrenchingly, a pet dog identified a child by curling up next to a small body.

And so, the painstaking identification process continued. In the end, each of the missing was found and identified except for nineteen children and one teacher, Katherine Weiler. Some of them were thought to have burned to ashes - ashes

**A row of bodies laid out in the Lake Shore Railroad shop used as a makeshift morgue.**

that would remain in the ruins of the school. Many authorities believed that several mistaken identifications had taken place, but often the children were buried before the blunders could be corrected.

In the end, 172 children lost their lives as a result of the Lake View School fire. Two teachers were also lost, Grace Fiske and Katherine Weiler, whose body was never recovered. A rescuer was also lost. John Krajnyak, one of the first people to respond, last seen running into the burning building in an attempt to rescue children, had been missing since the fire. However, it was not known that he had given his life until his body was recovered from the debris.

With a need to find someone or something to blame, whispers and rumors started to rumble amongst the townspeople and grieving parents. With no evidence at all, the blame was first laid at the doorstep of Fritz Hirter, the school's custodian. Soon after the fire was extinguished, a crowd of nearly five hundred people gathered outside his home and a contingent of police were called upon to protect him and his family. By the second day, however, when the Hirter family emerged from the house, along with three small coffins bearing the remains of his own children lost in the fire, hearts were softened and the crowd dispersed without incident. Walter, Helena and Ida Hirter were found huddled together on the second floor. It was later determined that Mr. Hirter bore no fault in the cause or spread of the fire.

The Collinwood Board of Trade and the town council each approved $5,000 to help families without the means to bury their dead. The town of Collinwood had planned to buy a field in which to bury all or most of the victims of the fire during a public funeral. However, after many families chose private burials, the town instead purchased a large plot in the Lake View Cemetery that would serve as a mass grave for the unidentified remains. Several children from poor families unable to pay for a funeral were to be interred there, as well. White coffins were purchased for the bodies going into this plot and white ribbons were placed on the doors of each family who had lost someone in the fire. A canvas of victims' families was conducted, identifying needs, and thousands of dollars worth of coal and groceries were distributed.

On March 6, the people of Collinwood began to bury their dead. An average of four funerals, some for multiple family members, were held every hour from sunrise to sunset and continued for three days. There were not enough funeral carriages available so many had to use wagons and even streetcars to transport the small coffins to the various cemeteries and churchyards. The last private funerals were held on March 8, a Sunday.

Monday was the day set aside for the memorial service and public funeral that was held in the Lake View Cemetery. The white coffins were placed side by side in a shallow arc with numerous white wreathes and huge arches of white flowers adorning the site. Thousands of people came to mourn the passing of so many young and innocent souls.

A movement was started to collect money from Cleveland area school children to pay for the erection of a monument dedicated to the memory of the lost children and teachers. The plan was broadened to include all the schools in northern Ohio, with each child asked to donate one penny. Word of the fund spread and soon envelopes containing pennies were arriving from schools from all over the country.

Collinwood needed a new school. The site chosen for it was next to where the Lake View School had stood. Several grieving parents tried to stop the plan and find a different location for the new school. They said they could not bear the thought of their younger children attending school next to where the ashes of their brothers or sisters lay. However, construction began on the chosen site and the school was completed in 1910. The school was named Collinwood Memorial.

To further memorialize the tragic loss of life, a public garden was built on the site of the fire. The garden contains a lovely lawn area with trees and plantings, benches and peaceful walkways. There is a large memorial in the garden. Around the sides of the memorial are 175 tiles, each inscribed with the name of someone who died in the fire.

Fritz Hirter continued working for the school system as a custodian until he retired at age 70. He rarely spoke of the fire. He passed away at the age of 96.

The devastating loss of life in the Lake View School fire was truly tragic but as often happens, there was some good that came of it. The fire not only touched the hearts of a mourning nation, it also caught its attention. Public awareness for fire safety and prevention was vastly increased leading to safer building and improved fire

## 10 MOST DEADLY AMERICAN STRUCTURAL FIRES

1. Killed: 602 - Dec. 30, 1903 - Iroquois Theatre Fire - Chicago, IL
2. Killed: 492 - Nov. 28, 1942 - Coconut Grove Fire - Boston, MA
3. Killed: 322 - Apr. 21, 1930 - Ohio Penitentiary Fire - Columbus, OH
4. Killed: 278+ - Dec. 5, 1876 - Brooklyn Theatre Fire - Brooklyn, NY
5. Killed: 209 - Apr. 23, 1940 - Rhythm Night Club fire - Natchez, MS
6. Killed: 175 - Mar. 4, 1908 - Collinwood School fire (AKA Lake View School) - Collinwood, OH
7. Killed: 171 - Jan. 13, 1908 - Rhoads Opera House - Boyertown, PA
8. Killed: 168 - July 6, 1944 - Hartford circus fire - Hartford, CT
9. Killed: 165 - May 28, 1977 - Beverly Hills Supper Club fire - Southgate, KY
10. Killed: 148 - Mar. 25, 1911 - Triangle Shirtwaist Factory fire - New York City, NY

codes. Cities and towns all across the United States instituted inspections of schools, theaters, nickelodeons and public buildings. Most were requiring the installation of exit doors that swing outward, noncombustible exterior fire escapes and in some cases additional fire escapes. It is impossible to determine how many lives were saved because of these changes.

Over one hundred families lost children on that terrible day in March. Sometime after the fire, families began talking softly amongst themselves about strange things happening in their homes. Several of them described catching brief glimpses of their lost children or hearing their voices from another room then finding no one there when they went to look. They never knew if their children returned to them to say goodbye or as a comfort. Over time, the visits became less frequent.

The Collinwood Memorial School was closed in the 1970s and remained abandoned for decades. The old school had developed a reputation for being haunted. Neighbors who live near the school have told of often seeing a light   appear in a window on the second story in the old building. The light would slowly move along the halls then disappear. This light was seen many times by many people over the years but no "natural" cause has ever been determined.

As the building had been abandoned for so long and the neighborhood around the school had deteriorated over time, few people have taken the opportunity to wander through the building at night to investigate the haunting.  However, an intrepid few who dared to do so reported a sudden onset of chills and cold spots and occasionally, they said they heard the faint sounds of screaming children.

People walking through the memorial garden, located on the actual site of the school fire, have told of smelling the strong odor of smoke in the area. This smoky smell occasionally becomes a putrid stench, so strong that it drives visitors from the garden.

In 2003, the memorial garden was rededicated. In 2004, the Collinwood Memorial School was demolished.  A brand new school, also named the Memorial School, now stands at the site to serve the area's children. Only time will tell if the children from so long ago will return, again, to this new school named in their memory.

# 1908: THE RHOADS OPERA HOUSE FIRE

All of Boyertown was in mourning. No one was without loss -- a parent, a sibling, a grandparent, an aunt, uncle or cousin, a friend or a sweetheart. To some, this day would forever be remembered as "Black Saturday." The ghastly parade had started at dawn and hadn't stopped until darkness had fallen. No floats or bands or smiling children were in this parade, only horse-drawn hearses, one after another, in a seemingly endless procession of the dead, winding its way to the Fairview or Union cemeteries. *The Press* of Philadelphia reported: "No bands played funeral marches. The measured beating of the horses' hooves, the grinding of the vehicles'

**Rhoads Opera House**

wheels and the tread of the many feet alone broke the silence of the day."

Outside the cemetery gates, hearses were lined up, waiting their turn to enter. Inside, clergymen stood in the frigid winter wind for more than eight hours, performing one funeral after another. They read a piece of scripture or two and said a brief prayer, then on to the next grave, and the next, and the next. They continued all day and there still wasn't time enough to complete their sorrowful task. They would begin again in the morning.

The town was burying its dead. One hundred and five people were laid to rest on that single day with over 15,000 mourners present. There had been 171 men, women and children who were victims of the Rhoads Opera House fire just five days earlier. The funerals would eventually end, but the pain and grief and anger would continue for this small town for a very long time.

Boyertown in 1908 was a thriving community of a little over 2,000 residents. Located between Philadelphia and Reading, Pennsylvania, it was in the heart of an industrialized area, though far from the sweatshops of New York. Many folks worked in small stores and businesses or in the cigar factory. But the largest employer in town was the Boyertown Burial Casket Company, one of the largest casket factories in the country. As with most small towns of that era, individuals were likely related to half the people in town and friends (or enemies) with the other half. It was a tiny place but prosperous and had a bright future ahead. You knew things were going well as soon as you arrived, as Boyertown had just acquired newly paved streets. In fact, the economy was doing so well, they even had an opera house. All was well in Boyertown.

Dr. Thomas Rhoads owned the large, three-story brick building on the corner of South Washington Street and Philadelphia Avenue. At street level, the building housed the Farmers National Bank and a hardware store. To the rear of the bank were four large apartments, or dwelling houses, as they were called at the time. A small fraternal lodge and the Rhoads Opera House took up the second and third floors. There was no electricity in the building so the opera house stage lights and foot lights were all oil lamps, fed through a metal trough from a five-gallon barrel of lamp oil off to the side of the stage.

**Typical Stereopticon in the early 1900s.**

The structure had recently had a building inspection, and with much persuading, Dr. Rhoads had reluctantly installed fire escapes. The landings were at floor level but escape could only be achieved by first crawling through a window three feet above the floor.

People in town were greatly excited by an extravaganza that was to take place on the evening of January 13. The event was sponsored by St. John's Lutheran Church and it promised to be the highlight of the winter season. Harriet Monroe, an internationally famed dramatist from Washington, D.C., was presenting her latest production, "The Scottish Reformation," at the Rhoads Opera House. This was to be her second production on that stage. Anticipation for the drama had been building for quite some time as some of the children and church members would be performing and they had been rehearsing for months.

Mrs. Monroe had hired Harry Fisher to operate a stereopticon. Also known as a "magic lantern," this was an early type of slide projector that used glass plates with pictures burned into them. The device had its own light source from a small, but very bright calcium-oxygen flame behind the glass plate. The night of the play, Fisher was set up at the rear of the auditorium, behind the audience. He would be projecting pictures of Scotland and Germany on a screen between acts. Few of the people attending the play had ever seen anything like a projected picture so this would truly be a special treat.

January 13 was a Monday but the audience arrived in their Sunday best. It was going to be a glorious evening.  The house was sold out and 312 excited spectators filled every seat, but there were an additional hundred people or so present, including actors and support personnel for the play, opera house employees and tenants in the apartments on the ground floor.

The play continued through the first two acts without problem and the audience was pleased. The curtain had been lowered about 9:30 p.m. to prepare for the third act. Fisher had resumed his slide show with the stereopticon when he turned a knob to adjust the flame within the projector. He made the adjustment improperly and the machine let out a very loud hiss that was heard throughout the auditorium. Several members of the audience were startled by the unknown sound and panicked.

The people who were frightened by the unknown noise rushed away from the device and toward the stage. The actors behind the curtain also heard the hissing caused by the projector and the shouts of the disturbed audience members. A young actor raised a lower portion of the curtain and peeped out to see what was happening. The curtain had a long bar running from one end to the other along the floor and when he lifted the curtain, the bar  accidentally knocked over one of the oil lamps.

The Reverend Adam Weber, pastor of St. John's Lutheran Church, which had sponsored the event, had taken six of his own children to the program. He described what happened first a little differently, but the end result was essentially the same. "I was sitting in the front row of the Opera House with three of the little children who were to take the part of pages. Suddenly there came a hiss from the rear of the house, where the stereopticon lantern was placed. Immediately all the people around arose to see what was the matter. The curtain was lowered, and when the people on the stage heard the noise they raised it. Just then, a wave of the crowd broke upon the stage and together with the raising of the curtain, upset the tank of oil which fed the eight burners used for footlights. Two of these burners immediately began to blaze up. I threw one of the little girls with me upon the stage and then followed her myself. Seizing a cap, I started to beat out the flames, which were shooting from the two burners. Someone threw down a piece of carpet and tried to assist in extinguishing the fire. When the blaze got beyond control, four men and myself tried to lift the oil tank, and throw it out of the window. The heat of the fire, however, had melted the soldering, and the hole blazed up in a burst of flame that shot up to the ceiling. There was no hope of saving the building now."

The fire ate through the stage as if it were kindling then moved into the auditorium like a beast stalking its prey.

The central section of seats ran from front to back with the best view of the stage. Tickets for these seats were higher priced. The central section was separated from two side sections, running along the walls to the right and left, by two four-foot-wide aisles. The more comfortable seats in the central section were bolted to the floor, but the seats in the two side sections were quite flimsy and were not secured to the floor, making it easy to move them about as needed.

At the first sign of fire, those seated in the central section packed the narrow aisles so quickly and tightly that movement was next to impossible. As bad as that was, it was far worse for those in the side sections. They jumped up and frantically crashed about. The frail seats scattered and collapsed, tripping up the frenzied mob and many of them went down, unable to regain their feet. The side sections became battlegrounds. The *New York Times* reported that: "Men used the chairs which had entangled their feet as weapons with which to clear a way to the open.   Several women say that they saw men respected in the community raise the chairs high over head and bring them down with crushing force on the heads of women and children. These men are reported among the missing, and probably died in the flames or were suffocated."

Many of those who had fallen, or were battered down, were so severely injured that they were unable to continue their struggle toward the exits. They lay where they fell, screaming and thrashing in terror as they waited hopelessly for the raging inferno to reach them.

As often happens when the cry of "fire" is heard, the crowd panicked as one. Frantic people fought and struggled against each other, trying to get to the main entrance at the rear of the auditorium. Survivor Randy Stover said, "Everyone seemed to have lost control of himself. The flames first consumed the flimsy scenery and then came toward the crowd like a great wave, and the suffocating smoke dropped men, women and children in its path. The flames did the rest. It was a terrible sight, and I shall carry the recollection as long as I live. Once the crowd began to fight its way toward the doors no power on earth could have saved all the lives, but I believe that if the men had not lost control of themselves, the loss of life would have been very small."

The exterior fire escapes were very poorly marked and many inside the already smoke-filled room could not distinguish the windows as portals to safety. Someone who did remember about the fire escapes called out to others to come to the windows. Some of those who were struggling at the rear entrance did brave the flames above and around them and rushed toward the windows opening onto the fire escapes. Once there, they still had to climb over the three-foot windowsill and out onto the landing. A bottleneck formed at these windows and in several cases, fights broke out as people struggled to make their escape.

Frank Cullen, the local blacksmith, had attended the program with his wife and four-year-old son. When Cullen realized the seriousness of the situation, he picked up his boy, and making his way to a window, tossed the child out. He believed that a quick death would be preferable to being burned alive. However, the youngster landed on a fire escape landing and climbed his way down to safety. By the time Cullen had returned to rescue his wife, she was helplessly trapped in a teeming mass of terrified humanity and he was unable to reach her. He never saw her alive again.

People who reached the main entrance doorway leading onto Philadelphia Avenue were unable to open the inward-swinging door. Witnesses insisted that the door was bolted, that the doorkeeper had become so interested in the play that he had bolted the door and taken a seat in the back to watch. A man whom newspaper accounts described only as a "big German," was among the first to be stopped by the bolt. He pounded with his fists and tried to force the door open with his shoulder while others tried to unfasten the bolt, but the door stood fast. Within seconds, their attempts were useless, as an increasing number of people pressed in upon them and against the door that could only be opened inward.

The crowd continued to build up behind them and the crush of people became so intense that the door finally collapsed outward. When the door gave way, those closest to it fell through and were thrown down the steep, narrow staircase, where they landed in a heap at the bottom. The continuing press of the crowd carried more people to the top of the stairs and they, too, were hurled down on top of those who were trying to regain their footing. The pile grew as people continued to tumble down the stairs, crushing those at the bottom. A dozen bodies were later found trampled to death where they had fallen.

Several people who were passing on the street heard the screams and saw the smoke. They rushed into the building to help but were quickly stopped by the pile of bodies wedged into the staircase in front of them. They were able to untangle and free a few people but were soon forced back into the street by the heat and smoke.

Reverend Weber told of his escape and of trying to help others, "When I was halfway down the fire escape I saw a little girl sitting on a windowsill above me and crying. I called to her to jump. She did so. I caught her by her dress. It tore as I grasped it, and the girl fell to the ground below. At the same time, a woman seated on the same windowsill made the same leap, and was caught between the fire escape and the wall."

When Weber was finally able to get home, he found five of his six children safe but one daughter had been lost to the fire. He was so badly burned about his hands and face that he was not able to officiate over any funeral, save that of his own child.

The fire seemed to bring out the worst in some. Men became brutes, batting away women and children in their rush to safety, women clawed and scratched at those in front of them to get by and children were trampled in the manic crush. The race to safety had become survival of the strongest.

But there were heroes inside that smoke-filled furnace, too. Dr. Charles Mayer, a local druggist, fought valiantly to get through the flames and terrified masses to carry his wife to safety. Once she was safely outside, he rushed back into the building in search of their daughter. We will never know if he found her, but we do know the fire found them and neither was able to escape alive.

**(Left) The interior of the building after the fire.   (Right) The burned-out shell of the Rhoads Opera House**

Many of the heroes did not survive to tell their stories, but many of their stories survived the fire. Witnesses told of numerous incidents of self-sacrificing acts as people who might have been able to save themselves, choose instead to stay to help save others - and were lost. Witnesses later recalled mothers and fathers searching for their children, brothers trying to rescue their sisters, friends clinging to friends and sweethearts unwilling to flee without their beloveds. Many who had reached the outside and safety, ran back inside in desperate attempts to save others and never returned.

Within five minutes of the first alarm, the Boyertown Volunteer Fire Department was at work pumping water onto the building. Sadly, also within the first five minutes, the building had become almost fully engulfed in fire. A few hours later the Reading and Pottstown Fire Departments arrived to assist in the fight but no amount of effort or water could quench the fire and their energies shifted to protecting the surrounding buildings from falling victim as well.

The fire had raged for over seven hours when the roof collapsed. An hour later, firefighters believed that the fire was under control but it wasn't until nearly 8:30 a.m. before the first recovery team was able to enter the remains of the building.

Almost immediately, they began taking in large muslin bags to hold the charred remains and bones. They knew they were going to find scores of bodies inside but nothing could have prepared them for the carnage that awaited them. Just inside the second-floor entry doors to the opera house, the same entry doors that had burst under the crush of the crowd, almost eighty bodies were found in a mass over seven feet high. They found torsos with their limbs completely burned away and others with only bits of bones. In the areas where the aisles and side seating once were, dozens of bodies were found with multiple broken or crushed bones, having been trampled where they fell. The most devastating things they saw were the children. Their tiny bodies seemed to have been particularly ravaged by the flames - and the loss of children is always the hardest.

Several factors made the recovery effort even more difficult. The fire had burned for so long that some bodies crumbled when touched. With others, limbs just pulled away when an attempt was made to lift the bodies. In some cases, the condition of the bodies was so poor that the recovery teams had to literally scoop up bone and ashes.  There were few ladders tall enough to reach the second story so getting the bodies down to the ground was particularly slow. Progress was also impeded the huge crowd of onlookers pressing in around the building.

Aid arrived later in the day from a group of surgeons and trained nurses, bringing with them a large stock of hospital and first aid supplies. Also arriving was a detachment of Troop C of the state constabulary, bringing with them additional ladders. The doctors and nurses set to work tending to the burned and injured. The constables roped off the area around the building and pushed back the crowd that had thus far been hindering the recovery efforts.  Boyertown was too small to have a morgue or any structure with much open space, so the workers filled one temporary morgue after another. The public school was called upon to serve as the fifth and final morgue.

The end of the second day brought with it several disturbing realizations. It was believed that all the bodies had been removed from the ruins and the total was shocking. There were 167 victims wrapped in white muslin and lying side by side on the floors of the temporary morgues. One fireman, fighting to save lives, became trapped in the building and sacrificed his own. Of the dead, the ratio of women and girls to men and boys was three to one.  Nearly one-tenth of the residents of Boyertown were now dead.

Berks County Coroner Robert E. Strasser went to work immediately, inspecting the morgues, counting bodies and putting in motion a system for identifying the remains and getting them to their families. Only ten of the corpses were recognizable but Strasser believed that most of the victims had been identified through personal items or fragments of clothing. Twenty-five bodies were so badly burned they couldn't be reassembled or separated from ash and debris, but the names of those still missing or unidentified were known.

The disaster would become a permanent part of the history and culture of Boyertown, but the immediate impact was almost unbearable for many. Several children were orphaned overnight and entire families had been wiped out.  A group of six cousins, all girls, perished in the fire. Charles Nuse along with his wife and three-year-old son were buried in a common grave. J.J. Becker, a member of the cast, saw the flames spread from the stage into the audience and envelope his wife and daughter, who were sitting in the front row. A woman had come to the play to surprise her husband, who was playing the piano for the production. Her husband survived but his surprise became a nightmare when he learned that his wife was among the dead. Even Harriet Monroe, author of the drama performed that night was not without loss. Her sister, Stella Mayers, who had been in charge of the school children in the play that night, was lost.

The number of known seriously injured neared 75 but it was assumed that several other persons were injured but were able to get home to be nursed by family members. The *New York Times* described how pain brought on by loss affected at least one man: "Warren Wein of Boyertown went insane tonight as a result of the tragedy. He knew that his sisters Carrie and Florence were in the burning building. He made efforts to climb the fire escape to get inside. Later he learned that his mother was also among the missing. He then became violently insane."

Within the first few days, Dr. Daniel Kohler, Burgess of Boyertown, an election position, realized that there were going to be many challenges for the town and for its residents. He appointed a group of men to form the Citizens Relief Committee. The group had several duties, starting with collecting the names of missing persons and crosschecking them with the known dead and getting these lists published. They also worked to arrange "proper and speedy burial of the dead." They purchased a large burial plot in the Fairfield Cemetery for $500. The unidentifiable bodies, still mixed in with remnants from the fire, would be buried together in a mass grave. The committeemen then arranged a special funeral for the unknowns for Sunday. They were

**Preparation for the mass grave in Fairview Cemetery.**

also delegated the duty of collecting and dispersing the $22,075 in donations - a huge amount in 1908 - that had flooded in from all over the country.

A common concern when any disaster occurred with great loss of life became a cruel irony in Boyertown. There was customarily a problem securing large numbers of caskets quickly enough to bury an abnormally large number of people. However, one of the largest casket manufacturing companies in the country was located in Boyertown, so finding enough would not be a problem they would have to face. The sad reality was that several of the men who died in the fire were buried in caskets that they themselves had made.

Coroner Strasser quickly convened an inquest in hopes of discovering the cause of the fire, and to determine who, if anyone, was at fault. The images of the carnage were still fresh in everyone's mind, just as the pain from the incredible loss was still fresh in their hearts. Anger was the dominant emotion during the inquest. Someone had to carry all the blame.

Three names rose swiftly to the top of the list. Dr. Thomas Rhoads had already been arrested as the owner of an unsafe building. How many more people might have survived if only the entrance doors hadn't swung inward, trapping scores of people? How many others might have been saved if the fire exit windows had been more clearly marked or the climb over the windowsill to the fire escape lower? But by the standards of the day, the building construction and design was considered acceptable. The structure had been inspected only a short time before and with the addition of the exterior fire escapes, it had been approved.

A warrant for the arrest of Mrs. Harriet Monroe was issued. She was the author and organizer of the production in progress when the fire started. Although she was not present the night of the fire, and she had lost her beloved sister to the flames, she was still found partially culpable for the tragedy. It was alleged that she had hired an incompetent stereopticon operator and that the oxygen tanks had ruptured and ignited the fire. She argued vehemently that this was not true - that the tanks had been found in the debris and they were intact. But Frank Moyer, the prosecutor who had lost his daughter in the fire, was not to be easily swayed.

The third supposed culprit was the hapless Harry Fisher, the stereopticon operator. When he was accused of literally starting the fire at the inquest, his guilt was believed to be so great that he was cursed and hounded by crowds at a train station in Philadelphia. Fisher was again mobbed while trying to board a ferry to his home in New Jersey. Philadelphia's *Evening Bulletin* reported that Fisher, his face swaddled in bandages from burns he received in the fire, turned to the mob and appealed to them, "As God is my witness, I am not to blame for this thing. I did not cause the deaths of those poor people."

Though the coroner's inquest had laid the blame for the terrible loss of life on those three people, the Grand Jury did not agree. Given more time to investigate the evidence and ferret out the facts, they came to a different conclusion. They found that there were inherent problems with the design of parts of the building, but there was no indication of negligence or ill intent. Further, they determined that: "While the calcium lighting outfit was the cause of a slight panic, it was not the fault of this mechanism that caused so much desolation. It was the upsetting of the lamp oil tank feeding the footlights with oil which set the fire to the building and cremated the spectators." This determination absolved Mrs. Monroe and Fisher of fault, as well. No one was ever criminally prosecuted for the fire.

The lessons learned from the Rhoads Opera House fire were not lost. The Pennsylvania legislature got to work and sixteen months after the fire, Governor Edwin Stuart signed the state's first fire safety laws. The laws covered landings, lighting, curtains, fire extinguishers, aisles, marked exits and doors. The part of the law that had the most impact required that all exit doors open outward and must remain unlocked when a business was in operation.

The day of the final burials was Sunday, the end of a weekend that would always be remembered as "Black Saturday" in Boyertown. By Sunday morning, there were 25 people left to be laid to rest. Neither the coroner nor the funeral directors were able to reassemble the last bodies so the remains were separated into 25 coffins, one for each person, along with fire debris that they felt might include human remains. Reading's *The Eagle* published the following description of the final funeral for the victims of the fire:

Unrecognized but not un-honored, Boyertown's unidentified dead were laid to rest on Sunday morning in Fairview Cemetery while a vast concourse of people stood with bared heads mourning those who had passed through the valley of the shadow of death.

Promptly at 9:00 a.m. thirteen hearses drove up to the school on Washington Street. All along that section of Washington Street on which the school is located hundreds of residents and strangers stood at silent attention, waiting for the march of the dead... Members of the local lodges of the Modern Woodmen of America, the Patriotic Sons of America, and the Independent Order of Odd Fellows acted as bearers at the request of the Citizens Relief Committee. These men met at the Town Hall and, headed by the committee, marched in a body to the school house. They filed into the temporary morgue, two by two, bent on a mission of brotherly love, a last duty of the living to the dead. Fifty-two they were and mostly young men, too. Each one borne by four carriers, 13 caskets were brought out in quick succession and deposited in the waiting hearses which, 100 feet apart, moved in a slow procession to Philadelphia Avenue and thence westward to Fairview Cemetery, the bearers walking two to the right and two to the left of each hearse.

After the first caskets were lowered into the grave, the hearses returned to the school for the remaining caskets. Four community pastors conducted the funeral service.

The caskets had no names on them, simply the words: "At Rest."

The fire was out, the cause of the fire discovered and the victims were buried. All that was left to do was to clean up, rebuild and try to move past the terrible tragedy. But some remained behind who would not let the living move on or forget. A few chose to stay where they had died. For many months, passers-by heard moans and screams of pain coming from the fire-gutted shell of the opera house. Reports of these cries were frequent and they continued until the building's remains were completely demolished and the opera house was rebuilt on the same site.

Before construction could be started, however, an elderly gentleman had to be repeatedly forcibly removed from the ruins, and later from the cleared lot. He insisted that his wife's ghost had been appearing to him, telling him to go to a specific spot to visit with her. He was frantic to talk to her. He continued to come to the site until the new building was completed.

A short distance from the Rhoads Building, a woman who had lost a child in the fire told friends and neighbors that she was unable to sleep at night for all the commotion. She believed that a number of fire victims had taken refuge with her and her house was now virtually overrun with ghosts.

**The reconstructed Rhoads Building as it looks today.**

The lingering spirits had not limited themselves to the place of their deaths. For many decades, Boyertown police have received reports of cries and moans emanating from the mass grave of the Rhoads Opera House fire victims. No explanation for this phenomenon has ever been found.

The inscription on each coffin read "At Rest" but it seems some of those lost have sadly not yet found their peace.

# 1909: THE CHERRY MINE FIRE

Coal has long been one of the great resources of Illinois but over the years, the rich veins of black gold have been soaked with the blood of those who have labored for them. Illinois's worst coal mine disaster occurred in the small northern Illinois town of Cherry, a place that within a few short days saw the best --- and the worst – of human nature. The disaster was caused by an electrical failure and fire but human error and panic would lead to the deaths of 259 men, a number of whom died heroically while trying to save the lives of others.

CHERRY MINE DISASTER 11-13-09

The coal mine opened in 1905 in a town that was named for the mine's developer, James Cherry. In those days, most miners were European immigrants and the Cherry miners were typical, representing sixteen different nationalities. The miners had come to the new town, located about eight miles northwest of the LaSalle-Peru area, because the mine was a good place to work. The entire output from the mine, owned by the St. Paul Coal Company, was used to fuel locomotives of the Chicago, Milwaukee & St. Paul Railroad. Because of this, unlike most mines at the time, there were no lay-offs in the summer time. The operation provided good, steady work and had a good safety record, as well.

There were three veins of coal in the mine but only the second vein, at 324 feet down, and the third vein, at 485 feet, were being worked. The second vein had proven to be the richest and in November 1909, the men were laboring a mile east and a mile west of the main shaft. About two hundred feet from the main shaft was a smaller airshaft that also served as an emergency exit and had a line of wooden steps that ran from bottom to top. In addition, the mine also featured the relatively new innovation of electric lights. Power plants were constructed directly on the site but unfortunately, the lights only worked sporadically. In the fall of 1909, the lights had been out for nearly a month because of trouble in the main wiring cables. The replacement parts finally arrived on November 14 --- one day too late.

Around noon on the afternoon of November 13, six bales of hay were lowered down the mine's main shaft to feed the mules who pulled the underground coal cars. The hay was piled into an empty coal car and the car was pushed to another shaft, where it was supposed to be lowered to the stable below. Unknown to anyone at the time, the car with the hay in it was parked under one of the kerosene torches that were being used in the absence of the electric lights. It was a common practice to turn the lighted torches horizontally so that the oil would keep the wicks soaked for a brighter flame but this also meant that the kerosene would often drip. On this day, a little of the oil dripped onto the hay and the hay caught on fire.

The hay in the cart was soon burning but unbelievably, everyone ignored the flames. The fire could have been easily extinguished, but small fires were commonplace and two men working close to the shaft just left it to burn. One man actually walked past the fire without a backward glance. He was in a hurry to catch the hoisting cage to the surface and couldn't be bothered.

Finally, two other men on their way to surface passed by and decided to push the car to the shaft so that it could be dumped into the water-filled pit below. The tracks were littered with debris, however, and they had trouble getting the car to move. As the flames grew and smoke began to fill the tunnel, the men worked more frantically. Finally, they managed to get the hay to the water, where it was immediately snuffed out. Tragically, it was too late.

Pieces of wooden planking, as well as support timbers and scattered chunks of coal, had started to burn. A large fan on the surface above kept a strong and steady current of air flowing through the mine, fanning the flames. Within minutes, the mine was burning.

Earlier that same day, 481 men had gone down into the mine for the work shift. They were scattered out in various areas when the horror began. Even after the men at the bottom of main shaft became aware of the fire, they continued to haul out coal. They believed the fire was nothing to be concerned about. From the time the fire was discovered, 45 minutes passed before attempts were made to start warning the workers who were spread out through the mine. When the seriousness of the fire was finally realized, a mad scramble for the surface --- and for life --- began.

At last the signal to clear out the mine was given, but for many, it was too late.

In an attempt to slow the spread of the fire, someone ordered the fan that was located at the top of the emergency airshaft to be reversed. This was a tragically flawed move as the reversal served only to suck the flames up into the shaft, burning the wooden steps. For a short time, though, the reversed air flow did keep the flames away from the main shaft. But as the heat that was pulled upward scorched the fan, its bearings began to melt and the fan ground to a stop. The flames then swept back into the main shaft.

A sixteen-year-old miner named Peter Donna was one of the ones who made it out. He later told of leading his father through the smoke and darkness toward an escape route: "After my father and I got to the second level the fire blocked us off. It singed my hair on the side of my face and my head. We circled around the burning section and made our way to the main lift. The smoke almost overtook us. I led the way.... All the lights were out and our matches wouldn't stay lit. We met only a few others who came with us on the way. When we finally reached the lift, there was no trouble getting on it and up the shaft. It took several seconds for my eyes to get adjusted to the bright light of the surface. When I finally could see, I couldn't find my father. I wanted to go back down into the mine and get him, but they stopped me. After a couple more cage-loads of men came up, my father stepped off with an old man he had saved."

About two hundred of the miners escaped but more than two hundred and sixty remained underground when the elevator stopped working, trapping twelve miners in the cage and leaving others with no escape route.

On the surface, the mine's shrill whistle cut through the afternoon air, carrying a dreaded alarm to the

**Crowds began streaming into Cherry as word of the disaster began to spread.**

community. The people of Cherry flocked to the mine. Wives, daughters, sons and loved ones crowded to the edge of the company property as clouds of black smoke billowed from the mineshafts. Panic ran through the crowd and necks were craned, hoping to catch a glimpse of anyone who had emerged from beneath the ground.

The hoisting cage, normally not used to carry passengers, with twelve brave volunteers inside, descended into what must have seemed like the pit of hell six times and each time, managed to bring up a few desperate survivors. Communication between the man operating the hoist on the surface and the men in the cage depended on a wire that rang a bell. The number of times the bell rang, the operator responded accordingly. On the seventh trip down, the clanging of the bell made no sense and the panicked operator, not knowing what to do and being assailed by threats and curses from those nearby, waited almost five minutes before bringing the cage back up. The men inside were horribly burned to death.

Finally, with no one else being allowed into the mine, the shaft was sealed at 8:00 p.m. in an attempt to smother the flames. Several attempts were made to reopen it, but each time it was unsealed, the fire flared up again. There was little hope that anyone could survive under such brutal conditions.

News of the disaster swept through the nation and a multitude of relief workers, including the American Red Cross, doctors, nurses, clergymen, reporters and even other miners, arrived in Cherry. Everyone wanted to help. They all wanted something to do but there was little that could be done. The crowd milled about on the surface as the men beneath the earth burned to death, choked on the smoke or simply suffocated as the fire literally pulled the air from their lungs.

Over the course of the next week, volunteers equipped with oxygen masks tried to descend into the mine but

**Volunteers equipped with oxygen masks tried to descend into the mine but were continually driven back by the smoke and flames.**

**(Left) Rows of dead men were laid out in tents so that they could be identified. (Right) Scores of funerals were held. This photo is captioned "Three dead from one family."**

"Dead Row" in Cherry. According to the original photo caption, on this street of more than 30 cottages, only four men survived the fire.

were continually driven back by the smoke and flames. The blaze was finally extinguished seven days after it started. The rescuers assumed there could be no survivors – but they were wrong. Twenty-two miners had managed to retreat to the deepest recesses of the mine, where they found a small amount of water, and sealed off the shaft behind them. On Saturday, November 20, near death, they attempted to escape. As they broke through the wall, they heard the sounds of a rescue party. In their haste to get out, one of the miners was killed when he struck his head on the opening. The others, however, found their way to the exploration party. On the early evening of November 21, one week after the fire had started, 21 miners were brought out of the mine alive. One of them later died.

News of the survivors exhilarated the town for a short time but no other men were rescued. By Thanksgiving Day, twelve days after the fire broke out, one hundred and fifty bodies had been recovered from the depths of the mine. The inner depths of the mine continued to smolder and rescue work remained dangerous. Many feared that the air from the surface would cause the fire to flare up again. Finally, the difficult decision was made to seal the mine with concrete in order to permanently extinguish the fire. All hope had been lost that anyone else could have survived.

Time passed and the remaining bodies were not brought to the surface until the following April. At least one of them was not found until July. Many of them were never recovered at all. Of those who were, their funerals seemed to go on and on. The men were laid to rest in a cemetery that remains today on the south side of Cherry. A sculpture of a mourning woman adorns a monument that was constructed in memory of the disaster victims, men who left one hundred and sixty anguished widows and three hundred and ninety fatherless children behind.

Illinois' worst mine disaster – and the third worst coalmine disaster in American history – had been caused by six carelessly placed bales of hay.

# 1911: THE TRIANGLE FACTORY FIRE

The Triangle Shirtwaist factory was a typical sweatshop, just like any of the hundreds of other sweatshops on the island of Manhattan in the early 1900s - that is, until it caught fire. What happened during that fire so shocked the nation that it literally changed history for the safety of millions of industrial workers and likely saved thousands of lives.

The Asch building, on the corner of Greene Street and

Washington Place, was a rather nondescript ten-story building. The owners, Max Blanck and Isaac Harris, rented or subcontracted out the lower seven floors of the building to various other similar enterprises. They saved the eighth, ninth and tenth floors for the Triangle Shirtwaist Company factory, which they operated to make ladies blouses, then known as shirtwaists. One unique aspect of this particular building was that it was constructed to be "fireproof." History has shown us so many times, that this kind of arrogance has proven to be deadly. Fireproof buildings didn't need the usual precautions and devices. The irony in this case was that the factory building's being considered fireproof led directly to the death of one 148 people.

**Garment workers at the factory before the fire.**

After that terrible fire was extinguished, the building did indeed seem to have been fireproof. Even inside, the floors and walls were left virtually intact. There was little visual evidence of the conflagration in the outward appearance of the structure and none of the floors below the eighth were damaged by the fire. The only signs of what had happened that day were the piles of broken bodies on the pavement below and the charred remains of people and burned stock and machinery later found on the upper three floors.

Employees of the Triangle Shirtwaist Company were not allowed to leave the building by the main doors. At the end of the work day they were required to go to the rear exit door, which was kept locked during the hours of operation for fear of theft. Here, the employees were routinely searched before leaving, lest they try to steal something. This situation created a terrific bottleneck during the fire and cut off one of the few means of escape. As the structure was deemed fireproof, it had only a single, flimsy fire escape.

There had already been four fires reported in this particular factory and the fire department had determined it to be unsafe because of insufficient fire escapes. However, because there were no meaningful legal requirements it was difficult, if not impossible to enforce any changes that should have been made. Also, as the previous fires were rapidly extinguished and no one was killed, the factory's routines remained unchanged.

March 25, 1911 was a Saturday and a fine day according to all accounts. Most sweatshop workers in the city were released by lunchtime for their Saturday half day-off, including those who worked on the lower seven floors of the Asch Building. However, the owners of the Triangle Shirtwaist Company, Max Blanck and Isaac Harris, who were known to be harsh employers, kept most of their employees hard at work until 5:00 p.m. Most of the factory employees, nearly five hundred women and one hundred or so men, were at work that day. Most of the women were very young, aged sixteen to 23, and very few of them spoke English. They were largely Italian, German, Russian and Hungarian immigrants and many of them were the primary wage earners for their families. The men employed there worked mostly in the capacity of office workers and management.

Around 4:40 p.m., just ten minutes before the end of the workday, cries of "fire!" rang out on the eighth floor. No one ever learned exactly how the fire started but most speculated that it was caused by a carelessly discarded cigarette or match. The fabric debris had not been removed for quite some time and finished clothing was hung on overhead lines so there was ample fuel everywhere.

Max Rother, a tailor working on the eighth floor, where the fire started, described this sight, "...hanging over the heads of the operators at their machines in the room was a line of clothes ablaze." He and another man tried putting the fire out with buckets of water but when the line burned through, the burning clothing fell onto them

**The fire department rushed to the Asch Building after the first fire alarm was sounded.**

and the workers. Rother fled to the stairs and was able to escape to safety but very few others followed him.

Within a few minutes, flames were pouring from windows of the top three floors of the Asch building. Four fire alarms were sounded immediately but the fire was already so intense that the first five women to jump to their deaths did so before even the first fire truck had arrived.

Of the two elevators in the building, only one was in working order. A few minutes after the fire began, the only stairwell was full of flames and smoke, making it impossible to flee using that route. Some survivors reported that the elevator only made one trip down that

afternoon but Thomas Gregory, an elevator operator from another building who was on his way home, ran into the building and said he made three more trips with the elevator before it broke down. He described leaving masses of terrified, panic-stricken people trying to fight their way onto the elevator but was only able to take fifteen or so people on each trip.

Even though the elevator was no longer operating, the shaft doors were forced open and several people attempted to escape by sliding down the elevator cables. At least two people were

**(Left) The Fire department works hard to put out the fires on the third floor of the Asch Building.**

**(Right) A photo showing that while multiple hoses are trained on the building, few of the streams are effective for the upper floors.**

successful in their attempt. A young woman, later pulled from the shaft alive, said she passed out on her way down the cables and had no memory of what happened next but she believed that she survived because she landed on several of the dead bodies of her fellow workers, which cushioned her fall. Another man reported using the same cables to flee. Unfortunately, as he slid down, the body of a young woman falling from above, knocked him from the cables and he fell the final few floors. After the fire, 25 bodies were pulled from the bottom of the elevator shaft, many of whom had simply jumped to their deaths to escape the flames.

Both Harris and Blanck, the building's owners, were in the building when the fire started, along with Blanck's children and their nanny. All escaped by making their way to the roof, a means of escape that was not known to most of the factory workers. The doors to the roof were kept locked on all but the top floor.

About two hundred workers did eventually make their way to the roof, most of them from the tenth floor. The New York University Law School building was located just across a small courtyard but was one story higher. As the fire raged, several law students led by Charles Kremer and Elias Kanter rushed to the aid of the victims. They tied two short ladders together so that the victims could climb to the roof of their building. Kremer climbed down onto the lower roof to help them up the ladder, and in this way they were able to save one hundred and fifty men, women and girls. Kremer then made his way down into the tenth floor to look for more survivors. He saw only one young girl, her hair ablaze. She ran toward him screaming and then fainted in his arms. He put out her burning hair then carried her to safety, believing there to be no one else surviving left behind on that floor. Meanwhile, at the other end of the roof, about fifty people had gathered and were fighting to scale the five feet to the roof of the adjoining building. Several of the law students reported seeing men kicking and biting the women and girls, knocking them out of the way as they escaped to safety.

After the fire department arrived, many attempts were made to save trapped or falling victims. Unfortunately, their ladders only reached a little above the sixth floor. Several people tried to jump to the ladders but none were able to catch hold and all fell to their deaths. Safety nets were also employed but to little or no avail. The great height was just too much and many of the nets split or were shredded as bodies fell through them, crashing to the pavement. In one case, a young girl was caught in a net but three others who jumped just after, landed on her and all four toppled onto the ground, dead. A few bystanders tried to stretch blankets or tarps but the results were nearly all the same. The number of people saved in this manner could be counted on one hand. One woman fell with such force that she ripped through a safety net and crashed through the thick glass vault in the sidewalk, finally coming to rest in the basement of the building.

Several rescue workers were injured when falling bodies struck them. People were falling faster than the firefighters could get into position to try to catch them. The firefighters' rescue efforts were further hindered by the growing number of corpses strewn about the sidewalks, making it difficult for them to move the safety nets. The bodies were left lying where they fell until later that evening, as the firefighters were busy fighting the fire. It was believed none of those who had fallen could still be alive. A few hours later, however, a young woman was pulled from a pile of bodies, still breathing. A great cheer arose as she was loaded into an ambulance.

**Police officers examine a cluster of bodies found on the street at the base of the building. Terrified workers flung themselves to their deaths.**

**(Left) A Five-foot diameter hole was broken in the sidewalk, caused by the impact of falling bodies.**
**(Left) Police officers continue the gruesome task of identifying bodies that have fallen from above.**

Sadly, though, she died a few minutes later.

As the upper floors of the building burned, a crowd of thousands, gathering in the streets below bore witness to the carnage that was unfolding before them. They screamed in horror as they watched, helpless. Many eyewitness reports of the tragic deaths of the people who fell to their deaths from the windows of the Washington Place and Greene Street sides soon followed. Some jumped, some were thrown or pushed and others were forced out by the panic-stricken crowds shoving their way toward the windows. A majority of those who fell did so with burning clothing and hair. Some continued to burn as they lay on the sidewalk until they were extinguished by the water dripping down from the fire hoses, their blackened bodies left lying there until late in the evening.

Five young women on the Greene Street side of the building climbed out onto the windowsill, wrapped their arms around each other and jumped together. They crashed through the sidewalk cover into the basement, their clothes and hair burning as they fell. Another girl leaped very far out but her dress got tangled up in some wires and she was left suspended high above as the crowd watched, unable to help. Eventually, her dress burned through and she fell to her death. A man on the same side was seen from an adjacent building, running from window to window picking up women and throwing them out the windows. Eventually, when no other women were left, he himself climbed onto the ledge, paused a moment then jumped. It was never known if he believed that there would be nets to catch them or if he was trying to shorten their suffering.

A young girl of about thirteen was seen hanging by her fingertips from a ninth-floor windowsill for a few minutes. Then the fire reached her fingers and she fell into a waiting net, only to be crushed by two other women who fell immediately after her, adding all three to the death list.

Frank Fingerman, an employee from a nearby business, reported, "As I ran past, I saw a boy and a girl standing together at a Greene Street window. He was holding her, and she seemed to be trying to jump. They were still there when I came back from the firebox (after calling in the fire alarm). As the smoke began to come out of the window above them the boy let the girl go, and she jumped. He followed her before she struck the ground. Four more people came out of the same window immediately and jumped."

Some of the girls who jumped from the Washington Place side crashed through the vault light in the sidewalk. As women continued to fall or jump from the same window, their bodies eventually created a hole nearly five feet in diameter. Later in the evening, firefighters pulled several partially nude and burned bodies from this hole.

On his way home from work, Dr. Ralph Fralick became a witness to horrific events he would never forget. He saw the heads of many screaming girls extending out of windows on the ninth floor. He stood frozen as he watched as several of them climbed out. "They stood for a time on the little ledge. Then one girl jumped, then another, then another. Some of them fell straight as a plummet and smashed through the vault lights of the street into the basement under the sidewalk. Most of them turned many times, shrieking as they fell." One girl, he said took off her hat and carefully laid it on the ledge before she jumped. Dr. Fralick stayed at the building, checking everybody he could get to after they struck the pavement, attempting to render first aid when possible and administered injections for pain. He later told officials that he was not able to save anyone but felt that he had helped a few young girls pass with a little less pain.

Another pair of girls climbed out of a window on the ninth floor, overlooking Greene Street. The older of the two seemed calm and composed as she tried to subdue the younger girl as she "shrieked and twisted with fright." As the crowd called to them not to jump, the older girl wrapped her arms around her and pulled her back toward the building. The younger girl, in her panic, twisted free, took a few steps away and then she jumped. The older girl remained standing on the ledge until the flames came so close that her hair was scorched. She looked skyward, placed her arms to her sides, and jumped straight down, feet first. Her name was Bertha Weintrout and she was the girl who was later found alive, if only for a few minutes, buried amid a pile of corpses on the sidewalk.

Samuel Levine, a machine operator who worked on the ninth floor survived to tell this tale, "I was at work when I heard the shout of "fire!" The girls on the floor dropped everything and rushed wildly around, some in the direction of windows and others toward the elevator door. I saw the elevator go down past our floor once. It was crowded to the limit and no one could have got on. It did not stop. Not another trip was made. There were flames all around in no time. Three girls, I think from the floor below, came rushing past me. Their clothes were on fire. I grabbed the fire pail and tried to pour the water on them but they did not stop. They ran screaming toward the window. I knew there was no hope there, so I stayed where I was, hoping that the elevator would come up again." Levine eventually escaped down the elevator cables, to be saved hours later when rescuers cut into the shaft.

Similar eyewitness stories began to rapidly accumulate. During the early stage of the fire, police officer Jimmy Lehan ran up the stairs to the eighth floor and forced open a locked stairway door. Just inside the door he found a group of terrified girls huddled together. He yelled for them to run down the stairs but they were in a state of shock and remained frozen to the spot. Officer Lehan was forced to use his club to "beat them down to safety." All in this group were saved, but within seconds, the stairway became engulfed in flames so no others could leave that way.

Six girls, after getting to a window on the ninth floor made their way out onto an eight-inch-wide ledge that ran the length of the building. Slowly, they edged their way along this ledge, more than one hundred feet above the ground, toward a swinging electric cable. When all had arrived, they grabbed the cable simultaneously in an attempt to swing to the safety of the adjacent building. The cable snapped as they swung out and all six perished below.

**The eighth floor of the building as it looked to the first firefighters who arrived on the scene.**

**The scene as the morgue as families and loved ones line up to try and identify the bodies of the dead.**

A few windows down, on the same floor, a man and a woman appeared on the sill. The man kissed, then hugged the woman, threw her to the street and jumped himself. Both were killed. Just around the corner, from another window, a young girl, a man and a woman, and two other women with their arms wrapped around each other leaped to the ground together. The young girl was found alive after her fall and was rushed to the hospital where she died upon arrival.

A small group of men tried to make a human bridge between the burning building and the window of another building. They were successful in saving a number of women but eventually the weight of the women became too great and the bridge broke, the center man tumbling to the ground with a broken back.

The fire was extinguished within an hour and by 7:00 p.m., less than two hours after it started, firefighters were able to force their way up the stairs and into the burned floors. They reported that, "50 roasted bodies were found on the ninth floor alone." The charred bodies of nineteen victims were found piled against locked doors and 25 more were found huddled together in a cloakroom. Each body, as it was found, was carefully lifted from the burned surroundings, wrapped in cloth and hoisted to the ground using a pulley system. They were then taken to one of a hundred wooden coffins lining the street. The bodies were then moved to the morgue at Bellevue Hospital or the Charities Pier morgue, which hadn't been used since the burning of the General Slocum steamship.

One unnamed reporter wrote in the *New York Times* that the "...remains of the dead, it is hardly possible to call them bodies, because that would suggest something human, and there was nothing human about most of

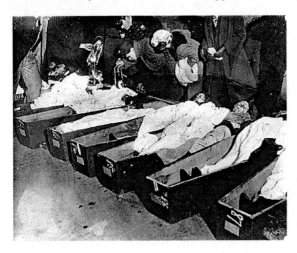

these, were being taken in a steady stream to the morgue for identification." Fire Chief Edward F. Croker, one of the first men to reenter the building following the fire left the building in obvious distress, stating that in all his years, he had never seen anything like what he had seen on those upper floors.

The police estimated that as many as 200,000 people; devastated family and friends, as well as the morbidly curious public, entered the makeshift morgue at the pier and filed past the over one hundred wooden coffins containing bodies that had been recovered. They walked past the bodies that were at least partially recognizable in the hope of finding a lost loved one. Tens of thousands were turned away by the police in an attempt to keep more of the general public away. Over forty human forms too badly burned to be recognizable, were covered with a white canvas tarp with the hope that they might be identified through trinkets, jewelry or articles of clothing.

Stories of unbelievable anguish were published in newspapers across the county. A young girl was identified by a family heirloom signet ring found clinging to the charred flesh of a badly burned body. A young woman screamed as she collapsed after identifying her fiancé by his ring, having become engaged only the night before. She asked if a watch had been found with his body. When she was given the watch, she opened it and "gazed upon her own portrait." A man, having waited in line for over five hours, identified his daughters by their clothing. After collapsing with grief, he attempted to kill himself on the spot. He was restrained by police until he calmed down enough to continue looking for his wife, also lost in the fire. A man with a fresh burn on his cheek, identified his brother. He told the police that he and his brother had fought the fire, standing side by side, with buckets of water. A man who had barely escaped with his own life identified his fiancée by her engagement ring. In her hand, she still clutched her handbag, her weekly wages of $3 remained inside, intact. A sobbing brother stumbled away from the mangled bodies of his two sisters left propped up in their coffins to search for their mother. The fire took his entire family.

As a growing number of people became hysterical or suicidal, a makeshift hospital was set up at the pier to deal with this unexpected problem. Doctors and nurses from Bellevue Hospital worked for days trying to help keep these grieving family members from being added to the list of lives stolen by the fire.

Thirty-one victims remained unidentified after the last of the survivors claimed their family and friends. The Hebrew Free Burial Association paid for the burial of 23 of these victims in a special section of Mount Richmond Cemetery. The remaining eight bodies were interred in the Cemetery of the Evergreens in Brooklyn.

As the blaze began, the only safety measures within the Asch Building available to those still inside were 27 buckets of water and one fire escape that collapsed almost immediately. Most of the exits were locked and those that weren't, opened inward so they remained closed under the crush of people pushing toward the doors.

It was not the 95 charred bodies found inside the building that so outraged the public, but rather the heaps of bodies along the sidewalk and rows of mostly young girls laying dead in the street. By the end, 53 people had jumped, fallen or were pushed from the upper floors and

**This gruesome photograph was captioned "The Picture that Changed the Future of the American Industrial Worker."**

thousands of people were there to witness each one of them fall and strike the pavement. The average age of those killed in the fire was nineteen. The public outrage was carried like a wave across the country as reports and pictures of the tragedy appeared in newspapers everywhere.

In a later interview, survivor Pauline Cuoio Pepe gave testimony, "It was all nice young Jewish girls who were engaged to be married. Those were the ones who threw themselves from the window. What the hell did they close the door for? What did they think we were going to go out with? What are we gonna do, steal a shirtwaist? Who the heck wanted a shirtwaist?"

The resulting public pressure proved to be too much to overcome and dramatic changes were in store for the existing fire codes and their enforcement in the workplace. The New York State Legislature formed the "Factory Commission" in 1911, which developed many requirements linked directly back to the Triangle Shirtwaist factory fire such as all exit doors must be left unlocked during operating hours and sprinklers were to be installed if a factory employed more than 25 people. The memories of the young women who perished in that terrible fire resulted in a major change in the way many people thought about protecting workers. Prior to the fire, the government left businesses alone regarding the safety of their workers. Afterwards, the government had little choice but to begin instituting sweeping safety laws that changed history for American workers.

In the end, no one was held accountable for the Triangle deaths. In December of 1911, Max Blanck and Isaac Harris, the Asch Building owners and Triangle Shirtwaist Company owners were charged and tried for manslaughter. Despite a mob of people outside the courthouse chanting "Murderers! Murderers!" the two were acquitted of all charges by the jury after only two hours of deliberation. Twenty-three individual civil suits for damages against the company were settled for an average of $75 per life lost.

Blanck and Isaac completed their association with the Triangle Shirtwaist Factory by filing an insurance claim in excess of their losses, garnering them a profit from the fire of more than $60,000 -- a hefty sum in 1911. Blanck continued on in the clothing manufacturing business. He opened another factory on Fifth Avenue. In 1913, just two years after the Triangle fire, he was arrested for locking the exit door in his factory during working hours. He was fined $20.

On February 22, 2001, Rose Freedman, the last living survivor of the fire died after having been a lifelong crusader for workplace safety.

The Asch Building still stands at the corner of Washington Place and Greene Street, but its name has been changed to the Brown Building. No longer are the floors of that building home to sweatshops employing poor and desperate immigrant women and girls, overworked and underpaid. Today, the Brown Building is full of young university science students as it has become a part of the New York University as a science lab -- the same university that was located next door and provided a means of escape to nearly one hundred and fifty people fleeing the fire with the aid of many of the students.

On the corner of the building a plaque has been placed, commemorating the tragic events that took place on that site on March 25, 1911, and the lives lost that day. The Triangle Shirtwaist Fire continues as a turning point in United States history.

There are other reminders of the fire for those who pay close enough attention. Even though the use of the building and the occupants have changed dramatically, bits and pieces of its history still linger, many of these believed to be supernatural. It is not uncommon for the smell of smoke to waft through the halls of the upper floors and more than once fire warnings have passed through the building. On occasion, people have reported a different kind of odor accompanying the smell of smoke. This odor can only be described as that of burning flesh -- then the odors simply disappear as quickly as they began.

Often, doors that are supposed to be locked are found unlocked, sometimes within minutes of being locked! Could it be that the spirit of someone lost in the fire is trying to keep the current occupants from meeting the same tragic fate by being trapped behind a locked door in an emergency?

A few people over the years have described a most peculiar experience. While sitting at a desk or workstation they have seen, out of the corner of their eye, something large flutter downward past their window. Upon going to the window to look down and see what it was, there is nothing there.

The most striking ghostly experience was related by "Susan" (not her real name), a secretary who worked in the building for many years. She explained that she had been working later than usual one evening and by the time she left to go home, most of the other employees and students had already left. As she walked out of the building, she noticed a young woman walk past her with a slight stagger and a dazed look on her face. She was very dirty and her hair and clothes appeared to be singed or burned. Susan called to her to see if she needed help but the young woman didn't respond; she just kept walking and turned the corner. Susan, thinking that the woman might be injured or in trouble, ran after her but upon turning the corner, she was met by an empty sidewalk. The young woman had simply vanished.

We will never know for sure if these occurrences are directly related to the Triangle Shirtwaist factory fire. However, it does appear that the most important thing is that we never forget what happened there, nor the lessons learned. We may even get a little reminder now and then --- just to make sure.

# 1929: THE CLEVELAND CLINIC FIRE

In his dedication speech at the opening of the Cleveland Clinic in 1921, Dr. George Washington Crile said that the purpose of the clinic was "to give assistance in solving the problems of the patient of today and through its investigations, its statistical records and laboratories to seek new light on aiding the problems of the patient of tomorrow."

**One of the Cleveland Clinic's Founders, Dr. George Washington Crile**

The Cleveland Clinic had been founded by four renowned Cleveland, Ohio, physicians. Three of the founders, George Washington Crile, Frank Bunts, and William Lower, were surgeons who had worked together in an army medical unit in France during World War I. When they returned to the United States, they decided to establish a group practice and invited an internist, John Phillips, to join in their endeavor. The concept of group practice in medicine was relatively new at the time. Only the Mayo Clinic and military units were known to follow this model. The founders established the clinic with the vision: "Better care of the sick, investigation of their problems, and further education of those who serve."

The clinic saw rapid growth in its early years but suffered a major setback in 1929 that almost closed its doors permanently. On May 15, 1929, a fire started in the basement of the hospital caused by nitrocellulose X-ray film that spontaneously ignited. The fire claimed 123 lives, including that of one of the founders, Dr. Phillips.

Dozens of people had come to the clinic for healing, but found death instead.

On May 15, 1929, about three hundred patients were within the walls of the Cleveland Clinic, an institution that everyone in the city had reason to be proud of. Some of them lay on operating tables, others rested in beds and some sat nervously in waiting rooms, unsure of what diagnosis awaited them. At 11:30 a.m., a resounding explosion occurred in the basement where the clinic's X-ray films were stored. The films immediately burst into flame. Several theories were later advanced to explain the initial explosion. A leaky steam pipe, authorities reasoned, overheated and caused the highly combustible X-ray films in the room to catch on fire. Others believed that a carelessly discarded cigarette or match caused the fire. No one was ever blamed – the impact lay in the tragedy itself.

When the X-rays caught fire, they began to release deadly fumes. The poisonous yellow gas penetrated to the waiting room on the floor above and then swirled throughout the clinic. The hollow center of the building soon filled with gases as the intense heat from below sent the fumes upward. Before anyone had an opportunity to escape, a second blast blew out a skylight. Every corner of the clinic filled with a deadly bromide gas.

People were quickly overtaken by the gas. They ran for the windows, seeking oxygen, but few were able to

**The Cleveland Clinic in the middle 1920s**

**Rescue workers scrambling to save survivors on the day of the deadly fire in 1929.**

reach them. They were enveloped in the fumes and collapsed. The fire in the basement burned up the air supply and combined with the choking gas, began to claim victims. The fumes poured in through ventilator shafts, up stairways, through halls, and then the fire found the woodwork in the stairways and began to devour it, climbing upwards into the building. Windows burst and passersby on the street in front of the clinic were also overcome by the fumes. Witnesses on the scene after the explosion said that they could hear terrified screams from blocks away.

The first explosion in the clinic was heard by police officer Henry Thorpe, who was walking two blocks away. He immediately turned in the alarm and ran towards the building, which was located at Euclid Avenue and 93rd Street. Thorpe was still a block away when he was blinded by the gas.

Firefighters arrived within minutes of the call. They turned in a second alarm and police, hospital and county morgue ambulances soon began to arrive. Meanwhile, firefighters were trying to enter the building. Battalion Fire Chief James P. Flynn, with his driver, Louis Hillenbrand, were the first to go inside. They found sixteen bodies packed in the space between the elevator and a stairway, where occupants of the clinic had tried in vain to escape. One of the people found near the elevator was Dr. J.L. Locke. He was taken outside and revived. Five of the others, who were still breathing, were taken to the roof, where firefighters were hard at work.

Flynn directed his men to scale the roof and enter the hospital through a skylight. They lowered themselves from the roof, but it was not an easy entry. From the skylight, the firemen suspended themselves and then swung their bodies to gain momentum in order to drop with minimum injury inside the mezzanine rail that encircled the fourth floor. The firefighters then searched the trap door that allowed access to the roof. While searching for the door, they found a mass of bodies of people who had attempted to make it to the roof on their own. One of the firefighters was horrified by the sight: "I hope to never have to look at anything so horrifying again. Lord help me, as far down the stairway as you could see were bodies, bodies, bodies. Twisted arms and legs, screaming men and women. Bodies and screams."

The firemen managed to lift out fifteen survivors from the top of the pile of bodies. The jam at this failed escape route was so great that many of those at the bottom of the pile were crushed to death. Oxygen tanks were rushed to the roof, but for many of the survivors, it was too late. They did not live for long. Battalion Chief Flynn lowered himself into the building and was appalled at the condition of the people his men found, most of them barely alive. He ordered the firemen to concentrate all of their efforts on saving the trapped and getting people out of the clinic. They could hear screaming coming from the third floor and crews went down the stairs. By now, the flames had reached the third floor and the men had to battle the fire while their comrades worked to revive those who had been overcome by the smoke and fumes.

Some of the firefighters described their efforts on the lower floors of the building as "a descent into Hell." Many victims were found collapsed at the windows, unable to find fresh air. Both entrances to the street were blocked by tangles of panic-stricken patients and personnel. The doorways had simply not been wide enough for everyone to exit at the same time. Trapped, they were overcome by the fumes and then burned to death by the fire. The fire had done its damage to the clinic, too. The woodwork and masonry walls were charred and blackened by the heat. Hardened plaster was blistered and peeled from the walls. Fumes that had filled a hollow compartment between the balcony roof and the roof of the building exploded and ripped apart the brick and mortar. The casings of the skylight above and buckled and warped under the force of the explosion and broken glass had rained down on the waiting room, three floors below. The suction of the explosion shattered glass doors reinforced with steel. Compression in the hollow center of the building packed air into the halls and staircases and when this force was released by the blast of air rushed back into the center of the building, smashing doors with the force of a battering ram.

Heavy fumes hung about the building for almost two hours after the blast. Rescuers were unable to stay inside for long intervals and frequently had to use the oxygen tanks that had been brought for the victims. All of them firemen continued to go back inside and look for survivors, though, risking their own lives.

The clinic's front lawn was soon covered with the dead and dying. Any available vehicle in the area, including taxicabs and personal automobiles, was commandeered by the police to be used as a transport from the burned-out clinic to other Cleveland hospitals. It took almost three hours to lift the bodies, one by one, through the damaged skylight. One police officer, a war veteran, described the scene as worse than his experiences on the front lines. He personally carried out 25 bodies from the building.

The poison gas from the X-ray films did not claim all of its victims immediately. Some people walked out of the building healthy and even aided firefighters in their rescue work, only to collapse and die hours or days later. A professional football player, Ben Jones, helped with the rescue efforts at the scene, felt fine and considered himself fortunate when he returned home. He died 48 hours later from the gas that he inhaled. Several firemen were also hospitalized because of ill effects from the gas.

Other, personal tragedies, occurred. Dr. Carl Helwig, a doctor at another hospital, came to the scene to aid in the rescue effort and discovered that his wife was at the clinic that morning for a routine check-up. She died as he worked to save her. One of the clinic's founders, Dr. George Crile, helped in the aid and rescue and later, visited fire victims at the city's hospitals. His close colleague, Dr. John Phillips, another of the clinic's founders, was in critical condition. Dr. Crile donated blood to save his friend, but Dr. Phillips died despite all of the efforts to save him.

The clinic, founded by these two men and dedicated to the welfare of its patients, was witness to 123 deaths on May 15.

What could have been the end of the clinic turned out to be only the beginning. The remaining founders responded to the tragedy with brave optimism and within days, they resumed operation of the clinic in the temporary quarters of an old school. The Cleveland Clinic was rebuilt and regained momentum to become nationally recognized as a leader in the fight against cardiovascular disease. In the decades since World War II, the clinic has grown to become internationally prominent and is currently the second-largest medical group practice in the world, after the Mayo Clinic.

# 1930: THE OHIO STATE PENITENTIARY FIRE

The Ohio Penitentiary opened in late October 1834, when 189 prisoners were marched under guard from a small frontier jail to the partially completed building. As they walked along the banks of the Scioto River, they must have been amazed and dismayed by the stone walls of their new place of incarceration, as many other men would be in the years to come. Hundreds of thousands of men were sent to this prison over the next 150 years and thousands of them died, usually violently, behind the high walls.

The prison was first condemned by reformers in the early 1900s but was not closed down until 1979. For years afterward, it stood empty and decaying, awaiting the wrecking ball to make room for the sports complex that now stands on the site.

If prisons are truly haunted because of the death and tragedy that takes place in them, then the Ohio Penitentiary, once located on Spring Street in Columbus, must have been one of the most haunted buildings in the region. Even though the prison itself is no more, this has not stopped the stories of murder, brutality and of course, ghosts, from being told. The prison may be gone, but some say the spirits of the past still linger.

The penitentiary that was located on Spring Street was actually the third state prison in Ohio and the fourth jail in early Columbus. The first jail in the city had been built in 1804 and was a two-story log stockade that was surrounded by thirteen whipping posts. Author Dan Morgan noted that "horrible stories were told about this primitive prison" and said that men, women and children were all brought there. They were stripped of their clothing and then tied to the posts. This was followed by whippings that left their backs resembling raw beef. Further torture was inflicted with hot ashes and coals that were spread onto their bleeding flesh. It was obviously a horrifying place.

Between 1813 and 1815, the first state prison was built along Scioto Street, which later became 2nd Street. It was a simple structure that housed prisoners in thirteen cells on the third floor. The prison was full within a year so the General Assembly commissioned a larger structure, designed for one hundred prisoners, that was completed in 1818. This building provided unheated cells, straw mats on the floor, infestations of lice and rats and was plagued by several cholera epidemics. It also had several subterranean places of punishment, called "holes," where conditions were even worse.

The prison remained in use until a new building was constructed on Spring Street, however an odd occurrence took place there in 1830. At that time, a fire of "incendiary origin" destroyed most of the prison workshops. Strangely, a century later in 1930, another fire of "incendiary origin" destroyed an entire cellblock and claimed 322 lives at the new penitentiary. It is still considered the worst fire in the history of American prisons.

The prisoners worked in factory shops, located behind the walls, to make leather harnesses, shoes, tailored goods, barrels, brooms, hats and other common goods that were not manufactured by legitimate business in Ohio. The paltry food the prisoners ate usually consisted of cornbread, bacon and beans and was served on "rust-eaten tin plates" and eaten with crude implements fashioned from broom handles. They slept on hay sacks and although fold-down beds were installed around the time of the Civil War, blankets were only issued in the wintertime. The clothing and the bedding were filthy and were major carriers of disease as laundry facilities were non-existent in the early days. There was also no medical treatment to speak of and epidemics, dysentery and diarrhea killed many. In 1849, a cholera outbreak killed 116 of 423 prisoners. The guards fled the grounds and the prisoners begged for pardons.

The inmates were routinely punished for both major and minor infractions. Whipping remained the major form of discipline until 1844, but was replaced by no less cruel methods of causing pain. These included dunking inmates in huge vats of water, hanging them by their wrists in their cells and of course, the sweatbox. In 1885, the prison would begin carrying out executions, as well.

The "golden age" of the prison came during the tenure of Warden E. G. Coffin, from 1886 through 1900. A number of flattering books were written about the institution during this era and visitors who came to tour the place could even buy picture postcards and souvenir books. One section of the souvenir book stated: "It is to Mr. Coffin's revolutionary methods of inaugurating, perfecting and successfully establishing humane but repressive methods in the management of the prison that the Ohio Penitentiary owes its world-wide celebrity."

On Christmas Day 1888, Columbus newspapers reported that Warden Coffin had decided to do away with such punishments as the dunking tub and the stretching rings. Coffin said, "A hard box to sleep on and bread and water to eat will cause them to behave themselves. It may not be so speedy but it is more humane."

Despite the fact that things at the Ohio Penitentiary seemed to be changed from the outside, the prisoners had a different story to tell. In 1894, a newspaper reporter learned that prisoners were still being locked in sweatboxes as punishment and that the ball and chain were also in use. The newspaper denounced the state of Ohio for "a partial return to the dark ages when the stocks and pillory were used for punishment." In addition, the prisoners were still being given bad food and medical care was still very poor. They also complained of pay-offs and political graft that resulted in some prisoners being blindfolded and tortured with water hoses, while well-connected inmates were given large cells and special privileges.

It was also during this era when the Death House was brought within the walls. Prior to that, the gallows had been set up on a place called Penitentiary Hill, located in a ravine near the present-day intersection of Mound and 2nd streets in Columbus. The first execution in the county had been carried out in 1844, when a convict was hanged for murder. The day of the hanging was regarded as "truly the greatest event in the history of Columbus" and was remembered as a day of "noise, confusion, drunkenness and disorder" during which a bystander, Sullivan Sweet, was reportedly trampled to death by a horse. Two sets of physicians were anxious to obtain the remains of the hanged man. One of the groups went to his grave and exhumed him and while they were making off with the body, they were shot at by the other doctors. The first party ran off, leaving the body to the second group, along

**(Left) The Ohio State Penitentiary "Death House"   (Right) The Penitentiary's electric chair, which sent many convicts to their deaths. (Ohio Historical Society)**

with the now-empty grave. The dead man's foot was, for many years, preserved in alcohol and kept on display by Drs. Jones and Little, who had an office on East Town Street.

In 1885, the gallows were moved behind the walls of the Ohio Penitentiary. Starting with Valentine Wagner in 1885, 28 men, including a 16-year-old named Otto Lueth, were hanged at the end of the prison's East Hall. The electric chair (considered a humane form of execution) replaced the gallows in the hall in 1897 and 315 men and women were put to death in it.

This aspect of prison life became hated and feared by guards and prisoners alike. Corrections Major Grover Powell, who spent 31 years as a guard at the Ohio Penitentiary, told reporter David Lore in 1984,   "Nobody ever really wanted to work the executions; nobody ever volunteered." Death House duties, such as staying with the prisoner during the last meal, fastening the straps or flipping the switch, were rotated. The warden would get $75 overtime pay to split among the attending officers. Powell recalled that many of the men, even during the lean days of the Depression, when extra money was desperately needed, did everything they could to get out of working the executions.

The 1930s saw more problems at the Ohio Penitentiary. On September 22, 1934, two members of John Dillinger's gang of bank robbers, Charles Makley and Harry Pierpont made a daring escape attempt from the prison. As Dillinger had done at the Crown Point, Indiana, jail, the men tried to bluff their way of the cellblock with fake pistols. They made it less than one hundred feet from their cells before they were met with gunfire and ripped to shreds. Both men fell bleeding to the floor. Makley was killed instantly but Pierpont survived and was taken back into custody.

Pierpont had been brought to the penitentiary under National Guard escort for his part in the murder of Sheriff Jess Sarber. The killing occurred during Dillinger's 1933 escape from the Allen County Jail. On October 17, sufficiently recovered from his wounds, Pierpont was executed in the electric chair.

Pierpont was just one of the many gangsters and bank robbers who ended up at the Ohio Penitentiary during the 1930s and 1940s. The best known of them was George "Bugs" Moran, Al Capone's lucky rival who arrived too late to be killed at the St. Valentine's Day Massacre. Moran came to the Ohio prison in the 1940s to serve out a sentence for bank robbery.

This era began to see an increase in problems at the prison. Many believe that the growth of the "rackets" and the general disrespect for the law in the 1920s and 1930s resulted in an upsurge of prison terms that had the available prisons filled to overflowing. The one-man cells at the prison were converted to handle three or more men and the average daily count swelled to 4,100 inmates by the end of the decade. In 1939, Warden William

Amrine once again recommended the construction of a new prison, stating that, "conditions at the Ohio Penitentiary are a disgrace to the state of Ohio." His request was turned down, but World War II marked the beginning of a new era for the prison.

The 1930s had been a horrendous time but changes came about because the inmates were now desperately needed to produce goods for the war effort. Warden Ralph "Red" Alvis is credited for the major changes in the prison, eliminating lock step marching, the strict requirements of silence and striped prison uniforms. And while many of the restrictions were lifted and the men were kept productive during the war, the food became worse. Wartime restrictions and rationing were hard on the ordinary public, but even worse on the prisoners. Gentry Richardson, a prisoner who began serving time at the prison in 1942, recalled, "They would give us butter beans with a piece of fat sowbelly in there with hair on it, big hairs up to an inch long." Bad food, in fact, was a reason for the 1952 Ohio Penitentiary riot, the first of three to rock the institution over the next two decades. It would not be until after this incident that the rations would start to improve.

Warden Alvis began to implement recreation programs for those incarcerated in the Ohio Penitentiary and began to assume a more humane posture toward the prisoners. His goal was to improve prisoner morale and to encourage a sense of dignity in the men. He believed this was the best way to rehabilitate the inmates and hopefully to release changed men back onto the streets. Holiday boxing and wrestling matches came about as early as 1940 and a bandstand was built on the O. Henry Athletic Field, the home of the inmate's baseball team, the "Hurricanes."

For years, the Ohio Penitentiary drew celebrities, athletes and performers like boxing champions Joe Lewis and Jack Dempsey and entertainers such as jazz musician Lionel Hampton. Ohio State University students performed classical music and opera behind the walls and pilots from the Lockbourne Air Force Base led literary discussions. Legendary coach Woody Hayes even once offered to help start an inmate football team. The high point of each year was always the inmate Christmas show, which was performed by the prisoners and always played to a full house. A few outsiders were allowed in for each show and the tickets were always in high demand.

Despite all of this, the conditions of the prison building continued to deteriorate and overcrowding became more of an issue. The prison population reached a record high of 5,235 in April 1955. Classrooms and visiting areas had to be used as dormitories and many of the programs fell apart. With more men came more danger. One former prisoner stated, "I saw a lot of men die behind the walls. How many? I can't even remember half of them, but there was a lot of killing."

On June 24, 1968, the worst series of riots in the prison's history began in the print shop, forcing a number of political decisions that would end with the closing of the penitentiary 16 years later. The initial June riots led to at least $1 million in fire damage and the destruction of nine buildings and damage to six others.

Tensions continued to mount through July and led to more riots in August, when inmates not only started fires, but also took nine guards hostage. This forced a 28-hour standoff between the leaders of the convicts and the authorities that ended with an assault on the prison on August 21. Officers blew holes in the south wall and the roof and invaded the prison with deadly force. Five of the convicts were killed but the guards managed to make it through alive. This strengthened the conviction that the prison needed to be closed down.

Governor James A. Rhodes ordered a new maximum-security prison to be built in remote Lucasville, Ohio, and placed the old prison under the control of Warden Harold Cardwell, who immediately cancelled the Christmas shows, the exhibitions and the team sports. The prison was now under a permanent lockdown and would remain that way for the rest of its existence.

In 1972, most of the prisoners were transferred out and sent to the Southern Ohio Correctional Facility in Youngstown, which had just been completed. The old prison now housed only the sick, the psychotic and the troublemakers. Except for the most secure areas, the place was falling into ruin. Finally, in 1979, the prison was ordered closed down for good, bringing an end to years of brutality, pain and death.

And there was nothing in the history of the prison, even the macabre execution devices, that matched the carnage and horror of April 21, 1930 – the day of the worst fire in the history of the American prison system.

Anyone who came to the Ohio State Penitentiary in 1930 couldn't help but be chilled by the atmosphere of desolation that permeated the place. A penal reform organization had recently proclaimed that the prison was one of the worst in the country and it remained untouched by the social reform that had changed prisons in other states. Life on the inside of the fortress-like structure was one of hard, weary routine – menial and meaningless labor at the rate of five cents an hour, terrible food, brutal guards, sickness and a lack of any real medical care. But the worst part of the deplorable conditions was the overcrowding. The men were packed into cells under horrific and unsanitary conditions. Much of the prison's foundation dated back to the 1830s and the bleak penitentiary had been designed to hold a maximum of 1,500 prisoners. In April 1930, it held nearly 4,300.

Discontent and anger ran through the prison. Several times, escape attempts were made. Prisoners, whether detained by murder or petty theft, wanted only to be let out of the "cage", as one prisoner called it. On one occasion, when the huge gates opened to let visitors inside, prisoners stormed the entrance and thirteen of them managed to get free. Warden Preston Thomas, the administrator at the time, promptly shot down four of the escapees with his own shotgun. Another was apprehended on a nearby side street and returned to the prison by a plainclothes police officer.

Life in the prison went on as bitter resentment grew on both sides. Informers to the warden told of elaborate plots to escape by digging tunnels under the walls or setting fire to the prison. The warden discovered that many of the threats were fabrications – but not all of them. As time went on, the rumors of escape plans became more numerous and more convincing. One prisoner allegedly confessed to the warden of stealing candles from the soap shop and handing them out to prisoners, who also had oil and gasoline in their possession.

Many of the prisoners worked in cellblock construction, which was finally being carried out to ease some of the overcrowding. Scaffolding had been erected from green lumber next to the six-story tier of cells. On April 21, between 5:20 and 5:50 p.m., a fire broke out in the scaffolding. Smoke was spotted curling ominously from the construction area and a fire alarm was raised at 6:00 p.m. The men had just returned to their cells from the evening meal and were locked in for the night. Some of them were reading, playing checkers or munching on after-dinner candy bars from the commissary.

The faint drift of smoke soon turned into flames, thanks to a strong wind from an open doorway. The flames rushed toward the tiers of occupied cells and soon the prisoners were screaming and pounding on the bars of their cells, begging the guards to let them out. Their screams and agonized cries echoed throughout the prison – and throughout the Columbus neighborhood that surrounded it.

There was confusion among the guards about what to do – should they free the prisoners, or was the fire really serious enough to risk the escape of the inmates? At the start of the fire, no one was alarmed since it was generally believed that the penitentiary was fireproof. There was also the matter of locating the keys. One guard possessed the set of keys that could have saved the prisoner's lives in the fire area, but he could not be located. When he finally arrived at the scene, he claimed that his superior ordered him to keep the cells locked. (After the fire, the prison official would deny giving such orders) Regardless, the other guards wrestled the keys away from him and proceeded to unlock the cells in the lower tiers. One guard was reported to have hastily run down the corridor unlocking cells until he was overcome by smoke. He gave the keys to one of the prisoners, who heroically continued to free the men.

The released prisoners were taken to the prison yard and placed under heavy guard. However, these were only the men from the lower tiers. The upper tiers were consumed by flames and the screaming that had been reverberating from those cells soon stopped. There was no one left alive to scream.

The fire department arrived within two minutes of the alarm being sounded but there was nothing to be done in the confusion and no one left to save. The highly flammable prison roof had caught fire and had roasted the prisoners alive in the upper tier cells.

The penitentiary was a scene or horror and heroism. The lower tiers, one and two, in the doomed cellblocks were opened and prisoners were staggered or crawled to safety or were carried out by guards and fellow inmates. Heroism cropped up in unexpected places. Through miraculously escaping from what seemed certain death, most of the liberated convicts gasped fresh air into their lungs, armed themselves with sledge hammers and crowbars and rushed back into the burning building to help rescue the less fortunate. Locks were knocked off. Case-hardened steel bars were spread. Cell doors were ripped away and convicts and guards plunged into the inferno to drag out or carry screaming men to safety. The bravest of the prisoners were members of Company "K," a group of incorrigibles, who were isolated from other prisoners as "troublemakers." They inspired past riots and escape attempts, but during the fire, their courage came through. Grievances were forgotten and guard and prisoner fought side by side under a common bond.

The fire department, however, was close to useless. The streams of water from the prison yard were of little help and there was no way to get the hoses into the building. They did manage to contain the fire for a brief time, but strong winds hampered their efforts.

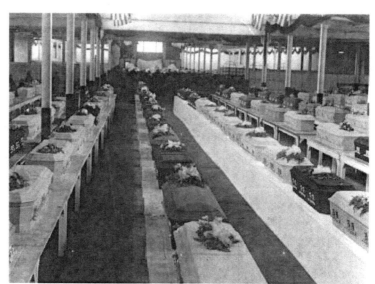

A morgue was set up at the Ohio State Fairgrounds for victims of the fire at the Penitentiary (Ohio Historical Society)

It was 8:00 p.m. before the fire was under sufficient control to enable guards and firemen to see what damage the blaze had done. They saw men, dead and dying, piled in grotesque heaps, some of them charred, others unscathed but dead from smoke and poisonous gases.

There bodies of the dead and injured, swathed in blankets were deposited in the yard with the prisoners from the lower tiers while doctors and nurses and first aid crews passed among them, administering to them. Every available physician was called to the scene and trucks and private automobiles laden with spirits of ammonia (used for treatment of blistered skin) sped through the prison gates into the yard. For most of them the ammonia was too late. Carbon monoxide or flames had seared their lungs or their bodies were badly charred. Following behind the physicians and nurses were priests and ministers -- the former dispensing the last sacrament of the Church, and the latter seeking to comfort the dying with prayer.

The men who had been herded into the prison yard were outraged at barely escaping in time. The guards had a near-riot on their hands but it was said later that Warden Thomas overreacted to the situation by calling for federal troops. A cordon of penitentiary guards was thrown about the towering prison walls. Other squads took up vantage points in sentinel towers and soon, five hundred soldiers from Fort Hayes, a local military post, arrived on the scene. Machine guns were mounted at the gates and on the walls. Bayonets were fixed and the troopers were ordered to shoot to kill. A troop of National Guardsmen soon augmented the regulars, and a half hour after the fire started the prison was completely surrounded. Thankfully, an actual riot never materialized.

All of the guards survived, but 322 prisoners died, many of them within days of completing their sentences. It was suggested that all could have been saved if the guards had unlocked the cells at the first sign of fire. One of the guards said, "I saw faces at the windows wreathed in smoke that poured through the broken glass. With others I tried to get to them but we could not move the bars. Soon flames broke into the cell-room and convicts dropped t o the floor. They were literally burned alive before our eyes." The mad confusion in the prison after the fire began was largely due to the fact that no training, instruction or fire drills had ever been carried out.

Not surprisingly, prison officials claimed that the fire had been set deliberately by the prisoners to cover an escape plan. According to this theory, three prisoners had set the blaze in hopes that it would really start to burn around 4:30 p.m. They hoped that it would divert the guards' attention from their escape, which they planned to take place when most of the prisoners were still in the dining hall. The fire smoldered too long, though, and didn't erupt for an hour after that, just after the hundreds of prisoners had been returned to the cellblock.

These claims were made months after the fire and of the three inmates who were blamed, two committed suicide after the tragedy. This was used by officials to point more fingers at the prisoners. The actual cause of the fire was never established, although many suggested that it had been accidental and that prison officials had blamed the disaster on the prisoners to cover up their own incompetence.

The Ohio State Penitentiary Fire was the worst fire in Ohio history and the worst in the history of American prisons. Most blamed the horrible overcrowding for the conditions that led up to the fire. The attention on the prison in the days that followed led to a repeal of judicial control over minimum sentences, which was thought to have contributed to the overcrowding. A package of new laws in 1931 established the Ohio Parole Board and established parole procedures, which by 1932 released 2,346 prisoners from the Ohio Penitentiary alone.

The doors were finally locked for good on December 31, 1983. For the first time in more than 150 years, the Ohio Penitentiary was completely silent and empty. Or was it? Not long after the last of the inmates departed, new stories began to be told about the legendary place. These weird tales were spread by local officials who had business inside the aging walls and by urban explorers who couldn't resist the urge to check out the now abandoned site.

While some stated that the only ghosts that remained in the prison were those of legend – remnants of the history and memories of the place, others soon began to argue that point. They believed that the executions, the stabbings, the shootings, the quiet, desperate suicides and, of course, the devastating fire that snuffed out hundreds of lives behind the prison walls, was being relived. These horrors had become imprinted on this terrible place and the spirits of the angry and often sinister men who had been incarcerated here had remained behind.

Stories began to spread about the old prison site. Those who wandered too close to the old buildings or who dared to go inside began to believe that the otherwise empty cellblocks were haunted by the spirits of the men who died in the prison. There were those who claimed to experience the phantoms connected to the horrendous fire of 1930. It was said that if you stood in the prison yard, you could hear the roar of ghostly flames from inside and the screams of the men who burned alive in their cells. Whiffs of smoke and burning flesh were often encountered in the old cellblocks.

These stories continued for several years until finally the prison was torn down and the site where it stood was cleared away. A sports arena was built where the prison once stood and in the fall of 2000, the arena became the home of the Columbus NHL hockey team. All traces of the old prison were finally destroyed.

Or were they?

According to reports, witnesses have spotted apparitions and have heard disembodied screams echoing across the arena's parking lot at night. This has led many to believe that the site continues to be haunted today.

Years ago, when it was first proposed that a tourist attraction or development would take the place of the prison, one of the former guards spoke up, "I wouldn't care if they dynamited the place. It's the entrance to Hell itself... I can't tell you what is there, what is seen and unseen..."

Could the destruction of the prison have erased the ghostly memories and restless souls that once lingered here? Or do they remain, still hoping for some sort of redemption to appease their troubled pasts?

# 1937: AMERICA'S WORST SCHOOL DISASTER
# THE NEW LONDON SCHOOL EXPLOSION

On March 18, 1937, the worst disaster to ever occur in a school in American history took place in New London, Texas. The horrific disaster – caused by the cancellation of a $300 a month natural gas bill – claimed the lives of at least 295 students and teachers. It was a catastrophe that the people of Texas would never forget.

New London was a blue-collar community in the middle 1930s. Even though the country was in the midst of the Great Depression, the local school district was one of the richest in America. Most of the residents of this East Texas town had been drawn there during the late 1920s and early 1930s when jobs dried up in other parts of the country. New London's oil fields were expanding and offered more jobs than could be filled.

At a time when small, often one-room rural schoolhouses were common, New London had a brand-new school. With the onset of Franklin D. Roosevelt's New Deal, community leaders successfully combined state, county and federal funding to build a new, large, one million dollar school complex. The new facilities offered the

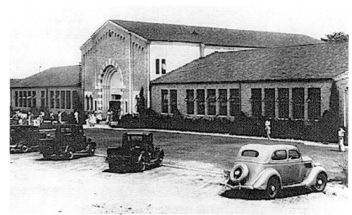

**The New London School before the explosion.**

most up-to-date curriculum for the students, from first grade through high school. It offered the most modern course of studies available, allowing students to choose between vocational and college preparatory courses in the later grades. This kept students in school longer and prepared them for jobs and college when they graduated. The campus became a great source of pride for area parents who had generally only had limited access to education during their own childhoods.

The new school was built on sloping ground and a large dead-air space was located beneath the structure. It would be learned later, during the investigation that followed the disaster, that in spite of the large initial investment in the project, planners had taken many dangerous shortcuts during construction. The school board had overridden the original architect's plans for a boiler and steam distribution system, instead opting to install 72 gas heaters throughout the building. Early in 1937, the school board canceled their natural gas contract and had plumbers install a tap into the Parade Gasoline Company's residue gas line in order to save money. This practice, while not explicitly authorized by local oil companies, was widespread in the area. The natural gas extracted with the oil was seen as a waste product and was flared off. As there was no value to the natural gas, the oil companies turned a blind eye. This "raw" or "wet" gas varied in quality from day to day, even from hour to hour.

Natural gas in its original state is both odorless and colorless, and because of that any leaks would be undetectable. The odor that most associate with gas today is added as a safety precaution by the commercial companies that sell it. In those days, there was no warning about a leak. Students had been complaining of headaches for some time, but no paid much attention to this. Unknown to everyone, gas had built up inside the crawlspace that ran beneath the entire 253-foot building.

Between 3:05 and 3:20 p.m., on March 18, Lemmie R. Butler, a manual training instructor, turned on an electric sander in one of the school's vocational workshops. It is believed that the sander's switch caused a spark that ignited the gas-air mixture.

Reports from witnesses stated that the walls of the school actually bulged outwards and the roof lifted off of the building, cartoon-fashion. But this was no cartoon. In seconds, the ceiling came crashing down on the seven hundred children and forty teachers inside. The main wing of the structure collapsed. Flames that were ignited by the explosion quickly died out since the building was fireproof but the strength of the explosion's concussion and pieces of falling debris instantly killed most of the adults and children inside. The force of the explosion was so great that a two-ton concrete block was thrown clear of the building and crushed a 1936 Chevrolet parked nearby.

The explosion was its own alarm, heard for miles away. The most immediate response was from a group of mothers who were gathered for a PTA meeting in the cafeteria building, which was about 300 feet from the main

**Hundreds were killed in the initial explosion.**

**People rushed to the scene to try and help with rescue efforts.**

**The body of one of the students, crushed under tons of stone and debris.**

building. They helplessly watched as the building collapsed on everyone inside. The women screamed and raced toward the school, digging for hours to reach victims who were alive under the rubble and could be heard screaming for help.

Within minutes, area residents started to arrive and began digging through the rubble, many with their bare hands. Roughnecks from the oil fields were released from their jobs and brought with them cutting torches and heavy equipment needed to clear the concrete and steel. A crowd of nearly 10,000 area residents quickly gathered at the site of the explosion, desperate to help. Their cars and pickup trucks clogged the roads and blocked the highways leading in and out of town.

Assistance poured in from outside the immediate area. Governor James Allred dispatched Texas Rangers, the state highway patrol, and the Texas National Guard. Thirty doctors, 100 nurses, and 25 embalmers arrived from Dallas. Airmen from Barksdale Field, deputy sheriffs, and even Boy Scouts took part in the rescue and recovery.

Most of the dead and injured were children and teachers who had been gathered in the auditorium. Some were rescued and cared for in hospitals as far away as Shreveport, Louisiana. However, hopes of finding more survivors dimmed as the sun began to go down. Illuminated by the powerful lights from the school's football field, a crowd of grief-stricken parents, relatives, friends and onlookers stood near a lengthening line of bodies covered by white sheets.

Most of the bodies were either burned beyond recognition or blown to pieces. One mother had a heart attack and died when she found out that her 16-year-old daughter's body had been found. Only part of the girl's face and some of her bones were still intact. Another boy was identified by the pull string from his favorite toy top, found in his jeans pocket.

Rescuers worked through the rainy night until, seventeen hours later, the entire site had been cleared. Buildings in the neighboring communities of Henderson, Overton, Kilgore and as far away as Tyler and Longview were converted into makeshift morgues to house the enormous number of bodies, and everything from family cars to delivery trucks served as hearses and ambulances. Mother Frances Hospital in nearby Tyler was scheduled to open the next day, but the dedication was canceled and the hospital opened immediately.

Reporters arrived to cover the calamity, but found themselves caught up in the rescue effort. Former *Dallas*

**(Left) An automobile that was crushed by debris from the explosion.   (Right) The New London school, days after the deadly explosion.**

*Times Herald* executive editor Felix McKnight, then a young Associated Press reporter, recalled, "We identified ourselves and were immediately told that helpers were needed far more than reporters." A 22-year-old reporter named Walter Cronkite also found himself in New London, on one of his first assignments for United Press International. Although he went on to become one of America's most beloved newsmen, covering everything from World War II to the Kennedy Assassination and Vietnam, he was quoted as saying decades later, "I did nothing in my studies nor in my life to prepare me for a story of the magnitude of that New London tragedy, nor has any story since that awful day equaled it."

The people of New London recovered as best they could. Not all of the buildings on the school campus had been destroyed. One of the surviving structures, the gymnasium, was quickly converted into multiple classrooms. Inside   tents and the modified buildings, classes resumed ten days later. A new school was completed on the property in 1939.

Families also received an outpouring of support from nearby communities, from people all over Texas, and from well-wishers across American and the world. Adolf Hitler, who was at the time the German Chancellor, paid his respects in the form of a telegram. It remains on display in the New London museum today.

Almost as the dust was still settling in New London, investigations began seeking a cause for the explosion. Experts from the United States Bureau of Mines concluded that the connection to the residue gas line was faulty. It had allowed gas to leak into the school, and since natural gas is invisible and is odorless, the leak was unnoticed. To reduce the danger of future leaks, the Texas Legislature began mandating that thiol, a strong-smelling sulfur compound, be added to natural gas. The practice soon began to be used all over the country.

A group of parents brought a lawsuit against the school district and the Parade Gasoline Company, but the courts ruled that neither could be held responsible. In the aftermath of the disaster, school superintendent W. C. Shaw was forced to resign amidst threats that a lynch party would be sent after him. Sadly, Shaw himself had lost a son in the explosion.

Over the years, the New London School explosion has received relatively little attention given the magnitude of the event. Explanations for this are speculative, but most center around residents' unwillingness to discuss the tragedy. It was a memory that most simply did not want dredged up. In addition, many of the parents left the area in the years that followed since most were transient oil workers. Another reason for the lack of attention was believed to be the overshadowing effect of the Hindenburg disaster, which happened two months later.

The school disaster remains a haunting memory in New London, even after all of these years. Many questions remain unanswered, even the exact number of those who died in the blast. It may actually be much higher than the nearly 300 that has been estimated over the years. Many of those killed were the children of temporary residents, oilfield workers who moved from one place to another, depending on what work was available. It's believed that some of these "roughnecks" may have collected the bodies of their children after the disaster and returned them to be buried near their respective homes.

The true magnitude of this disaster may never be known.

# 1942: DINNER, DANCING & DEATH
# THE COCOANUT GROVE FIRE

**The Cocoanut Grove Nightclub in Boston**

t was the place to be in Boston throughout the thirties and early forties. The Cocoanut Grove was one of the city's most elegant nightclubs and everyone went there. It was a place where all sorts of people from many walks of life could mingle indiscriminately, Irish with Jews or Italians, Protestants with Catholics, the wealthy with the middle class, athletes with movie stars and gangsters with politicians. Equally indiscriminate was the fire that swept through the crowd of over a thousand patrons on that icy November night, killing nearly half and seriously injuring over a hundred more. It took little more than fifteen minutes for the fire to eat its way through the 10,000 square feet of public spaces and do its deadly work.

The Cocoanut Grove, named after the famed Cocoanut Grove nightclub in Los Angeles' Ambassador Hotel, started out as a Boston restaurant turned speakeasy. Musician Mickey Alpert had conceived of an idea for a roaring twenties'-style nightclub for Boston. With hundreds of thousands in financing provided by California mobster and swindler Jack Berman (hiding out in Boston), Mickey turned a vacant building near the Boston Common, located in what is now Bay Village, into a fine eatery with top-notch entertainment. On advice from his brother, George, a New England lawyer, Mickey was determined to maintain a "classy" environment by refusing to serve alcohol. Patrons wishing to drink something with a little more kick had to bring their own. Opening in October of 1927, the new establishment flourished for the first few years, until it was hit hard by the Great Depression. In 1930, Charles "King" Solomon offered to buy the floundering nightclub for a mere $10,000, and Mickey and his partners jumped at the offer.

King Solomon was a Russian-born Jewish gangster who had risen through the ranks of the New England mob to become one of the most powerful gang bosses of the day. He ruled over most of Boston's illegal gambling, prostitution and narcotics operations. More importantly, the King had control of most of the bootlegging in the region, which had proven to be an extremely lucrative operation during Prohibition. King bought the Cocoanut Grove as a personal amusement. Soon after taking it over, he turned it into a speakeasy, albeit a classy one, using his bootlegging connections to keep the alcohol flowing. At the time, there were at least 4,000 speakeasies in Boston -- one for every 185 residents, and all of them illegal. This one had to be special. King hired entertainers with real star power, bringing in some of the biggest names in the country including Rudy Vallee, Guy Lombardo, Jimmy Durante and Sophie Tucker. Despite the large crowds, the soaring entertainment budget and poor business practices turned the Cocoanut Grove into a real money pit. Solomon, however, didn't care. It had become a personal playground for himself and his cronies and he spent much of his time there, hobnobbing with the Boston elite and Hollywood stars.

King Solomon's reign over the nightclub was short lived, as was he. In 1933, just three years after acquiring the Grove, he was gunned down by four gangsters in the men's room in Boston's Cotton Club. Solomon's mob kingdom was divided up between rival gang members but his estate was handled by his Boston attorney Barnett "Barney" Welansky.

Barney had worked for Solomon for many years but had kept himself well insulated from King's mob dealings and only handled his legitimate businesses. Within days of acting as pallbearer at Solomon's funeral, Barney emerged from a private meeting with the probate judge as the new owner of the Cocoanut Grove nightclub, having "inherited" the club from the Solomon estate, explaining that the estate "didn't want it." Just how he determined that the estate didn't want it, no one ever knew, but by the end of 1933, the legendary Cocoanut Grove had a new master and Prohibition had been repealed.

Barney Welansky was determined to turn the old speakeasy into one of Boston's most important and stylish hot spots and to make a profit while he was at it. Over the next nine years, he made many changes. He reduced the cost of the entertainment by hiring musicians and establishing a house band that was led by none other than Mickey Alpert, the Cocoanut Grove's original creator and owner. Angelo Lippi, known as "the Count," had worked as maitre d' at the Grove since it had opened and he agreed to continue to work for Welanskyy. The Count managed the floor employees and kept the customers feeling welcomed, happy, and eager to return.

The floor space of the Cocoanut Grove was multiplied several times as adjacent buildings were acquired and added to the Grove's original footprint. With three major expansions, Welansky hired the famous nightclub designer Reuben Bodenhorn to renovate the spaces as each was added. His ultimate vision for the interior of the club was a theme reflecting the tropical setting of Casablanca. The walls were lined with imitation leather and the ceilings were draped with thousands of yards of satin. Six pillars, three on each side of the dance floor, were designed to look like palm trees, with large paper palm fronds extending far out over the floor in a circular pattern. An elevated area called "the terrace" was inside the main dining room just off the foyer. Wrought iron railings had been installed along the edges of the terrace, which created a feeling of separation and maintained prime views of the floorshow for VIPs.

Since the original structure had been designed during Prohibition, there was no bar so this had to be changed, as well. Bodenhorn designed the 48-foot Caricature Bar within the main room. It was covered with red leatherette and commanded an excellent view of the floorshow.

When Welansky decided to carve out space for a new bar in an old storage room in the basement, he wasn't quite sure it would pay off. Would customers really want to leave the bright and gay atmosphere of the main dining room and dance floor to go down into a dark, claustrophobic area? He decided to give it a chance and created the Melody Lounge in the recesses of the Cocoanut Grove basement. The idea turned out so well that he had the bar enlarged twice, finally ending up with an octagon shape that was roughly 35 by 18 feet, in the center of the lounge. This place was to be a bar, pure and simple. No floor show, no dancing and no fancy food. The only entertainment was a singer, playing the piano on a small revolving stage.

With the growing success of the Melody Lounge, Welansky again hired Reuben Bodenhorn to design the interior of his subterranean enterprise. Bodenhorn wisely decided to embrace the dark, windowless space and created a dim, intimate lounge with an exotic feel. There was one soft light in the center of the room, aimed at the floor, and neon lined the underside of the bar. The only other illumination was from the tiny seven and one-half watt lights that twinkled out from the fronds of the imitation palm trees in the corners. It was so dark in the lounge that customers had a longstanding joke that you had to light a match to find your drink!

Bodehorn hid the dingy walls with flimsy paneling and covered the ceiling by draping nearly two thousand square feet of dark blue satin over wooden slats, twelve and eighteen inches below the low ceiling. This was meant to give the customers a feeling of sitting beneath a star-filled night sky. The draped satin extended up the ceiling of the staircase leading from the Melody Lounge to the main floor. He placed zebra print settees along the outer walls of the lounge, along with several tables and chairs.

The final renovation to the Cocoanut Grove came in 1942 when Barney Welansky annexed the last building and constructed the New Broadway Lounge. As with his two previous renovations, he failed to apply for a building permit. He did submit plans to the city, however, which called for an emergency exit to be built that could accommodate the New Broadway Lounge patrons. However, as the renovations progressed, he decided to keep the door locked and to have a coat check room built across the exit, thus blocking the door and concealing it from sight. Since the new lounge was connected to the main dining room through a narrow corridor next to the stage, a fusible fire door was required by the licensing board. In the event of a fire, the heat would cause the door to fuse to the frame, preventing the fire from spreading in either direction. No fusible door was installed but Welansky was granted the license extension on the mere say-so of his brother, Jimmy.

As Welansky expanded his domain, he did so without concern about what he was forming. He paid no attention to the original layouts of the different buildings the Grove had consumed; he just kept adding and adding. The result was a confusing maze of coat check rooms, dressing rooms, restrooms, service rooms, kitchens and store rooms connected to each other and the three large public rooms by winding and twisting corridors, and to the basement Melody Lounge by a single narrow stairway.

Welansky apparently paid no attention to Boston's building codes or fire codes, either. With his growing business, he had ceased practicing law and had become a respected Boston businessman. He had forged friendships with many Boston politicians during his nine years at the Grove. Those "friendly" connections that seemed to be the most beneficial to the nightclub owner included Mayor Maurice J. Tobin, Fire Commissioner Arthur Reilly, Building Department Commissioner James Mooney and Mary Driscoll, chair of the licensing board.Though none of these prominent names ever appeared on the list of indictments following the fire, their influence, or one might say their lack of attention to what was going on with the building or the decorating and operation of the nightclub seemed all too apparent. But this ignorance did not stop them from enjoying many long evenings of dining and dancing at the wonderful Cocoanut Grove. Welansky was able to complete three major renovations without once applying for building permits. He was granted extensions to his liquor license twice, first to cover the Melody Lounge and again for the New Broadway Lounge -- and all without a single building inspection, which was a requirement of the licensing board.

By 1942, shortly before it was reduced to ashes, the single-story Cocoanut Grove was an amalgam of six interconnected buildings, fronting on the south by Piedmont Street, on the north by Shawmut Street and Broadway Street on the east. The Grove's original size had nearly tripled. There were three large public rooms with three bars, a dining room, a dance floor and a stage for the band. During fair weather, the roof above the dance floor could be electrically rolled back, revealing the night sky and allowing patrons to dance under the stars. The basement had been converted into the dark, intimate Melody Lounge. The newest expansion, The New Broadway Lounge, had opened only eleven days before the fire.

Saturdays were always packed at the Cocoanut Grove and November 28, 1942 was no exception. Legal occupancy was listed as 460 but on that evening, with extra tables and chairs covering every square foot of floor space, over a thousand patrons were enjoying a night out at the Grove. Among the merrymakers was Buck Jones, the famed cowboy celebrity, star of more than two hundred movies. In town promoting war bonds on a bond tour, he was having dinner with a group of fellow promoters. As a VIP, he was seated with his party on the terrace.

The nightclub was packed but two key people were conspicuously absent. Club owner Barney Welansky had been admitted to the Mass General Hospital twelve days earlier after collapsing from a heart attack, leaving his brother Jimmy in charge. Also missing was the Grove's long time maitre d', Angelo Lippi, who was home suffering from arthritis.

In the Melody Lounge, people drifted back and forth between the basement and the dining room or the dance floor or the restrooms, but as the night went on, the lounge filled up with

The corner of the Melody Lounge where the fire started. The 'trunk' of the cocoanut tree is still visible. The furniture was hardly touched by the fire.

nearly four hundred guests. In one corner, a sailor and his date were enjoying the privacy created by the dim lighting. As their passions heated up, or because the young woman grew shy, the sailor reached up and unscrewed the tiny light in the artificial palm tree over their heads. Goody Goodelle had just started playing the piano and singing Bing Crosby's new hit, "White Christmas," when head bartender John Bradley looked up and noticed that their corner was now pitch black.

Annoyed with the sailor but too busy serving the customers lined up four deep around the bar, Bradley called out to Stanley Tomaszewski, a sixteen-year-old bar boy, and told him to get the light back on right away. Tomaszewski  walked over to the corner and politely explained that it was dangerous having the light out and he had to get it re-lit. Unfortunately, the bulb had fallen completely out and it was far too dark for young Stanley to see the socket inside the tree. Striking a match, he found the socket and got the bulb back on. He blew out the match, dropped it to the floor and stepped on it to make sure it was out.

As Tomaszewskiy returned to work, he heard someone shout that there was a fire in the top of the palm tree. John Bradley ran from behind the bar and together, the two young men pulled and batted at the tree attempting to put the fire out. As other employees ran to help by throwing pitchers of water on the tree, the scene became almost comedic and witnesses chuckled at their hapless attempts. As the burning fronds were finally pulled down, Bradley looked up in time to see the satin fabric above the tree start to smoke and then burn. A ball of fire erupted from the corner, feeding on the fabric-covered ceiling, and rapidly spread across the room heading for the open staircase.

It was 10:15 p.m.

Don Lauer, a Marine private, jumped onto a chair and tried to use his pocket knife to cut the fabric down to stop the fire from spreading, but he was too late. In mere seconds, the entire ceiling was a sheet of blue and orange flame, dripping fire onto the frantic patrons below. Almost immediately, the crowd panicked as hair and clothing began to burn. The crowd moved toward the only exit they knew -- the narrow staircase -- and the fire did the same.  As the fire reached the staircase, it continued on its path, burning away at the fabric ceiling over the stairs. The staircase quickly became jammed, as four hundred people tried to escape the inferno, not knowing that the fire was taking the same route, in search of the fresh oxygen on the main floor.

Ruth and Hyman Strogoff were Wednesday and Saturday night regulars at the Melody Lounge. They spotted

**Narrow staircase leading out of the Melody Lounge.**

**Locked emergency exit at the top of the Melody Lounge staircase.**

the "little fire" and deciding not to take their chances, headed toward the stairs. Ruth believed that she and Hyman were among the first to reach the foot of the stairs but by that time, the fire had spread and the crowd began a mass rush behind them. In their frenzy to escape, several people grabbed and pulled at Ruth and Hyman to get past them and    Hyman went down. Though Ruth pulled hard on his arm, she was unable to get him up. He was held fast to the floor as screaming men and women trampled on him to get past, or by those who simply collapsed on top of him. Within a matter of seconds, there was a growing tangle of bodies at the bottom of the stairs. As Ruth's hat and jacket caught fire, she was pushed up the stairs by the moving mass, after which she rolled on the floor to put her own fire out.  Knowing there was nothing she could do for her husband and that he was likely already dead, she was forced to leave him behind. Before the night was over, hundreds of others would have to face the same terrible choice of having to leave loved ones behind that they might themselves survive.

Gunner's Mate Matt Lane was farther back in the crowd. When he finally reached the bottom of the stairs, the way was completely blocked with bodies, some dying, some already dead. He jumped onto the railing and used it to pull himself along as he climbed over the others to make his escape. He had come to the Cocoanut Grove with his friend Don Lauer, who had tried to slice the fabric from the ceiling only moments before. He would never see Don alive again.

The way to safety wasn't easy. The frightened patrons had to make their way up a narrow flight of fifteen steps, past the locked emergency exit at the top, then make a U-turn to the right and down a ten-foot hallway, then another right turn around an office and coat check room for 28 feet, then another right turn and twelve more feet across the foyer to the revolving door opening onto Piedmont Street. All of this with a fire raging over their heads and thick black smoke filling the air around them.

Barney Welansky had ordered all the service and emergency exits to which the public had access to be locked while the club was open. This was intended to keep patrons from sneaking out without paying their check.

Many terrified, confused people never made it out of the basement Melody Lounge. They were overcome by the thick choking smoke or by the near-eighteen-hundred-degree heat resulting from the fire. They weren't aware that there was an exit door in the back of the lounge, as it was disguised with the same paneling used on the walls. It would have taken them down a hallway, up three steps and to an outside exit. The exit door was partially blocked by a sewer pipe so it only opened about eighteen inches. But none of that mattered. No one found the door so no one was able to escape that way.

Two of the people who survived inside the Melody Lounge were Daniel Weiss, a bartender, and singer-pianist Goody Goodelle. They dowsed napkins with water and held them to their noses and mouths to breathe through and then lay on the floor until the fire had passed out of the room and up the stairs. They then crawled along the

**(Left) Piedmont Street entrance during the fire.   (Right) Cocoanut Grove dining room.  The ceiling is charred but most of the chairs and tables are relatively untouched.**

floor and into the kitchen, where they escaped through a barred window. The fire had been mainly limited to the ceiling so when firemen made their way down the steps to recover the bodies, they found much of the furniture was hardly damaged. The fire had moved on in little more than a minute or two.

When Melody Lounge customers finally stumbled to the main entrance off the Piedmont Street foyer, only the first few were able to make their way through the revolving door before it was completely clogged by the crush of people behind them. They were unaware that there was a conventional exit door right next to the revolving door. Welansky had installed a coat check room in front of it, with a large wooden coat rack blocking the door from sight.  It is questionable however, whether this door would have saved many lives as it swung inward and would have been forced shut by the crush of the crowd.

In a strange irony, at 10:15 p.m., while Stanley Tomaszeswky and John Bradley were trying to put out the small fire in the palm tree, the fire department was responding to an alarm for a car fire just three blocks from the Cocoanut Grove. It only took a few minutes to put out that small fire, and a firefighter noticed what he thought was smoke coming from the area of the Grove. As the firefighters headed toward the club to investigate, people started running toward them to report the fire. When they arrived, they found heavy black smoke pouring out of the building and patrons and employees scrambling out into the street. In short order, the fire chief on site ordered a third alarm to be issued, skipping the second alarm as he realized the scale of the disaster. A fourth alarm was issued at 10:24 p.m. and the fifth alarm went out at 11:02 p.m. By this time, the fire was largely extinguished and the departments responding to the fourth and fifth alarms were called for the rescue and recovery efforts.

While the fire department was assembling outside, the fire continued to rage through the club.

As the fire arrived at the main floor in search of fresh oxygen and fuel, several hundred unsuspecting revelers were just beyond the foyer, not knowing that many of them would be dead within minutes, and the rest would be frantically searching for any way out of the blaze. Just as the fire entered the main public room, the lights went out, tumbling everyone into near total darkness, except for the firelight.

The dining area, dance floor, bandstand, and the Caricature Bar were all in the main public room. Customers complained that the tables and chairs had been packed in so tightly that they had to twist and turn and walk sideways just to get through the room to the dance floor. Tables were added along the side walls as well, some blocking emergency exits. But it would not do to turn anyone away -- after all, the Cocoanut Grove was the place to be!

Some heard the screams first, commenting that there must be a fight. Then they smelled the smoke. Then they saw the flames blast through the doorways and charge across the room. The fire was feeding off the fabric on the ceilings and walls. With the flames came extreme heat that seared flesh and lungs as people tried to breathe. The fire gave off carbon monoxide and toxins as the air filled with thick, acrid smoke, making it even harder to breath.  The flames moved through the room so rapidly that many were overcome with heat or smoke before they even had a chance to leave their chairs. Some bodies were found burned beyond recognition while others were found next to their tables without any signs of injury.

Movie star Buck Jones was one such victim. A popular story about Jones circulated after the fire. As the story went, he had escaped the fire but ran back into the building several times, carrying out injured victims until he collapsed on the sidewalk and was rushed to the hospital, where he died a short time later. In reality, Buck Jones was at the club that night having dinner, even though he would have preferred to be resting in his hotel room, nursing a bad head cold. Instead, he found himself sitting at a table on the terrace when the fire advanced across the room. He was rapidly overcome by the heat and smoke and fell to the floor next to his table. Firefighters found him where he had fallen, barely alive. The only accurate part of the story was that he was taken to the hospital where he died.

It is well known to firefighters that unless directed otherwise, a panicked crowd will attempt to leave a building the same way they came in. The Cocoanut Grove had only two public entrances -- the revolving door in the main foyer on Piedmont Street and the exit leading from the New Broadway Lounge opening onto Broadway Street. This exit entailed a single, inward-swinging door that led into a small vestibule then to double doors opening onto the street.  Most of the patrons had entered the club through the Piedmont entrance with only a single revolving door. These two exits were nearly a full city block apart.

Men and women who were able to run did so. They were desperate to find a way out -- any way out. And some of them did get out. All but twenty of the club's employees survived the fire, largely because they knew where the hidden exits were and where windows would open. Some of the patrons were able to follow employees to safety.  The rest were on their own -- lost in the dark.

As the Piedmont foyer continued to fill with people, bodies continued to pile up against the revolving door. Eventually, under the extreme pressure, the door mechanism gave way and collapsed outward. Nathan Greer saw the collapse and jumped forward onto the sidewalk. Sadly, a ferocious wall of fire followed him through the opening as a blast of fresh air rushed in from outside, burning up most of the people in or around the opening.

A set of emergency doors was located along the Shawmut Street wall behind the terrace. These double doors

were covered with wooden slatted doors and were blocked off with tables that were added to accommodate the large crowd. Even so, several people were able to find the doors. Each door was only twenty inches wide and the door on the right was bolted near the top of the frame, where no one could find the bolt in the dark. Joyce Spector witnessed the chaos in the dining room. "The men were the worst. Honest. There were men pushing and shoving to get out." She was knocked down and started crawling across the floor, lungs burning, eyes stinging, until she felt fresh air on her face. She had found the Shawmut Street exit. As she struggled to get out someone outside pulled her through the door and "threw me across the sidewalk, and grabbed for more people inside. It seemed like an hour I lay there.  I couldn't tell. More people were pulled out and tossed down beside me." Joyce survived her ordeal but her fiancé, Justin

**Double door exit to Shawmut Street, hidden behind Venetian slat doors.**

Morgan, did not.

Charles and Peggy Disbrow found themselves descending the service stairway to the kitchen where they joined a group of people already there. After searching the kitchen in the dark, they found a small window above a counter that had been boarded up. Knocking the boards away, they saw that a pipe was blocking the opening, except for about eighteen inches. Still, most were able to climb through and into a blind alley behind an apartment building. Margaret Foley, sitting in her living room, was unaware of what was going on only a few feet from her home when a woman burst through her back door, ran through her apartment and out the front door. Stunned, Margaret watched as another person, then another, repeated the performance. She later estimated that at least fifty people had escaped through her home.

Don Jeffers, also having made his way to the kitchen, dropped to the floor as the room filled with smoke. Crawling around trying to find a way out, he heard a voice in the darkness. Following the voice, he joined four other people hiding in the walk-in refrigerator. They waited there until the fire department entered the kitchen and escorted them out.

Two more exits were located on the main floor but both proved useless. One was a service door located to the left of the stage platform. This door also opened inward but it, too, was locked. The other door was in the New Broadway Lounge, locked and well hidden behind a coat check room. Barney Welansky had this built to serve the patrons entering through the Broadway Street entrance, earning him an extra $4.50 a night.

The 250 or so customers enjoying themselves in the New Broadway Lounge remained blissfully unaware of the carnage that was taking place on the other side of the adjoining wall for several minutes. Meanwhile, the fire in the dining room was getting hotter. When it reached the velour-lined passageway into the Broadway Lounge, extreme heat built up a massive amount of pressure that blasted the flames and hot gasses down the short passage and into the lounge like a torch. That room did not contain the large amounts of flammable decorations that the other rooms had, but the pressure, hot gasses, and scorching temperatures created an environment that caused the fire to burn more completely than in any other area of the club. Twenty-five bodies, burned to blackened cinders, were found where they fell. Dozens of bodies were piled against the only unlocked exit in the room.

Next to the Broadway Street entrance, two large windows had been replaced by glass block. One man was able to break a small hole through the glass block and attempted to crawl out but became stuck. Firefighters found the man reaching partially through the hole but were unable to get him out. They doused him with water

**(Left) Broadway Street entrance and (Right) Piedmont Street entrance after the fire.**

**Firefighters inside the Cocoanut Grove after the fire.**

**Chaotic crowds outside the club**

but in the end they had to watch helplessly as the man burned to death.

A long wall on the Piedmont Street side of the building contained four large plate glass windows. These windows, if broken out would have provided an excellent escape route for those trapped in the dining room area. Unfortunately, they had been covered with wood panels and no one knew they were there. Experts estimate that if these windows had not been covered, hundreds could have been saved.

Firefighters needed to get hoses into the building quickly to save anyone trapped by the fire. Early on, wherever they tried to break through, they were driven back by the extreme heat and thick black smoke. When they were finally able to enter, they went through the area where the revolving door had collapsed. They had to climb over a six-foot-high stack of bodies to get to the dining room area. By the time they were able to enter the foyer, the fire had nearly burned itself out.

Less than half an hour after it started, the fire was largely extinguished, inside and out. Rescuers now needed to clear the entrances. They pulled body after body from the stack blocking the doorway, piling them on the sidewalk in the cold November night. Police officer Elmer Brooks remembered rescuers lifting bodies and having arms and legs come off in their hands.

Clearing the entrances had been a terrible job in itself, but nothing could have prepared them for the gruesome task that lay ahead. As they moved through the building, they found bodies everywhere. Some were piled up against locked doors, while others were by themselves. Some were horribly burned, while other were unmarked by flames. Some were found where they had been sitting when the fire started while others were in found in the far reaches of the club. Firefighter Winn Robbins saw a dead woman, propped up in one of the Grove's phone booths, still holding a telephone receiver in her hand.

Firefighters, police officers and volunteer military men began removing the bodies, piling them on the sidewalks. Some of the victims were still alive but there wasn't time to separate the living from the dead (except for badly charred bodies) so they were all loaded into ambulances and trucks and taken to area hospitals. Medical professionals triaged the victims as they arrived, sorting out the dead and determining the level of medical care required by the living.

Everyone who died at the Cocoanut Grove, died as a result of the fire, but there were several causes of death. The most straightforward were those who were physically burned. Some died from smoke inhalation or carbon monoxide poisoning and still others died from internal burns - burned lungs and nasal passages from breathing the superheated air. Several bodies showed signs of being crushed by a mass of people pushing in on them, or at the bottom of a pile as people collapsed upon them. Even more disturbing was the number of people who had fallen and were trampled to death by the stampeding crowd.

As they went about their work inside with stunned calm, outside it was rapidly becoming chaotic. The temperature was falling and the water on the cobblestones was making the roads icy. Fire hoses froze to the ground as smoldering bodies, living and dead, were doused with frigid water. Family members, friends and bystanders were pressing in on the building, forcing officials to form a human chain to stop people from entering the building to search for loved ones or to satisfy their curiosity. Unfortunately, some of the bodies piled on the sidewalk suffered the further indignity of being stripped of their money and jewelry as they lay dead or dying by ghouls in the crowds.

Over the next few hours, nearly 450 fire victims were transported to hospitals. Massachusetts General Hospital received 114 of which 75 were already dead or died soon after. Of the 300 bodies to arrive at Boston City Hospital, 168 were dead on arrival and 36 more died within hours. Some were sent directly to temporary morgues but were found to be alive and transferred to hospitals; a few of those eventually made it home.

For several days, newspapers were filled with stories of those who lived and those who died.

Stories of those who lost their loves and those who lost their families.

Stories of how some survived and of how some died.

Eleanor Chiampa, only fifteen years old, was very excited to be there that evening. This was her first visit to the famous Cocoanut Grove and to top it off, she was sitting on the same terrace as movie star Buck Jones! Her big brother, home on leave from the war, had taken her to the Grove along with his wife and another couple. The two men were the only people from their party to survive. Eleanor lived for a few days in the Mass General Hospital before she became the youngest victim of the fire.

Married earlier that evening, John O'Neil and his bride, Claudia Nadeau O'Neil, had originally planned to celebrate their wedding at the Latin Quarter, another fashionable Boston nightclub. However, at the last minute, they decided to move the celebration to the Cocoanut Grove. Their marriage had lasted only a few hours as neither of them left the Grove alive. Their bodies were found in the dining room, next to those of their best man and maid of honor.

Harold Thomas was in the main dining room and Thomas Sheehan, Jr. was in the New Broadway Lounge when the fire started. As people dashed madly about, each of them was knocked to the floor and were unable to get up as others fell on top of them. This likely saved their lives. They were shielded from the flames and heat by the layers of bodies above, and from the bottom of the piles, they were able to breathe the cleaner air near the floor. Both men walked away from the fire that night with only a few burns.

Pvt. Harry T. Fitzgerald of the Army Air Corps, was home on leave from Florida. He had not been home for several months and his three older brothers were anxious to welcome him home and show him a good time. James, John and Wilfred Fitzgerald treated Harry to a night at the Cocoanut Grove. None of the four brothers or their dates survived the night. Their mother, a widow of twenty years, lost her entire family to the fire.

A few found interesting ways to save themselves. One young soldier reportedly urinated into a handful of napkins and placed them over his mouth and nose. Another young man found a container of ice cream to bury his burning face in as he searched for an exit. Both men survived the fire without injury to their lungs or throats.

A party of ten, members of a family of funeral directors from a nearby town, were enjoying a night out, dining and dancing at the Grove. One of the couples decided not to stay for the second floor show, opting to see a program at a theatre just a few blocks away. When they returned, nearly their entire family had been wiped out.

Two young couples were at the Grove to celebrate their wedding anniversaries. Helping them celebrate were eleven of their friends and family, including five brothers and sisters and their spouses. One member of their party had risen to walk to the Caricature Bar when he noticed the fire moving rapidly across the ceiling. He shouted for his group to follow him out of the room, but none of them did. He was the only one from the group of fifteen to survive. The others were found later, still at their table.

Coast Guardsman Clifford Johnson, who was at the Grove that night on a blind date, got out safely but went back into the inferno four times looking for his date. He wasn't aware that she had already gotten out safely. He aided others in their escape until he finally collapsed onto the pavement with third degree burns over fifty percent of his body. No one had ever survived such severe burn injuries but Clifford became a medical miracle. Twenty-one months later, he was discharged from the hospital. In an ironic twist of fate, fourteen years later, back in his home state of Missouri, Clifford was killed when the car he was driving left the road, rolled over and burst into flames.

Francis and Grace Gatturna were waiting for the floorshow to begin when they smelled smoke. Francis grabbed Grace by the hand and attempted to pull her from the room. As they tried to make their way out, they became separated. Francis made it to safety but Grace did not. After Francis was dismissed from the hospital, he became very depressed, telling family members that he should have either saved his wife, or died with her. His family became worried and checked him back into the hospital. He seemed to be improving with the help of therapy when on January 9, 1943, he jumped through a closed hospital window to his death.

The last Cocoanut Grove victim died in the hospital on May 5, 1943.

By the time it was over, the fire had involved 187 firefighters, 26 engine companies, 5 ladder companies, 3 rescue companies, 1 water tower and countless volunteers. The property losses were in the hundreds of thousands. The cost in human suffering was immeasurable.

Just twelve hours after the fire was extinguished, Arthur Reilly, Boston's Fire Commissioner, convened a series of public hearings to determine the cause of the fire and find who was to blame. More than one hundred witnesses gave testimony, including several public officials and over ninety survivors. The results of the inquest revealed that club owner Barney Welansky manipulated local politicians to his advantage and cut corners, putting his customers at risk, to save a buck or make a buck.

At the same time, the politicians and public officials were busy playing pass the buck. Everyone had a good story that seemed to be designed to leave the teller free of any blame or questionable activities.

Lieutenant Frank Linney, an inspector for the fire department had inspected the Cocoanut Grove just eight days before the fire. His report gave new meaning to "cursory inspection." The entire report took only one page. Linney passed every topic and made only two specific notations.

1.   *No flammable decorations.*
2.   *Sufficient number of exits.*

The testimony of the 93 survivors corrected Linney's erroneous observations.

Perhaps the most bizarre testimony was in the form of an opinion offered by James Mooney, commissioner of the Boston Building Department. "I don't believe a panicked crowd would get out even if there were no exterior walls. They would get entangled among themselves and not get out anyway." Mooney's department had allowed the New Broadway Lounge to open without the fusible fire door, no new fire exit, no final inspection and the only emergency exit blocked by a coat check room.

The only person who came forward and told the truth as he knew it, regardless of the implications, was sixteen-year-old Stanley Tomaszewski. He testified to exactly what happened just before the fire started. Tomaszewski had been vilified in the newspapers but he stood tall and told the truth about lighting the match near the paper cocoanut tree in the ill-fated Melody Lounge. He insisted that he had carefully blown out the match and stepped on it. In the end, he admitted that he believed that this was probably how the fire started.

Fire Commissioner Reilly did everything he could to ease the strain on Tomaszewski and ease his fright. He praised him and described him as an honorable young man. The *Boston Globe* advanced the idea that the blame should not be placed on the shoulders of this fine young man, but rather on the heads of the corrupt officials. Even with high praise and reassurances supporting the shy young man, his life was threatened. For the next several months he was kept under protective guard in a Boston hotel.

On New Year's Eve, a Suffolk County Grand Jury handed down ten indictments, carrying charges from neglect of duty to twenty counts of manslaughter. Barnett "Barney" Welansky and his brother, Jimmy, received the harshest charges. Indictments were distributed to such officials as Frank Linney and James Mooney. Also charged were interior designer Reuben Bodenhorn, and the construction contractor and construction foreman. Stanley Tomaszewski was officially exonerated of all blame.

Barney Welansky alone was found guilty on nineteen counts of manslaughter and was sentenced to twelve to fifteen years in prison. Nearly three years into his sentence, he was diagnosed with lung cancer. Governor Tobin, mayor of Boston at the time of the fire, quietly pardoned Welansky. When he walked out of prison, Barney was a sick, bitter man. While speaking with reporters, he told them "If you were wrongfully convicted, framed, you'd feel you had a perfect right to be free. I only wish I had been at the fire and died with those others." Welansky got his wish and died just nine weeks after being released from prison.

Stanley Tomaszewski died in 1994 at the age of 68. He had gone to college, married, and raised three children and led a responsible life as a federal auditor. No matter what he did or how he lived, he was never able to escape the shadow of the tragedy. He had escaped the fire without injury but was terribly scarred just the same. For decades, he had been called "every bad name in the book" and had received threats and phone calls in the night. Shortly before he died, he said he had suffered enough and wished to finally be left alone.

As we so often see, out of tragedies there sometimes comes a positive side. Within two years, new fire safety laws were passed for public gathering structures placing a ban on flammable decorations. Inward-swinging exit doors were no longer allowed, exit signs were to be visible at all times and revolving doors were to be flanked by regular swinging doors or they were to be retrofitted to fold flat in an emergency.

Several medical advancements came about as a direct result of the fire. Dr. Oliver Cope developed and tested new and innovative treatment methods for burn patients. These advancements were in four distinctive areas: fluid retention, infection prevention, treatment of respiratory trauma and skin surface and surgical management. These new treatments were credited with saving countless Cocoanut Grove victims, including the first use of Penicillin on a patient. Also, the first serious research was conducted into what we now know as Post Traumatic Stress Disorder.

The burned shell of the infamous Cocoanut Grove was finally demolished in September of 1945.

In 1996, Fire Modeling Specialist Doug Seller, working with the National Fire Protection Association (NFPA), attempted to develop a model to describe the fire's progression through the structure and possible alternative causes. Using modern technologies and improved understandings of fire dynamics and fuels, Seller determined that there might be another possible cause for the fire. In 1942, freon was the refrigerant of choice, however all freon was being allocated to the military for the war effort. The Cocoanut Grove was using Methyl Chloride as an alternative to cool its drinks, its food, and its customers.

Seller found several indicators pointing to the Methyl Chloride as being a significant factor in the fire, its rapid spread and the large number of deaths resulting from respiratory lesions. Doctors treating the survivors in 1942, noted that the inhalation traumas caused by the fire were strikingly similar to those caused by Phosgene, a toxic gas. Several survivors reported that something in the smoke smelled sweet and four others were able to protect their lungs by breathing through wet towels or napkins. When Methyl Chloride burns, it emits phosgene, smells sweet, and is water-soluble so it could be stopped by wet cloth.

The last clue might have been the most important. After the fire, inspectors found cracked and melted refrigerant tubing in the basement behind a false wall. This was the same wall that survivor Gloria Deagle Doherty had been leaning against just before the fire started and had described it as being very hot -- the same wall located directly behind the artificial palm tree containing the tiny light removed by an amorous sailor, the same palm tree in which young Stanley Tomaszewski needed to replace the light bulb. So, he lit a match...

Whether the fire was caused by a rupture in the refrigerant lines, by Stanley's match, or by a combination of the two, we can never be certain. But one has to wonder how this new theory might have affected Stanley, had he lived two more years, just long enough for the report to be made public.

Today, the streets that used to box the Cocoanut Grove nightclub have been reconfigured to allow for the construction of the Boston Radisson Hotel and Theater Complex. The Grove's original footprint has been swallowed up by the much larger hotel along with a tiny parking lot. The only physical reminder of what happened on the site is a small bronze plaque with the Cocoanut Grove's floor plan. The plaque was prepared as a memorial by the Bay Village Neighborhood Association and embedded in the brick sidewalk next to the parking lot in 1993.

Though all other physical reminders of the Cocoanut Grove are now gone, there are other reminders that still linger. Hopefully, most of those who lost their lives have moved on in peace. So many lives were snuffed out before they could know what was happening; bodies were found still sitting where they had been sitting or collapsed where they had been standing when the smoke and fumes found them. It is considered by many that these unfortunate victims are still wandering the site, trying to find their way to safety, or maybe discover a friend or loved one.  Several employees of the Boston Radisson Hotel might agree that they are. On a few occasions, people have witnessed strange appearances throughout the hotel. Disheveled and confused men or women, seeming to appear out of nowhere, wander past and disappear just as mysteriously. There have been other experiences reported in the hotel bar and in the kitchen, odd noises, flashes, and loud popping sounds, without any discernible cause.

The Stuart Street Playhouse, the Radisson's theatre, is another location where fire victims make their presence known. On occasion, the quiet, shadowy form of a man can be seen passing a doorway or walking down an empty hall. When approached by employees, he fades away to nothing. Other phenomena include water -- unexplained flooding in different areas within the building and a singular water faucet in a restroom on the second floor that reportedly turns itself on, even when no one is in the room. On one occasion, employees entered the auditorium and found a seat completely soaked, with no explanation. Others have described hearing their names called while working in the theatre at night, with no one else around.

It seems that not all of those who stayed behind after the fire remained at the Cocoanut Grove. Another Boston location believed to be haunted by victims of the fire is Jacques Cabaret, just a few blocks away from where the tragedy occurred. Not everyone at Jacques is willing to discuss the ghostly happenings there, but one former bartender said that, "spooky stuff happened there all the time." The most significant experience he had while working at the bar happened late one night when he was cleaning up after closing. He had left the bar area for a moment and when he returned, he saw bodies lying in long rows all across the floor. He turned to switch on the overhead lights and when he turned back, everything had returned to normal.

The night of the fire, as bodies were pulled from the building, some were taken directly to hospitals while others were taken to a temporary morgue or to one of the designated mortuaries. Many who were believed to be still alive and taken to hospitals were already dead, and conversely, some of those taken to the morgue or mortuaries were still alive. A film distribution garage located near the Cocoanut Grove was set up as a temporary morgue on the night of the fire. The bodies were laid out side by side in rows on the tile floor to await identification and transportation.  That garage is now known as Jacques Cabaret.

There is a record of every person who was killed or injured in the Cocoanut Grove fire, but there will never be a complete list of everyone who was inside when it started. Some of the people who escaped the building unharmed, or with only minor injuries, left the scene and went home. In this case, lists didn't matter. What bound these people together for the rest of their lives was the common experience. They went from joy and celebration to horror in a matter of seconds. Most of those who saved themselves lost someone dear. They had to contend with their own horrifying experience while simultaneously grieving their loss.  They wondered at the randomness of who was taken and who was spared. And none of them ever forgot...

# 1944: DEATH UNDER THE BIG TOP
# THE HARTFORD CIRCUS FIRE

On the hot, humid afternoon of July 6, 1944, a crowd of almost 9,000 people, mostly children, crowded under a huge tent in Hartford, Connecticut, for a special matinee performance of the Ringling Brothers, Barnum & Bailey Circus. Mothers and grandparents brought their young ones to the Barbour Street fairgrounds for a day of joy and merriment and to forget about the war overseas for a while. But later that afternoon, the day turned into horror and death as a fire broke out under the big top tent. The ensuing inferno killed 168 people and injured another 484. Five bodies still remain unclaimed and unknown in Hartford today. The Hartford Circus Fire would turn out to be the worst tragedy to ever occur in the history of the American circus.

The circus began its history in American in 1790. Since then, more than 1,000 circuses have toured the country and have become a part of colorful part of America that few can resist. In the first half of the twentieth century, the mere rumor that a circus might be coming to town was enough to excite every child in the community.

P.T. Barnum

Perhaps the best-known showman connected to the circus was Phineas Taylor Barnum, an eccentric promoter who became known for his novelty museums and engaging hoaxes. Barnum eventually became the founding father of the spectacular traveling show that would develop into the renowned Ringling Brothers, Barnum & Bailey Circus. Before leading the life of a showman, Barnum was a storekeeper and when he failed in business, he started a weekly magazine, which folded under the weight of several libel suits that landed him in prison.

In 1834, Barnum relocated to New York and one year later, he became involved in putting on shows. His first venture involved the exhibition of an African-American woman who was purported to be the 160-year-old nurse of George Washington (she wasn't) and he enjoy short-lived success with this exhibition. Unfortunately, his attraction died and her age was proven to be no more than 80.

Several years of failure followed and then, in 1841, he purchased Scudder's American Museum on Broadway in New York and he re-named it "Barnum's American Museum." Word quickly spread across the city about the numerous fascinating exhibits on display and it soon became one of the most popular attractions in New York.

In 1842, Barnum's museum became the talk of the town with exhibits like the midget "General Tom Thumb" and the Fiji Mermaid, a crudely concocted mummy, part monkey and part fish, which was alleged to be the preserved body of an actual mermaid. He also showcased the original Siamese twins, Chang and Eng Bunker, and continued to expand his offerings with the likes of Native American dancers and the giantess, Anna Swan.

Barnum may have been the first to promote the sort of exhibits that would become circus staples, but he was also the first to suffer the kinds of calamities that would also be connected to the circus – fires, train wrecks and storms. His museum burned so many times that it was nearly impossible for him to obtain fire insurance. But what would become the tradition of "the show must go on" always prevailed. After his museum burned the first time, he moved to a new building. However, a second fire put him out of business.

After the loss of his last museum, Barnum attempted to take a break from show business, but looming debt wouldn't allow him to leave. Finally, Barnum was convinced to create a partnership with William Cameron Coup, who owned a circus in Delavan, Wisconsin. With his famous name and Coup's financial backing, the "P.T Barnum's Grand Traveling Museum, Menagerie, Caravan & Hippodrome" was born. His closest competition at the time, James Bailey, would later become an ally.

In 1872, Barnum coined the phrase, "The Greatest Show on Earth," as his traveling circus and sideshow toured the world, undergoing a series of name changes and billings in the process. In 1881, a significant merger took place when Barnum joined forces with James Bailey and James L. Hutchinson. The original name, "P.T. Barnum's Greatest Show On Earth, And The Great London Circus, Sanger's Royal British Menagerie and The Grand International Allied Shows United" was shortened to "Barnum & London

Circus" for obvious reasons. A series of splits ensued until the "Barnum & Bailey Greatest Show on Earth" and later "Barnum & Bailey Circus" became the final name for the show.

When P.T. Barnum passed away in 1891, Bailey purchased the circus from his widow. He successfully toured the eastern part of the United States until he transported the circus to Europe in 1897 and began a lengthy tour of the continent. He remained abroad until 1902 and when he returned to the United States, he found that the Ringling Brothers, a new circus that had been formed by five brothers, had established a reputation in the east. The new rivalry forced Bailey to tour the Rockies for the first time during 1905. The next year, Bailey passed away and the Barnum's much-loved circus was sold to Ringling Brothers in 1907 for the sum of $400,000.

In a few short years, the Ringling Brothers show became the most popular circus in American. As was the method of the times, the circus traveled from town to town, setting up their tents and sideshows in whatever venue was available. They started out touring the Midwest, where they achieved great success, and eventually began traveling all over the United States. The circus eventually became so large that a train was needed to transport the bulk of their business. It is through this mode of transportation that the Ringling Brothers became known as the largest traveling show of their day.

The Ringlings purchased the Barnum & Bailey Circus in 1907 and kept the circuses separate for several years. In 1919, the last remaining Ringling Brothers, Charles and John, decided to combine the two circuses into one grand enterprise. The "Ringling Brothers and Barnum & Bailey Combined Shows" made its debut at Madison Square Garden in New York City on March 29, 1919.

Throughout the 1920s, the circus continued to generate great success and when Charles passed away in 1926, John Ringling became recognized as one of the richest men in the world. Although the circus was affected by the Great Depression of the early 1930s, it managed to do well, largely because people counted on the circus to take them away from their troubles for awhile. After the United States entered World War II, the lure of the circus stayed strong. Despite travel restrictions that were created by the war, President Franklin Roosevelt made a special declaration to allow the circus to use the rail system.

People still wanted to escape from reality, which is what they came seeking that July afternoon in Hartford, Connecticut.

**The circus arrived in Hartford**

July 6 was a hot day in Hartford, but no one wanted to miss the show. The previous day's performance had been cancelled because the circus had arrived six hours late from Providence, Rhode Island. The circus management had decided to offer a special afternoon show to make it up to the disappointed children and adults who had planned to come the night before.

People began arriving at the Barbour Street fairgrounds several hours before the circus was scheduled to begin. Children ate hot dogs and cotton candy and mothers purchased tickets for the sideshows and the rides. When it came time for the show to begin, thousands hurried into the tent while the Wonder Band played "The Star Spangled Banner."

The nineteen-ton big top tent was almost as wonderful an attraction as the animals and performers inside. The massive canvas tent had cost more than $60,000 and was carefully maintained by the circus crews. It had been weatherproofed the previous April with a coating of paraffin, thinned with gasoline, to keep out the rain. Most of the crowd sat on bleachers under the tent, while those with reserved seats sat on folding chairs in the front. On the long north side of the tent were three exits, although all of them were blocked with chutes that were used to bring the animals into the tent. On the south side were three additional exits, one of which was blocked with cables.

The performance began with Alfred Court's wild animal act, which was hugely popular with the crowd. As the animals were being escorted out through the steel enclosures that would take them back to their cages, the Flying Wallendas, the famed aerial act that was known for their seven-person pyramid on the high wire, were climbing the poles and getting ready for their performance. Emmett Kelly, America's most famous hobo clown, was busy going through his antics, which brought laughter to children and parents alike. He was one of the stars of the circus and a universal favorite. Ironically, he never smiled during a show, always making others laugh with his deadpan expression.

Suddenly, a cry of "fire!" was heard in the tent.

A spot of flame appeared on the tent at the main entrance. A Hartford police officer was on duty there and said that when he saw it, the hole was no bigger than a cigarette burn. Slowly, the tiny flame traveled up the canvas wall, increasing in size as it climbed toward the tent's roof. It was still a small fire at first and most of the performers and the audience were not even aware of it. The spotlights were focused on the Wallendas.

Merle Evans, the circus bandleader, saw the fire at about the same time the policeman saw it. He instantly led the band into a lively rendition of "Stars and Stripes Forever," the song traditionally used in the circus world to warn performers and circus employees that something was amiss under the big top.

Almost immediately, someone threw several buckets of water (which were kept in place inside the tent in case of just such an emergency) but it had no effect. Trainers tried desperately to hurry the wild animals out of the ring. All personnel knew that any impending tragedy would be made worse by animals in the tent's center. Unfortunately, time was lost when two leopards proved reluctant to leave. Trainers had to turn a water hose on them in order to prod them into the chutes. Meanwhile, the Wallendas had descended speedily on their ropes and were hurrying to safety.

The crowds who previously did not know that the band was playing the "disaster march" now were undecided whether to watch the trainers struggling with the animals or to watch the growing fire. Buckets of water were still being thrown on the blaze, which had now climbed to a height of five or six feet. Circus hands ran back and forth, trying to decide what to do. Perhaps this was why there was no panic from the audience – the fire was still small and it was being dealt with by people who surely knew what they were doing. Though the fire was still growing, and was about two feet in width, there was no mass migration toward the exits. Before that actually happened, a strong wind whipped into the enclosure and the fire suddenly swept across the top of the tent with alarming speed. It rose across the west end and moved toward the northeast corner. Soon, the "entire top became a mass of flames," as one witness later recalled.

Burning bits of canvas and liquid paraffin began to rain down onto the now-panicking crowd, inflicting severe burns on everyone they struck. The band gave up on their music and proceeded to march calmly from the tent in hopes of encouraging the audience to do the same – but it was too late for that. As support ropes burned, the tent's six huge poles began to fall, taking flaming pieces of canvas with them as they toppled over. Screams filled the tent as the frightened crowd began to run. Hundreds climbed around the circus wagons, stumbled over the animal chutes and became tangled in the metal folding chairs that had been tossed aside in front of the bleachers. Parents tossed their children into the open arms of strangers at the bottom of the grandstands. Some of these parents and children left the black smoke unscathed, while others were trampled and burned amid the confusion.

Many children, separated from their parents, wailed and screamed. One little boy tried to shield his fallen grandmother from the stampeding crowd, begging someone to help him get her to her feet. Pieces of flaming canvas continued to fall and women, their hair and dresses on fire, shrieked and wept. The human barricade that had been caused by the knocked-over folding chairs prevented many from reaching the exits. Many rushed to the entrances on the north side, only to arrive there and find them blocked by the animal chutes. Hundreds of bodies were later found piled there.

**The fire quickly began to burn out of control, engulfing the entire tent.**

One by one, the heavy support poles crashed over. As the sixth and final pole toppled, the entire tent, which was now engulfed in flames, swooped down on the crowd, blanketing them in fiery canvas. Those trapped and screaming beneath the collapsed tent were doomed and soon they fell silent. It had taken the fire only ten minutes from the time the first warning cry had gone up to wreak its havoc.

Sirens screamed at the five alarms triggered and fire trucks raced to the fairgrounds, but they were too late to save lives. All they could do was spray water on the charred ruins. To make matters worse, there were no hydrants on the fairgrounds and the firefighters had to use hydrants located almost three hundred yards away.

Ambulances lined up to take victims to the hospital. Hartford hospitals were prepared for such a disaster. It was wartime and major hospitals were instructed in burn treatment in case of enemy air raids. Victims were given morphine, wrapped in sheets and given plasma injections.

The dead numbered 168 – half of them children. All of them had come to the circus that day for an afternoon of carefree fun. All of the circus people escaped alive, although the Wallendas had barely made it out safety. The villainous and heroic acts of the fire became apparent in the hours, days and weeks following the disaster. Some threw chairs at others to clear from their escape route. Some jumped from the tops of the bleachers into the crowds of people, not knowing or caring if they hurt someone. On the other hand, Emmett Kelly, the famous clown, rallied performers to get buckets of water and help however they could. Some grabbed scared and crying children and stayed with them until they could be reunited with a loved one.

The aftermath of the fire was grim. The Connecticut State Armory was turned into a temporary morgue and families filed through, lifting white sheets and trying to identify the charred remains. State and city investigators followed clues about the causes of the fire, which ranged from a tossed cigarette, a motor that was left running near the tent that ran out of oil, and even arson. The likely cause was determined to be a cigarette that was tossed into some dry grass at the edge of the tent. The rapid spread of the fire was blamed on the improper weatherproofing of the canvas and the use of highly flammable materials. State investigators listed eight causes of the fire and issued citations to Ringling Brothers for various offenses, including failure to flameproof, location of the animal chutes, insufficiency of personnel, failure to maintain an organization to fight the fire,

**Mass funerals were held for the local victims of the fire but many believe that the dead still do not rest in peace.**

lack of firefighting equipment, failure to distribute firefighting equipment, and the location of the supply wagons. Five circus employees were charged with manslaughter and arrested and warrants were issued for four more. Later, seven of the defendants received one- year prison sentences. Legal claims against Ringling Brothers, Barnum & Bailey totaled nearly $4 million.

The fire captured America's attention in 1944 and was ranked tenth among all stories reported by the Associated Press that year. It was the only one not related to the war.

In Hartford and the Connecticut River Valley, the story was more than just a news report. It was a heartbreaking occurrence that touched almost every family in the region in one way or another. Flags flew at half-staff for weeks and funeral parlors were forced to hold services at fifteen-minute intervals. The burning of the big top on July 6, 1944 was the worst circus disaster in history and it continues to haunt the people of Hartford even now, more than 65 years later.

And not all of those haunting memories are physical scars, mental trauma and bad memories.

Several legends grew in the wake of the fire, including one that stated that the ghosts of the fire victims remained behind at the site of the tragedy. Two years after the fire, a housing project was erected nearby and many claimed the place was haunted. Residents told of hearing screams, strange cries, disembodied weeping and they spoke of seeing apparitions of people who seemed to be smoldering, or on fire. One man stated that he was unlocking his door one night and looked up to see a little boy go running past his apartment. The boy left a trail of smoke behind him, as though his clothing was burning. The man dropped the bag of groceries that he was carrying and hurried off to see if the boy needed help. When he turned the corner in the direction the "burning boy" had gone, he was shocked to see there was no one there. The man who recounted the story had recently moved to Hartford and was unaware that the 1944 fire had occurred a short distance away.

A few years later, the housing project, which had been a temporary arrangement to ease the home shortage being experienced by returning war veterans, was torn down and replaced by a school. The weird haunting tales also plagued the school and it was generally accepted that the ghosts were victims of the fire.

A memorial to the fire victims now stands at the site and some say the ghosts remain, lingering at the place where their lives were cut short so tragically.

# 1958: INNOCENCE LOST
# THE OUR LADY OF ANGELS FIRE

There is no question that the most soul-crushing type of fire is one that claims innocent children as its victims. There have been far too many school fires in the history of America and one of the most devastating occurred in Chicago on December 1, 1958. On that day, 92 children and three nuns died in a fire on the West Side of the city at the Our Lady of Angels School. The horrific event shattered scores of lives on that day and the neighborhood where the school was located has never fully recovered.

Our Lady of Angels was located at 3820 West Iowa Street. It was surrounded by a quiet Catholic parish of about 4,500 families from mostly Irish and Italian backgrounds. They lived modestly in apartments and brick bungalows until after the fire, when many of these hardworking families abandoned the neighborhood, never to return.

On December 1, between 1,200 and 1,300 students were sitting through their last hour of classes for the day at the parochial school. The fire started around 2:25 p.m., about twenty minutes before class was going to be dismissed. Like many other schools of that era, Our Lady of Angels was tragically without many of the safety measures that exist today. The forty-year-old building had no smoke detectors, no sprinkler systems, no outside fire alarm and the building had only one fire escape. Unbelievably, the school had passed a fire inspection two months before. By 1958 standards, the building was legally safe.

Two students on an errand returned to their classroom and said that they smelled smoke. The teacher took them seriously and after consulting with a teacher in the room next door, both decided to evacuate their students. The rest of the school was not, at this time, alerted to the fire. The two classes left the building – one using the fire escape, the other an inside staircase – and reported to the church, which was on the same grounds. The janitor entered the school building and noticed that it was on fire. He told the parish housekeeper to call the fire department. It was suggested later that she may have delayed calling for a few minutes since an alarm was not received until 2:42 p.m. This was the same time that the building's fire alarm was also sounded. It was a manual alarm and not connected to the fire department. This was the first warning received by the rest of the school that the building was in danger.

It is believed that the fire started in a trash can at the bottom of the basement stairwell. There, it smoldered for a good part of the day and then spread to the stairs, thanks to air from an open window. Once it was ignited, the fire quickly spread and burned up to the second floor, devouring the building as it went. By the time the first fire trucks arrived, the upper floor of the north wing was engulfed in flames. The fire had already been burning for a number of minutes before the alarm went off and more precious time was lost when the fire department trucks mistakenly pulled up to the church rectory, and not the school. The dispatchers had been given the wrong address by the person who phoned in the report. Then, when the first trucks arrived at the school, they had to break through a locked gate to get inside.

**Two photographs taken in front of the school on the day of the fire. As firefighters battled the blaze, worried neighbors and desperate parents flooded the area.**

Inside the classrooms, which were rapidly filling with smoke, the students heard the sound of the fire trucks approaching, but then nothing, as the trucks went to the rectory instead. At that desperate moment, the nuns asked the children to bow their heads in prayer. When the trucks finally arrived, and the extent of the blaze was realized, another alarm was sent out, ordering all available vehicles to the scene. Before it was over, 43 pieces of fire equipment were at the school.

When the firefighters arrived, they saw children calling for help from the second-story windows. Since it was the rescue of the children that most concerned the firemen on their arrival, the fire continued to spread and eventually burned off a large portion of the roof.

Occupants on the first floor of the school were safely evacuated in orderly fire drill formation but the situation was more difficult on the upper floor, which was now filled with thick clouds of smoke. The fire escape had become unreachable through the burning hallways. The only way out was through the windows and soon, screaming children were plunging to the frozen ground below. The desperate firemen, icicles hanging from their helmets, behaved heroically and managed to save one hundred and sixty children by pulling them out the windows, passing them down ladders, catching them in nets, and breaking their falls with their own bodies. One rescuer who climbed a ladder up to the building's second floor was Lieutenant Charles Kamin. When he reached the window of Room 211, he found a number of eighth graders were crammed together and trying to squeeze out. He reached inside and, one a time, began grabbing them, swinging them around his back and dropping them onto the ladder. He saved nine children, mostly boys, because he could grab hold of their belts. He was only stopped when the room exploded and the students fell back out of his reach.

In one classroom, the children were so gripped with fear that they refused to leave. The teacher instructed them to crawl to the staircase and she pushed them down and out, saving the entire class. Math was being taught in another room when the fire broke out. The quick-thinking teacher ordered the students to pile books around the doors where the smoke could seep in. She told them to put their desks in front of the doors to keep out the smoke and the tremendous amount of heat that was starting to come in. The alarm had not been sounded at that point, so she convinced all of her students to loudly chant in unison that the school was on fire; that way, she told them, they would help by alerting students and teachers in other classrooms who might not know what was going on. By keeping the children occupied, and by quick actions that increased their confidence in her, she was able to keep them calm while they awaited rescue. Some safely jumped to a staircase a few feet below, while others waited at the window for fire department ladders. After all of the students had been rescued, the teacher descended the ladder. Even though this room was heavily damaged by smoke and fire, only one child died. The

Heroic firefighter Richard Scheidt, who later became Captain of Engine 121, carries the body of a young boy from the school.

A priest delivers Last Rites over the body of a deceased child.

students in the classroom across the hall were not so fortunate – the teacher and 29 students burned to death.

A nine-year-old girl named Margaret Chambers had stayed home that morning with a cold but she hated missing school and begged her mother to let her go for the afternoon session. Her mother, Rose Chambers, agreed and Margaret never returned home.

Max Stachura, father of a nine-year-old boy who attended Our Lady of Angels, rushed to the school as soon as he heard about the fire. He was able to save twelve children by either catching them as they jumped or breaking their falls. He couldn't save his son, Mark, however. He found the boy standing at the window of his classroom and shouted for him to jump. Mark either didn't understand what his father wanted him to do or was too frightened to jump. He perished in the fire.

Firemen groped their way through smoke and fire, searching for children who might be trapped. Hallways and rooms were filled with smoke and gases but the firemen remained, looking in every room for signs of life. They found many groups of children still alive but, unfortunately, they were too late for many. They fought their way into one classroom to find 24 children sitting dead at their desks, their books open in front of them. It was a scene that members of the rescue party would never forget.

The scene outside the school was one of chaos. Between children jumping from windows and screams and cries for help, firefighters also had to deal with the terrified parents who began to arrive. They hampered the efforts of the firefighters as they rushed the police lines, hysterically trying to reach their children who were trapped in the building. It took the crew a little over an hour to put out the fire. The blaze had consumed the second-story classrooms, claiming the lives of dozens of children and nuns.

For the hundreds of parents and relatives who stood outside, the huge loss of life was soon apparent as cloth-covered stretchers began to emerge from the smoldering building. A long line of ambulances and police squadrons slowly collected the bodies and took them to the Cook County Morgue, where family members could identify them. Confusion and mystery made the tragedy even worse. Many parents had no idea if their children were dead or alive. Some of them were discovered standing in the street outside the school. Others were given shelter in nearby homes. However, many parents had no choice but to search the seven hospitals to which the injured were taken or, worse yet, to wait in the grim line at the county morgue.

Chicago was stunned by the appalling loss of life and word of the disaster spread around the world. In Rome, Pope John XXIII sent a personal message to the archbishop of Chicago, the Most Reverend Albert Gregory Meyer. Four days later, Meyer conducted a mass for the victims and their families before an altar set up at the Northwest Armory. He called the fire "a great and inescapable sorrow."

Nearly as tragic as the fire itself was the fact that no blame was ever placed for the disaster. In those days, there was no thought of suing those responsible (the Catholic Church, which ran the school) for the conditions that allowed the fire to happen. Outwardly, the families accepted the idea that the fire had been simply "God's will," but it cannot be denied that a number of those involved left the Church, their faith as shattered as their lives. No one dared to challenge the Church over what happened and life moved quietly on.

But in January 1962, the fire was news again when police in Cicero questioned a thirteen-year-old boy about a series of fires that had been set in the city. When they learned that he had been a troubled student at Our Lady of Angels at the time of the fire, their interrogations took another direction. The boy's mother and stepfather hired an attorney, who recommended that the boy submit to a polygraph test.

In the interview, polygraph expert John Reid learned that the boy began starting fires at the age of five, when he set his family's garage alight. He had also set as many as eleven fires in buildings in Chicago and Cicero, usually by tossing burning matches on papers at the bottom of staircases. This was exactly how most believed the Our Lady of Angels fire started and so Reid pressed him harder. The boy denied starting the fire at first, but test results indicated that he was lying. Later, the boy admitted that he had set the blaze, hoping for a few extra days out of school. He said he hated his teachers and his principal because they "always wanted to expel me from school." His attendance record had been poor and his behavior was described as "deplorable."

In his confession, he said that he had started the fire in the basement after leaving his classroom to go to the bathroom. He threw three lit matches into a trashcan and then ran upstairs to his second-floor classroom, which was soon evacuated. When Reid asked him why he had never told anyone about setting fire to the school, the boy replied, "I was afraid my dad was going to give me a beating and I'd get in trouble with the police and I'd get the electric chair or something."

Reid turned the confession over to the police and the boy was placed in the Arthur J. Audy Juvenile Home. Charges were filed against him, but after a series of hearings that ended in March 1962, Judge Alfred Cilella tossed out the boy's confession, ruling that Reid had obtained it illegally. Also, since the boy was under the age of thirteen at the time of the fire, he could not be tried for a felony in Illinois. He did charge the boy with starting the fires in Cicero, and he was sent away to a home for troubled boys in Michigan. The boy's identity has never been released, but there are those who know it. Despite pleas from surviving family members of the Our Lady of Angels victims, it has never been publicly released.

Despite the passage of time, the fire has never been forgotten. A new parish school was constructed on the site in 1960, but it was closed in 1999 because of declining enrollment. The only memorial to the victims of the fire is located in Queen of Heaven Cemetery in Hillside, where 25 of the victims are buried. It was constructed from private donations in 1960 and to this date, no official memorial to the fire has been erected.

For those who survived the fire, or lost friends or family members to the blaze, the Our Lady of Angels disaster remains a haunting memory that has been impossible to shake. To this day, they continue to hold reunions and services in memory of those who died, and many of those with connections to the fire tell strange stories and personal experiences with those who died in 1958.

One woman recounted how her parents were relieved to see that she and her brother had survived the fire when they found them on the street outside the school. Her mother later told her that, shortly after arriving, she saw her son running from the building and heading toward his parents. He had a big smile on his face, thrilled to have escaped the burning school with his life. The parents and son became separated in the confusion and after the fire was out, they were unable to find the boy. Hours later, it was learned that he had died in his second-floor classroom and had not left the school at all. Until the day she died, the woman's mother was convinced that she saw her son outside the school that day.

Others with a first-hand connection to the fire have also spoken of encounters with loved ones who did not survive. Mothers claimed their children came to visit them and some who were children at the time of the fire stated that they were consoled by perished brothers and sisters, who stayed only briefly before moving on. Some visitors to the fire memorial at Queen of Heaven Cemetery say that they sometimes smell the strong presence of smoke nearby.

Are such stories merely imagination, or perhaps wishful thinking? No one can say for sure, but there is no denying that the Our Lady of Angels Fire remains one of the most poignant and heart-breaking in Chicago's history and will continue to be a wound that cannot be healed for many years to come.

# WATER

## 1853: THE SINKING OF THE SAN FRANCISCO

In 1848, Americans began a mass exodus to the wild frontier of the region known as California. Nearly all of them had one thing on their minds: gold. At Sutter's Mill, just northeast of Sacramento, workers accidentally discovered the precious metal, sparking a gold fever that stretched all the way back to the eastern states. Prospectors and fortune seekers – often referred to as "49ers" since the gold rush began in earnest in 1849 – began flooding the state.

Ships offered the fastest form of transportation to California. The land route could take months for a prospector who wanted to get rich quick and so most favored travel by sea. In those pre-Panama Canal days, there were two methods of water travel to the West Coast. The first was to go around the continent of South America. The other was to cross the isthmus of Panama from the Gulf of Mexico to the Pacific and board a vessel bound for California. Once in California, the gold fields beckoned. In fact, so many sailors jumped ship to run to the gold fields that crews for ships were scarce. A ghost fleet of abandoned and unmanned vessels was anchored in San Francisco Bay.

With the number of ships making the trip to California at one time, it's not surprising that tragedy sometimes occurred. The *Winfield Scott* was one of the many vessels that helped bring prospectors to the West. Sent to California in 1850, she shuttled passengers back and forth between Panama and San Francisco. She was a modern, well-constructed ship.

In early December 1853, she was bound from San Francisco to Panama where the passengers would disembark. After leaving the vessel, the passengers would cross the isthmus to the Gulf of Mexico and board ships for the journey to their final destination. The steamer sailed through the foggy channel at top speed. The captain, Simon Blunt, boldly asserted that fog does not slow a steamship. Blunt had helped survey the waters for the government a few years earlier and knew them well.

During the evening and into the night, the ship passed the islands of San Miguel, Santa Rosa, and Santa Cruz. At about 11:00 p.m., it grounded bow-first on a submerged ledge close to the north side of Anacapa's middle island. The impact jarred the hundreds of passengers out of their sleep and most fled to the deck, where ship's officers moved about in the darkness, trying to restore calm and reassuring the passengers that everything was all right. Passengers returned to their cabins and grabbed saddlebags and satchels filled with gold – just in case the ship went down.

Meanwhile, Captain Blunt worked to back the ship off the ledge but the stern collided with a rock and the rudder was torn away. Water soon began pouring into gaping holes in the bow. The *Winfield Scott* soon began to sink and Blunt knew that the ship was doomed. Members of the crew began lowering lifeboats and trying to keep the passengers from rushing into them. The passengers stayed on a few outcroppings of rock until morning. As the sun rose, a beach was found and the castaways established a shore camp, salvaged what they could, and shot seals and caught fish for food. Within a few days, the rescue of the more than three hundred passengers began.

Luckily, no one was killed in the incident, but the same cannot be said for the worst disaster of this era, the sinking of the *San Francisco,* a steamer that was being used to ferry passengers from the East to California in 1853.

On December 22, 1853, the *San Francisco* departed from New York City on its maiden voyage, bound for San Francisco. She had 718 passengers and crew on board. Unlike many ships that were carrying prospectors bound for the gold fields of the region, the *San Francisco* had been chartered by the U.S. government to transport eight companies of the Army's 3rd Artillery Regiment, along with officers and their families, to the West Coast. The recent influx of settlers and gold hunters had created chaos in the area and the soldiers were being sent to maintain order.

The *San Francisco* was designed by William H. Webb for the firm of Aspinwall & Co. One of America's foremost naval architects and builders, Webb designed clipper ships, warships and steamships. William Henry Aspinwall was a businessman who owned the Pacific Mail Steamship Company, which had received the government contracts to deliver mail to the West Coast of the United States. He also founded the Panama Railroad in Central America, the aim of which was to cut traveling time between New York and California by eliminating the need to sail all the way around the tip of South America. Ships would journey southward along the Atlantic coast to Panama, transfer mail and passengers by rail to the Pacific side, and then ferry the cargo northward by ship up the West Coast to California. The *San Francisco* was built with the intention of it serving the West Coast leg of the trip after its maiden voyage around Cape Horn.

The ship was innovative for the time. It was two hundred and eighty feet long and had three decks, including a super-structure above the hull that housed a main saloon. The ship was powered by two oscillating steam engines that turned two 28-foot diameter paddle wheels, each capable of producing 1,000 horsepower. A massive ship, the *San Francisco* had stateroom accommodations for three hundred and fifty people and steerage berths for an additional 1,000.

Under the command of Captain James Watkins, the ship left New York on Thursday, December 22. The passengers were mostly Army personnel, including officers and their families. Only about half of the available passenger space was being used. The rest of it was filled with military equipment and supplies that were meant to last the regiment for a year.

About 36 hours out of port, the ship encountered strong gales as it headed south. The first officer, Edward Mellus, later testified that in his twenty years at sea, it was the heaviest storm that he had ever seen. The seas had first turned rough on Friday afternoon but by 3:00 a.m. on Christmas morning, the mainmast was lost and the rudder chain was broken. Thirty minutes later, the engines failed and the foremast was lost, causing the ship to swing broadside to the seas. Because of the extra military cargo below deck, soldiers were forced out of the berthing area to the saloon on the upper deck. About 9:00 a.m., a huge wave crashed onto the *San Francisco* and swept off all of the upper works, taking with it all of the lifeboats and about one hundred and sixty people, including officers, women and children and nearly one hundred soldiers. Most were probably killed instantly by the crush of timbers from the collapsed saloon and those that weren't drowned beneath the waves. Survivors later stated that they heard no cries for help and saw no one struggling in the sea.

The *San Francisco* floundered for three days, during which time more than sixty of the remaining passengers died from an outbreak of cholera. Newspaper accounts of the time stated that the outbreak was induced by overindulgence on preserved meats and pickles that were taken from a storeroom on the ship.

On December 28, the *Kilby,* a commercial ship from Boston, came upon the ship and lay over until about one hundred of the passengers from the *San Francisco* could be brought on board. Unfortunately, the *Kilby* was too small to carry any more but crew members promised to alert the authorities, and any other ships it encountered, of the remaining wreck victims' plight.

On December 31, another ship, the *Three Bells* from Glasgow, arrived. This ship had also been through the storm and was leaking badly. Short of provisions, Captain Creighton of the *Three Bells* refused to leave the scene and remained on hand, doing what he could to aid the sick and dying for four days. Soon after, the *Antarctic,* a New York ship bound for Liverpool arrived. The two ships rescued the remaining 398 survivors, after which the *San Francisco* sank beneath the waves.

The ship's fate was relayed by telegraph as soon as the survivors made it to shore on January 6. This was the first time that news of a maritime disaster had been transmitted by wire in the United States.

# 1854: WOMEN AND CHILDREN LAST
# THE WRECK OF THE *ARCTIC*

One of the greatest maritime disasters of the nineteenth century was the wreck of the *S.S. Arctic* in 1854. The steamship went down in heavy fog off the coast of Newfoundland on September 27 after colliding with a French fishing ship, the *Vesta.* Nearly three hundred passengers and crew members, all from the *Arctic,* perished in the accident, which stunned the public on both sides of the Atlantic.

And what made the disaster so shocking was that not a single woman or child aboard the ship survived. Lurid tales of panic aboard the sinking ship were widely publicized in newspapers. Members of the crew had seized the lifeboats and saved themselves, leaving helpless passengers, including eighty women and children, to perish in the icy North Atlantic.

It was a tragedy that destroyed a steamship company and changed the custom of the sea forever.

The *Arctic* had been built in New York City, at a shipyard at the foot of 12th Street on the East River, and was launched in early 1850. It was one of four ships of the new Collins Line, an American steamship company determined to compete with the powerful British steamship line run by Samuel Cunard.

The businessman behind the new company, Edward Knight Collins, had two wealthy backers, James and Stewart Brown of the Wall Street investment bank of Brown Brothers and Company. Collins had managed to get a contract from the American government that would subsidize the new steamship line as it would carry the U.S. mail between New York and Britain. Collins Line steamers could cross the Atlantic in nine or ten days and since they carried mail, they had to make at least twenty crossing each year.

When the Collins Line began sailing its four new ships in 1850, it quickly gained a reputation as the most stylish way to cross the Atlantic. The *Arctic*, and her sister ships, *Atlantic*, *Pacific*, and *Baltic*, were hailed for being plush as well as reliable. The ships were designed for both speed and comfort. The *Arctic* was 284 feet long, a very large vessel for its time, and its steam engines powered large paddle wheels on either side of its hull. Containing spacious dining rooms, saloons, and staterooms, the *Arctic* offered luxurious accommodations never before seen on a steamship.

The company benefited from the outbreak of the Crimean War in 1854 because Cunard Line ships were requisitioned by the British government for military uses. The *Arctic* disaster, however, would destroy this temporary advantage.

On September 13, 1854, the *Arctic* arrived in Liverpool after an uneventful trip from New York. Passengers departed the ship, and a cargo of American cotton, destined for British mills, was offloaded. On its return trip to New York the *Arctic* would be carrying some important passengers, including the manager of the line, Edward Knight Collins, his wife, and one of their sons. Also along on the voyage was Willie Luce, the sickly eleven-year-old son of the ship's captain, James Luce. They would be joined by one hundred and fifty crew members and 233 passengers.

The *Arctic* sailed from Liverpool on September 20, and for a week it steamed across the Atlantic in its usual reliable manner. On the morning of September 27, the ship was off the Grand Banks, the area of the Atlantic off Canada where warm air from the Gulf Stream hits cold air from the north, creating thick walls of fog. Visibility was only about one-half to three-quarters of a mile, according to the testimony of Captain Luce. He ordered lookouts to keep a close watch for other ships but despite the conditions, he kept the ship at her top cruising speed of 13 knows. This order followed company directions that high speed be maintained in order to keep trip time to a minimum and to clear fog conditions as quickly as possible.

Shortly after noon, lookouts sounded alarms. Another ship had suddenly emerged from the fog, and the two vessels were on a collision course. The other ship was a French steamer, the *Vesta*, which was transporting French fishermen from Canada to France at the end of the summer's fishing season. The ship carried fifty crew members and 147 fishermen. The propeller-driven *Vesta* had been built with a steel hull, which made it a terrible danger to the wooden-hulled *Arctic*.

Due to the high rate of speed of both vessels, the foggy conditions and their head-on course – the *Arctic* westbound and the *Vesta* eastbound – a collision became unavoidable. The *Vesta* rammed the bow of the *Arctic*, and in the collision, the steel bow of the *Vesta* acted like a battering ram, spearing the *Arctic's* wooden hull before snapping off. The impact tore a five-foot hole in the *Arctic's* bow below the waterline and two smaller holes above the waterline. The crew and passengers of the *Arctic*, which was the larger of the two ships, believed the *Vesta*, with its bow torn away, was going to sink. Yet the *Vesta*, because its steel hull was built with several interior compartments, was actually able to stay afloat.

The *Arctic*, with its engines still steaming, sailed onward. When it became clear that the damage would doom the ship, Captain Luce ordered the vessel to make its best speed toward shore. This decision ran contrary to an unwritten rule of the sea to aid other ships in distress. Leaving the *Vesta* to its own fate, the *Arctic* proceeded at 15 knots toward land.

Unfortunately, the damage from the collision proved fatal for the ship. Two hours after leaving the *Vesta* to her own devices, the rising water in the engine room put out the boiler fires. The paddlewheels stopped and the ship began to sink.

The *Arctic* only carried six lifeboats. Yet had they been carefully deployed and filled, they could have held approximately one hundred and eighty people, or almost all the passengers, including all the women and children aboard. Launched haphazardly, however, the lifeboats were barely filled and were generally taken over entirely by crew members. Passengers, left to fend for themselves, tried to fashion rafts or cling to pieces of wreckage. Many drowned in the frigid water.

The *Arctic's* captain, James Luce, who had tried to save the passengers and crew by steaming toward land and had tried to get the panicking and rebellious crew under control, went down with the ship, standing atop one of the large wooden boxes housing a paddle wheel. In a quirk of fate, the structure broke loose underwater, and quickly bobbed to the top, saving the captain's life. He clung to the wood and was rescued by a passing ship two days later. His son, Willie, perished.

The next day, two nearby ships, the *Huron* and the *Lebanon*, rescued the survivors from the *Arctic*. The most reliable estimate is that about three hundred people died in the sinking of the *Arctic*, including every woman and child aboard. It is believed 23 male passengers and about sixty crew members survived. Mary Ann Collins, wife of the Collins Line's founder, Edward Knight Collins, drowned, as did two of their children. Collins himself survived.

Word of the shipwreck began to hum along telegraph wires in the days following the disaster. The Vesta reached a port in Canada and its captain told the story. And as survivors of the Arctic were located, their accounts began to fill newspapers. The tragedy hit the public quite hard, mostly due to stories of cowardice by crew members. The fact that no women or children survived did not sit well with the American public. In a search for heroes in the disaster newspapers noted the bravery of young Stewart Holland, who stood on the sinking ship's deck firing the distress cannon, until the ship went under water. Holland did not survive.

Captain Luce was rescued by the *Cambria* on September 29. He never went to sea again. He was, however, hailed as a hero, and when he traveled from Canada to New York City aboard a train, he was greeted at every stop. However, other crew members of the Arctic were disgraced, and some never returned to the United States.

A grand jury investigation into the disaster in 1855 determined that the *Arctic* had too few lifeboats for its passengers, even though it was following maritime regulations of the day, and too few crew members who knew how to handle the boats. New shipping lanes were created for east- and westbound ships but were only used by the Navy for many years. Fixed routes for steamships were not adopted until 1898.

Cunard ships returned to the transatlantic passenger trade at the end of the Crimean War in 1856. Renewed competition from the British line, as well as the loss of the *Arctic* (and the scandal surrounding the disaster) and the disappearance of the *Pacific*, a second Collins Line ship, in the North Atlantic in 1856, pushed the firm into bankruptcy one year later.

Even with the Collins Line gone, the memory of the *Arctic* tragedy refused to go away. Public outrage over the treatment of the women and children aboard the ship resonated for decades, and led to the familiar tradition of saving "women and children first" being enforced in other maritime disasters.

# 1865: THE SINKING OF THE *S.S. SULTANA*

In the dark of night on April 27, 1865, nearly 1,800 souls were either blown apart, burned by fire, scorched by steam or drowned in the cold waters of the Mississippi River. The explosion and subsequent sinking of the *SS Sultana* became the worst maritime disaster in America's history - and arguably the least known. How is it possible for such a horrific accident to go nearly unnoticed at the time, and remain unknown or forgotten even today? The answer is really quite simple: the *SS Sultana* was a victim of the times.

When the *Sultana* exploded and sank, the country had been embroiled in the death and destruction of the Civil War for over four years. People had become accustomed to the long lists of the dead following battles during which soldiers were killed by the thousands. People were weary of war and death; tragedies became statistics.

The same month that the *Sultana* sank, the country had experienced extreme highs and extreme lows. On April 9 at Appomattox Courthouse, Virginia, General Robert E. Lee surrendered to General Ulysses Grant, essentially ending the Civil War and the long years of bloodshed. Just five days later, the North reeled in shock as news of the assassination of President Lincoln spread. Over the next few weeks, the country was consumed with the drama surrounding the burial of President Lincoln and the hunt for his killer, John Wilkes Booth, who was finally captured and killed on April 26. That same day, General Joseph Johnson surrendered the last of the Confederate Army. In the South, remnants of the Union army searched for and captured Confederate President Jefferson Davis and much of his cabinet.

The war was over. The President was dead. His killer was dead. There was a new President in the White House. Confederate President Davis was in prison. Tens of thousands of soldiers from both sides headed home. Half of the country rejoiced while the other half worried about how to rebuild. Newspapers in both the North and the South were filled with such stories. News of the sinking of a steamboat on the Mississippi was relegated to the back pages, if mentioned at all.

The loss of life from the Sultana disaster was tragic indeed, but the true sense of tragedy deepened with the death list. Nearly all of those who perished were Union soldiers on their way home, having been recently released from the most notorious Confederate POW camps: Andersonville and Cahaba (aka Cahawba).

The *Sultana* was a wooden, sidewheel-design steamship constructed in 1863 in Cincinnati, Ohio. She weighed 1,710 tons, carried a crew of 85 and had

a legal passenger limit of 376. She was built to run the cotton route between St. Louis and New Orleans, although she had been frequently commissioned by the U.S. Department of War for troop transport.

In late April 1865, the government was making every effort to get Union soldiers home, especially the former POWs. A commission of $5 per soldier was offered to all steamships headed north on the Mississippi River from Vicksburg, Mississippi (the port city closest to the Confederate prison camps) to Cairo, Illinois. The arrangement created opportunity for corruption among riverboat captains and the Union officers in charge of loading the boats.

The *Sultana* was piloted by Captain J. Cass Mason of St. Louis, who had a reputation of being a "good and careful riverman." She left New Orleans headed for Vicksburg on April 21 with 75 to one hundred passengers on board, along with a sizable amount of cargo to be unloaded at Vicksburg. Unfortunately, by the time the *Sultana* reached Vicksburg, she had a seriously leaking boiler with a badly bulging boiler plate that would need to be repaired or replaced before she could continue on.

At the Vicksburg dock, the steamships were loaded with soldiers in the order in which they arrived. When the *Sultana* steamed in on the 24th, she was last in line. Captain Mason made an ominous decision to hastily patch the bulging boiler plate, rather than to replace the plate entirely, which would take up to three days to complete. It was more profitable to be able to leave sooner, to cash in on the traveling soldiers, who were in a hurry to return to their loved ones. The soldiers would eventually be picked up by the steamboats scheduled to arrive within the next two days. If this happened, the *Sultana* would miss out on the financial bonanza.

With the hasty repair completed, the former POWs could be loaded onto the ship. The government commission of $5 per soldier was big money in those days, so the captains wanted to carry as many of these men as they could. To do this, the captains paid a kickback of between $1.00 and $1.15 per soldier to the officers in charge of loading the boats. Even though they knew of the *Sultana's* boiler problems, the officers could not resist the lucrative deal made with Captain Mason. The captain claimed he had carried that many men before without a problem; they believed Captain Mason to be a capable man and trusted that the *Sultana* was a good sound ship.

When the *Sultana* steamed out of Vicksburg at 9:00 p.m. on April 24, she was carrying nearly 2,400 people. She had been built to carry only 372. At least 2,134 of these passengers were Union soldiers, returning home after being released from prison camps. The men were tightly packed on the hurricane (top) deck, the second deck, and the main (bottom) deck. There was scarcely room for them to move about or even sit down. This forced them to sleep sitting or standing while leaning against each other. However, these circumstances seemed minor after their experiences in combat and later as prisoners of war. They gladly accepted their plight with hopes of a rapid return to home and family.

Adding to their discomfort, most of the men were in extremely weakened states, suffering from severe malnutrition and disease caused by the hardships of war and their incarceration in the Confederate prison camps. Andersonville, officially named Camp Sumter and Castle Morgan, also known as Cahaba, were notorious for the

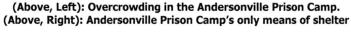

**(Above, Left): Overcrowding in the Andersonville Prison Camp.**
**(Above, Right): Andersonville Prison Camp's only means of shelter**

**(Left) Infamous photograph of a survivor of Andersonville Prison Camp.**
**After his release, he was returned to his family.**

deplorable conditions in which the prisoners were forced to live. The camps, vastly overcrowded, were essentially open pens with no shelter, other than makeshift tents built by the prisoners. In Andersonville, the only source of drinking water was from a small stream that ran through the camp. The stream was also used for washing and often as a latrine by the prison guards who were posted upstream from the camp. Food rations were small and soldiers who did not succumb to disease died of starvation. Similar conditions existed in Union prison camps but were much less noted by the general public.

Shortly before the end of the war, both sides initiated a prisoner exchange that continued to the end. This resulted in reduced overcrowding but the conditions were still horrible. The prisoners released at the end of the war were weak, malnourished and diseased from living in the camps. These were the men who boarded the *Sultana* for that fateful trip.

Although the Sultana passengers came from all over the Union, more than seven hundred were from Ohio, including Companies C and G of the 115th Ohio Volunteer Infantry. These men seemed to have led charmed lives for most of the war, given special duty safeguarding Union bridges and instillations. However, later in the war they were captured almost en mass and taken to Andersonville and Cahaba. Nearly all survived their time as prisoners only to end their days in the dark, frigid waters of the Mississippi River.

With great difficulty, the drastically overloaded ship was able to maneuver away from the Vicksburg wharf and started her steam upriver. The currents were much stronger than usual as spring rains had swollen the Mississippi nearly to flood stage and her waters were icy cold, making her progress slow and sluggish. Despite all this, the next 48 hours were fairly uneventful with a single exception.

The *Sultana* narrowly avoided disaster during a short stop at Helena, Arkansas, when a photographer set up his camera to take a photograph of the ship and the men aboard. When the men learned of the photographer, many of them moved to the shore side of the ship to be in the photo. The ship was so severely overloaded that the weight of the men moving to one side nearly caused the *Sultana* to capsize there at the dock. That would have been a potential disaster in itself, but the death toll would have been significantly lower.

The ship made a few more scheduled stops before docking at Memphis to take on coal on April 26. The problem boiler, again leaking badly, needed to be repaired. Yet again, Captain

**The photograph of the Sultana, taken in Helena, Arkansas, just days**

Mason opted to have a quick patch job done rather than the major repair. Because of the delay for the repair, some soldiers seized the chance to go into Memphis to see the sights. A few of them, not knowing at the time how lucky they were, didn't make it back to the ship in time and were left stranded on the dock. Repairs completed, the *Sultana* cast off from the Memphis wharf at midnight. Less than two and a half hours later she was gone.

The *Sultana* struggled to make headway against the strong current of the flood waters. Her paddle wheels churned up the water as she rounded a bend in the river and headed for a series of small islands known as the "Hen and Chickens" just seven miles outside Memphis. The passengers had had time to settle down again, and one supposes, were trying to get some sleep, when her first boiler blew just after two in the morning.

As the men were resting, a monstrous explosion rent the night air. Arthur A. Jones, a survivor of the *Sultana* disaster later wrote, "What a crash! My God! My blood curdles while I write, and words are inadequate; no tongue or writer's pen can describe it. Such hissing of steam, the crash of the different decks as they came together with the tons of living freight, the falling of the massive smokestacks, the death cry of strong-hearted men caught in every conceivable manner."

The initial blast destroyed much of the ship, killing many men instantly and sending many more into the frigid Mississippi waters. Most of the men who found themselves blasted into the river couldn't swim or were too weak or sick to hold out for long. The force of the explosion caused the *Sultana's* two smoke stacks to smash onto the hurricane deck, which collapsed, crushing several hundred men. When the deck collapsed it created a steep ramp upon which a number of men and pieces of wreckage slid down into the hottest part of the fire. Burning coals were blasted onto the remaining deck, setting the ship on fire. The second and third boilers exploded within minutes of the first. Passengers remaining on the ship were faced with deciding what to do next: stay on the ship and risk being blown up or burned, or jump overboard and risk drowning in the flooding Mississippi. Many were trapped under debris from the explosions, unable to escape the inferno, never having the chance to make that choice as they were burned alive.

William H. Norton, another *Sultana* disaster survivor described the scene, "Men were rushing to and fro, trampling over each other in their endeavors to escape. All was confusion. The river was full of men struggling with each other and grasping at everything that offered any means of support. As I arose to the surface, several men from the boat jumped upon me and we all went down together." Another survivor recalled, "When I got about 300 yards from the boat clinging to a heavy plank, the whole heavens seemed to be lighted up by the conflagration. Hundreds of my comrades were fastened down by the timbers of the decks and had to burn while the water seemed to be one solid mass of human beings struggling with the waves."

One man, who had clung to the upper deck for as long as he could, described what he saw: "On looking down and out into the river, I would see men jumping from all parts of the boat into the water until it seemed black with men, their heads bobbing up and down like corks, and then disappearing beneath the turbulent waters, never to appear again." Another wrote, "The men who were afraid to take to the water could be seen clinging to the sides of the bow of the boat until they were singed off like flies."

It was reported that hundreds of men, horribly burned and scalded, were left on board in the burning wreckage. Some had enough remaining strength to tear pieces from the ship, toss them into the water and jump in after them. Others remained aboard, frantically moving toward the bow and away from the flames, praying and screaming for help that would not come.

Some of the men were able to make it to riverbanks while others clung to floating debris, praying for rescue. Private William Carter Warner, a teenager who had lied about his age so he might enlist in the Union Army, woke up floating in the river after being blown from the deck of the ship and knocked unconscious. The entire area was alight from the flames of the *Sultana*. He removed his long-john bottoms and used them to lash together two pieces of wood blown from the ship and held on for dear life. He was later rescued wearing only a shirt, shivering, but alive.

As the river filled with bodies and men fought for their lives, the fire made quick work of the *Sultana*. It took only twenty minutes for the burning remains of the ship to float to the west side of the river and sink just outside the tiny village of Mound City, Arkansas.

The sound of the explosions and the glare from the fire were heard and seen as far away as Memphis, where rescue ships and smaller boats were launched immediately. The first ship to arrive was the *Bostonia II*, steaming down from the north. She arrived an hour after the first explosion to find a river full of debris, bodies and still-struggling survivors. The *Bostonia II* fished dozens of men from the water before any other ships arrived. The rescue effort was aided by the steamers *Arkansas, Jenny Lind* and the *Essex*. A short time later the Navy gunboat *USS Tyler* arrived, manned by volunteers; her regular crew had been discharged several days earlier. Many other smaller boats arrived to help pull the half dead men from the icy waters. It was said as many as fifteen Union soldiers were rescued by a former Confederate soldier.

The rescue efforts continued through the night and the next day. Between five hundred and six hundred survivors were pulled from the water or taken from the riverbanks. A few men were plucked from trees along the Arkansas shore, where they had been thrown by the first explosion. The survivors were taken to hospitals in Memphis with severe burns, broken bones and hypothermia. Within a short time, over three hunded of the passengers who had survived the disaster succumbed to their injuries and died, adding to the growing list of the dead.

Though the Civil War had been raging only a few weeks earlier, with the North and the South bitter enemies, newspaper accounts described the sympathy and the many kindnesses of the people of Memphis toward the remaining survivors. The number of injured overwhelmed the Memphis hospitals, so several victims were taken in and nursed by private citizens. The mayor of the city took in three injured soldiers.

As many bodies as possible were recovered at the scene. A barge left Memphis each morning with the morbid task of picking up mutilated bodies littering both shores of the river, and returned to Memphis each night with its gruesome cargo. This continued for several days and though they did their best, many more bodies were found floating or washed down shore for several months. Unfortunately, a large number of victims were never recovered. The remains of a few of the soldiers were found floating as far south as Vicksburg -- the very place where their final trip home had begun on the ill-fated *Sultana*.

Because of the circumstances in which the large number of men was being transported on the *Sultana*, no "official" passenger log was kept. The exact death toll will never be known. Following the disaster, there were estimates of between 1,300 and 1,900 dead. The United States Customs Service determined an official death toll of 1,547. Modern historians now believe that the correct figure is likely closer to 1,800. Those killed included Captain Mason, all of his officers and nearly all of his crew. Only six hundred people lived to tell the tale of this terrible disaster about which so few people living today have heard.

When she exploded, the *Sultana* was fitted with what was, for that day, considered to be an advanced boiler system design and the most modern safety equipment. She had pressure valves on her boilers, three fire-fighting pumps, a metal lifeboat, three hundred feet of fire hose, thirty water buckets, five fire-fighting axes and seventy life jackets – all of which were useless on that fateful night.

There were many causes for the explosion. The gross overloading of the ship made her extremely top heavy. This in turn caused her to list heavily from side to side. Her newly designed boiler system had all four boilers interconnected. It is believed that as she rounded her last corner, she listed heavily to one side, so much so that most of the water ran out of the first boiler -- the damaged boiler -- causing a hot spot. When the ship listed to the other side, water flowed back into the damaged boiler, hitting the hot spot and turning instantly into steam. The pressure surge inside the weakened boiler caused it to explode with enough force to destroy most of the ship.

As with any major disaster, there are always rumors of conspiracy and sabotage and the sinking of the *SS Sultana* was no exception. In 1888, 23 years after the disaster, just such a tale began to circulate. William Streetor of St. Louis claimed that Robert Louden, his former business partner, had made a deathbed confession concerning the *Sultana*. Louden, Streetor said, claimed that he had sabotaged the *Sultana* using a coal torpedo.

There may have been some credence to that story. Louden was a former Confederate agent and saboteur who had operated against Union shipping in the St Louis area during the Civil War. He did his dirty work at the same time as Thomas Edgworth Courtenay, another Confederate saboteur working in the St. Louis area. Courtenay had invented the coal torpedo, a weapon designed to be used against Union shipping interests. "Torpedo" was a name given to all sorts of Civil War era explosive devices. The coal torpedo was a hollow iron casting in the shape of a lump of coal, covered with coal dust and filled with blasting powder. Confederate agents would hide the torpedo in piles of coal designated for use in Union steamships. When the torpedo was shoveled into the ship's firebox with the other coal, the resulting explosion could result in anything from disabling a boiler to killing crewmen and sinking the vessel.

Additional support for Louden's claim came from eyewitnesses who said they had seen a piece of an artillery shell in the ship's wreckage before it sank. While Louden certainly had motive and opportunity, there is no direct evidence that his confession is anything more than fancy and most modern day historians support the official cause.

Many of the victims were buried in Memphis cemeteries but a large number of others were buried near where their bodies were recovered. Still others were collected and taken by their families to be buried.

Survivors eventually melted back into society and continued on to become builders, farmers, merchants, law men, lawyers, husbands and fathers. Some spoke at length about their near-death experience but others kept it to themselves. Some were able to recover from the trauma of that terrible night but many were haunted by the tragedy for the rest of their lives. A handful of survivors decided that they would end their haunting memories on their own terms. In 1887, Charles Heberth having suffered from nervous attacks since the tragedy, shot himself to death at only 42 years old. At 65, Horace Tifft committed suicide by jumping into a gorge in 1910. Both men indicated that they were driven to their actions by their experiences aboard the *Sultana*.

The *Sultana* herself disappeared into the mud and silt of the Mississippi River bottom and the location of her burned-out hull was lost. Repeated flooding over many decades caused the river to change its course several times, making it even harder to locate her remains. The main channel of the river in that area has shifted over two miles from its position in 1865.

Although the tragedy of the *Sultana* remains largely forgotten, there are those who have worked to help us remember. Many of the soldiers who perished in the dark waters of the Mississippi that late April night were buried in towns all along the river from Memphis to Vicksburg. Eight separate commemorative monuments and markers were placed in communities including Memphis, Tennessee; Muncie, Indiana; Hillsdale, Michigan; Mansfield, Ohio; Knoxville, Tennessee; Marion, Arkansas; Vicksburg, Mississippi; and Cincinnati, Ohio, dedicated

# 10 MOST DEADLY US MARITIME DISASTERS

1. Killed: 1700 - Apr. 27, 1865 - *SS Sultana* - Mississippi River outside of Memphis, TN
2. Killed: 1517 - Apr. 15, 1912 - *RMS Titanic* - North Atlantic Ocean
3. Killed: 1021 - May, 15, 1904 - *SS General Slocum* - New York City, NY
4. Killed: 835 - July, 24, 1915 - *SS Eastland* - Chicago, IL
5. Killed: 400 - Sept. 8, 1860 - *SS Lady Elgin* - Chicago, IL
6. Killed: 260 - Oct. 15, 1898 - *USS Maine* - Havana, Cuba
7. Killed: 260 - Sept. 5, 1622 - *Nuestra Senora de Atocha* - Florida Keys, FL
8. Killed: 250+ - Apr. 16, 1854 - *Powhattan* - off the NJ coast
9. Killed: 250+ - Nov. 7-11, 1913 - (19 ships sunk, 19 ships disabled) US Great Lakes
10. Killed: 129 - Apr. 10, 1963 - *USS Thresher* submarine - North Atlantic Ocean

to that terrible loss of life. Across the country, other memorials have been erected in remembrance of the Civil War dead, including those lost on the Sultana.

A group of Sultana survivors formed an association and met several times on the anniversary of the sinking until the 1930s. In 1987, The Association of Sultana Descendants and Friends resumed the tradition and began meeting annually in Memphis to commemorate the terrible tragedy that touched the lives of their ancestors, and their lives as well.

The tragic explosion and sinking of the *SS Sultana* has left what many people believe to be a strong paranormal presence that continues today. For decades, Mississippi River tugboat captains and crew have reported a golden-orange glow appearing in an Arkansas field a few miles north of Memphis. They describe the glow as if it is a fire that slowly fades away to darkness. Many local residents have also reported seeing this glowing phenomenon and have added that a particular part of that field seems to be warmer than the surrounding land.

Hunters in the area have reported hearing ghostly sounds such as screams and choking. Some have passed the sounds off as effects of the wind and nature around them but others admit that there seems to be no natural explanation for the eerie sounds.

Another common phenomenon witnessed by many just after dawn, is the appearance of apparitions in human form, wandering the same field, apparently sifting through the dirt as if searching for something. When seen clearly, they appear to be scarred, disfigured and wearing old, shredded clothing. These apparitions are witnessed briefly before disappearing into the fog along the river bottom.

For many years, there had been no reasonable explanations for these ghastly apparitions and terrifying noises. Then in 1982, a team of archeologists working about four miles from Memphis unearthed fire-blackened deck planks and timbers that they believed to be the remains of the wreckage of the *Sultana*, 32 feet beneath that very same Arkansas soy bean field.

Because of the high costs of excavation, it is unlikely that the complete remains of the *Sultana* will ever be unearthed. But maybe that is as it should be, the burned out hulk remaining in its own burial site in the isolation of an Arkansas field. The peace of its final resting place broken only by the spirits of soldiers lost, reluctant to leave their last ties to the lives they lost so tragically.

There is no marker or monument in this lonely field to memorialize the tragic loss of life and the disaster that happened there. For many, the lingering spirits are the only reminders necessary.

# 1889: HISTORY OF THE JOHNSTON FLOOD
## 'I HAD GREAT FAITH THAT I WOULD NOT BE ABANDONED..'

Like so many other American tragedies, the terrible Johnstown Flood was the culmination of several factors, each with roots spreading out in many directions. To make sense of how and why 2,209 men, women and children suddenly and unexpectedly lost their lives on that fateful day in May, we need to consider the different causes, natural and man-made, and how they all came together to create a horrific entry in our nation's history.

This story had many beginnings...

It began in Philadelphia.

Pennsylvania lawmakers wanted to increase the expansion of the nation as well as the state, so they devised and constructed a faster, safer route for the transportation of goods and people between Philadelphia and Pittsburgh. Unfortunately the Allegheny Mountains, cutting through the middle of the state, were going to make that difficult.

The Pennsylvania Main Line of Public Works was built between 1826 and 1834. A passenger or piece of freight that started the 395-mile trip by boarding a canal boat in Philadelphia could stay aboard the same boat until disembarking in Pittsburgh. The boat would leave Philadelphia aboard a horse-powered railroad, reaching the Susquehanna River, where it was floated for the first time. From there, the boats were fastened together to form a "boat train" traveling through connecting rivers and canals until they reached Hollidaysburg. Here, the boats were loaded onto the Allegheny Portage Railroad and hauled 36 miles over the Allegheny Mountains using five inclined planes on each side and passed through a 950-foot tunnel; the first railroad tunnel built in America. They were finally refloated in the canal basin at Johnstown. The canal then carried them to the Allegheny River upon which they continued their journey into Pittsburgh. When the main line, as it became known as, was completed, the traditional 21-day wagon trip was reduced to four and a half days.

The main line allowed for larger and heavier quantities of freight to be shipped west with much greater ease compared to hauling it with Conestoga wagons. It didn't take long for the line to carry large numbers of passengers west as well. Unfortunately, the line was incredibly expensive and labor intensive to maintain. There was frequent damage caused by floods and the constant worry that during dry spells, there might not be enough water to keep the canals flowing. Reservoirs needed to be constructed to supply water to the canals. The entire operation became a money pit for the state. Within a few years after the main line's completion, it became obsolete when in 1854, the Pennsylvania Railroad opened an all-rail service connecting the same points but cutting the travel time down to three and a half days. The railroad was also far less expensive to travel and maintain. Three years later, the state sold the main line land and structures to the Pennsylvania Railroad, including the dams and reservoirs.

It began at the South Fork Dam.

The South Fork Dam, started in 1838, was originally built by the main line to create the Western Reservoir, which would in turn feed into the Johnstown canal basin when rain was scarce. The design for the dam was sound but there had been problems from the start. Two years after completion, the culvert that passed through the base of the dam to dispel the water collapsed on the lakeside and the dam was damaged. The lake was drained and repairs were begun, but by then, there was no longer any need as the main line was being closed. The dam was abandoned.

After passing through a few private hands, Benjamin Ruff bought the property and applied for a permit to repair the dam and refill the reservoir. Ruff's master plan was to create an exclusive club, a vacation resort for wealthy Pittsburgh families wishing to escape the heat, and grit and smoke of the city during the summer months. Ruff named this new corporation The South Fork Fishing and Hunting Club. He was able to convince many of the richest and most well-connected industrialists and business men to purchase two shares, at $100 each, in his new venture.

Ruff began repairs on the dam in 1879 but the work was shoddy and the repairs washed out later that year.

**(Left) South Fork Fishing and Hunting Club clubhouse where most of the members stayed.
(Right) Privately owned "cottages" on the lake.**

The next year, repairs were resumed under the direction of Edward Pearson and by 1881 the dam was completed, the lake was filled and stocked with 1,000 black bass from Lake Erie. The dam had been built back up in the center, where it had washed out before but the damage caused by the collapsed culvert was never corrected. Further, the previous owner had pulled the metal discharge pipes out of the base of the dam and sold them for scrap. The pipes had not been replaced, so if there were any problems with the dam, there would be no way to drain the lake to make repairs or to release excess water if it rose dangerously high.

While the dam was being repaired again, Ruff had a large, elaborate clubhouse built. The ideal place for the building was on the opposite side of the lake from the nearest railroad station in South Fork. The top of the dam was just wide enough for a one-lane carriage road -- except for the gaping hole over the spillway, the section of the dam designed to allow excess water to flow out of the lake. Ruff had a bridge built across the spillway so that carriages could carry club members across the top of the dam. To keep the expensive game fish from escaping down the river and into the valley, he had metal screens installed across the spillway.

It began in Pittsburgh.

Steel, coal, coke and railroads. The magical combination that kept so many people impoverished but gilded the lives of an elite few. Andrew Carnegie for example, rose up from the slag heaps of Pittsburgh to became one of the most powerful men in the world, though many would have said he got there on the backs of tens of thousands. He brought select men to the top with him, while others made it there on their own. It never really mattered how they got there, though, only that they worked together once they arrived. The history of the coal, steel, and railroad barons, lawyers, bankers and business owners illustrated a web of interaction and self-preservation in the business world of the late nineteenth century.

The families of these powerful men were reflective of their businesses. Their wives and children lived lives that orbited each other, as well. Their mansions, estates, schools and even churches were set apart from the working class. They attended parties together and their children intermarried. They could afford whatever they wanted and could do as they pleased without ever having to leave their ivory towers. But in Pittsburgh, the grit, smoke and soot from all that industry turned those lovely towers gray and choked off the fresh air at the top, just as it did down at the bottom. The difference was that these families were wealthy enough to escape, even if just for a little while, to somewhere cool; somewhere clean; somewhere relaxing; somewhere that allowed them to leave home but still stay isolated from the outside world -- and most importantly, somewhere that would allow them to be do all this with the select group of people they knew. Somewhere like a mountain resort, with a lovely lake...

It began at The South Fork Fishing and Hunting Club.

Membership was by invitation only and by 1889, the 61-member roster read like the "Who's Who" of the business world and included Andrew Carnegie, the richest man in the world. Other prominent members and recognizable names were Edward Jay Allen, organizer of the Pacific and Atlantic Telegraph Company; John Chalfant, President of People's National Bank; Henry Clay Frick, the coke king; Philander Knox, prominent

**Lake Conemaugh and the South Fork Dam. The clubhouse is visible in the background across the lake.**

lawyer and later the U.S. Secretary of State; Andrew Mellon, founder of the Mellon bank and on the boards of over sixty companies; Henry Phipps, Jr., chairman of Carnegie's company and Robert Pitcairn, Superintendent of the Pittsburgh Division of the Pennsylvania Railroad, to name a few.

The club owned the South Fork Dam, the Western Reservoir, renamed Lake Conemaugh after the river that fed it, and one hundred and sixty acres of woods surrounding the lake. They also owned the magnificent 47-room clubhouse, where most of the members stayed when visiting. There were sixteen privately owned cottages, on club- owned land. The cottages were really fairly large houses, typically with three stories and twelve to fifteen rooms each. They looked out upon the lake through cool, deep porches and large windows. The only requirement club members had was that all meals were to be taken in the clubhouse dining room.

Members of the South Fork Fishing and Hunting Club did fish and hunt, but they also spent much of their time on the lake. A few steam-powered boats had been brought up the mountain so lengthy excursions were common as families steamed back and forth across the lake. They held regattas, had picnics, played games and put on pageants. Young men courted young ladies and mothers chased after babies. The dam's broad, stony spillway was a favorite spot for families to sit back and enjoy the sound of the water, cascading down the rock face.

The train ride from Pittsburgh to South Fork, the nearest railroad station, took a little more than two hours. Once they arrived in South Fork, they boarded carriages and rode the 2-1/2 miles to the dam, across the dam and on to the clubhouse or cottage. After a while, as the membership grew and families spent more time at the club, the narrow road across the top of the dam became a bit of a nuisance. If an oncoming carriage was already on the dam, other carriages had to wait until the first one was driven off before gaining access to the road on the dam. The members decided that this was too bothersome so they had the top of the dam lowered between three and four feet, thus widening the road sufficiently to allow two carriages to pass side by side.

It began in the plain states of Kansas and Nebraska.

A nasty storm was brewing in the Midwest on May 28. As the storm moved east, it picked up momentum and moisture. When it reached the Conemaugh River Valley, it let loose with a vengeance. Few people living in the valley had ever experienced rain that hard or steady. The storm dumped between six and eight inches of rain across the mountain and valley in less than 24 hours. The rivers and streams coming down from the mountains drained a 657- square mile watershed and flowed right into Lake Conemaugh.

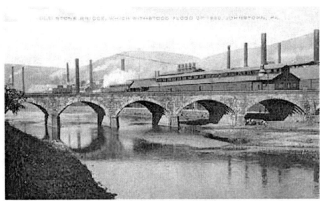
**Famous stone bridge with the Cambria Iron Company behind it.**

This story had many beginnings but only one ending – Johnstown, Pennsylvania.

The prosperous community of Johnstown, founded in 1794, was located in the Conemaugh River Valley, where the Little Conemaugh meets the Stony Creek. Johnstown was located just below the Allegheny Mountains in western Pennsylvania and was originally populated largely by Germans, Welsh and Irish.

In 1889, Johnstown boasted a population of thirty thousand and was so closely packed together that there was hardly room for any more buildings. The Cambria Iron Company was the centerpiece of city, employing over seven thousand men and producing more high-quality steel than anywhere in the United States -- even more than Pittsburgh. A branch of the company was making nearly of the barbed wire used in the country. Railroads were king, and most of the public traveled by rail, along with all that steel and wire. The valley was full of smoke and the iron works glowed around the clock. The men were doing well, earning at least $1.50 a day and wore suits and ties to the pay window each week to pick up their checks, a sign of respect for the job they did and for their community.

Johnstown was a progressive town and a fine place to raise a family. There were new electric lights in the downtown streets, seventy telephones, 25 churches, three newspapers, two railroad stations and over 123 saloons. The people of Johnstown were thriving but their lives were very different from those just up the valley at Lake Conemaugh. Though only a short distance apart, the folks around the lake up on the mountain lived a world away from the folks in the valley below. What happened up at the lake was a constant source of fascination, but the only way anyone from Johnstown or the surrounding area was allowed inside the mysterious community, was to cook, or clean or change the sheets of the residents of the lakeshore community. Any man found hunting or fishing in the area was unceremoniously sent on his way.

Thousands of people lived downstream from the South Fork Dam and Lake Conemaugh. The lake was fourteen miles from Johnstown and nearly five hundred feet higher up the mountain, but for all intents and purposes, the lake was a thousand miles away from the people living in the valley below. When the spring rains came, the Little Conemaugh River and Stony Creek overflowed their banks nearly every year, filling the downtown Johnstown streets with water. Every time this happened, warnings came down from the mountain that the dam was in danger of failing. The years came and went and the dam never failed. It was not surprising that most of the people in the valley didn't pay much heed to the warnings.

The only member of the exclusive club to take an active notice of the condition of the dam was Robert Pitcairn. He would occasionally stop his buggy as it crossed the dam and do a visual inspection. He also discussed maintenance issues with Benjamin Rupp, the club president and overseer, and asked about conditions and repairs. Rupp repeatedly boasted of the dam's excellent condition and its meticulous upkeep. Pitcairn was satisfied with Rupp's answers and never investigated any deeper.

The club did conduct periodic maintenance on the dam but they also made some dangerous modifications. The fish screens that had been installed across the spillway to keep the expensive game fish in the lake also collected debris that would have otherwise passed on through and away from the dam. The clogged fish screens created serious obstructions that kept the excess water from flowing freely from the lake if they weren't periodically cleared. A bridge was built over the spillway to create a carriage road. The bridge piers were planted into the spillway and also caught debris, further inhibiting the flow of water.

Then they made the most dangerous alteration of all. They lowered the top of the dam to less than four feet above the top of the spillway. The danger here lay in the possibility of heavy rains, falling at rate too great for the shallow spillway to relieve the pressure on the dam from the extra water. The face of the spillway was all rock to prevent erosion of the dry face of the dam as water poured out of the lake. If there was too much water, the spillway might not be able to handle it all and the lake would "top" the dam, pouring over parts that were not safe from erosion. The water topping the dam in places other than the spillway could eat away sufficient material from the face that the dam would be weakened and possibly fail. The discharge pipes had been removed years earlier and were never replaced so there was no other way to quickly remove water from the lake safely other than the spillway. The wealthy club members had purchased a defective dam but those who were in charge weren't particularly concerned with its safety.

Pitcairn may have been the only club member who was concerned about the safety of the dam, but he wasn't entirely alone. Daniel J. Morrell, the most important person in Johnstown and head of the huge Cambria Iron Company, was also worried. He requested that his own engineer, John Fulton, be allowed to study the dam and inspect it for defects and potential problems. Fulton met with Ruff and saw the dam for himself. After questioning Ruff, he was certain that the damage caused by removing the drainage pipes had never been repaired. He also observed that wet areas around the dam were not coming from small springs in the as Rupp stated, but instead were from leaks in the dam. Fulton was not informed that the dam had been lowered or about the fish screens. He left convinced that the dam was an accident waiting to happen, even though he wasn't aware of all the damaging modifications that had been made to it.

Morrell passed Fulton's assessment on to Rupp and proposed sharing the cost of the repairs with the club. Rupp however, refused to acknowledge the problems, and insisting the dam was perfectly safe, he declined Morrell's offer and apparently kept the report to himself. Benjamin Rupp didn't live long enough to see how wrong he was, or the damage resulting from his stubborn attitude. Nor did Daniel Morrell live to see his concerns become founded. Both men were cold in their graves years before the waters of Lake Conemaugh rushed down the valley.

The next man to hold the office of president and overseer of the club was Colonel Elias J. Unger, who insisted on the title even though he had never served in the military. Unger was a local farmer. His farmhouse was situated atop a nearby hill, overlooking the dam and the lake. He had not only assumed Rupp's office, he also assumed Rupp's attitude about the dam. Nothing was done to correct the damage or dangerous modifications under Unger's watch.

When Unger went to bed on the night of May 30, it had been raining most of the day and the hills and mountains were already water-logged. Lake Conemaugh was filling up. Down in the valley, Johnstown, too, was filling up with water. People were working frantically to move their possessions onto their second floors and out of the water's way. They had experienced water in their streets many times before, but never this bad.

Early the next morning, May 31, Colonel Unger rose from his bed and looked out his window. To his utter horror, he saw that the lake had risen dramatically. He called for all the assistance he could muster to shore up the dam. There happened to be a group of men described only as "twenty Italians" on the club's property, working on the sewer system. They were also enlisted to work on the dam. With horses, wagons and a plow, they first tried to cut a groove into the hillside on the opposite side of the dam, hoping this would allow water to escape the lake faster without damaging the dam. However, at just four feet deep, they struck rock and could go no deeper. Water began rushing through the cut, but not nearly enough to relieve the pressure.

The section of the dam that had been repaired years before had settled, just as it was supposed to, but was never built back up. Now, with the water nearing the top, Unger realized that the settled area was now noticeably lower than the rest of the dam. He and his men frantically dumped wagon load after wagon load of soil onto the dam, trying to raise the level of the low area, as well as the entire dam.

Debris was washing down the mountain and into the lake. With the newly established current created by the water rushing over the spillway and the groove cut in the hillside, the debris headed directly for the spillway. In very short order, the fish screens and bridge piers became so clogged that the amount of water escaping the dam was significantly reduced. The rivers were rising at a rate of one inch every hour, but the lake was rising about one inch every ten minutes. By 10:00 a.m., the water was only one foot below the lowest level of the dam. Unger ordered his men to get into the water to clear the fish screens but they refused, fearing for their lives.

At 11:30 a.m., Unger ordered John Parke, the club's resident engineer, to take his horse and ride to South Fork and send a message down the river to Johnstown, warning the people there that the condition of the dam was approaching a critical stage and was likely to fail at any moment.

While Parke was gone, the dam was finally topped. With water pouring over the top of the dam, it only took a few minutes to wash away all the soil the men had hauled in to raise the dam's level. After the new soil was gone, the velocity of the escaping water increased dramatically. The tons of water rushing over the top began to quickly erode the soil face of the dam. The surging water cut deep grooves into the face and it began to be washed away. It was now only a matter of time before the dam gave away completely.

Telegraph lines were down all over and trackmen were out searching for breaks in the lines. Emma Ehrenfeld, the South Fork telegrapher, was only able to send the message four miles down the line to Mineral Springs. From there, a trackman ran the message 1-1/2 miles to the next telegraph tower, where it was forwarded to East Conemaugh and then on to Johnstown.

A copy of the telegraphed warning was also sent to Robert Pitcairn, who was sitting in his private railroad car just a few miles outside of town, unable to move forward because the track ahead was washed out. He immediately ordered that his car be attached to another train and he headed back to Pittsburgh. But first, he telegraphed ahead to his office to gather one thousand of his own railroad men and get them ready to go to Johnstown to help with the rescue and cleanup from the impending disaster. He then ordered his home office to contact every newspaper to let them know that Johnstown was about to be wiped out and that they should call for immediate aid of all kinds. Pitcairn's quick thinking and efforts to get rescuers and aid flowing into Johnstown as fast a possible was credited with saving many lives and organizing aid even before the waters had begun to recede.

In Johnstown, the flooding from the Little Conemaugh River and Stony Creek was growing steadily worse. George Swank, owner and editor of the *Johnstown Tribune*, looked out his second-story office window and watched as the streets turned into rivers. People were being rescued in boats and livestock was washed down the street toward the Little Conemaugh River and on out of town. Flooding in town was common, but never had it been this bad.

Trains were being held up along the line. One was held in South Fork and two others, including the Day Express, had been held at East Conemaugh, with the track washed out both in front of and behind the train. It had nowhere to go so the passengers simply sat in the cars and waited.

By 2:45 p.m., all hope of saving the dam was gone. Unger had pulled his men from the dam when the water

**(Left) The destroyed South Fork Dam. (Right) Looking east through the hole in the South Fork Dam. The line in the back shows where the top of the dam had been and behind that, where Lake Conemaugh had been.**

had topped it. With nothing else they could do, he sent them to find shelter and returned to his home and collapsed from exhaustion.

The Western Union telegraph lines went down in Johnstown at 3:00 p.m. They had received three warning messages about the impending failure of the dam, but had neither time nor any method of warning many people. If the residents had heard the warning, it is likely they would have waved it off as another false alarm, like every other year.

At approximately 3:10 that afternoon, the South Fork Dam finally let go and crumbled. Witnesses said that it seemed as though the face of the dam just moved away. The roar that followed was deafening. There were only six or seven club members there at the time and

A mud flat created by the giant wave of water as it moved through a previously inhabited area, wiping out almost everything in its path.

unable to do anything, they stood watching, dumb struck. It only took a matter of minutes, forty minutes to be exact, for Lake Conemaugh to empty through the break in the dam, and to fall out of existence. Almost instantly, twenty million tons of water surged through the opening in the dam, rushing down the valley, headed for Johnstown and wiping out everything in its way. The wall of water was at times as high as sixty feet and was moving at nearly forty miles per hour.

The water first slammed into a hillside, and the backwash dragged a bridge two hundred yards upstream. The first town to be hit was tiny South Fork. Fortunately, most of the town was perched on the side of a hill and out of the path of destruction. And since many of South Fork's residents were watching the dam when it gave way, they were prepared and had gotten to higher ground. Between thirty and forty houses were destroyed and four people were killed.

The water continued its rampage until it struck its next target: the small mill town of Mineral Springs. All of Mineral Springs was erased except for one city block. After the water passed on, sixteen more people were dead.

The water was picking up debris as it raged down the valley. Rolling across the giant wave was an already growing mass of trees, chewed-up houses, smashed bridges and even railroad cars. With all this, the water next struck the Little Conemaugh Viaduct, a 78-foot-long railroad bridge. The bridge became so packed with the debris dragged from upriver that it created a dam and slowed the progression of the flood. The bridge held for seven minutes, and then it, too, succumbed to the pressure of the water and crumbled. The rush of water resumed its course through the valley with renewed vigor.

As the water continued down the valley, a train farther down had become stranded on the washed-out tracks. The railroad men were out walking the track, trying to determine where they needed to make repairs when they heard a tremendous roar approaching them. Realizing what must have happened, everyone scrambled up the hill toward safety -- everyone except John Hess, the train's engineer. He ran to his locomotive, tied open the train's whistle and steamed down the track in reverse, as fast as the engine would go, trying to warn as many people as possible. It is believed that Hess saved many lives with his heroic run. Hess was injured but he survived the day, even though the water eventually caught up with him and tumbled his locomotive end over end, as if it was a toy.

Next in line for the water's wrath was the town of East Conemaugh. By the time the behemoth arrived, witnesses said that the water was almost completely obscured by the wall debris it carried with it, and much of East Conemaugh was added to growing mass as it moved on toward its next victim. Here, the destruction was

**(Left) Destroyed train amid mass of wreckage left behind by the giant wave of water.**
**(Right) Destroyed Cambria Iron manufacturing building.**

much worse. Half the town was destroyed including at least forty houses, two hotels and the railroad station. As the wave moved through the town, witnesses said it looked like a massive, rolling hill of debris, forty feet high and half a mile long, just rolling and rolling and rolling. East Conemaugh was home to a large Pennsylvania Railroad roundhouse. When the water hit, the roundhouse was housing many eighty-ton locomotives. The force of the water crushed the roundhouse and carried all 32 locomotives along with it, some for one hundred yards, and a few of the locomotives were found as far as a mile away.

The two parts of the Day Express train had been stranded on the tracks on the edge of East Conemaugh. When the water hit the train, the results were truly bizarre. Those passengers in the first section of the train who ran for their lives survived, and those who stayed on the train were drowned. But in the second section of the train, those who ran were drowned and those who stayed on the train were left unharmed.

When the flood of water had moved on, it left more than fifty bodies in its wake, 25 of them had been passengers on the stranded train.

The wave began to pick up speed as it continued down the valley. It smashed into Woodvale without warning. Of the 1,100 residents of Woodvale, 314 were killed, along with 89 horses that were trapped in a stable. When the water passed, nearly all that remained of the town was a mud flat.

Sixteen-year-old Victor Heiser was working in his family's barn, getting the animals fed and bedded down as they, too, were waiting out the storm. He heard his father yelling to him from a second story window in their house. He was waving wildly for Victor to climb onto the roof of the barn, which he did. Victor could then see what his father had already seen -- a massive wall of water and debris barreling down on them. He looked over just in time to witness his family home crushed and swept away with his parents inside. The barn was also smashed to bits but Victor managed to stay on top of a piece of the barn's roof. He rode the wave of water down the valley, narrowly missing being knocked off or crushed by rolling freight cars and other wreckage. Clinging to his flimsy raft, he saw a two-story brick house, still standing solidly. He made a desperate jump toward the roof of the house and just made it. He spent the rest of the night huddled in the attic of the house with nineteen other people, praying that the house continued to stand.

The leading edge of the water was now approaching Johnstown. But first, it hit the Gauliter Wire Works, a part of the Cambria Iron Company. There the giant wave picked up miles of rolled barbed wire to add to its collection. The rolling action of the wave caused the barbed wire to tumble around and around, twisting tightly in and about the wreckage. When the cool water doused the giant boilers, they exploded, sending a cloud of black sooty mist and dust into the air, where it hung above the wave of water and was sucked along with it into the city. People who witnessed the wave roaring into town, called the black cloud the "death mist."

It was 4:07 in the afternoon. As the wave entered Johnstown, it slammed into another hill, creating a second backwash that traveled along Stoney Creek in both directions destroying the small settlement of Kernville, and then returned to rejoin the rest of the wave.

The Rev. H.L. Chapman and his family lived in the downtown parsonage of the Franklin Street Methodist Church. His first clue that the dam had broken came when he opened his front door to check on the rising waters and saw a boxcar rolling down the street in a rush of water. A man was standing on the roof of the car but as it approached a large overhanging tree, the man grabbed a branch and managed to get into a second-story window of the parsonage. Rev. Chapman screamed for his family to get to the attic as he ran into the hall to turn off the gas. Just as he did so, the front doors flew open and a rush of water burst into the house. The Reverend was able to run to the kitchen stairs, with the water hard on his heels, and was reunited with his family in the attic. They were joined by the man from the boxcar and a few other people who had rescued themselves as well.

They huddled together for hours, listening to the roar of the water and the crunching, grinding noises of debris as it passed by, or slammed into the house. They were all terrified by the frightening noises coming from the outside and feared their house could not withstand the pressure. Reverend Chapman later wrote: "I think none of us was afraid to meet God, but we all felt willing to put it off until a more propitious time." When the noises finally ceased, they looked outside and saw "a scene of utter destruction." The Franklin Street Church had also survived the flood, and had, in fact, borne the brunt of the wave's impact and sheltered several smaller buildings including the Chapman house and Alma Hall.

The Rev. David Beale, pastor of the Presbyterian Church on Main Street, was also in his church's parsonage when the wave hit. He and his family had retreated to the third floor of their house, well above the highest water. While there, they were able to pull several people who were floating into the safety of their home. As the night wore on, they felt that the house was nearing collapse and decided to evacuate. They walked on top of debris in the street for a block, until they came to Alma Hall, Johnstown's tallest building, also on Main Street. Before the night was over, 264 survivors had sheltered in Alma Hall, bring comfort to each other as they had no food, blankets or supplies of any kind.

Possibly the strangest incident in the disaster happened in Alma Hall. James Walters, a local lawyer, was in his home on Walnut Street. When the wave hit, the rush of water carried him out of his house and to where he was able to climb onto a floating piece of roof. A short time later, a surge of water propelled him into the air and through an open window and into his own office in Alma Hall. Surviving today, Alma Hall stands as a local landmark and symbol of the town's strength and resilience.

George and Belle Waters had spent the much of the morning and part of the afternoon moving their furniture and valuables to the second floor of their house. George heard a neighbor outside screaming a warning that the dam had burst. He quickly got Belle and their three young daughters up the ladder and into their unfinished attic. The floor had never been finished so they had to balance on the floor joists to keep from falling through the ceiling below. The water was washing through the house and had risen nearly to the ceiling of the second floor when the house suddenly gave a great shudder as something heavy struck it from outside. Belle, still holding her baby, Eva, fell between two joists, through the ceiling and into the dirty water. The whole house was now sitting at an angle and Belle was able to keep her face above water by standing on her toes in a raised corner of the room. She stood, holding little Eva above her shoulders. Soon, Mary and Margaret followed their mother and sister into the swirling, cloudy water. Panicked, George reached down and grabbed two feet, hoping to save at least one of his young daughters, when he found he had grabbed one foot of each girl and was able to save them both. With the two girls safe, he climbed down into the water-filled room and pulled his wife and youngest daughter to the ladder and back up to safety, where they all remained until the danger had passed. The next day, they found that their son, Merle, who had been playing at a neighbor's house when the wave hit, had also survived.

Gertrude Quinn Slattery, a six-year-old girl who was caught in the flood and separated from her family, later wrote a description of her wild ride on what she called a "raft with a wet muddy mattress and bedding." She later told her story:

"I had great faith that I would not be abandoned. A large roof came floating toward me with about twenty people on it. I cried and called across the water to them to help me. This, of course they could not do. The roof was big, and they were all holding on for dear life, feeling every minute that they would be tossed to death. While I watched I kept praying, calling, and begging someone to save me. Then I saw a man come to the edge, the others holding him and talking excitedly. I could see they were trying to restrain him but he kept pulling to get away which he finally did, and plunged into the swirling waters and disappeared. Then his head appeared and I could see he was looking in my direction and I called, cried, and begged him to come to me. He kept going down and coming up, sometimes lost to my sight entirely, only to come up next time much closer to my raft. The water was now between fifteen and twenty feet deep."

"As I sat watching this man struggling in the water my mind was firmly fixed on the fact that he was my savior. At last he reached me, drew himself up an over the side of the mattress and lifted me up. I put both arms around his neck and held on to him like grim death. Together we went downstream with the ebb and flow of the reflex to the accompaniment of crunching, grinding, gurgling, splashing and crying and moaning of many. After drifting about we saw a little white building, standing at the edge of the water, apparently where the hill began. At the window were two men with poles helping to rescue people floating by. I was too far out for the poles, so the men called: 'Throw that baby over to us.'

My hero said: 'Do you think you can catch her?'

They said: 'We can try.'

"So Maxwell McAchren threw me across the water (some say twenty feet, others fifteen. I could never find out, so I leave it to your imagination. It was considered a great feat in the town, I know.)"

In the aftermath, not only had Gertrude Slattery lived to tell her thrilling tale, but Maxwell McAchren, her personal hero, had survived as well.

Thousands of people were in the path of destruction as the wave wound through the lower river valley. Some chose to ride the flood out in their homes or businesses and others raced for the hills and ran for their lives. As with the passengers on the stranded train, their survival was as random as their choices. Families ran up the stairs of their home, having nearly been swept away as the water surged through their houses and were saved if their houses withstood the onslaught. Others making the same choice of moving to a higher floor became trapped in their own piece of floating, rolling debris is their house was knocked from its foundation and taken along with the wave. Some people who chose to run were able to get to higher ground just ahead of the water while others didn't make it and were swept up in the tumult. Pieces of debris in the mass slammed together and crushed some of the people who were taken by the water, but for others, floating pieces of wreckage provided makeshift rafts or material for them to cling to.

John Fenn had gone to a neighbor's house to help them move their furniture upstairs and out of the rising water. When the wave hit, he was washed away with no chance to save himself. His wife, Anna Fenn, had remained in their home with their seven children. When the wave hit their house it rapidly filled with water. Anna clutched her youngest, only a toddler, and the other six children held on

**Six of John and Anna Fenn's children. All of the children died in the flood plus one not pictured and one not yet born.**

**(Left) Tumbled freight car in front of the destroyed Cambria Iron Company offices.    (Right) So many houses had been knocked off their foundations and moved around by the water and heavy debris, they ended up literally stacked up against each other.**

to her clothing, trying to stay afloat.

One after another, each of her children drowned as she struggled to hang on. Anna described what happened inside that hell, "The water rose and floated us until our heads nearly touched the ceiling...It was dark and the house was tossing every way. The air was stifling, and I could not tell just the moment the rest of the children had to give up and drown...what I suffered, with the bodies of my seven children floating around me in the gloom can never be told." Anna's sorrows did not end when the water receded. She soon learned that her husband had not survived the flood. Then, a few weeks later, the final blow came when she gave birth to a daughter who did not survive -- another victim of that horrible night.

In Johnstown, escape on foot was difficult because of the already flooded streets, with water levels from two to seven feet deep. One witness, watching from an upper floor explained, "the streets grew black with people running for their lives." Dozens of people became ensnared in the tangle of barbed wire as it twisted its way through the surging carnage. Many people were pulled under water and drowned while others were tangled so tightly that they were unable to work themselves free. "People were hanging from rafters or clinging to rooftops and railcars, trying to keep their balance as their rafts floated in the turbulent waters," recalled one witness.

Soon after the backwash of water rejoined the main current with renewed energy, the wave next slammed up against the stone railroad bridge near the Cambria Iron Company's main buildings. This bridge held fast and stripped the floating wreckage from the wave and dammed up the water as it continued to rush forward. Johnstown became a lake of more than fifty acres with water between ten and thirty deep. As pressure built up behind the stone bridge, water cut through a section of an earthen embankment and shot off again, this time striking Millville and Cambria City with another violent blow. The devastation of lower Johnstown had taken only ten minutes. Factories, houses, business and entire neighborhoods had been destroyed.

After passing through Cambria City, the valley opened up and the land spread out -- and the killer wave did the same. The water's rage was spent; its energy depleted. The monster lay down and died.

But the floodwaters were not finished with Johnstown just yet. Thousands of people were clinging to roofs or shivering in attics of homes that had withstood the initial attack. They watched in terror as the twenty-foot-deep river washed through town as the rest of Lake Conemaugh followed the giant wave out of the valley. The current remained strong and massive chunks of debris and wreckage collided with the foundations and lower walls of their homes. Other buildings around them surrendered to the near-constant barrage.

The water had quieted somewhat and the giant wave had moved on, but for those poor, ravaged people, there was one more blow yet to come. When the debris-laden wave had struck the stone bridge, thousands of tons of wreckage became trapped behind the bridge. The pile was mammoth, rising to nearly forty feet high and covering thirty to forty acres of land. It represented the accumulation from the entire valley. Mixed into the pile were whole and fractured houses, pieces of bridges, trees, animals, telephone poles, several freight cars, over fifty feet of railroad track, machinery from the iron works, miles and miles of barbed wire, and people. Nearly five hundred people had been driven along by the massive wave, some still huddled in the fragments of their own homes.

Once the mass was stopped at the stone bridge, those who could get out, headed for the shore, but it was going to be next to impossible for the people tangled in barbed wire and trapped in the ruins behind the stone bridge to free themselves. The swift current held the mass tight to the bridge and the rolling effect of the debris in the water had wrapped it in the barbed wire so tightly that it was as if it was one solid piece. And everything was coated with oil and grime. Oil tankers from up river were dragged along by the wave and had ruptured, emptying thousands of gallons of oil into the tumult, complicating the rescue even further. It was going to take a while to figure out how to get them out and besides, most of the surviving population was still trying to do what they could to stay alive themselves as people all around them were still dying.

At a little after 6:00 p.m., rescuers had started moving through the pile to try to free at least some of the people before nightfall. They were true heroes, venturing out onto the unstable mass to save others when just minutes before, they had been in fear for their own lives. And then the inconceivable happened. The oil in the wreckage caught fire. The flames spread rapidly across the pile as the rescuers worked frantically to save whomever they could before having to flee for their lives -- again! A Johnstown newspaper reported that..."the fire burned with all the fury of hell!" Eighty of the survivors who had escaped a watery death died in the fire.

The fire burned off the oil and then burned itself out, having only waterlogged fuel left. Night finally fell, ending the longest day in any of these people's lives. They were left to wonder what the next day would bring and how their lives would be changes from that moment forward.

The next morning, the survivors woke to an eerie quiet. During the night, the waters had receded. Everywhere they looked, there was nothing but death and destruction, mud and muck and wreckage -- and bodies. There were bodies of men, bodies of women, and the most difficult to look upon -- bodies of children and babies. Thousands of people were buried in muck and rubble and would need to be dug out. Others started crawling out of their homes, or wherever they had found shelter, and surveyed the damage. They were stunned by what they saw; it seemed that nothing had remained intact. Entire city blocks were gone.

**(Left) Mass of wreckage piled up against the stone bridge. The debris field around the bridge covered thirty acres of land.  (Right) Recovery workers remove a body is removed from the wreckage stopped by the stone bridge.**

People came together, trying to learn anything they could about their lost families. Wives searching for husbands, husbands searching for wives, parents searching for their children and children searching for their parents. Nine morgues were set up all over town in churches, schools and saloons. Survivors wandered from morgue to morgue, hoping against hope that they would not find whomever they had lost, at least not in a morgue. Mrs. Fenn had lost her husband and seven children. A man lost his wife and eight children. Undertakers and embalmers arrived by the dozen and worked in shifts around the clock.

**Johnstown's Main Street on the morning after the flood.**

But they also saw something they didn't expect to see, at least not yet. There were strangers everywhere. They had come from Johnstown, from Pittsburgh, and from everywhere in between. That had learned of what had happened in that lovely river valley and had come in the night to do whatever they could do. Robert Pitcairn had notified newspapers of what was to happen even before it had happened, so the rescue effort had gotten a head start.

As invariably happens, when a deadly disaster strikes, disease follows. Typhoid had the biggest impact, causing forty more deaths, beyond the original 2,209. The later deaths have never been included in the death totals given, even though these people died as a result the flood just surely as if they had drowned. Doctors took to doing house-to-house searches of the homes not destroyed. They were dismayed to find that in many cases, there were thirteen or fourteen people living in one room with their windows tightly shut against the odor outside. This created a prime breeding ground for typhus or typhoid fever and other contagious diseases.

A team of doctors had descended on Johnstown, including the Dr. Benjamin Lee, head of the state Board of Health. Dr. Lee's chief concerns were with the spread of disease and contaminated water. As the days rolled on and the cleanup continued, five or six bodies were discovered and buried every day for several weeks. The layer of mud left behind by the floodwaters was in most places two feet thick, providing for ample space for bodies to be concealed until an unsuspecting worker shoveled away the muck or moved a piece of wreckage.

The water supply had been seriously compromised by the catastrophe. The Little Conemaugh River, which later emptied into the Allegheny River, provided water for four hundred thousand people and it was now severely contaminated, and stayed that way as it continued to flow through and over the putrefying bodies of people and animals that had not yet been uncovered. The river had also become the sewer system for most of the valley because the cesspools had been overrun by the floodwater. The rivers became so bad that in places as far away as Pittsburgh, people were being told to filter and boil their drinking water.

There was a shortage of disinfectants in Johnstown. Dr. Lee called for all the disinfectants in the state to be sent there directly, and special trains were appointed to fetch any and all that could be found. Interestingly, tar was considered an absolute must for the process of disinfecting the air of the "death carrying odor." They believed that smoke would help clean the air of germs but it needed to be a heavy smoke. The *New York Times* reported, "There are many bonfires ablaze now but their smoke has no quality for good. The odor which would arise from the burning tar would, according to Dr. Lee, be of incalculable value to the hill dwellers, as well as to the temporary residents of the destroyed city." With much work, cleaning, and the education of the public, general

**Quite possibly the most well-known photo taken following the Johnstown Flood.**

**A Johnstown family standing in front of their "Oklahoma house."**

good health was restored to the people of Johnstown and the rivers that flowed through it.

Robert Pitcairn's own railroad men helped tirelessly to clean up and rebuild Johnstown. They started with the railroad. He understood that without the rails, recovery and rebuilding would be greatly slowed. His men had rebuilt the railroad bridges and viaducts in a matter of a week and within another three or four days, the trains were steaming along at full speed again. Work on the debris field behind the stone bridge had proven to be impossible until "Dynamite Bill" Finn, a demolition expert, came in and did his magic, blasting the mass apart with black powder so his nine hundred-man crew could haul it away. Volunteers flocked to the valley to care for the survivors and help clean up the mess.

Five days after the waters receded, a new organization came to town to render aid. An organization that would in time, become familiar throughout the world in the wake of disasters. Clara Barton, the "angel of the battlefield," arrived with the newly formed American Red Cross. They set up tent hospitals and Red Cross hotels, distributed food, clothing and other supplies. Clara Barton became so invested in the welfare of the people of Johnstown that she stayed there for five more months, even though she was nearing seventy.

Donations of food, medical supplies, construction supplies, clothing, shoes, bedding, pots and pans, cleaning supplies, and everything else anyone could think of, poured into town. The Red Cross had to set up distribution centers to handle it all. Money poured in, too; citizens from around the country and the around the world gave generously, donating over $3.7 million.

Today, when we think of emergency housing following a disaster, we picture rows upon rows of FEMA trailers sitting in parking lots or in the driveways of wrecked houses. But the first real emergency housing appeared in Johnstown. "Oklahoma houses" started appearing all around the town. These were manufactured houses designed by a Chicago company for the Oklahoma Land Rush. They were simple, unattractive houses in two sizes: sixteen by twenty-four feet and ten by twenty feet. Never intended to be long-term homes, they did not stand up well to the harsh Pennsylvania winters, but they did put a roof over many heads and provided a secure place to sleep.

A large plot of land was secured in the Grandview Cemetery for the unidentified victims. All 777 of them were buried in individual graves with individual headstones. There had been no massive recovery of bodies in a short amount of time, but instead, a smaller number were found every day for weeks. They had to be buried as they were found.

Three years after the flood, a large memorial monument was erected, the Monument to the Unknown Dead, in Grandview Cemetery. The plot, funeral, headstones and monument were paid for by the state flood commission. Ten thousand spectators came to pay their respects at the unveiling of the monument. The identified victims were buried in a number of cemeteries all over the valley with dozens of funerals performed simultaneously and almost around the clock but a very large number were also buried in Grandview. Numerous priests and ministers came to Johnstown to help bury its dead.

X.J. Swank lost his wife and four children to the floodwaters. In an attempt to make one last statement, condemning those whom he blamed for his loss, Swank put up a sign next to his wife and children's grave stones that read: "Family of X. J. Swank. Wife and 4 children drowned by the South Fork Fishing and Hunting Club. May 31, 1889."

When the results of the flood are put in quantifiable terms, the terrible cost is undeniable.
- 99 entire families were killed, including 396 children
- 124 women and 198 men were left widowed.
- 777 victims were never identified -- one-third of the total lost
- 1,600 homes were destroyed
- $17 million in property damage was done (In 1889 dollars)
- Bodies were found as far away as Cincinnati, Ohio (600 miles away) as late as 1911

**Burial site for the wife and children of X.J. Swank. The sign he posted condemning the club members can be seen on the left.**

The club members who were at the lake the day the dam broke went home to Pittsburgh. The other club members, except for Robert Pitcairn, never came back. Their first response was to donate a thousand blankets. Andrew Carnegie donated $10,000 immediately and later paid for the new library. Pitcairn spent much of his time over the next several months in Johnstown, serving on planning committees and overseeing the reconstruction.

Sadly, only about half of the members donated money to the relief and recovery funds, some as little as $100. And they never came back. Not even to see for themselves what their elitism and disregard had caused and no member ever agreed to any personal, or organizational responsibility for what had happened. The Johnstown Flood became a symbol of a new found expression of resentment and outrage against the giant trusts and corporations. It became the standard bearer for what many Americans thought was going wrong with America. The general consensus was that most of the members of The South Fork Fishing and Hunting Club were simply robber barons who had gotten away with murder.

After the flood, most of the club's assets had been wiped out. The land and buildings were abandoned. Some of the townspeople went up into the mountain to take out their frustrations out on the buildings by breaking windows and trashing some of the furnishings, but little real damage was done. It wasn't possible to sue an abandoned club so a few of the survivors tried to sue individual club members, but they had to show that the individuals had intended to do harm, and this they could not do. No club member was ever held accountable for what they had allowed to happen.

Victor Heiser, the young man who made the dramatic ride on the roof of his family's barn, found that his parents were not among the survivors. His home was gone as was the family store. The only thing he had to left to his name was a single trunk that held some family memorabilia and his father's Civil War uniform. As the last remaining member of his family, it would not have been surprising if Victor had given up and let life pass him by, but he was made of stronger stuff than that. He left town to attend college and later became a physician. He became a hero in his own right when he developed the first effective treatment against leprosy and is credited with saving at least two million lives.

Johnstown not only rebuilt and recovered astoundingly quickly, it prospered again and grew. Within a few years, the population of Johnstown doubled and the Cambria Iron Company quadrupled its steel output. Businesses rebuilt and families settled back in to a happy routine. But the town had not finished with floods. In 1936 and 1977, the Little Conemaugh and Story Creek rose up again and claimed several more lives, but never has anything come close to the killer destruction of the Johnstown Flood of 1889.

# 10 DEADLIEST AMERICAN FLOODS

1. Killed: 2,209 - May 31, 1889 - South Fork Dam collapse - Johnstown, PA
2. Killed: 1,464 - Aug. 29, 2005 - Levee failure due to Hurricane Katrina, LA and MS
3. Killed: 1,100 - April 1927 - Mississippi Valley Flood
4. Killed: 467 - Mar. 23-27, 1913 - Great Ohio Floods (AKA Great Dayton Flood), OH
5. Killed: 450 to 600 - Mar. 12, 1928 - St Francis Dam collapse - Santa Paula, CA
6. Killed: 400 - June 27, 1957 - Storm surge from Hurricane Audrey - East TX and Southwest LA
7. Killed: 385 - Late January to Early February 1937 - Ohio River Flood.  Pittsburgh, PA to Cairo, IL
8. Killed: 238 - June 9-10, 1972 - Black Hills Flood - Rapid City, SD
9. Killed: 200 - May 16 to June 1, 1903 - Kansas City, MO
10. Killed: 200 - April & May, 1912 - Mississippi Valley

The bodies were buried, the town was cleaned up, and the houses and businesses were rebuilt. But that doesn't necessarily mean that everything went back to normal and the dead all rest in peace. The death and devastation caused by the Johnstown Flood was spread over fourteen miles and tens of thousands of square acres of land.  There are dozens of stories and legends of ghosts and hauntings spread throughout the valley, from the dried bed of the once-lovely Lake Conemaugh to the lower valley beyond Johnstown. It is difficult to determine which of the many spirits were of people who had died a watery death in 1889. The valley itself has much reason to be haunted, with Native American battlegrounds and burial mounds, a deadly coal mine explosion and Revolutionary War deaths -- and several other floods.

There are however, several accounts that we can comfortably connect with this terrible disaster. On or around the anniversary of the flood, people commonly report having difficulty spending much time in the downtown area in Johnstown. They experience feelings of anxiety and discomfort. Occasionally, these feelings are so strong that they begin to have trouble breathing and the air around them feels thick and heavy. The only cure is to leave the area.  Another recurrent manifestation is that of a terrible odor. While walking along a downtown sidewalk on any given day or night, one might catch a whiff of death and decay. One woman explained that she thought she had walked through a "pocket" of putrid odor. It was so strong that it penetrated her sinuses and clung to her clothing. She went straight home to change and wash her clothes. The smell in her nose faded over time.

It is not recommended that you walk along the old stone bridge at dusk, for that is the time of day when the flood victims seem to prefer. Faint shouts for help and cries of pain and anguish can sometimes be heard in the vicinity of the bridge, along with soft sounds of wood smashing against wood or stone and an eerie grinding noise.  The odor of death and burned flesh sometimes permeates the air around the bridge.

In one particular house, along a lonely side street just below Johnstown, it sometimes sounds as if a family is preparing for death. On very quiet nights, if you stand just outside in the yard, you may hear the voices of a panicked man and woman, and sounds of children screaming for help...

There is nowhere more closely associated with spirits of the flood victims than Grandview Cemetery. It is here where many of the victims were buried along with the 777 unidentified bodies. These people were buried with no living persons knowing their names or anything about them. They not only died suddenly and tragically, but they went to their graves having had their lives become no more than a smudge in our history, with no one there to miss them, no one to remember them. A number of apparitions have been witnessed in area of the unknown graves in Grandview over the years. An older couple, walking with their arms linked; a young boy or girl, dressed in fragments of clothing and seeming to be frantically looking for someone or something; men and women wandering the rows of the unknown; a baby, sitting on one of the unknown graves, crying inconsolably. Sometimes, they are not seen, just heard. There are quiet sobs, names called out, cries for help, and sighs of frustration.

There is always the hope that the lost and unknown will eventually find who they are looking for, or someone who knows them, and they will finally rest in whatever peace they can make for themselves. But in over a century, that time has still not come.

David McCullough, historian and author of one of the most respected books about the Johnstown Flood, believed that the greatest tragedy was that the flood was completely avoidable, that not a single person needed to die. He further suggested that of the many lessons learned, maybe the most important lesson was that, "it is a grave mistake to ever assume that just because there are people in positions of responsibility, they are therefore behaving responsibly."

# 1904: THE BURNING OF THE *GENERAL SLOCUM*

If you were to ask a group of native New Yorkers to name the city's worst disaster prior to the September 11, 2001 terrorist attack, nearly all of them would answer with the Triangle Shirtwaist Factory fire in 1911. Indeed, that was a terrible disaster in which 148 factory workers, mostly young women and girls, were killed. This tragedy drew the attention of the nation, if not the world. And yet the loss of life in the Triangle Shirtwaist Factory fire is diminished by the number of lives lost on the *SS General Slocum* as it burned in the Hell Gate area of the East River in New York City only seven years earlier.

The Knickerbocker Steamship Company needed a second passenger steamship to carry visitors back and forth from New York City to Rockaway Beach during the summer resort season. The *SS General Slocum* was commissioned and built in Brooklyn to fulfill that need. Before and after the Rockaway Beach season, the *General Slocum* was an excursion ship carrying visitors around New York City and was available for private charter.

The ship had a 235-foot-long wooden hull, three expansive decks and a passenger capacity of three thousand. The *Slocum* was, by design, a "sidewheel" boat. This means her paddlewheels, 31 feet in diameter, were located on each side, just aft of the center of the ship. Launched in 1891, her white hull with brilliant gold lettering and bright orange paddlewheels made her a spectacular sight as she steamed around New York. As an excursion ship, she was one of the most popular and recognizable steaming the New York City waters. At the time the *General Slocum* burned, at least half of the people living in New York had either been aboard her or had seen her close up.

Many believed the *General Slocum* was a cursed ship, however that idea never made it into print until after the fire and sinking. In support of these claims, during her fourteen years afloat, she did experience a series of unfortunate mishaps. The first in a long succession of problems that plagued the *General Slocum* involved the drowning of a young girl, who had been accidentally pushed overboard by an overzealous crowd.

It turned out that 1894 was a very bad year for the ship. In July, while carrying 4,700 passengers, she ran onto a sandbar so hard that her lights were completely knocked out. The *New York Times* reported, "A panic followed, in which women who fainted were trampled upon, and men fought with each other to get to the boats. Pandemonium reigned for half an hour, until order was restored by the crew. Then it was found that hundreds had been injured in the wild scrimmage." In August, she ran into another sandbar off Coney Island during a terrible storm. Panic again ruled the night until the storm eased and the passengers were transferred to another boat. The very next month, the *Slocum* collided with a tugboat, the *R.T. Sayre*. She drifted helplessly about the East River, nearly running aground on the rocks off Governor's Island before another tugboat was able to push her to safety.

The *General Slocum* suffered only minor scrapes over the next four years; however, in 1898 she collided with the lighter *Amelia*, just off the Battery. The two ships struck each other so hard that they became locked together and had to be separated by tugs. Then in June of 1902, during a return trip from Rockaway Beach, she again ran aground on yet another sandbar. As it was already dark, the four hundred passengers on board had to camp out on deck all night until they could be rescued the next morning.

On August 17, 1901, a bizarre event occurred aboard the *General Slocum*. The ship had been hired to take a group of four hundred people, mostly men, to Rockaway Beach. The men, immigrant workers from the silk mills of Paterson, New Jersey, were reportedly already drunk when they boarded the vessel. As the ship steamed into open waters, she was met by a storm with heavy seas. The drunken passengers, whom news reports dubbed the "Paterson Anarchists," for their rowdy behavior and labor union affiliation, panicked and insisted that the captain turn around. When he refused, a group of them stormed the bridge in an attempt to take over the ship. The crew fought the group off successfully and was able to lock them in cabins until the captain could land. At least seventeen of the so-called anarchists were arrested and most of those ended up in jail.

St. Mark's Evangelical Lutheran Church was located in Little Germany, also known as *Kleindeutschland*, a New York community of eighty thousand German inhabitants located along the Lower East Side near Tompkins Square. St. Marks held an annual celebration to commemorate the conclusion of their Sunday school year. In 1904, the parishioners chose to charter the *General Slocum* to take them to Locust Point on Huntington Bay on the North Shore of on Long Island for a picnic. The charter cost them $350 and for most of them, their lives.

On the morning of June 15, 1904, Captain William Van Schaick and his crew of twenty docked the *General Slocum* for boarding at the Third Street and East River pier. The scene was that of great fanfare with excited parents and children. The *Slocum* band played German favorites. Because it was a Wednesday and most men were at work, a majority of those boarding the ship that day were women and children. In all, 1,358 souls were on the *General Slocum* that day. Only 337 were still alive just two hours later.

The ship was loaded and underway by 9:30 a.m. One survivor recalled the *General Slocum*, "glided through the water so smoothly that the children were allowed to move around and play as they wished about the deck." As it turned out, her smooth sailing was not so fortunate, as families who had wandered apart towards the beginning of the journey would later spend much precious time frantically searching the parts of the ship not burning, trying to

**The General Slocum docked and loading passengers, providing a good view of her three passenger decks.**

**(Left)** The *General Slocum*, still upright but burning to the water line. **(Right)** The General Slocum continued to burn as fireboats tried to extinguish the last of the fire.

find their children.

Less than thirty minutes after casting off, twelve-year-old Frank Prawdzicki was the first to notice signs of fire. He tried to warn the captain but was pushed away from the bridge and told not to bother the officers again. Ten minutes later, a general fire alarm spread through the ship. Young Frank Prawdzicki and his mother survived the fire but his four sisters, Annie, age fifteen, Henrietta, age thirteen, Gertrude, age three and one-year-old Johanna, were all lost.

The fire spread through the ship faster than anyone could have possibly imagined. Feeding the flames further was the highly flammable paint with which the ship had recently been repainted. However, the main reason the flames spread with such ferocity was because of what Captain Van Schaick did next. Many believed that he badly mishandled the fire and the situation that followed.

When the Captain was first notified of the fire in the forward compartment, they were steaming past a large set of piers where he could have docked in time to possibly save countless lives. Instead, he steamed ahead at full speed for nearly five minutes before beaching the ship on the shores of North Brother Island. He later tried to explain, "I started to head for 134th Street, but was warned off by the captain of a tugboat, who shouted to me that the boat would set fire to the lumber yards and oil tanks there. Besides, I knew that the shore was lined with rocks and the boat would founder if I put in there. I then fixed upon North Brother Island."

Unfortunately, as the ship steamed ahead at full speed, the wind fanned the flames fiercely and caused them to move toward the aft (rear) part of the ship where most of those aboard had taken refuge from the smoke and heat. The fire ate away at the decks with amazing speed. A flotilla of small boats and tugs followed the raging inferno as she sped down river.

It would not be one single thing that doomed the ship. Even though the *General Slocum* had experienced a variety of mishaps during her short life, Captain Von Schaick had received a number of safety commendations as he was ultimately in charge of safety on board the ship. Little did anyone know that the Captain had become very lax in regard to safety. In reality, the *General Slocum* had become a floating deathtrap. The crew had never been trained in the required safety drills or with the safety equipment, most of which was aged and rotted. The ship's life boats were originally lashed in place with ropes, but as the ropes had begun to rot, they were reattached with wire and could not be released during the fire.

The times were also a factor in the large number of lives lost. In the early twentieth century, very few people knew how to swim, especially those living in the city. The clothing worn by the women and young girls also proved to be a great hindrance to their survival. Long, heavy skirts and the petticoats worn underneath grew heavy in the water and clung to their legs, pulling them down and making it impossible to for them to swim or even stay afloat. And these were Victorian times. Devout, church-going women would never have considered stripping down to their undergarments before jumping, even to save their own lives. Also, many waited on the ship too long and were killed when the decks burned through and collapsed. Others were mauled to death by the still-turning paddle wheels as they jumped over the side.

The first action taken by the crew was to try to put out the fire using the on-board fire hoses. Having never been used before or replaced as needed, most crumbled as they were taken from their racks. The hoses that didn't crumble into pieces, burst apart when the water pumps were turned on. After this first course of action failed, a majority of the crew abandoned ship leaving the passengers to fend for themselves. One survivor related, "...it seemed to me that the crew of the boat lost their heads -- they were undisciplined, and did not do what sane men would have done to stay the panic and restore order."

Three thousand life preservers were hung along the interior deck walls near the ceilings. Passengers climbed onto deck chairs and camp stools to take them down but found that many of them were stuck to the walls, evidently put back too soon after the recent paint job. Others simply fell apart in their hands, the fabric shredding, releasing the granulated cork inside. At that time, solid pieces of cork were sewn inside life preservers and maritime law required a minimum amount of cork be placed in each, measured by the weight of the finished jacket. The Nonpareil Cork Works, makers of the life preservers used on the *General Slocum*, had used useless lightweight granulated cork instead of the required solid cork. It was later discovered that in order to reach the required minimum weight, the company had placed iron bars and pieces of stone inside the jackets.

A few of the life jackets did stay intact for a while. Mothers strapped their babies and young children into the remaining life preservers, took them to the rail of the ship and dropped them over the side. To their utter horror, they stood and watched as their children hit the water's surface and immediately sunk from sight, pulled down by the weighted jackets that were supposed to keep them afloat.

Joseph Halphusen, the church sextant described the scene as "pure panic." He further described how a sheet of flame followed rolling clouds of smoke. A rush began towards the sides of the boat during which women and children were thrown down and trampled. He said that many were pushed overboard and even more jumped into the river. Mr. Halphusen waited till the last minute before he dropped his two daughters over the side and jumped himself, just as a rescue tug arrived in time to fish all three from the water.

Because this was to be a cheerful family-oriented outing, George Maurer, the *Slocum* bandleader, brought along his wife. Margaret, and daughters Clara, age twelve, and Matilda, age fourteen. Margaret died a few days after the fire from burns. His daughters drowned, as did Maurer himself. When his body was recovered, his forehead carried the imprint from a boot heel. It was believed that after he was already in the water, someone landed on him as they jumped.

As the *General Slocum* struck the shore of North Brother Island, Nicholas Balser was at the aft end of the ship, waiting till the last minute to jump. When at last he did jump, to his surprise he landed in water only up to his armpits and walked out onto the shore. "When I finally emerged, I looked back and to my dying day I'll never forget the scene. Around me were scores of bodies, most of them charred and burned. I helped as many as possible of those still living to land. From the stern of the boat, where hundreds of persons were huddled fighting like mad to leap into the water, I saw dozens of women and children throw themselves over the side."

Catherine Kassebaum, and the ten family members she brought with her that day, wanted to listen to the music, so they all gathered around the band. A woman's scream reached them before any smoke was noticed. Thinking that someone had fallen overboard, she and her family scanned the waters below. Within seconds, the true nature of the problem became apparent when smoke began billowing toward them and they heard general panic on the forward part of the deck. Catherine, realizing that she had to stay calm if there was any chance for survival, called her family together, instructing the strong to care for the weak, but they were soon overtaken by a mass of screaming women and children rushing toward them in an attempt to escape the oncoming smoke and flames.

Catherine's family disappeared as the crowd swept past her. She was able to climb onto a rail for a better vantage point, trying to spot any of her family. Her hands and face were scorched and blistered, holes were burning in her clothing; she finally decided to take her chances by jumping into the water. She described the feeling that she would never again surface when she saw a flash of light and something solid above her. She was later found alive, clinging to the ship's paddle box. Her daughter Nettie had waited until she saw a tugboat approach the burning ship and jumped onto the deck, breaking her leg. Though mother and daughter were reunited, the remaining nine members of their family perished.

The family of Anna Weber was slightly more fortunate than the Kassebaums. At the first puff of smoke, Anna began rushing about the deck searching for her children. The heat was so intense that her face was scorched and her hair caught fire. Hoping that her husband had found their children, she went to the side of the boat and tried to lower herself down by a rope. Her flesh blistered every time her hands or face touched the side of the boat. She finally dropped when her rope burst into flames. Anna was soon pulled to the shore of North Brother Island by an unknown savior where she found her husband with his clothes burned off, wandering about looking for their children.

Frank and Anna Weber lost both their son and daughter, along with her sister. Their friends, Paul and Anna Liebenow, whom the Webers had invited along as a special treat, lost two daughters but their six-month old daughter Adelia was miraculously saved. The following year little Adelia Leibenow (later Witherspoon) unveiled the Steamboat Fire Mass Memorial. She went on to live a full life and was the last known *General Slocum* survivor. She died in 2004 at the age of one hundred.

The Reverend George Hass, pastor of St. Marks, had been on a tour of the ship as it first got underway. As smoke began pouring up from below he was able to find his wife, Anna, and his sister, Emma. They waited on the middle deck, searching for George and Anna's thirteen-year old daughter, Gertrude. When they realized that the deck above them was about to collapse, they jumped together into the water. Rev. Hass described how he

**Bodies are pulled from the water and laid out on the North Brother Island Hospital lawn.**

thought he must have put on his life preserver incorrectly because it seemed to be pulling him deeper under water. He was able to free himself and floated to the surface, but by that point, had lost track of his wife. Of the entire Hass party, only Rev. Hass and his sister survived the ordeal.

By the time the *General Slocum* was beached on North Brother Island, she was fully engulfed in flames. She ran aground in about 25 feet of water, just off the shoreline. Fireboats arrived shortly, along with other small boats and tugs. These smaller boats maneuvered around the bodies and wreckage, plucking any survivors they found from the water. Captain Van Schaick jumped to the deck of an approaching tug, with an injury to his eye that left him blind on one side, but otherwise unharmed and dry.

North Brother Island was a hospital island for contagious diseases. Many medical personnel and patients watched from the hospital windows as the *General Slocum* approached. They rushed the short distance to the shore to render any aid they could. City Health Commissioner Thomas Darlington happened to be visiting the hospital that day. "I will never be able to forget the scene, the utter horror of it," he said later. He described how the patients in the contagious wards "went wild at the things they saw from their windows." They screamed and beat at the doors until they were finally quieted by a number of staff members. They watched as the small boats were arriving with the survivors, and towing large numbers of bodies.

The island became a "scene of courage and panic." Many stories of heroism and cruelty were printed in the newspapers over the next week. A tugboat captain risked his boat and crew by pulling right up to the flames and is said to have saved nearly a hundred lives. Some quite ill patients left the safety of their hospital beds and ran into the water, rescuing as many children as they could. One newspaper reporter wrote of the actions of a particular hospital staff member, "A nurse who always wished she could swim ran into the river to grab some children, which she did again and again until she was swept into deeper water, where she discovered that she could swim, and continued saving lives."

Over the following few days, hordes of souvenir hunters made the recovery of bodies much more difficult as they washed ashore on North Brother Island and other sites down river. Thieves stripped many of the bodies of jewelry and other valuables as they lay at the high tide line. Hospital attendants chased away a man they found stooped over the body of a woman, attempting to steal the gold watch chain that she wore at her waist. Then there was the large and mysterious white yacht that was cursed by many as it lay just yards away without making any attempt to help with the rescue. A *New York Times* headline screamed from the page that the private captain "Kept His Yacht Back While Scores Perished: White Vessel's Captain Watched *Slocum* Horror Through Glasses."

The bodies that were pulled from the water or washed ashore on North Brother Island were laid out side by side on the grass outside the hospital. They were later moved to a makeshift morgue at the East 23rd Street Pier. Coroner William J. O'Gorman announced that more than $200,000 in cash and jewelry was recovered from the victims. Eva Eingler's body was found to have $30,000 in cash, securities and bankbooks on it. It is unknown why she took that much money with her on what was supposed to be a short excursion. The funds, jewelry and personal items taken from the victims were taken to the coroner's office to be held for the owners' survivors. A volunteer who was taking inventory of the victims' personal effects was startled to discover that fifteen-year-old Clara Hartman of East Ninth Street, pulled from the water and thought to be drowned, was still alive three hours after the fire on board the *General Slocum*.

Rescue volunteers and police openly sobbed as they moved bodies hour after hour. As morgue staff worked to lay out the bodies as they arrived, others were sent to search the city for wooden coffins. Still others brought back tons of ice to help maintain the bodies until they could be identified and claimed by family members.

While still burning, the hull of the *General Slocum* was washed a few thousand yards down river by the current until it became lodged in the mud. In following weeks the hull remained partially submerged just off of Hunts Point in the Bronx. Divers were sent down into the hull to search for and recover trapped bodies. Police continued to search the riverbanks for many weeks, collecting bodies and debris from the boat that continued to wash ashore.

While the divers were searching the burned-out hull, they discovered many bodies lying at the bottom of the river. Continuing their search they found a deep hole in the riverbed from which they retrieved more than fifty more bodies. All of these bodies were wearing life preservers. The very life preservers that were supposed to save

**(Left) The burned-out and partially sunken hull of the General Slocum.**
**(Right) Some of the metal work remained intact within the hull.**

their lives were weighing their bodies down, making the recovery that much more difficult.

When they heard about the disaster, huge numbers of people amassed at St. Mark's Church to await news of survivors. Still others rushed to the morgue trying to get information faster. Over the next week, thousands upon thousands of New Yorkers walked past the rows of bodies, hoping to find a lost friend or family member. Though many bodies were never recovered, assumed to have washed out to sea, 61 were never identified and were buried in a common grave in the Cemetery of the Evergreens in Brooklyn. The tragedy was further deepened as people committed suicide after learning they had lost their entire families. They may have died later but they were killed by the *General Slocum* as surely as if they had been killed by the flames.

Funerals were held every hour around the clock in Little Germany. With such a large number of dead, all having lived in the same community, nearly everyone in Little Germany had lost a friend or family member or knew someone who had. The deep sadness of the tragedy seemed to permeate the very fabric of the community and people started to leave. Within a few years, only a small handful of the original inhabitants were left and Little Germany was no more.

Of the 1,021 people who died as a direct result of the fire on board the *General Slocum*, over ninety percent of them were women, children and infants.

Outrage was the order of the day as people wondered how such a tremendous tragedy could occur within a few hundred yards of one of the most modern cities in the world. Someone had to be held accountable for such a great loss. City leaders vowed to bring to justice those who were to blame. Within a few weeks, the main executives of the Knickerbocker Steamship Co. were indicted along with Captain Van Schaick and a safety inspector. Also indicted were the top executives of the Nonpareil Cork Works, makers of the deadly life preservers. They were never convicted.

**Relatives wait outside the morgue for their turn to enter and identify their lost family members.**

During the trial, it was revealed that the Knickerbocker Steamship Company had falsified records, covering up its lack of concern for passenger safety. In return for their complicity in the tragedy, they received only a small fine.

Captain Van Schaick's story ended differently. Though he tried to explain his actions on that terrible day, the jury was not convinced. In the end, the captain was the ultimate authority for safety on his ship and he was held accountable. Convicted of criminal negligence and manslaughter, Captain Van Schaick was sentenced to ten years hard labor at Sing Sing Prison. Though he appealed for his release directly to President Theodore Roosevelt, a native New Yorker, he was repeatedly refused. After serving three and a half years, he was pardoned under President William Howard Taft and spent the rest of his life in seclusion, a broken man, until his death in 1927.

The cause of the fire was quickly discovered. The night before the *General Slocum's* final trip, deck hand Dan O'Neill violated fire regulations by storing a barrel of packing hay on board. He placed the hay in a closet with a stash of oil lamps. This proved to be the deadliest of mixtures.

Just one month before the fire, Henry Lundburg, Assistant Inspector of Hulls, performed a safety inspection of the *General Slocum*. During this inspection, he determined that the life preservers were "up to date and of good quality." When inspecting the water pumps and fire hoses, he didn't seem at all concerned that no water came out when he turned the valves on and off. Another part of the inspection required him to climb up to the lifeboats to check them. Instead, he merely glanced up and checked the box for "in good condition" on his form and walked on.

The great tragedy that occurred aboard the *General Slocum*, resulting in the horrific deaths of so many innocent men, women and children were in large part due to the illegal actions and corrupt behaviors of Henry Lundberg and Dan O'Neill. Neither of these men spent a single day in jail.

In 1906, a memorial fountain to the victims of the fire was erected at the north end of Tompkins Square Park.

The remains of the *General Slocum's* hull were recovered and rebuilt into a barge named the *Maryland*, which sank off of Sandy Hook, New Jersey, during a December storm in 1911. The curse, some said, continued.

Captain Van Schaick lived for twenty years after he was released from prison, though he didn't get much rest during that time. He privately told friends that his nights were frequently interrupted by the screams of women and children. His days were filled with shadows in the corners and the smell of burning flesh. In the end, it was said that he welcomed death. Was he being haunted by the victims of the great tragedy in which he was at least partially to blame, or was his tormentor his own conscience?

So many suffered to learn such harsh lessons. Perhaps the greatest tragedy of this disaster is that so much is left without rest, so many lost forever. But many were left witness, to remember the flames, to remember the screams, to remember the horror.

# 1912: TITANIC

Although not the most deadly disaster in maritime history, the sinking of the *Titanic* in 1912 is, without question, the most famous. The *RMS Titanic* was an Olympic-class passenger liner that was owned by the White Star Line and at the time of her construction, she was the largest passenger steamship in the world.

Shortly before midnight on April 14, 1912, four days into the ship's maiden voyage, *Titanic* struck an iceberg and sank in just two hours and forty minutes – carrying 1,517 people to the depths of the Atlantic Ocean. A shocked world learned the news on April 15, particularly stunned by the fact that the ship had been deemed "unsinkable." The frenzy on the part of the media about *Titanic's* famous victims, the legends about the sinking, the resulting changes to maritime law, the discovery of the wreck and one of history's highest grossing films based on her story have continued the notoriety of *Titanic* over the years.

And so have the ghost stories. For not only are strange tales told of sea where the ship sank, there are many who believe that many of the artifacts that were salvaged from the ship are haunted, as well. Truth? Legend? Perhaps more than a little of both, the story of *Titanic* may be one of the most puzzling tales in America's haunted history.

At four city blocks long and eleven stories high, *Titanic* was the biggest ship ever built when she was launched at the Harland and Wolff shipyards in Belfast, Ireland. The White Star Line wanted *Titanic* and her sister ship, *Olympic,* built to carry passengers between Europe and the United States in unprecedented comfort and safety. *Titanic,* the more luxurious of the two ships, had a gymnasium, Turkish bath, squash court and shipboard swimming pool. It also had a hospital and a darkroom for developing photographs taken on board the ship. The opulent staterooms, lounges and dining areas, as well as the attentive service reminded first-class passengers of staying in one of the world's finest hotels. Even the third-class accommodations far surpassed those aboard second class on *Titanic's* competitors.

First-class common rooms were adorned with ornate wood paneling, expensive furniture and other decorations. In addition, the Café Parisian offered French cuisine for the

first-class passengers, with a sunlit veranda fitted with trellis decorations. There were libraries and barber shops in both the first and second-class. The third class general room had pine paneling and sturdy teak furniture. The ship also had a number of features that were far ahead of its time. She had three electric elevators in first class and one in second class. She had also an extensive electrical subsystem with steam-powered generators and ship-wide wiring feeding electric lights and two Marconi radios, including a powerful 1,500-watt set manned by two operators working in shifts, allowing constant contact and the transmission of many passenger messages. First-class passengers paid a hefty fee for such amenities. The most expensive one-way trans-Atlantic passage was $4,350.

White Star ordered Harland and Wolff to build the ships for safety, as well as comfort. Theorizing that running aground and collisions were the greatest dangers that a ship could encounter, *Titanic* was engineered to withstand these two types of damage. She had a double-bottomed hull and the interior was divided by transverse bulkheads into a series of sixteen watertight compartments. According to its designers, *Titanic* could stay afloat with the first four compartments completely flooded, and in the event of a broadside collision, the ship could stay afloat with any two central compartments completely flooded. It was inconceivable to the owners and builders that *Titanic* would ever encounter a greater threat than this. These features caused *Shipbuilder* magazine to call *Titanic* "practically unsinkable."

Overconfidence in the seaworthiness of the ship led the builders and owners to send *Titanic* into service with only enough lifeboats for about half of the people on board. Although in her early plans she was to have 32 lifeboats for her full capacity of three thousand passengers and crew, they did not consider it necessary to provide lifeboats for all on board; they believed that in the event of a mishap, passengers would be safer staying on the ship than getting into small lifeboats on the tossing waves of the Atlantic. In addition, outdated regulations from

**(Left) Titanic's grand staircase  (Right) One of the spacious decks, "uncluttered" by lifeboats**

the British Board of Trade, the agency that governed safety matters for British ships, required only sixteen lifeboats on ships weighing more than ten thousand tons. The regulations had made no extra provisions for larger ships since 1894, when the largest passenger ship in existence weighed thirteen thousand tons. Sir Alfred Chalmers, nautical adviser to the Board of Trade from 1896 to 1911, had considered the matter "from time to time," but because he thought that experienced sailors would have to be carried "uselessly" aboard ship for no other purpose than lowering and manning lifeboats, and the difficulty he anticipated in getting away a greater number than sixteen boats in any emergency, he "did not consider it necessary to increase [our scale]."

Under these regulations, *Titanic,* which weighed more than 46,000 tons, had a total of twenty lifeboats, which exceeded the board's minimum requirements. Therefore, the White Star Line actually provided more lifeboats than was legally required.

But it would not be enough to save the lives of hundreds of passengers on board the doomed ship.

*Titanic* began her maiden voyage from Southampton, England, bound for New York on April 10, 1912, with Captain Edward J. Smith in command. As the ship left her berth, her wake caused the liner *SS New York*, which was docked nearby, to break away from her moorings, whereupon she was drawn dangerously close (about four feet) to *Titanic* before a tugboat towed the *New York* away. The incident delayed the departure for about an hour and marked an ominous start to what should have been a celebratory occasion.

# NOTABLES ABOARD *TITANIC*

**(Left to Right) Captain Edward Smith; White Star Managing Director J. Bruce Ismay;   Ship's Builder Thomas Andrews**

**John Jacob Astor & wife, Madeleine; Benjamin Guggenheim; Isidor & Ida Strauss; Margaret "Molly" Brown**

**Sir Cosmo Duff-Gordon; Lady Lucy Duff-Gordon; author Helen Churchill Candee; Silent film actress Dorothy Gibson**

After crossing the English Channel, *Titanic* stopped at Cherbourg, France, to board additional passengers and stopped again the following day at Queenstown (known today as Cobh), Ireland. As harbor facilities at Queenstown were inadequate for a ship of her size, *Titanic* had to anchor off shore, with small boats, known as tenders, ferrying the embarking passengers out to her. When she finally set out for New York, there were 2,240 people aboard.

*Titanic's* maiden voyage attracted some of the most prominent people of the day, all traveling in first-class, of course. Among them were millionaire John Jacob Astor IV and his nineteen-year-old pregnant wife, Madeleine Force Astor; industrialist Benjamin Guggenheim; Macy's department store owner Isidor Straus and his wife, Ida; Denver millionaire Margaret "Molly" Brown (known afterwards as the "Unsinkable Molly Brown" due to her efforts in helping other passengers while the ship sank); Sir Cosmo Duff-Gordon and his wife, fashion designer Lucy (Lady Duff-Gordon); George Elkins Widener and his wife, Eleanor; cricketer and businessman John Borland Thayer with his wife, Marian, and their seventeen-year-old son, Jack; journalist William Thomas Stead; the Countess of Rothes; United States presidential aide Archibald Butt; author and socialite Helen Churchill Candee; author Jacques Futrelle his wife, May, and their friends; Broadway producers Henry and Rene Harris; and silent film actress Dorothy Gibson, among others. American financier J.P. Morgan was scheduled to travel on the maiden voyage, but he cancelled at the last minute. Also travelling in first–class aboard the ship were White Star Line's managing director J. Bruce Ismay and the ship's builder, Thomas Andrews, who was on board to observe any problems and assess the general performance of the new ship.

The shortest route between Great Britain and the United States was a "great circle" that took ships far north in the Atlantic Ocean to take advantage of the curve of the earth. Ice was a frequent navigational hazard on this route. In fact, from January 15 to August 14, ships used the "summer route," which was farther south and longer than the "winter route" but provided protection from icebergs that would drift south from the late winter to late summer. In April 1912, however, *Titanic's* use of the summer route was not sufficient to avoid encountering ice. It had been an unusually mild winter and ice had drifted farther south than usual and into the shipping lanes.

Minor disorganization and occasionally shaky communications plagued the early days of the voyage and contributed to the disaster. All of it was attributable to the unfamiliarity of the crew with the new ship and with each other. For example, the lookouts high up in the crow's next had no binoculars. At Southampton, some of the binoculars of the officers on the bridge were lost when senior officers were changed at the last minute to bring in a more experienced crew. The officers kept the remaining pairs on the bridge, leaving the lookouts without any for the duration of the trip. Needless to say, binoculars might have made it possible for the lookout to spot the iceberg much sooner and perhaps the ship could have avoided it altogether.

In addition, even though *Titanic* was outfitted with a state-of-the-art, long range Marconi radio set, two critically important messages, which would have warned the ship's officers about ice directly in her path that Sunday, did not reach the bridge at all. During the voyage, the ship's wireless operators relayed and received several messages from ships encountering ice along the route, but there was no protocol giving priority to

messages with navigational information and delivering them immediately to the bridge. Unaware of how close the dangerous ice field was, Captain Smith saw no reason to slow down or to post extra lookouts on a clear night.

Weather conditions on the night of April 14 added to the danger. Visibility was clear, but there was no moon, and the sea was dead calm. This made it more difficult to spot icebergs that were a long way off and a ship as large as *Titanic* needed as much time as possible to turn and steer around any hazards in its path.

As *Titanic* sailed across the ocean that night, the captain and crew had no idea of what lay ahead of them. Earlier that afternoon, a message from the steamer *Amerika* warned that icebergs lay in the ship's path, but since Jack Phillips and Harold Bride, the Marconi wireless operators, were employed by Marconi and paid to relay messages to and from the passengers, they were not worried about relaying such "non-essential" messages to the bridge. Later that evening, another report, this time from the *Mesaba,* also failed to reach the captain.

At 11:40 p.m., while sailing about four hundred miles south of the Grand Banks of Newfoundland, lookouts Frederick Fleet and Reginald Lee, spotted a large iceberg directly ahead of the ship. It seemed to come from nowhere. Fleet sounded the ships' bell three times and telephoned the bridge, crying out a warning, "Iceberg, right ahead!" – but the warning came too late.

First Officer William Murdoch gave the order "hard-a-starboard", using the traditional tiller order for an abrupt turn to port, and adjusted the engines through the telegraph for "full reverse" or "stop." However, survivor testimony conflicts about this. The iceberg brushed the ship's starboard side, buckling the hull in several places and popping out rivets below the waterline over a length of 299 feet. As seawater filled the forward compartments, the watertight doors shut. However, while the ship could stay afloat with four flooded compartments, five were filling with water. The five water-filled compartments weighed down the ship so that the tops of the forward watertight bulkheads fell below the ship's waterline, allowing water to pour into additional compartments.

Captain Smith, alerted by the jolt of the impact, arrived on the bridge and ordered a full stop. Shortly after midnight, following an inspection by the ship's officers and its builder, Thomas Andrews, the lifeboats were ordered to be readied and a distress call was sent out.

Unfortunately, neither the passengers nor all of the officers initially knew the full gravity of the situation, so assembling the passengers and readying and loading the lifeboats at first went slowly. Many of the boats were lowered half empty by officers who, never informed that they had been tested by Harland and Wolff, did not trust them to hold the stated capacity. The fact that there were no assigned placed on the boats and that there had been no boat drill for either passengers or crew during the voyage added to the confusion of the process, as did the apparent lack of seamen experienced in lowering and handling small boats. Of the crew of nine hundred, fewer than seventy were actually seamen. Most were stewards, cooks, bellboys, janitors and the service workers needed to run a floating luxury hotel. Without a drill and with too few sailors to guide them, third-class passengers found it difficult to make their way to the lifeboats. As a result, the poorer, steerage passengers suffered a much higher casualty rate. Only a few of the third-class male passengers, and less than half of the third-class female and child passengers survived, despite the emphasis on loading women and children first into the lifeboats.

At first, there was little sense of urgency. Passengers, confident of the massive ship's safety, were reluctant to be lowered almost seventy feet down to the surface of the icy water in what seemed to be precarious boats. The crew didn't force them to go. It was warmer inside the ship and, at least in the first-class lounge, where the ship's band played music to keep everyone's spirits up.

As the bow of the ship sank lower and lower it became clear that *Titanic* was sinking. By this time, most of the lifeboats – some of them barely filled – were gone. As the final boats were loaded, ship's officers had to use the threat of firearms to keep order among the tense and panicking passengers.

While all of this was happening, wireless operators Jack Phillips and Harold Bride were busy sending out CQD, the international distress signal. Several ships responded, including *Mount Temple, Frankfurt* and *Titanic's* sister ship, *Olympic*, but none of them were close enough to reach *Titanic* before it went down. The closest ship to respond was Cunard's *Carpathia*, which was 58 miles away. It arrived in four hours, long after those in the freezing water had perished. The only land–based location that received the distress call from *Titanic* was a

## EERIE PREDICTIONS OF *TITANIC'S* DEMISE?

Did as book predict the *Titanic* disaster? American author Morgan Robertson, who was known for his novels of adventure on the high seas, published a short fictional book called "Futility," which chronicled the sinking of the British ship *Titan*. The fictional ship was eerily similar to the *Titanic* in size, speed, equipment, number of passengers and number of those lost in the wreck.

Both the real ship and the fictional ship were British and sailed in April with a top speed of 24 knots. They had the same passenger and crew capacity of three thousand but sailed with a little over two thousand. Also they were between eight hundred and nine hundred feet long and driven with triple propellers. Each also sank about 95 miles south of Greenland – after being pierced by an iceberg on their starboard side.

"Futility" tells the story of a luxury ocean lined named *Titan*. It was the largest ship afloat and had the best in modern technology, including watertight bulkheads that made her virtually unsinkable. She set off on a voyage across the North Atlantic, carrying many wealthy and influential passengers. Moving at her full speed through cold waters on an icy April night, *Titan* collided with an iceberg on the fore-starboard side close to midnight, tearing gashes in the ship's hull below the waterline. *Titan* lacked enough lifeboats for all of those aboard, and eventually sank resulting in a tremendous loss of life, despite the watertight compartments. There were few survivors.

With all of these obvious similarities, you might think that Robertson 'borrowed' the story of *Titanic* for his book, but in that theory there is just one problem: "Futility," Robertson's account of the doomed *Titan*, was written in 1898 --- fourteen years before *Titanic* sank.

From the bridge, the lights of a nearby ship could be seen off the port side. The identity of this ship remains a mystery, but it was subsequently identified by the British Board of Trade as the Boston-bound liner *Californian*. However, the *Californian's* captain denied it and told a different story. Since the mystery ship did not respond to wireless calls, Fourth Officer Joseph Boxhall and Quartermaster George Rowe attempted signaling the ship with a Morse lamp and later with distress rockets, but the ship never responded.

According to Stanley Lord, captain of the *Californian*, his ship was nearby and stopped for the night because of ice. He also saw lights in the distance. The *Californian's* wireless was turned off, and the wireless operator had gone to bed for the night. Just before he went to bed at around 11:00 p.m., the *Californian's* radio operator attempted to warn *Titanic* that there was ice ahead, but he was cut off by an Jack Phillips in *Titanic's* radio room, who had fired back an angry response, "Shut up, shut up, I am busy; I am working Cape Race," referring to the Newfoundland wireless station. When the *Californian's* officers first saw the lights of an unidentified ship, they tried signaling her with their Morse lamp, but never appeared to receive a response. Later, they noticed the ship's distress signals over the lights and informed the captain. After much discussion, they decided the distress flares must be fireworks being set off to entertain the unknown ship's passengers. Even though there was much discussion about the mysterious ship, which appeared to the officers on duty to be moving away, the master of the *Californian* did not wake her wireless operator until morning. Whether the mystery ship was indeed the *Californian* or some still-unidentified vessel, why it did not assist *Titanic* is a puzzle that remains unsolved.

Around 2:10 a.m., with the bow filled with water, *Titanic's* stern rose up out of the water, exposing the propellers and within minutes, the waterline had reached the boat deck. The last two lifeboats floated off the deck, upside down and half-filled with water. Shortly afterwards, the forward funnel collapsed, crushing part of the bridge and people in the water. On deck, people were scrambling towards the stern or jumping overboard in hopes of reaching a lifeboat. The ship's stern slowly rose into the air, and everything unsecured crashed downward, tumbling and spinning and knocking down those who were clinging to anything that would keep them from falling into the sea. While the stern rose, the electrical system finally failed and the lights went out. Shortly afterwards, the stress on the hull caused *Titanic* to break apart, and the bow went completely under. The stern righted itself slightly and then rose vertically. After a few moments, at 2:20 a.m., this, too, sank beneath the waves.

Survivors splashed desperately in the bitterly cold water but only two of the eighteen launched lifeboats rescued people after the ship sank. One of them picked up five people, two of whom later died. Nearly an hour later, another lifeboat went back and rescued four people, one of whom died afterwards. A few people managed to pull themselves into the lifeboats that floated off the deck. There were some arguments in some of the other lifeboats about going back, but many survivors were afraid of being swamped by people trying to climb into the lifeboat or being pulled down by the suction from the sinking ship.

When the *Carpathia* arrived at the scene, all of those who had been left in the water had long since succumbed to hypothermia. The *Carpathia* saved seven hundred and five survivors of the sinking, all of them in lifeboats.

As the *Carpathia* steamed toward New York, rumors and inaccurate newspaper reports quickly spread. Throughout the day on April 15, there was hope that *Titanic* was only damaged and under tow and that all passengers and crew were safe. Finally, a short message to White Star's New York office from the company's managing director, himself a survivor on *Carpathia*, dashed these hopes.

On April 18, *Carpathia* docked at Pier 54 at Little West 12th Street in New York with the survivors. It arrived at night and was greeted by thousands of people. As news of the disaster spread, many people were shocked that *Titanic* could sink with such great loss of life, especially since it had been widely publicized that she was

## EERIE PREDICTIONS OF *TITANIC'S* DEMISE?

Another prominent writer of the day, William T. Stead, was also believed to have published two eerie premonitions of the *Titanic* disaster. However, Stead's predictions are even stranger because he was one of the victims who died on that very ship!

Stead was a British journalist and social reformer who distinguished himself by originating the modern journalistic technique of creating a news event rather than just reporting it, as his most famous "investigation," the Eliza Armstrong case, demonstrated. In 1885, he began a crusade against child prostitution by publishing a series of articles entitled "The Maiden Tribute of Modern Babylon." In order to demonstrate the truth of his revelations, he arranged the "purchase" of Eliza Armstrong, thirteen-year-old daughter of a chimney sweep. Though his action is thought to have furthered the passing of the Criminal Law Amendment Act 1885, it nearly destroyed his career. In fact, his exposure of the child prostitution trade led to his conviction and a three-month prison term. He was convicted on grounds that he had failed to first secure permission for the "purchase" from the girl's father.

Stead continued to campaign for social reform and later wrote a book to expose the red-light districts and vice in Chicago, which was considered America's most corrupt city. His book, "If Christ Came to Chicago," led to several sweeping reforms in the vice districts of the city. He also wrote several other sensationalistic books on various subjects and became an advocate for the Boer cause during the war in South Africa in the early 1900s.

Around this same time, Stead became a devout Spiritualist. He claimed to be in receipt of messages from the spirit world, and to be able to produce automatic writing. His spirit contact was alleged to be a girl named Julia. In 1909 he established "Julia's Bureau" where inquirers could obtain information about the spirit world from a group of resident mediums. After his death, a group of his admirers founded a Spiritualist organization in Chicago called the William T. Stead Memorial Center.

Stead made several possible predictions of the *Titanic* disaster. Oddly, in many of his spiritualist lectures and writings Stead sketched pictures of ocean liners and himself drowning. In March 1886, he published an article called "How the Mail Steamer Went Down in Mid-Atlantic, by a Survivor," where a steamer collides with another ship, with high loss of life due to lack of lifeboats. Stead had added "This is exactly what might take place and will take place if liners are sent to sea short of boats." In 1892, Stead published a story called "From the Old World to the New," in which a White Star Line vessel, *Majestic*, rescues survivors of a ship that collided with an iceberg.

Stead was a passenger aboard *Titanic* in 1912. He was on his way to the United States to take part in a peace congress at Carnegie Hall at the request of President William Howard Taft. After the ship struck the iceberg, Stead helped several women and children into the lifeboats. After all the boats had gone, Stead went into the first-class smoking room, where he was last seen sitting in a leather chair and reading a book.

"unsinkable." Newspapers were filled with descriptions of the disaster and reporters were eager to get the latest information. Many charities were set up to help the victims and their families, many of whom lost their husband and father, or, in the case of the third-class survivors, lost everything they owned.

In one case from the third class, a Swedish man lost his wife and his four children, all under ten. The father was waiting for them to arrive in New York. Newspapers wrote that his grief "was the most acute of any who visited the offices of the White Star, but his loss was the greatest. His whole family had been wiped out."

One survivor, stewardess Violet Jessop, who had been on board the *RMS Olympic* when it collided with *HMS Hawke* in 1911, went on to survive the sinking of *HMHS Britannic* in 1916.

There are no living survivors of the *Titanic* disaster today. The last was Millvina Dean from Southampton, England, who was only nine weeks old at the time of the sinking. She died on May 31, 2009.

Once the massive loss of life became evident, the White Star Line chartered the cable ship *Mackay-Bennett* from Halifax, Nova Scotia, to retrieve bodies from the North Atlantic. Three other ships joined in the search: the cable ship *Minia*, the lighthouse supply ship *Montmagny* and the sealing vessel *Algerine*. Each ship left with embalming supplies, undertakers, and clergy on board. In the end, 333 victims were eventually recovered from the icy waters. The Canadian ships found 328 of them and five others were found by passing steamships. The final three bodies were found by the *Oceanic;* they had been occupants of a lifeboat that was swamped during the last minutes of the sinking.

The cable ship *Mackay-Bennett* was the first recovery ship to make it to the site of the sinking. They found so many bodies that the embalming supplies on board were quickly exhausted. Health regulations allowed only embalmed bodies to be returned to shore, so the crew had a dilemma on their hands. After some discussion, Captain Frederic Larnder of the *Mackay-Bennett* and the undertakers on board decided to preserve all of the bodies of the first-class passengers, justifying this decision by stating that the wealthy men's remains needed to be returned in order to settle any disputes over their large estates. As a result, the bodies of crew members and third-class passengers were buried at sea. The selection was made of which victims would be embalmed and brought back to shore and which would be buried at sea based on who appeared to be wearing better clothing. The public was predictably upset by this decision, but Captain Larnder defended it by saying that as a seaman, he hoped that he would be buried at sea, as well. His statement did not stop complaints from family members and undertakers on shore. The family members had hoped to have the solace of a funeral and a grave to visit; the undertakers didn't like being cheated out of business. Later ships, like the *Minia*, found fewer corpses, requiring fewer embalming supplies, and they were able to limit burials at sea to bodies that were too badly damaged to preserve.

Before thinking the sailors on board the Mackay-Bennett to be heartless, consider that they were very upset by the discovery of a fair-haired toddler's body that no one claimed. They paid for a monument for this unknown child out of their own pockets and he was buried on May 4, 1912 in Halifax's Fairview Cemetery, with a copper pendant placed in his coffin by the sailors inscribed with the words "Our Babe." It wasn't until 2007 that the child was positively identified by DNA matching as nineteen-month-old Sidney Leslie Goodwin of Wiltshire, England. Sidney, his parents, and five of his brothers and sisters, were third-class passengers. He was the only member of his family aboard *Titanic* whose body was recovered and subsequently identified.

The bodies that were recovered and preserved were taken to Halifax, the closest city to the sinking with direct rail and steamship connections. The Halifax coroner, John Henry Barnstead, developed a detailed system to identify bodies and safeguard personal possessions. Friends, family and loved ones from all over North American came to identify and claim bodies. A large temporary morgue was set up in a curling rink and undertakers were called in from all over Eastern Canada to assist. Some bodies were shipped to be buried in their hometowns across North America and Europe and in the end, almost two-thirds of them were identified. Unknown victims were buried in three Halifax cemeteries, each grave marked with a number based on the order in which the body had been discovered.

The identities of nearly one hundred and fifty of *Titanic's* dead will never be known.

In the wake of *Titanic's* sinking, waves of anger and grief rolled across America. No one could understand how the great "unsinkable" ship could have been lost. What negligence and incompetence had caused so many to lose their lives? By the time that *Carpathia* docked on April 18, the U.S. Senate had already formed a committee to investigate the disaster. The hearings began in New York but were moved to Washington, D.C. The committee's final report, issued six weeks later, blamed misguided assumptions, errors in judgment and disorganization for the sinking. However, because of the regulations that were in effect in 1912, these problems did not constitute legal negligence under either United States or British law. Because of this, the Senate report could only make recommendations to increase regulations that would better protect the safety of passengers at sea. The British Board of Trade held its own hearings about the tragedy and its findings exonerated the owners and crew and also made recommendations to increase safety on the high seas.

All of the recommendations later led to legislation that required more lifeboats for large ships and 24-hour manning of wireless equipment at sea. Lifeboat drills became mandatory and laws required speed to be altered in the event of ice reports.

Of course, all of these new regulations came too late for the 1,517 people who died either in the North Atlantic or aboard *Titanic.*

The story of the *Titanic* disaster was never far from the minds of the public. Interest remained strong in the form of books, articles and films but there were two events that seemed to spark interest in the minds of people who were not even alive when the sinking occurred: the blockbuster film by James Cameron in 1997 and the discovery of the ship's wreckage in 1985.

The idea of finding the wreckage of *Titanic,* and even raising the ship from the ocean floor, had been around since shortly after the ship sank. However, no attempts were successful until September 1, 1985, when a joint American-French expedition, led by Jean-Louis Michel and Dr. Robert Ballard, located the wreck using side-scan sonar from the research vessels *Knorr* and *Le Suroit.* Earlier that summer, *Le Suroit* began systematically crossing a one hundred fifty square mile target zone with sonar and was later joined by the *Knorr.* The wrecked ship was found at a depth of 2.5 miles, slightly more than three hundred seventy miles from Mistaken Point, Newfoundland. It was thirteen miles from fourth officer Joseph Boxhall's last position reading, where *Titanic* was originally thought to rest. Video cameras on an unmanned submersible called *Argo* were the first to document *Titanic's* current state on the bottom of the ocean. In 1986, Ballard returned to the wreck site aboard the *Atlantis II* to conduct the first manned dives to the doomed liner in the submersible *Alvin.*

The most notable discovery that the team made was that the ship had split apart. The stern section was found resting about 1,970 feet from the bow section and facing in the opposite direction. There had been conflicting witness accounts of whether the ship broke apart or not, and both the American and British inquiries concluded that the ship sank intact. Up until the discovery of the wreck, it was generally assumed that the ship did not break apart.

The ship's bow section had struck the ocean floor at a position just under the forepeak and had embedded itself sixty feet deep in the sand. Although parts of the hull had buckled, the bow was mostly intact. The collision with the ocean floor had forced water out of *Titanic* through the hull below the well deck.

The stern section was in much worse condition, and appeared to have been torn apart during its descent. Unlike the bow section, which was flooded with water before it sank, it is likely that the stern sank with a significant volume of air trapped inside it. As it sank, the external water pressure increased but the pressure of the trapped air could not. This caused some sections of the hull to implode because of the pressure difference. Further damage was caused by the impact of hitting the seabed and the decks collapsed when it landed on the ocean floor.

The wreck was surrounded by a large debris field with pieces of the ship, furniture, dinnerware and personal items scattered over an area of about one square mile. Softer materials, like wood, clothing and human remains had been destroyed by marine life many years before. Ballard and his team did not attempt to bring up any artifacts from the site, believing it would be the same as grave robbing. The artifacts, once found, however, would not remain at the bottom of the ocean for long.

Under maritime law, it was necessary to establish salvage rights to a shipwreck before artifacts could be removed from it. In the years after the discovery of the wreckage, a number of court cases were filed concerning the ownership of the artifacts and *Titanic* herself. In 1994, *RMS Titanic,* Inc. was awarded ownership and salvaging rights of the wreck. While criticized for disturbing the site, the salvaging expeditions have managed to remove about six thousand artifacts from the site of the wreck. Many of them were put on display and became a part of a traveling museum exhibit that began touring the country in the late 1990s, creating stories of a mysterious haunting that is still being experienced today.

## GHOSTS OF *TITANIC*

Strange tales about the area of the North Atlantic where *Titanic* went down began to be steadily reported in the early 1970s, although it's possible that a haunting in the area began much earlier than that. In 1990, an American historian in Strasburg, Germany, found the 1943 diary of a Nazi U-Boat commander who fired on a suspicious ship in the North Atlantic that subsequently vanished – almost exactly where *Titanic* had sank years before.

Many believers in ghosts and hauntings accept the idea that ghosts are often linked to events of extreme emotion and turmoil, which explains why so many can be found on battlefields and at locations of historical significance. Is it possible that the sinking of *Titanic* caused such a traumatic disturbance that the energy of the event imprinted itself on the atmosphere of the place where she sank beneath the waves?

In 1972, a crew member aboard a Canadian trawler on the North Atlantic made a notation in the ship's log about hearing screaming voices one night. It was a quiet, still night and while the sounds could have possibly have carried from some distance, the ship was then almost directly above at the location where the *Titanic* sank.

On another night in 1972, the *SS Hitchcock* was traveling past the location where *Carpathia* rescued survivors from the disaster and a young woman claimed to encounter the ghost of a young boy in old-fashioned clothing, clinging to the ship's rail. That same night, a man and a woman encountered an elderly couple in period clothing as they walked on the ship's deck. The old couple greeted them warmly and walked on. When the man and woman looked back at them, the couple had vanished.

Fourteen years later, in 1986, a ship from Nova Scotia reported seeing "vague balls of bright light" dancing on the horizon behind them "as if from a ship in trouble." In April of 1989, 57 witnesses on a British passenger ship described nearly the same thing: "the ghostly spectacle of a vast ship concealed in an unearthly fog just a mile off starboard."

In 1977, Second Officer Leonard Bishop of the *SS Winterhaven* was asked by a cordial, white-haired man with a neatly trimmed beard, whom he thought to be a visiting British sea captain for a tour of his ship. The ship was crossing the North Atlantic at the time, just where *Titanic* had gone down in 1912, but this thought was the furthest thing from Bishop's mind. He was happy to oblige the man with a tour, leading him through the bridge and down to the engine room. A bit later, he was asked to resume his duties and turned to his guest to apologize. When he did, he discovered that the man had vanished. Crew members searched the engine room, thinking he had wandered off, but he was ever found. Years later, Bishop recognized a picture of Captain Edward J. Smith from *Titanic* as his guest on the tour that day.

There have been many other reports from ships that cross this region. Crews and passengers have often experienced hearing strange sounds, including old-time band music and calls of distress that come out of the night and are heard crackling over radios and transmission devices. In 1982, the radio system of the *Queen Elizabeth* reportedly shorted out in the area and as the radio officer tried to fix it, he heard the sounds of people screaming and shrieks of desperation cutting through the static. Moments later, the radio went dead. Strangely, as the ship neared New York, the radio crackled to life and was in perfect working order once again.

Since the discovery of *Titanic's* wreckage in 1986, there have been at least 25 explorations of the ship's remains and debris field and almost all of them have had private experiences that are usually undocumented. In most cases, researchers and historians are not interested in connecting ghost stories to the seriousness of the tragedy and are willing to either shrug off their personal encounters as an imagination working overtime or are simply not willing to talk about it for fear of looking foolish.

However, some stories do manage to make the rounds. In addition to several encounters on the sea with eerie sounds and sightings, there have been rumors of undersea incidents that have been quickly hushed up by scholars trying to preserve the sanctity of the disaster. Sailors and engineers have spoken about whispers and voices in submersibles that didn't belong to any of the crew members or scientists present. An oceanographer sitting in a sub on the deck of *Titanic* briefly commented on a shadow racing between the on-deck structures, later denying it and calling it a figment of his imagination. In one ascent from the depths, music similar to the hymn "Nearer My God To Thee" was heard reverberating in a submersible as it rose to the surface; the music stopped only when it emerged from the sea. According to accounts from survivors, the song was played on deck by *Titanic's* orchestra in an attempt to keep passengers calm as they loaded the lifeboats.

But there are no ghostly tales as prevalent as those connected to the artifacts that have traveled all over the country since the late 1990s. Many don't realize that the *Titanic* Exhibit, which journeys from one major city to next, giving people the opportunity to view many of the artifacts from the wreckage, seems to be perpetually haunted. It seems that at least some of the ghosts of the more than fifteen hundred people who died in April 1912 have chosen to attach themselves to the only remaining tangible objects from that fateful voyage. Or perhaps the haunting is merely residual energy from the tragedy of the shipwreck. Regardless, the exhibit is one of the only haunted traveling exhibits in the world.

The exhibit began touring the United States in the late 1990s, taking advantage of the new interest that had been generated in *Titanic* after the release of James Cameron's film. Almost as soon as the exhibit opened in various museums, newspaper stories began appearing that described the haunting effects that were being experienced by exhibit visitors. An overwhelming number of them claimed to get an eerie feeling while viewing the artifacts, as if being watched, or feeling an immense sadness around specific objects or areas of the exhibit. Most assumed it was the general somber mood brought about by the disaster, but as more and more reports came in with similar claims, it began to be realized that something very unusual was taking place. Visitors told of intense cold spots, sensations of being touched, pushed, and brushed past by invisible people.

Some even told of seeing actual apparitions of the doomed *Titanic* passengers. One visitor to the exhibit, who came with her daughter and four-year-old grandson, stated that she firmly believed the artifacts to be haunted. According to her story, they were viewing the first-class quarters and she and her daughter thought little of the young boy's repeated questions of, "Who is that lady?" and "What is she doing?" They assured the boy that what he saw was only a dress on display but later, after learning of other people's experiences with the exhibit – and recalling the detailed description that the little boy gave of the "woman" he saw – they realized that he might have seen one of *Titanic's* ghosts.

While no one can say for sure who the ghosts are that haunt the *Titanic* exhibit, there are some who believe that at least one of them may be Frederick Fleet. The young man was on duty on the night of April 14 as a lookout and it was Fleet who had telephoned the bridge with the dire warning of "Iceberg, right ahead!" Fleet remained in the crow's nest for twenty minutes after the ship struck the iceberg, waiting to be relieved.

When he came down, he made his way to the Boat Deck, where Second Officer Charles Lightoller ordered him to help Quarter-Master Robert Hitchins load and launch the first lifeboat from the port side. After loading some 28 women and children, the boat was lowered to the water. As it was being lowered, Lightoller realized that it was undermanned and called for an experienced seaman. Fleet ended up on the boat and he survived the disaster.

From June 1912, Fleet served briefly as a seaman on the White Star liner *Olympic*. He found that White Star looked at *Titanic's* surviving officers and crew as embarrassing reminders of the disaster and he left the company in August 1912. For the next 24 years, Fleet sailed with Union-Castle and various other companies, finally leaving the sea in 1936. Ashore, he worked for Harland and Wolff as a shipbuilder, and later was the shore master-at-arms for Union-Castle Mail Steamship Co. As an old man, he sold newspapers on a street corner in Southampton.

On December 28, 1964, Fleet's wife died. Her brother, with whom the couple lived, then evicted Fleet, and in a state of despondency, he committed suicide two weeks later, his body being discovered on January 10, 1965. He was buried in an unmarked pauper's grave at Hollybrook Cemetry, Southampton. In 1993, a headstone was erected through donations by The Titanic Historical Society.

According to those who knew him, Fleet spent his entire life consumed by guilt over what happened on the night of April 14, 1912. He always believed that he had not been alert enough during his watch and that if he had only seen the iceberg sooner, perhaps the tragedy could have been avoided. Some believe that his suicide was not only caused by his wife's death, but by his guilt over the wreck of *Titanic*, as well.

Since the 1990s, some have come to believe that Fleet is one of the ghosts who haunt the *Titanic* exhibit. Psychics believe that it is his spirit who touches people who come through the displays, making sure that everyone is safe.

Is this really the case? No one can say, but there does seem to be some sort of lingering energy around the remains of *Titanic* and weird encounters still continue to occur around the exhibit today.

## 1915: DEATH IN JUST 18 FEET OF WATER THE *EASTLAND* DISASTER

July 24, 1915 was a special day for thousands of Chicagoans. It was the afternoon that had been reserved for the annual summer picnic for employees of the Western Electric Company. Officials at the utility company had encouraged workers to bring along as many friends and relatives as possible to the event, which was held across the lake at Michigan City, Indiana. In spite of this open invitation, they were surprised to find that more than seven thousand people showed up to be ferried across Lake Michigan on the three excursion boats that had been chartered for the day. The steamers were docked on the Chicago River, between Clark and LaSalle streets, and included *Theodore Roosevelt*, *Petoskey* and *Eastland*.

*Eastland* was a rusting Lake Michigan steamer that was owned by the St. Joseph-Chicago Steamship Company. It was supposed to hold a capacity crowd of 2,500 people but it is believed that on the morning of July 24, more than 3,200 climbed on board. In addition to being overcrowded, the vessel had a reputation for being unstable. Years before, it was realized that design flaws in the ship made it top-heavy. In July 1903, a case of overcrowding had caused *Eastland* to list and water to flow up one of its gangplanks. The situation was quickly rectified, but it was only the first of many such incidents. To make matters worse, the new federal Seaman's Act had been passed in 1915 because of the *RMS Titanic* disaster. This required the retrofitting of a complete set of lifeboats on *Eastland*, as well as on other passenger vessels. *Eastland* was so top-heavy that it already had special restrictions about how many passengers it could carry. The additional weight of the mandated lifeboats made the ship even more unstable than it already was.

**Two views of the Eastland after she rolled over in the water of the Chicago River. Rescuers were immediately on the scene but they were too late to prevent the deaths of hundreds of people who had been on board.**

The huge crowd, the lifeboats and the negligence of the crew created a recipe for disaster.

On the unseasonably cool morning of July 24, *Eastland* was moored on the south side of the Chicago River in downtown Chicago. After she was loaded with passengers, the aging vessel would travel out into Lake Michigan, heading for the Indiana shoreline. Excited, happy passengers lined the riverside docks, eager to get on board. The morning was damp, but better weather was promised for the picnic in the afternoon.

After the passengers were loaded on board, the dock lines were loosed and the ship prepared to depart. The crowd, dressed in their best summer clothes, jammed onto the decks, calling out and waving handkerchiefs to those who were still on shore. Many of the passengers went below decks, hoping to warm up on this cool, cloudy morning. As the steamer eased away from the dock, it started to list to the port side. Unknown to the passengers, the crew had emptied the ballast compartments of the ship, which were designed to provide stability, so that more passengers could be loaded on board. They didn't count on a sudden shift in weight that would cause the vessel to lean even farther toward the port side. That sudden shift was caused by a passing fireboat, which fired off its water cannons to the delight of the crowd. The passengers hurried over to the port side for a closer look and moments later, *Eastland* simply rolled over. It came to rest on the river bottom, which was only eighteen feet below the surface.

The passengers who had been on the deck were thrown in the river, thrashing about in a moving mass of bodies. Crews on the other steamers, and on passing vessels, threw life preservers into the water, while those on shore began tossing lines, boxes, and anything that would float to the panicked and drowning passengers. The overturned ship created a current that pulled many of the floundering swimmers to their doom, while many of the women's long dresses were snagged on the ship, tugging them down to the bottom.

The unluckiest passengers were those who had been inside the ship when it turned over. These ill-fated victims were thrown to one side of the vessel when it capsized and many were crushed by the heavy furniture below decks, which included tables, bookcases and a piano. As the river water rushed inside, those who were not immediately killed drowned a few moments later. A few managed to escape to the upturned side of the ship, but most of them didn't. Their bodies were later found trapped in a tangled heap on the lowest side of *Eastland*.

Firefighters, rescue workers, and volunteers soon began to arrive and started cutting holes in the ship's hull that was above the water line. A few who had scrambled to safety inside the ship emerged from the holes but, for most of them, it was simply too late. Those on shore eagerly watched for more survivors, but there just weren't any more. The men who had come to rescue the trapped and the injured had to resign themselves to pulling waterlogged corpses from the river instead. The bodies were wrapped in sheets and placed on *Roosevelt*, or lined

The body of a woman is pulled from the ship.

Divers searched for bodies along the bottom of the Chicago River. The pulled dozens of corpses to the surface.

Legend has it that one of the divers recovering bodies that day had a mental breakdown and had to be sedated -- overcome with grief by what he was seeing.

up along the docks. The large department stores downtown, like Marshall Field's, sent wagons to carry the dead to the hospitals, funeral homes and the makeshift morgues.

Corpses were fished out of the river using large grappling hooks, but those who had been trapped beneath the ship had to be pulled out by police divers and volunteers. According to newspaper accounts, one of these divers, who had been bringing up bodies from the bottom of the river for hours, went insane. He had to be subdued by friends and police officers. City workers dragged the river where *Eastland* had capsized, using large nets to prevent the bodies from being pulled out into the lake. By the time it was all over, 841 passengers and four crewmembers perished in the disaster. Many of them were women and children and 22 families were completely wiped out.

The hundreds of bodies that were recovered on the morning of the disaster were taken to the nearby Reid-Murdoch Building and to local funeral homes and mortuaries. The only public building that was large enough to be used as a morgue was the Second Regiment National Guard Armory, which was located on Carpenter Street, between Randolph Street and Washington Boulevard. The dead were laid out on the floor of the armory in rows of 85 and assigned identifying numbers. Any personal possessions that were found with the corpses were placed in envelopes bearing the same number as the body.

Chicagoans with loved ones who had perished in the disaster filed through the rows of bodies, searching for familiar faces, but in the mentioned 22 cases, there was no one left to identify them. Those families were completely wiped out, including grandparents, parents, children, aunts, uncles and cousins. The names of these victims were learned through the efforts of neighbors who came searching for their friends. The weeping, crying and moaning of the bereaved echoed off the walls of the armory for days. The American Red Cross treated thirty women for hysteria and exhaustion in the days following the disaster.

The last body was identified on Friday, July 30. A seven-year-old boy named Willie Novotny of Cicero, whose corpse was assigned the number 396, was the last. His parents and older sister had also died on *Eastland* and his identification came from extended family members, who arrived nearly a week after the disaster took place. After Willie's name was learned, a chapter was closed on one of Chicago's most horrific events.

Officially, the mystery of what happened to *Eastland* that day was never solved. No clear accounting was ever made to explain the capsizing of the vessel. Several hundred lawsuits were filed but almost all of them were dismissed by the Circuit

Court of Appeals, which held the owners of the steamer blameless in the disaster. After the ship was raised from the river, it was sold at auction. The title was later transferred to the government and the vessel was pressed into duty as the gunboat *U.S.S. Wilmette*. The ship never saw action but was used as a training ship during World War II. After the war, it was decommissioned and put up for sale in 1945. Finding no takers, it was scrapped in 1947.

*Eastland* was gone, but her story has continued to linger for years.

On the morning of the *Eastland* disaster, many of the bodies of the victims were taken to the Second Regiment National Guard Armory. As the years passed, there was no longer a need for a National Guard armory to be located so close to downtown Chicago. It was closed down by the military and the building was sold off. It went through several incarnations over the decades, including uses as a stable and a bowling alley, before being purchased by Harpo Studios, the production company owned by Oprah Winfrey. Winfrey is one of Chicago's greatest success stories and is the host of one of the most popular talk shows in television history, a film star, producer, publisher and well-known personality.

Unfortunately, though, the success of the show that is filmed in the former armory has done nothing to put to rest the spirits that linger from the *Eastland* disaster. A number of staff members, security guards and maintenance workers claim that the ghosts of the disaster victims who perished in 1915 restlessly wander this building. Many employees have had encounters with things that cannot easily be explained away, including the sighting of a woman in a long, gray dress who walks the corridors and then mysteriously vanishes into the wall. There have been many occasions when this woman has been spotted but each time she is approached, she always disappears. Some have surmised that she is the spirit of a mourner who came here looking for her family and left a bit of herself behind at the spot where she felt her greatest pain.

The woman in gray may not be alone in her spectral travels throughout the old armory. Staff members have also claimed to hear whispers, the sounds of people sobbing, moaning noises, and phantom footsteps. These footsteps, which sound as though they belong to a group of several people, are usually heard on a staircase in the lobby. Doors that are located nearby often open and close under their own power. Those who experience these strange events have come to believe that the tragedy of

**The 2nd Regimental Armory Building, which is now the site of Oprah Winfrey's Harpo Studios**

**The line of people that formed at the Armory to identify the dead from the Eastland Disaster**

**The dead from the Eastland were arranged in long lines so that they would be easier for grieving family members to identify.**

The recovery of the Eastland's dead continued long into the night, creating an "unearthly glow" on the river. Eerie lights are reported today that have no explanation. Could history be repeating itself as a haunting?

yesterday is still visiting itself on the former armory as it exists today.

The site of what became the Second Regiment Armory morgue is not the only location in Chicago that still resonates with chilling stories of *Eastland* disaster ghosts.

There were reports of the ship itself being haunted that date back to the time just after the disaster and prior to its sale to the Navy. During that period, it was docked near the Halsted Street Bridge and regarded with much superstition by passers-by. One lonely caretaker, Captain M.L. Edwards, lived aboard it and said he was awakened by moaning noises nightly, though he attributed them simply to the sound of the ship falling apart. Amused though he was to see people hurry across the bridge, terrified, when they saw a light in his cabin, he was very glad to move off the ship after its sale to the Navy in December 1915.

The site on the river where the disaster occurred has its strange stories, as well. For many years, people who have passed on the Clark Street Bridge have claimed to hear moaning and crying sounds coming from the river, along with bloodcurdling screams and pleas for help. In addition, some witnesses state that the cries are accompanied by the sounds of someone splashing in the river and even the apparitions of people helplessly flailing about in the water.

During several incidents, witnesses have actually called for help from emergency services, believing that someone was actually drowning in the river. At least one man jumped into the water to try and save what he thought was a person who was unable to swim. When he returned to the surface, he discovered that he was in the river alone. He had no explanation for what he had seen, other than to admit that it might have been a ghost!

In the same way that the former armory seems to have been impressed with a ghostly recording of past events, the Chicago River seems haunted, too. It seems that the horror of the *Eastland* disaster has left a memory behind at this spot and it continues to replay itself over and over again - ensuring that the luckless victims from the *Eastland* will never truly be forgotten.

## 1928: MULHOLLAND'S FALL
## THE ST. FRANCIS DAM COLLAPSE

At three minutes before midnight on March 12, 1928, the St. Francis Dam, which had been designed as a reservoir for the Los Angeles water supply, suddenly failed, releasing eleven billion gallons of water. Over the course of the next four hours, a roaring wall of water swept through the night, traveling 55 miles from the San Francisquito Valley in northeastern Los Angeles County, through the Santa Clara Valley, and on to the Pacific Ocean.

The dam had been built between 1924 and 1926 under the supervision of William Mulholland, chief engineer and general manager of the Los Angeles Bureau of Water Works and Supply. The concrete gravity-arch dam should have been impregnable, but Mulholland's arrogance and negligence led to disaster. The devastating flood killed more than six hundred people and its collapse is one of the worst American engineering failures in American history.

The collapse of the dam marked the end of Mulholland's career and the catastrophe has left an eerie haunting

in its wake.

The St. Francis Dam was built by the city of Los Angeles and was the brainchild of William Mulholland, an Irish, self-taught engineer who had fought his way through the ranks of the Los Angeles Department of Water and Power (then called the Bureau of Water Works and Supply). He had made a name for himself as a man with a penchant for thriftiness, an enormous capacity for innovation and for having the ability to bring in projects on time and under budget. His skills aided him in designing and building the Los Angeles Aqueduct in 1913, which at the time was the longest aqueduct in the world, bringing water 233 miles from the Owens Valley to L.A. The city had been built in the desert and the water was critical to its dreams of growth and glory. The aqueduct brought in fresh water, but the city always demanded more, forcing other, smaller ones to be built.

But the promise of more water was overshadowed by the deceit and corruption involved in taking away the water rights of the Owens Valley farmers and residents who also needed the water. Mulholland's financial backers became rich off of the water bonanza while the people of Owens Valley suffered financial ruin. Some called it "The rape of Owens Valley." At the opening ceremony for the aqueduct, Mulholland uttered his most enduring quote, "There it is. Take it."

The aqueduct and the series of small reservoirs built in the 1920s proved insufficient to quench the city's thirst and it was obvious that a larger reservoir was needed. When building and designing the Los Angeles Aqueduct in 1911, Mulholland had considered sections of the San Francisquito Canyon – beginning about thirty miles north of L.A. – as a potential dam site. Conveniently, the aqueduct ran along the canyon and two generating stations in the canyon used aqueduct water to provide power for the city. Mulholland quickly saw the potential of the canyon to serve as a reservoir that would provide ample water for L.A. in case of a drought or if the aqueduct was damaged in an earthquake.

In 1924, construction was quietly started on the dam so as to not attract the attention of the farmers who were dependent on the waters from San Francisquito Creek. The Los Angeles Aqueduct had already been the target of frequent sabotage by the angry farmers and landowners in the Owens Valley, who felt the city was stealing their water. Mulholland wanted to avoid costly repairs and delays caused by sabotage at the new dam – and avoid the scandal that surrounded by the building of the aqueduct – so almost no publicity was generated about the new project. The dam was named the "St. Francis," an anglicized version of the name of the canyon in which it was built.

The official plans for the St. Francis Dam describe a curved, concrete gravity dam. The basic principle of this type of dam was simple – the mass of the structure had to be great enough to hold against the pressure of the water behind it. However, rock at the dam site, both the red conglomerate rock and the sandstone on the western side of the canyon and the mica schist on the eastern wall, were less than ideal for construction. The conglomerate lost strength when it was wet and mica was a porous rock that was unstable under pressure. When water seeped into the rock below and alongside the concrete dam, pressure pushed it upwards, reducing its effectiveness against the water pushing behind it. There are several ways to counter this effect, but Mulholland used only one technique, installing drainage wells to reduce water in the material beneath the dam. In addition, during construction, the width of the dam was decreased and the height increased. Mulholland, the self-taught genius, had ordered these important changes, even though they were never formally studied by trained engineers. It was later determined that the unstable rock along the eastern side of the dam was what caused it to give way.

**The St. Francis Dam in 1927**

The St. Francis Dam project was a disaster in the making, although apparently no one ever noticed – or they were afraid to speak up. As the reservoir filled during 1926 and 1927, several cracks appeared in the dam and its supports, likely caused by temperature changes and the contraction of the concrete. The cracks and leaks were inspected by Mulholland

**The St. Francis Dam in 1928**

and his assistant, Harvey van Norman, but they dismissed them, stating that there were to be expected in a concrete structure the size of the new dam. By March 1928, the reservoir had reached full capacity. The water had risen steadily and uneventfully for almost two years but by the middle of March, motorists traveling along the east shore reported cracks and a sagging roadbed near the dam's east support. On March 12, the road was reported to have sagged more than one foot.

That same morning, the dam keeper, Tony Harnischfeger, discovered a new leak and immediately alerted Mulholland. He inspected the leak, along with his assistant van Norman, but convinced that it was relatively minor and normal for a concrete dame, Mulholland pronounced the structure absolutely safe.

At three minutes before midnight on March 12, the St. Francis Dam catastrophically failed. No one actually

**WEATHER FORECAST**
Virginia: Cloudy and warmer tonight followed by rain. Wednesday colder. N. Carolina: Cloudy with showers late tonight.

**The ☆ Bee.**

Annexation Will Give Danville Prestige of 40,000 Population

FOUNDED FEBRUARY, 1899. NO. 10,083.    ASSOCIATED PRESS    DANVILLE, VA., TUESDAY AFTERNOON, MARCH 13, 1928.    HOME EDITION.    PRICE: TWO CENTS.

# HUNDREDS PERISH WHEN DAM COLLAPSES

saw the dam collapse, but a motorcyclist named Ace Hopewell was riding about one-half mile upstream from the dam around this time and reported that he felt a rumbling and the sound of "crashing, falling blocks." He assumed that the sensation was either an earthquake or one of the landslides that were common to the area and didn't realize at the time that he would be the last person to see the dam intact – and survive.

Dam keeper Tony Harnischfeger and his family were, most likely, the first casualties caught in the wave of water that tore through the dam. The wave was at least 125 feet high when it hit their cottage in San Francisquito Canyon, about one-quarter mile downstream from the dam. Thirty minutes before the

**Remains of the dam after the collapse.**

collapse a motorist passing by the dam reported seeing lights in the canyon below the dam (the dam itself did not have lights) and many believe that the lights could have been Harnischfeger inspecting the dam immediately before its failure. He may have been nervous about the cracks that had been discovered earlier in the day. The body of Leona Johnson, who lived with the Harnischfegers and was later mistakenly reported to be Harnischfeger's wife, was found fully clothed and wedged between two blocks of concrete near the broken base of the dam. Neither the body of the dam keeper or that of his six-year-old son, Coder, was ever found.

As the dam collapsed, eleven billion gallons of water surged down San Francisquito Canyon, demolishing the heavy concrete walls of Power Station No. 2, destroying the Harnischfeger home, wiping out a camp of migrant workers and destroying everything else in its path. The flood surged south through the canyon, flooding parts of present-day Valencia and Newhall. The deluge then followed the Santa Clara River bed to the west, flooding the towns of Castaic Junction, Fillmore and Bardsdale. The water continued west through Santa Paula in Ventura County, emptying the victims and debris that it carried with it into the Pacific Ocean, 55 miles from the reservoir and dam site. When it reached the ocean, the flood was almost two miles wide. Bodies of victims were recovered from the ocean, some as far south as the Mexican border.

Many more were never found at all.

To this day, the exact number of victims remains unknown. The official death toll in 1928 was 385, but the bodies of victims continued to be discovered all of the way until the middle 1950s. Many bodies were swept out to sea when the flood reached the Pacific and were not discovered until they washed ashore. The remains of another victim were found deep underground near Newhall in 1992, and the current death toll is estimated to be more than six hundred victims. This number does not include the itinerant farm workers camped in San Francisquito Canyon, the exact number of which will never be known.

Immediately following the disaster, Los Angeles officials wanted to put it behind them as quickly as possible.

Because of this, official investigations and hearings were short and cursory. Mulholland publicly announced that he was willing to shoulder all of the blame. He said that he "envied those who were killed" and went on to say, "Don't blame anyone else, you just fasten it on me. If there was an error in human judgment, I was the human, and I won't try to fasten it on anyone else." Although he did imply that the dam had been cursed or that it had been sabotaged. A coroner's inquest ruled that the disaster was caused by the faulty rock on which the dam was built and blamed the governmental organizations that oversaw the dam's construction and the dam's designer and engineer, William Mulholland. However, Mulholland was cleared of any charges, since neither he nor anyone at the time could have known of the instability of the rock formations on which the dam was built.

At the time, Mulholland managed to escape severe criticism and he won accolades for his courage and the responsibility that he took for the disaster. It was not until much later that evidence emerged that his arrogance and negligence were the real causes of the dam's collapse. Perhaps because of his lack of formal education, Mulholland relied more on experience and guesswork than on scientific study and data. He discounted or ignored contemporary knowledge about the dangers of the uplift in the rock and failed to implement a wide variety of safety measures that were available at the time. Too proud and independent to hire expert consultants, as was the custom on large engineering projects, Mulholland forged ahead and never submitted any of his plans for an independent safety review. His authoritarian management style made sure that none of his subordinates would question his judgment.

The catastrophe haunted Mulholland and it marked the end of his career. He retired several months after the disaster and retreated into a life of self-imposed isolation. With almost no contact with the world, he died in 1935 at the age of 79.

With thousands of homes destroyed and hundreds of people dead, the St. Francis Dam Collapse remains a dark event in American history and was one of the worst disasters to ever take place in California. The calamity left an indelible mark on the landscape of Southern California --- and many believe that it earned a place in the annals of the supernatural, as well.

Over the years, San Francisquito Canyon has remained a sort of blighted spot near San Fernando. The area where the dam keeper's cottage was once located – and where many migrant workers were camped – has been turned into a public park. But it's a place where remnants of the past still make themselves known today.

It's been said that just about anyone who has lived in San Francisquito has a ghost story. In 1986, a local historian was videotaping in a small cemetery and his friend came out of a gulley with a mysterious acid burn on his arm. When the pair got back to town, the historian found his videotape was completely blank, even though frequent inspections during taping showed the video was good. He went back for a second shoot and this time, his camera caught fire in an odd case of spontaneous combustion. The owners of the property weren't surprised. They mentioned that a half-ton watering trough had been mysteriously moved in the middle of the night -- with no tracks. Another time, a man was painting his barn and he happened to look up and see the wet palm print of a child impressed on the wood. There were no children anywhere nearby at the time.

The large park located in the canyon is said to be one of the most haunted spots in the region. Here, where an unknown number of itinerant workers met their death in the floodwaters, visitors who have braved the place

**Ruined pieces of the old St. Francis dam can still be found in the public area where it once stood. Many claim that the ghosts of those who perished in the collapse still haunt this place today.**

after dark say that many of the flood victims have remained behind. According to reports, strange things occur here at night, especially when it's foggy. Eerie voices are sometimes heard, people are touched, pushed and caressed by invisible hands and on other occasions, shadowy forms are seen walking in the mist. When approached, they always vanish.

Who are these mysterious apparitions? Are they the doomed workers who perished in the flood? Or could they be the spirits of victims whose bodies have not yet been discovered? That particular mystery remains unsolved.

# BIBLIOGRAPHY & RECOMMENDED READING

Backes, Nancy (Editor of *Country Beautiful*) – *Great Fires of America; 1973*

Barry, John – *The Great Influenza*; 2004

Bellamy, John Stark II - *The Corpse in the Cellar*; 1999

--------------------------- - *The Maniac in the Bushes and More Tales of Cleveland Woe*; 1997

Benzaquin, Paul -- *Holocaust! The Shocking Story of the Boston Cocoanut Grove Fire*; 1959

Bixell, Patricia -- *Galveston and the 1900 Storm*; 2000

Bonasinga, Jay – *The Sinking of the* Eastland; 2004

Braatz, Werner and Starr, Joseph. *Fire on the River: The Story of the Burning of the* General Slocum; 2000

Bryant, William O.-- *Cahaba Prison and the Sultana Disaster*; 1990

Cadle, Lt. Cmdr. Gregory – *Navy Medicine's Connection to the Ghost of the Hindenburg*; 2002

Campbell, Ballard – *American Disasters*; 2008

Coppock, Mike – *Oklahoma's Deadliest Tornado / American History*; April 2007

Cromie, Robert – *The Great Chicago Fire*; 1958

Davis, Devra Lee -- *When Smoke Ran Like Water*; 2003

Dillon, Lacy. -- *They Died in the Darkness*; 1976

Drake, Benjamin -- *Life Of Tecumseh And Of His Brother The Prophet*; 2008

Eaton, John P. and Charles A. Haas – *Titanic: Destination Disaster;* 1996

Eckert, Allan -- *A Sorrow in Our Hearts: The Life of Tecumseh;* 1992.

Elder, Rob & Sarah – *Crash*; 1977

Esposito, John C. -- *Fire in the Grove: The Cocoanut Grove Tragedy and its Aftermath*; 2005

Everett, Marshall – *The Great Chicago Theater Disaster*; 1904

Feldman, Jay – *When the Mississippi Ran Backwards*; 2005

Fuller, John G. – *The Ghost of Flight 401;* 1976

Galloway, Lisa - *Ashtabula Train Disaster*; 2002

Gavenda, Walter and Shoemaker, Michael T.-- *A Guide to Haunted West Virginia*; 2001

Genoways, Ted and Genoways, Hugh H. -- *A Perfect Picture of Hell*; 2001

Guiley, Rosemary Ellen – *Encyclopedia of Ghosts & Spirits;* 2007

Green, Casey Edward and Kelly, Shelly Henley -- *Through a Night of Horrors: Voices from the 1900 Galveston Storm;* 2000

Hacker, Tonya & Tammy Wilson – *Ghostlahoma;* 2009

Halstead, Murat-- *Galveston: The Horrors of a Stricken City*; 1900

Hatch, Anthony P. – *Tinder Box*, 2003

Hauck, Dennis William -- *Haunted Places: The National Directory*, 2002

Hawes, Jesse. -- *Cahaba: A Story of Captive Boys in Blue*, 1888

Jackson, Carlton -- *The Dreadful Month*, 1982

Jenkins, Greg -- *Florida's Ghostly Legends And Haunted Folklore: Volume One: South And Central Florida*, 2005

Jones, James Gay -- *Appalachian Ghost Stories and Other Tales*, 1975

Keyes, Edward -- *Cocoanut Grove*, 1984

Korson, George Gorshon – *Black Rock*, 1960

Krist, Gary – *The White Cascade*, 2007

Langguth, A. J. -- *Union 1812: The Americans Who Fought the Second War of Independence*, 2006

Law, Anwei -- *The Great Flood: Johnstown*, 1987

Lord, Walter – *A Night to Remember*, 1956

Marvel, William -- *Andersonville: The Last Depot*, 1994

McCullough, David G -- *The Johnstown Flood*, 1968

Minutaglio, Bill -- *City on Fire*, 2003

Mooney, Michael McDonald – *The Hindenburg*, 1972

Musick, Ruth Ann-- *Coffin Hollow and Other Ghost Tales*, 1977

Nash, Jay Robert - *Darkest Hours: The Great Book of Worldwide Disasters From Ancient Times to the Present*, 1976

Nunis, Doyce, Jr. - *The St. Francis Dam Disaster Revisited*, 2002

O'Donnell, Edward T. – *Ship Ablaze*; 2003

Potter, Jerry O -- *The Sultana Tragedy: America's Greatest Maritime Disaster*, 1992

Reed, Charles B.-- *The Curse of Cahawba*; 1925

Reed, Robert C. – *Train Wrecks*; 1968

Rust, Claude – *The Burning of the General Slocum*; 1981

Schneider, Mary Jane -- *Midwinter Mourning: The Boyertown Opera House Fire*, 1991

Schorow, Stephanie --*The Cocoanut Grove Fire*, 2005

Scott, Phil – *Hemingway's Hurricane: The Great Florida Keys Storm of 1935*; 2006

Shaw, David – *The Sea Shall Embrace Them*; 2002

Stackpole, Edward – *Wreck of the Steamer San Francisco*; 1954

Standiford, Les – *Last Train to Paradise*, 2002

Stephens, Hugh W -- *The Texas City Disaster, 1947*, 1997

Sugden, John -- *Tecumseh: A Life*; 1997

Sutherland, Monica – *The Damndest Finest Ruins: The San Francisco Earthquake*, 1959

Taylor, Troy – *Dead Men Do Tell Tales*; 2008

------------- with Adam Selzer & Ken Melvoin-Berg – *Weird Chicago*; 2008

Telzrow, Michael E. – *The Peshtigo Fire / New American*; 2006

Tintori, Karen – *Trapped: The 1909 Cherry Mine Disaster*, 2002

Wade, Wyn Craig – *The Titanic: End of a Dream*; 1986

Williams, Docia Schultz -- *Ghosts along the Texas Coast*, 1995

Withington, John – *Disaster!*; 2010

Newspapers, Journals and Magazines:
*Boston Globe*. Boston, MA
*Brooklyn Daily Eagle*. Brooklyn, NY
*Brooklyn Union-Argus*. Brooklyn. NY
*Chicago Sunday Tribune*. Chicago, IL
*Chicago Tribune*. Chicago, IL
*Cleveland Sun*. Cleveland, OH

*Daily Independent.* Monesson, PA
*Daily Reporter.* Washington, PA
*The Democrat.* Doylestown, PA
*Galveston County Daily News.* Galveston, TX
*Harpers Weekly* Magazine
*Houston Daily News.* Houston, TX
*Houston Press.* Houston, TX
*Journal of Forensic Sciences*
*National Fire Protection Association Journal*
*National Geographic* Magazine
*New York Times.* New York, NY
*North and South* Magazine
*Philadelphia Inquirer.* Philadelphia, PA
*Pittsburgh Dispatch,* Pittsburgh, PA
*Pittsburgh Post.* Pittsburgh, PA
*Pittsburgh Post-Gazette.* Pittsburgh, PA
*The Press.* Philadelphia, PA
*The Reading Eagle.* Reading, PA
*Washington Reporter.* Washington, PA
*Tribune-Review.* Pittsburgh, PA
*Valley Independent.* Pittsburgh, PA

Special Thanks from Troy Taylor:
Jill Hand -- Editor
Mike Schwab -- Cover Design
Rene Kruse
Elyse Horath
Rachael Horath
Bethany Horath
John Winterbauer
Ken Berg
Derek Bartlett
Rosemary Ellen Guiley
Crusty & Herbie

& Haven Taylor

Acknowledgements from Rene Kruse:
For Adrian, who resides in the clouds and visits us in starlight.
   I would like to thank my children: Aaron, Bethany, Elyse and Rachael, for solving computer problems, proof-reading stories, patiently listening to ten different ways to phrase a sentence, helping me find that elusive perfect word, but also for all the extra cooking, cleaning, laundry and a hundred other little things they did so I could research, read and write.  To my grandchildren, Kaitlynn and Gavin, for pulling me away from the darkness of these tragedies with their hugs and smiles. To Cindy Stonick and Laura Baugher who read my stories and made sure they left home in their Sunday best.  To Marianne McCarthy, who drove around Brooklyn, NY to photograph special locations for me, then took me to visit them, that I might stand on the site of the Brooklyn Theatre fire and pay my respects at the mass grave of the theatre's unidentified victims.  To Daniel Rodriguez of the New York University campus police who listened to two strangers and chose to break the rules so that Bethany and I could stand on the ninth and tenth floors of the building that had once housed the Triangle Shirtwaist Factory.
   And finally, I would like to thank my dear friend Troy Taylor, who had more confidence in me than I did, and whose constant (and I do mean constant) encouragement and guidance kept me typing away into the wee hours of the night and feeling proud of my accomplishments.

CPSIA information can be obtained at www.ICGtesting.com
Printed in the USA
LVOW120059050612

284648LV00003B/2/P